Players
Making
Decisions

Game Design Essentials
and the Art of Understanding Your Players

ZACK HIWILLER

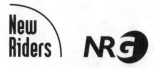
New Riders NRG

Players Making Decisions:
Game Design Essentials and the Art of Understanding Your Players
Zack Hiwiller

New Riders

www.newriders.com
To report errors, please send a note to errata@peachpit.com
New Riders is an imprint of Peachpit, a division of Pearson Education
Copyright © 2016 by Zachary Hiwiller

Senior Editor: Karyn Johnson
Development Editor: Robyn G. Thomas
Production Editor: Danielle Foster
Copyeditor: Rebecca Rider
Proofreader: Patricia Pane
Compositor: Danielle Foster
Indexer: FireCrystal Communications
Interior Design: Danielle Foster
Cover Design: Mimi Heft, with Zack Hiwiller

ISBN-13: 978-0-134-39675-0
ISBN-10:   0-134-39675-8

9 8 7 6 5 4 3 2 1

Printed and bound in the United States of America

Dedication

To my grandmother, Betty Hiwiller (1927–2014), who always wanted me to be a writer. Yes, textbooks count, Grandma.

Acknowledgments

First, I would like to thank my wife, Gloriana, and my parents, Dan and Jan Hiwiller, for always tolerating me and encouraging me. Although the former would have been enough, the latter is greatly appreciated.

I would like to thank everyone who provided comments and support on early drafts. Many helped, but Mark Diehr, Matthew Gallant, and Scott Brodie did a yeoman's job on a short turnaround, even though they have extremely busy professional careers. If *Uncharted 4* is delayed, please do not blame me.

Everything that looks professional within is thanks to the wonderful team at Pearson including Robyn Thomas, Rebecca Rider, Danielle Foster, Patricia Pane, and Karyn Johnson.

I would like to use this space to thank Jesse Schell for convincing me game design could yield a career and be intellectually interesting. I'd like to thank Jon Dean, James Hawkins, and Jason Barnes for being early examples to me of what leadership looks like among game industry professionals. I would also like to thank all my friends and colleagues at Project Horseshoe, the best community of game designers in the world.

Finally, I cannot forget the dedicated staff and faculty of the Game Design program at Full Sail University who have helped me refine my approach to communicating the practice of game design, including, but not limited to, Ricardo Aguilo, Dax Gazaway, D'Juan Irvin, Christina Kadinger, Michael Lucas, Kingsley Montgomery, Andrew O'Connor, Mark Pursell, Brian Stabile, and Lee Wood.

About the Author

Zack Hiwiller is a game designer, educator, and writer who lives in Orlando, Florida. He is a department chair for the Game Design degree program at Full Sail University and does consultant work for many large and small companies. Previously, in addition to independent projects, he was a designer at Gameloft and Electronic Arts. He holds a Bachelor's degree in Information Systems from Carnegie Mellon University and a Master's degree in Modeling and Simulation from the University of Central Florida. His writings at hiwiller.com have been reposted by Kotaku, GameSetWatch, and other sites and have reached over 2 million readers. You have probably seen something of his reposted without attribution on sites like 9GAG, BuzzFeed, TheCHIVE, and others. Mark Zuckerberg used an image from one of his blog posts in his keynote at the 2011 F8 conference, and although he would have liked to have been cited, he actually thought it was pretty cool. In the fall months, he serves as an official for high school football games in central Florida.

Contents

Preface

"If you wish to make an apple pie from scratch, you must first invent the universe."

—CARL SAGAN

This Carl Sagan quote from *Cosmos* intends to cheekily point out that even a simple object like an apple pie contains a multitude of layers, depending on your level of analysis. Although the baker feels that the apples, sugar, and flour are the fundamental building blocks of an apple pie, the physicist sees down to the atoms and fundamental particles that make up the pie itself. It is a profound and long-lasting quotation because of the disconnect that the listener experiences. Making an apple pie is prosaic. Inventing the universe is deity-level stuff.

Teaching game design offers a similar conundrum. Making games is fairly easy, as is apparent from looking at the number of available games. For example, when you look at the games available for just a single platform (iOS) in a single country (the US) at the time of this writing, you'll see that there are nearly 400,000 games available.[1] In addition, Over 110,000 analog games are listed in the BoardGameGeek.com database.[2] And, of course, the number of games children create every day on playgrounds all across the world is uncountable. With so many games coming out every day, games surely must be easy to make. As a result, teaching about games must be fairly straightforward and simple.

Unfortunately, that is not true.

The primary reason is that there is no reliable algorithm that we can use to create things as wildly disparate as *Chess*, *Grand Theft Auto V*, *Red Rover*, pole vaulting meets, and *Jeopardy!*. A cursory listing of the skills a game designer of any type will

---

1   App Store Metrics. (n.d.). Retrieved July 13, 2015, from http://www.pocketgamer.biz/metrics/app-store/app-count/.

2   BoardGameGeek. (n.d.). Retrieved July 13, 2015, from https://boardgamegeek.com/browse/boardgame.

find useful includes mathematics, psychology, computer programming, composition, rhetoric, drafting, architecture, art history, philosophy, economics, business, history, education, mythology, and animation. I stopped the list not because it was complete, but because I think the list—as incomplete as it is—makes the point that game design is remarkably multidisciplinary.

Because no algorithm exists, we have to attempt to shoehorn the facts and methods of a universe of disparate disciplines to make game design heuristics. Meanwhile, the impatient student just wants to make a simple apple pie.

When I first left the world of full-time development of video games to teach game design, I faced this very problem of distilling a vast universe down to a few salient points. I voraciously consumed every book I could find about design or game design and found that they largely talked about the process from a descriptive perspective. That was useful in some aspects, but not useful when I was looking to teach a prescriptive method. Most game design books were ludicrously padded with obvious statements that were not at all helpful to aspiring or professional designers. Some books, like Schell's *Art of Game Design* and Salen and Zimmerman's *Rules of Play* did a great job of merging descriptive and prescriptive insights from numerous areas of study and then backed up these anecdotes with external best practices.[3, 4] As my library expanded, I found more and more areas that I wanted to share with students, but unless I wanted to assign them hundreds of dollars worth of (sometimes overly academic, sometimes out-of-print) reading materials, I had no way to easily teach lessons that would have helped me professionally if someone had taught them to me in my apprentice years. This is the curse of a multidisciplinary field—the sources for insights are limitless, so collating knowledge into a curriculum eventually expands like a gas to fill whatever space you have.

I have created games professionally on over a dozen platforms. I have created large physical games for corporate retreats; I have created interactive books for tablets; and I have created free-to-play games in a brutally competitive market. These platforms seem like they share little in common. Some topics make sense only in terms of analog games, or single-player games, or multiplayer games. But some topics transcend platforms and are timeless. Less than ten years ago, mobile games had few established design patterns. Less than ten years ago, no digital social networks supported formal games. Less than thirty years ago, networked games in general were a quiet niche. What platforms will support the games ten years from now? Thirty years from now? What game design concepts

. . . .

3   Schell, J. (2008). *The Art of Game Design: A Book of Lenses*. Amsterdam: Elsevier/Morgan Kaufmann.

4   Zimmerman, E., & Salen, K. (2003). *Rules of Play: Game Design Fundamentals*. Cambridge, Mass.: MIT Press.

will help support the game designers of the future? I cannot possibly claim to know the answer to those questions. But I can provide tools to support game designers today, and I can present them in the most evergreen way I know in order to sustain their relevance. In time, concepts in this book will be updated, expanded, or even retired as the industry gains greater understanding of how we game designers complete our magic.

Teaching has been incredibly challenging and rewarding. Just as my career in game design stemmed from a need to constantly learn about as many things as possible, my teaching career has reflected that as well. Research is enlightening, but it is students who provide me with unparalleled perspective into how to explain what game design actually is and how to do it well. This book is another well-disguised ploy for me to learn more, to pull insights from multiple disciplines, and to share new ideas with others.

Thank you for the opportunity,

—Zack Hiwiller
November 2015

Who Is This Book For?

This book is for those who are interested in what elements are involved in the design of games. Its purpose is to introduce the knowledge areas that are most helpful for understanding game design. This book is not a manual on how to design a game. There is no such book possible. Neither is it a book that claims to let one in on all the "secrets" of successful game design. Anyone promising that should not be trusted. Nor is this a book to teach a specific programming language or scripting toolset. Those books can be incredibly useful, but go obsolete quickly. This book focuses on concepts that can be used to help you understand the design of any type of game—analog or digital.

How Is This Book Organized?

This book is split into eight sections, each of which covers a topic I feel is essential to being a game designer—no matter the platform—and is not completely obvious to new designers:

- Part 1,"Getting Started," is about how to start from nothing. Although some games are iterations of previous games, most start with just the seed of an idea. What should that seed look like? What are some prerequisite elements that will help you organize your ideas into an actionable project?

- Part 2, "Prototypes and Playtesting," talks about how to plan and test your game before it is a final product. There is a pervasive myth among novice designers that games are largely birthed finished from idea to product, with only moderate tweaking along the way. This section sets out to debunk that myth and provide designers with the tools and inspiration required to make quick, testable versions of their games.

- Part 3, "Meaningful Decisions," covers one of the most interesting topics in games: decision-making. It is incontrovertible that interactivity is one of the key-stone characteristics of games. Interactivity means that the players make some decisions that the game reacts to. How do designers present these decisions? What makes for interesting decision-making?

- Part 4, "Describing Game Elements," covers a number of topics concerning the different elements of games and different considerations thereof. There is little uniformity when talking with designers and academics about how game elements should be classified or applied, so this section takes a cross-section of the most pragmatic approaches for actually designing games.

- Part 5, "Game Theory and Rational Decision-Making," considers how players should behave were they to act rationally. By examining game decisions from this perspective, designers can remove elements that should be consistently never chosen. This leaves players with decisions between possibly interesting options.

- Part 6, "Human Behavior in Games," eschews the convenient fable of the rational player and looks to the realm of psychology to try to understand how real human players actually act. If games are truly about decision-making, then the whole branch of study spun off from psychology and economics that explores how humans actually make decisions is relevant to game design.

- Part 7, "Game Design Tools," considers the different tools designers use to document, analyze, and communicate ideas, such as the universally misunderstood game design document (GDD).

- Part 8, "The Game Design Business," considers the craft of game design as it relates to business. The old joke that is appropriated for nearly every industry is this: "How do you make a small fortune in the games business? Start with a large fortune." If a designer's craft is done for more than just a hobby, she must understand the requirements of the business aspects of game design.

PART 1

Getting Started

Ideas are like stars—numerous and dazzling,
but it takes a lot of work to confirm life near one.

—DANIEL SOLIS

I teach game design to students in one of the larger game design programs in the world. I see hundreds of students a year, and I see a fear in them. That fear is that they have a desire—to be a game designer—and they don't know what transition they will have to go through to become one. The role seems so glorious and fulfilling, so certainly there must be a change between their present, mundane self and their future-inspired "artiste" self. Many seem to believe that a professor will come down from a mountaintop with stone tablets, they will have some divine epiphany, and all will become clear. Even you, dear reader, likely have some watered-down version of that belief. Otherwise, why would you be reading a book about game design?

The problem with this meme is that game design itself has no gatekeepers. It doesn't need them. If you fail (and you will), so what? Ophthalmologists, for example, have hefty barriers for entry into their profession because their failures come with major consequences. If a game designer fails at making a game, then maybe someone just has less fun for a little while.

Game design requires little specialized knowledge. Plenty of specialized knowledge exists that helps (hence this book), but nearly all of it has been gleaned from the trial and error of designers who have come before and failed.

When I tell students that they can be a game designer *today*, I tend to get glassy-eyed stares. It is true: Anyone can make a card or board game with commonly found materials. Even digital games are easier to throw together these days than ever before with tools like GameMaker, Twine, and Perlenspiel. Where do you start? You make a game. You put one foot in front of the other.

1 What Is a Game Designer?

The best of men
That e'er wore earth about him, was a sufferer,
A soft, meek, patient, humble, tranquil spirit,
The first true gentleman that ever breathed.

—THOMAS DEKKER

Asking the question of what a game designer is seems pedantic, especially to someone who has chosen to read a book about game design. Yet so many people have misconceptions of game designers' role, abilities, and responsibilities, that it's necessary to address this topic right away.

Responsibilities of a Game Designer

Game designers have a myriad of responsibilities that often differ depending on the type of game and development environment. Making a print-and-play card game for free release on the Internet demands different skill sets than designing for a yearly, iterative, big-budget software title. However, many similarities bubble to the surface:

- **ESTABLISH DESIGN GOALS AND PLANS ON HOW TO REACH THEM.** Game design is rarely a jam session where you use automatic writing to document ideas as they come to you. Game design is problem solving to meet goals. Without clear goals and plans on how to achieve those goals, the game designer is just riffing. Many designers are content with riffing because it's more difficult to prove the design ideas wrong and it protects their ego. However, the most effective designers, those who end up with a game that reflects their original intent, are those who problem-solve within the framework of understood and well-defined problems.

- **THINK IN SYSTEMS.** Games are interactive systems. Some have more interactive depth than others. No matter how nuts-and-bolts the designer is in dealing with the day-to-day tasks of game development, it's absolutely essential that she have a deep understanding of how all the game's systems work together. It is not enough to know how a feature works in isolation or to apply normative values like "good" or "bad" to individual implementations or features.

  Here's an example: I once worked on a yearly iterative American football video game. A feature request was made where mistakes on the field would lower the probabilities that, say, the quarterback would hit his targets effectively, or receivers would run correct routes, and so on. This is fine in theory. However, a lack of understanding for positive feedback loops and how the game's unique systems function under-the-hood and are revealed to the player can lead to disastrous results. When implemented, the feature caused the first player who made a mistake to enter a death spiral of ineptitude as his onscreen players followed mistakes with more mistakes. Eventually, the game looked buggy as quarterbacks passed to empty field positions because their ratings dropped so low. Players had no idea what was going on because these systems were not revealed through the user interface, so they complained that the game was broken. The designer failed in understanding both the system internally (the feedback loop problem) and externally (the user-interface problem).

  A contingent of practitioners exists on both the bootstrap indie end and the mega-millions publisher end of the spectrum that has no time for any consideration of game design theory. How dare anyone tell these practitioners how to make a game? Their process boils down to a complicated dance of "guess and check." They put something they think is "good" into a game—maybe it's good or maybe it's not. It's the most rugged form of determinism—wherever they end up was where they meant to go all along.

Good design is not just whatever works or whatever sells. That is a koan at best. The study of game design is an attempt to find repeatable, predictive things that help game designers meet their design goals. These "things" may be immutable laws; but more than likely they'll just be helpful heuristics, bound to fail and be built upon until the originals have become as quaint and old-fashioned as imagining light as a particle traveling through ether or that behavior is regulated by four cardinal "humors."

- **SEE WITH THE PLAYER'S EYES.** Game development can be horribly tedious at times. Often in frustration at a non-functioning or poorly functioning feature, designers do whatever is the quickest that allows them to move on to the next task. But the designer's role is to understand how players will see this in the final product. What is the easiest solution is rarely the best solution. Should this menu take three clicks to navigate or is there a way to do it in one click? What if the three-click method is much easier to implement? Is it worth the trade-off? Tracy Fullerton, in *Game Design Workshop* calls this "be[ing] an advocate for the player" and cites it as the designer's most important responsibility.[1] It is difficult for you to see with the player's eyes because you are biased by having seen the game from embryo to finish. You have the luxury of comparing a game in its current state to what it was in an earlier unfinished state, so it will always look better to you than it will to a new player without all that information and baggage. The game designer often has to play the role of villain in telling the team (or even himself) that what they have made is not what is best for players.

- **EMBRACE BEING WRONG WITH HUMILITY AND UNDERSTANDING OF ALL OF ITS CONSEQUENCES.** Ego is great for promoting successes and inspiring others. It is horrible for remaining objective. Game design requires iteration. Designers are always tempted to treat their ideas as sacred. But when players experience those ideas and find them wanting, the designer must be OK with admitting the idea didn't work and changing it into a form that better meets the design goals. Playtesters are sometimes wrong. More often, they are right. A responsible designer knows when a playtest reveals that major changes need to be made.

. . . .

1   Fullerton, T., & Swain, C. (2008). *Game Design Workshop: A Playcentric Approach to Creating Innovative Games* (2nd ed.). Amsterdam: Elsevier Morgan Kaufmann.

- **COMMUNICATE WITH TEAM AND PLAYERS.** Understanding the game's systems and design goals has an additional responsibility: The game designer must be the one who helps the rest of the team understand those goals so they can work in concert. In large teams, this is often done by writing effective and clear game design documents and reiterating the goals and design focus when appropriate with every team interaction. This communicator-in-chief role extends also to communication with the players. The most brilliant, detailed system will fall flat with players if players do not understand it. The zeal with which the designer must carry the torch of the design goals and the means to achieve them must be duplicated by communicating clearly with the players through thoroughly tested user interface and content.

- **FILL IN THE GAPS.** Large "AAA" software titles can afford to be highly specialized due to the size of the team. They can hire narrative designers, user interface (UI) designers, designers who specialize in economies, and so forth. The smaller the team gets, the more the designer has to be a jack-of-all-trades. In the singular case, a team of one can rely only on the designer herself and the players. Anything the players cannot do on their own must be done by the game designer in this case. The game designer needs to have a polymath's skill set to fill in the gaps where the game's goals are not being met.

- **FACILITATE PLAY.** All of the previous similarities are applicable for any user-centered design process. With some change in nomenclature, those responsibilities make sense for designing a better ATM, or a website for ordering custom-tailored shirts. The difference in games is that the freedom that comes with play is fundamentally different than checking a box to determine whether a use case was satisfied. The game designer who errs on the side of staid checklists is just as remiss as the designer who riffs without having goals in mind and never finishes. Games are about play. That play can facilitate different types of emotions and aesthetics, but at its heart, it is still play. The designer shares in the producer's responsibility to keep the game on schedule. He shares in the engineer's responsibility to make the game functional. But the designer's unique responsibility is to ensure that the game is aesthetic and playful.

- **DON'T BE AN AUTEUR.** The common outside stereotype of a game designer is similar to the stereotype of the auteur film director. The auteur has tyrannical influence from beginning to end, dictating her unique vision to a team of cogs who implement her genius design. The auteur's ideas come from her mind fully formed. If the audience does not "get" it, then it's their fault for not being sophisticated enough. This is a stereotype without many successful antecedents in the real world. The successful game designer shares more traits with a successful scientist than an auteur.

Attributes of a Game Designer

As an administrator of one of the largest game design programs in the world, I constantly have different stakeholders (students, parents, admission representatives, and other university staff) ask what the qualities of a good game design student should be. Should they be mathletes? Should they be expert tinkerers? Luckily for nascent designers, my experience has led me away from the existence of any innate traits that make for a good designer. My answer tends to be just three elements, all of which can be cultivated by anyone: varied interests, persistence, and mindset and purpose.

Varied Interests

In my classes, I almost always ask the question of why the students want to design games. Quite often, students say, "I have been playing games since I was in the womb!" He (this is always a male student) claims that he has played every game released for every expensive console for the last 20 years. This, he claims, makes him extremely qualified to be a designer. These students tend to not care about game design theories because they know what a good game looks like already.

To this, I usually say how odd it is that I have eaten every day, maybe upward of 20 or 30 thousand meals by this point, yet I am just not a proficient chef. I have a refined palette, I know what I like and what I do not like, and I can even approximate it to some degree. Yet I often need a couple tries to make a good cake. It is almost as if experience in consuming something quite weakly correlates with the skill involved in making something!

In my experience, the best designers are not ones who are singularly interested in games. This is somewhat counterintuitive. The best designers are those who are interested in *everything* and can learn new skills and disciplines quickly. Not only does a designer often need to fill in and ramp up to a new responsibility quickly, but it is the core of creativity to draw from varied experience. Ernest Hemingway is quoted as saying, "In order to write about life first you must live it." Legendary designer Richard Bartle says, "Designers read up on every subject they can conceivably find. [...] They'll spend six hours absorbed in the details of the inner workings of the Palestine Liberation Organization in the 1970s because somehow they sense it will help their understanding of guilds, or orcs, or griefing, or terrain, or who knows what."[2]

---

2   Bateman, C. (2009). *Beyond Game Design: Nine Steps Toward Creating Better Videogames*. Boston, Massachusetts: Cengage Learning.

A technical term for this is *philomathy*. A *philomath* is a lover of learning. The goal of the philomath is to pursue varied skills and knowledge. Of course, a philomath can be a dilettante by not applying that varied knowledge. Therefore, a great game designer employs *practical philomathy*—applying the lessons of many different fields to a practical project.

Some, such as educational researcher James Paul Gee,[3] believe that games encourage learning because of their ability to teach the transfer of skills and knowledge between different domains. If this is true, then the game designer must also be comfortable transferring between domains of knowledge.

Persistence

> The rain to the wind said,
> "You push and I'll pelt."
> They so smote the garden bed.
> That the flowers actually knelt,
> And lay lodged—though not dead.
> I know how the flowers felt.
>
> **—ROBERT FROST "LODGED"**

Any successful creative endeavor is a slog. The most enjoyable times to be a game designer are at the beginning of a project, when the possibilities are endless, and at the end of the project, when the work is complete. Unfortunately, most of the project lies between those two points. The middle contains unfathomable bugs, bratty and rude playtesters, teammate squabbles, external flies in the ointment, and intense periods of self-doubt.

Poor designers settle or quit and then blame the bugs, playtesters, squabbles, and more for falling short of success. Excellent designers have the fortitude to stick with it when it gets tough and are generally rewarded for their hard work by better output. "Sticking with it" is not a measure of time. It is not a metric of how stone-faced you can be while you wait out your troubles. Ego-driven designers can wait out a tsunami of criticism, but if they do not adapt to that criticism, their work never improves. Instead, "sticking with it" is a measure of work. How can a designer adapt to all the obstacles in her path? That measure is a key attribute of a good designer. But it is not innate! It is something that can be trained.

. . . .

3   Gee, J. P. (2003). What Video Games Have to Teach Us About Learning and Literacy. *Computers in Entertainment (CIE)* 1(1),20.

Mindset and Purpose

I see a distinct difference among potential designers with two mindsets.

Some want to *design games*. They are perfect for the program at my university because that is exactly what our program teaches. They have no problem throwing together prototypes, and often many students I work with have a history of making games before I see them in our program. They embrace failure as a step toward success. The act of making games is what sustains them through the tough times.

The other type of potential designer is made up of folks who want to *be game designers*. These people I find much harder to help. All these folks want is the gravitas that comes with saying that you are a professional game designer. They want to tell someone what to make and have it made. They want to be the mythical "idea guy." These people shy away from or are dismissive of making things themselves. Often they claim they "don't have the skills" to make things. They want the title without the work. This comes from a common misconception of what game design actually is in practice.

▶ **NOTE** Spoiler: There is no gravitas. Sorry. It is a good icebreaker with strangers to say that you design games, but beyond that, it has its pros and cons like any other field.

The problem with being an idea guy is that everyone is one. Everyone has a great game idea that they have been itching to make. But actually making it is difficult. Sometimes it requires specialized knowledge; it always requires a significant amount of work and revision. Why should someone pay you for your ideas when everyone else has ideas? If you were a programmer, would you want to work on your ideas or someone else's? "But my ideas are great!" you may say. How do I know? Can you prove it? The way you can prove it is by making a playable prototype, which requires you to be someone who makes things, not just someone who talks about making things.

The concept of idea guys is a running gag in the industry. It is shorthand for people who want to work in games without actually doing any work. Either they are afraid of doing work or they are so afraid of their egos being damaged that they offshore and delay the work that might prove their idea is no good. There are a few notable idea guys in the industry today, but they earned that role by working really hard at implementing their now-famous ideas until they were successful. For example, Will Wright sometimes plays the role of idea guy, but he designed and coded *SimCity* by himself, not to mention tons of other games that never reached that level of success. There are no idea guys who started as "idea guys."

Before you continue on your journey toward learning about game design topics, take time to consider whether you want to design games or be a game designer.

Make Things

David Bayles and Ted Orland's book *Art & Fear* is a great collection of observations about creating things.[4] The following excerpt is about ceramics, but its lessons apply to almost any creative endeavor, especially making games:

▶ **NOTE** Thanks to Joël Franusic, as I originally found Art & Fear through his blog.

> The ceramics teacher announced on opening day that he was dividing the class into two groups. All those on the left side of the studio, he said, would be graded solely on the quantity of work they produced, all those on the right solely on its quality. His procedure was simple: On the final day of class he would bring in his bathroom scales and weigh the work of the "quantity" group: fifty pounds of pots rated an "A," forty pounds a "B," and so on. Those being graded on "quality," however, needed to produce only one pot—albeit a perfect one—to get an "A." Well, came grading time and a curious fact emerged: The works of highest quality were all produced by the group being graded for quantity. It seems that while the "quantity" group was busily churning out piles of work—and learning from their mistakes—the "quality" group had sat theorizing about perfection, and in the end had little more to show for their efforts than grandiose theories and a pile of dead clay.

At the start, ideas are exciting. It's easy to see an idea only for its promise. There is a honeymoon period where all the fun bits are coming together. But, extraordinarily, rarely does an idea go from form to product in a smooth transition. Most projects enter a period where the idea needs work: Either the code is not working, or the game is testing poorly, or there is just a lot of foundational work to complete. Those parts are no fun. At that point, the creator has a choice: Slog through the difficult parts and finish, or choose one of the other new, exciting ideas and start working on the fun parts that it promises. You can imagine what most people choose. It ends up leaving us with a graveyard of half-finished ideas. Sometimes giving up on an idea is justified and useful, but always chasing the next promising idea without ever finishing the one in progress is an easy mistake to make. Worse yet, if you abandon a project with a difficult trajectory for one with potential, you never learn the valuable lessons about the craft that the process of slogging through difficult and tedious tasks ends up often teaching you.

. . . .

4   Bayles, D., & Orland, T. (2001). *Art & Fear: Observations on the Perils (and Rewards) of Artmaking.* Eugene, Oregon: Image Continuum Press.

This is what Bayles and Orland are talking about. The "quantity" group probably made some terrible pots. That is okay. By doing so, they did not shame themselves or reveal that they didn't have it in them to create ceramics. Instead, they were able to build upon their mistakes. Their goal was not the one perfect pot, but better and better pots.

A similar, oft-repeated bit of advice is delivered by radio's Ira Glass:[5]

> Nobody tells this to people who are beginners, I wish someone told me. All of us who do creative work, we get into it because we have good taste. But there is this gap. For the first couple years you make stuff, it's just not that good. It's trying to be good, it has potential, but it's not. But your taste, the thing that got you into the game, is still killer. And your taste is why your work disappoints you. A lot of people never get past this phase, they quit. Most people I know who do interesting, creative work went through years of this. We know our work doesn't have this special thing that we want it to have. We all go through this. And if you are just starting out or you are still in this phase, you gotta know it's normal and the most important thing you can do is do a lot of work. Put yourself on a deadline so that every week you will finish one story. It is only by going through a volume of work that you will close that gap, and your work will be as good as your ambitions. And I took longer to figure out how to do this than anyone I've ever met. It's gonna take awhile. It's normal to take awhile. You've just gotta fight your way through.

Do not underestimate how difficult the evolution can be at times. Sometimes students cave in to the pressure that comes from the distance between where they are and where they want to be. They respond to it by lowering their expectations of their own work because they are "only students." Architect, designer, and professor Christopher Alexander has this fight often with his pupils:[6]

> In my life as an architect, I find that the single thing which inhibits young professionals, new students most severely, is their acceptance of standards that are too low. If I ask a student whether her design is as good as Chartres, she often smiles tolerantly at me as if to say, "Of course not, that isn't what I am trying to do.... I could never do that." Then, I express my disagreement, and tell her: "That standard must be our standard. If you are going to be a builder, no other standard is worthwhile. That is what I expect of myself in my own buildings, and it is what I expect of my students."

. . . .

5   Glass, I. (2009, August 18). "Ira Glass on Storytelling," part 3 of 4. Retrieved March 11, 2015, from www.youtube.com/watch?v=BI23U7U2aUY.

6   Gabriel, R. (1996). *Patterns of Software: Tales from the Software Community.* New York: Oxford University Press.

In this book, we'll discuss many of the fields of study that touch and inform game design. But these lessons are intended to guide your decision-making as you craft new games. These lessons are not intended to make you a game designer. Only you can do that through sustained, deliberate practice.

Abandon the common desire to achieve perfection. The Platonic ideal of your game only exists in your head. To approximate it is a worthwhile goal, but to demand adherence to it is not. Like Moses, your game can see the Promised Land but will never reach it. At some point, you must finish that game to have the experience of finishing. It needs to be released to the wild, not buried in a notebook or on a private thumb drive.

Additionally, your repeated practice in making games must be deliberate. If you make games, that is good. But if you make games with a purpose toward becoming better at making games, that is a whole lot better. Always challenge yourself to stretch outside your comfort zone. This is the only way to grow. As Susan Cain writes in *Quiet* about deliberate practice:

> When you practice deliberately, you identify the tasks or knowledge that are just out of your reach, strive to upgrade your performance, monitor your progress, and revise accordingly. Practice sessions that fall short of this standard are not only less useful—they're counterproductive. They reinforce existing cognitive mechanisms instead of improving them.[7]

Cultivate Your Gardens

Playing games is, of course, not the same as making them. You do not have to be a master at playing a game to understand why it works or to be able to describe and emulate its systems. But understanding what is being done in the field currently saves you a lot of time. And to do that, it is helpful to know how many different types of games solve their design problems. You do not have to reinvent the wheel if you can use best practices from other games. How does *Halo* do weapon switching? How does *League of Legends* implement end-game feedback? Perhaps you want to make a game by combining elements. It helps to know if that game already exists, or if a similar game exists and what it did right and wrong.

The most helpful research you can conduct is often to play bad games. Good games are similar, but bad games are different in a myriad of unique ways. Bad games teach you hundreds of things not to do. For instance, you can learn just as much about level

. . . .
7   Cain, S. (2013). *Quiet: The Power of Introverts in a World That Can't Stop Talking*. Broadway Books.

design from *Gunvalkyrie* as you can from *BioShock*. The other benefit of playing bad games is that it differentiates you as a designer. Most designers have played *Final Fantasy VII*, so most designers have internalized the same lessons. However, few will be able to tell you the lessons they learned from *Mario Is Missing, Dino Crisis 3, Rule of Rose*, or *Azurik: Rise of Perathia*.

> ▶ **NOTE** I try to be extraordinarily careful with the use of the terms "good" and "bad" since they are not only wildly subjective, but also serve as a means to eliminate all critical and helpful commentary from an object. In this instance, "good" games are games that match your tastes and do so in a way that is widely accepted as being successful. "Bad" games are those that are widely criticized or do not match your preferences.

In one class, I had students practice making presentations. At first, I let students select any topic of their choice that didn't violate university guidelines. Roughly 80 percent of the presentations ended up being about games they had played or games they wanted to design. It was the same presentation every month on the newest, hottest game. It was dreadfully boring. Then I changed up the assignment and forbid anyone from doing any presentation on games or game design. Instead, I challenged them to teach the class something new that was not about games or pop culture. I received a lot of push-back from students. They claimed that games were all they knew! I let these protestations fall on deaf ears. When I finally received the presentations, the topics were diverse and interesting: how to cook perfect chicken wings, the struggles in adopting three children from overseas, why greenhouse tomatoes are better than store-bought, tips on figure drawing—one memorable presentation even did an ethnographic study of Juggalo culture! People become more interesting if you push them away from what makes them wholly comfortable. Writer Geoff Dyer once wrote: "How can you know anything about literature if all you've done is read books?"[8] The same goes for games or any other creative endeavor.

Inspiration and guidance comes from every aspect of our lives. When we all do the same things, we mold ourselves into cookie-cutter patterns that make us identical to our neighbors. In some aspects, this is useful: We can communicate more easily using shared experiences, and we can understand the motivations of those who think like us. However, in creative endeavors, it can be a death knell. If you are identical to every other designer, then why should anyone hire you or play your games? Products that are identical to their direct competitors are called commodities. Commodities are priced as low as possible. Do you want to be paid as low as possible? Or do you want to be different and command the highest prices?

. . . .

8   Dyer, G. (1999). *Out of Sheer Rage: Wrestling with D. H. Lawrence.* New York, New York: North Point Press.

On Ontology and Dogma

Man only plays when in the full meaning of the word he is a man, and he is only completely a man when he plays.

—FREDRICH SCHILLER

Since the reality of play extends beyond the sphere of human life it cannot have its foundations in any rational nexus, because this would limit it to mankind. The incidence of play is not associated with any particular stage of civilization or view of the universe. Any thinking person can see at a glance that play is a thing on its own, even if his language possesses no general concept to express it. Play cannot be denied. You can deny, if you like, nearly all abstractions: justice, beauty, truth, goodness, mind, God. You can deny seriousness, but not play.

—JOHAN HUIZINGA

Many game design books start by posing this question: What is a game? Surely you have to know what you are creating in order to create it. So most game design textbooks have a chapter covering this question. The primary problem with designers considering this question is that no matter what the answer is, it's not instrumental in making better games. The main output of "what is a game" discussions is argument. We discuss it here only to give it some air, since it constantly comes up in nearly every generalist game design book. But this topic is only covered in a perfunctory way to make more time for concepts with direct application to craft.

Formalism

The topic of the essential features of a game is an important debate in the field of game studies. *Game studies* is an interdisciplinary catchall term for any research surrounding the cultural and ontological components of games and play. *Game design* is a subset of game studies that is most concerned with the normative aspects of how to make a game.

Scholars and lay folks have long attempted to pin down what exactly is meant when we say "game." Here are a few samples of what has been published:

* French sociologist Roger Caillois in 1961: "an activity which is essentially: Free (voluntary), separate [in time and space], uncertain, unproductive, governed by rules, make-believe."[9]

---

9   Caillois, R. (1961). *Man, Play, and Games*. University of Illinois Press.

- Games researcher Clark Abt in 1968: "any contest among adversaries operating under a limiting context for an objective."[10]
- Researchers E.M. Alvedon and Brian Sutton-Smith in 1971: "an exercise of voluntary control systems in which there is an opposition between forces, confined by a procedure and rules in order to produce a disequilibrial outcome."[11]:
- Philosopher Bernard Suits in 1978: "the voluntary attempt to overcome unnecessary obstacles."[12]
- Game designers Katie Salen and Eric Zimmerman in 2003: "a system in which players engage in an artificial conflict, defined by rules, that results in a quantifiable outcome."[13]
- Game designers Andrew Rollings and Ernest Adams in 2007: "a type of play activity, conducted in the context of a pretended reality, in which the participants try to achieve at least one arbitrary, nontrivial goal by acting in accordance with the rules."[14]
- Game designer Jesse Schell in 2008: "a problem-solving activity approached with a playful attitude."[15]
- Game researcher Jesper Juul in 2010: "a rule-based formal system with a variable and quantifiable outcome, where different outcomes are assigned different values, the player exerts effort in order to influence the outcome, the player feels attached to the outcome, and the consequences of the activity are optional and negotiable."[16]
- Game designer Stephen "thecatamites" Murphy at some point: "some combination of the following indivisible elements: skeleton, red key, score thing, magic door. If you see something that looks like a video game but isn't, you should immediately call the police."[17]

We could wander far into the weeds of philosophy, wondering if we are using the ruler to measure the table or the table to measure the ruler, but the point here is not to argue the validity or invalidity of any particular definition or definitions of games, but to understand why these definitions are not important for this exercise.

. . . .

10 Abt, C. C. (1968). "Games for Learning. Simulation Games in Learning," Sage Publications 65-84.

11 Avedon, E., & Smith, B. (1971). *The Study of Games*. New York: J. Wiley.

12 Suits, B. (1978). *The Grasshopper: Games, Life and Utopia*. Toronto: University of Toronto Press.

13 Zimmerman, E., & Salen, K. (2003). *Rules of Play: Game Design Fundamentals*. Cambridge, Massachusetts: MIT Press.

14 Adams, E. and Rollings, A. (2007). *Fundamentals of Game Design*. Upper Saddle River, New Jersey: Prentice Hall.

15 Schell, J. (2008). *The Art of Game Design: A Book of Lenses*. Amsterdam: Elsevier/Morgan Kaufmann.

16 Juul, J. (2010). *The Game, the Player, the World: Looking for a Heart of Gameness*. PLURAIS-Revista Multidisciplinar da UNEB, 1(2).

17 Murphy, S. (n.d.). "VIDEOGAMES." Retrieved March 16, 2015, from http://harmonyzone.org/Videogames.html.

Planetologists argue about the definition of planets (see the recent furor over Pluto), yet the planets keep their orbit regardless. Researchers Espen Aarseth and Gordon Calleja argue that we, as game designers, do not need definitions at all.[18] They say that fields such as literature, media studies, and planetology all have unsettled debates on definitions yet have no problems continuing on in the production of their field. They also argue that rigid definitions hurt multidisciplinary fields. As we have already covered, game design is a vastly multidisciplinary field.

As the cultural reach of games has increased, some works have been created that do not look at all like games, are familiar, and do not appeal to the same aesthetic goals and audiences. This is expected when a medium grows. However, in some sort of insane tribalism, some commentators use the previous definitions of games as a tool to exclude these works and creators from the community of creators.

A recent flare-up of this debate surrounded the indie game *Gone Home* by Fullbright. It was a top-seller and had wide-reaching critical acclaim,[19] yet it eschewed many of the features of mainstream games. There is no way to lose or win. There is no challenge in the traditional sense. Players explore a house and piece together the story of the home's inhabitants. There is no antagonizing force. There are no resources, per se. It fails some of the accepted definitions, yet many (including the creators)[20] consider it a game. Critics of the game often throw out that it is not a game at all and is thus somehow unworthy of praise or scrutiny.

Imagine an 18th century art critic who wrote that art was the depiction of images as a true depiction of their real elements. That was what art largely was up to that point. Then when abstract and surreal art came along in the 19th and 20th centuries, that definition had to change. A dogmatic following of the critic's rules would have denied the world the beauty of images like those popularized by painters like Salvador Dali, Piet Mondrian, or even fantasy artists like H. R. Giger or Frank Frazetta. Ironically, Frazetta's work has influenced almost every popular fantasy game since the dawn of the genre.[21]

If the purpose behind game formalism is to deny other works the light of day, then it is garbage scholarship. The medium needs boundary-ignoring works or it risks being

18 Aarseth, E., & Calleja, G. (2009). *The Word Game: The Ontology of an Undefinable Object.* In Lecture delivered at Philosophy of Computer Games Conference, Vol. 178, pp. 12–25.

19 Grant, C. (2014, January 15). "Polygon's 2013 Game of the Year: Gone Home." Retrieved March 16, 2015, from www.polygon.com/2014/1/15/5311568/game-of-the-year-2013-gone-home.

20 Gaynor, S. (2014). "Why Is Gone Home a Game?" Game Developer's Conference. San Francisco, CA.

21 "Tracing the Influence." (n.d.). Retrieved March 16, 2015, from www.hardcoregaming101.net/tracing/tracing2.htm.

stuck in an endless status quo. This should not be threatening to game designers. There is room for both the status quo and the new and original. Saying that something is "not a game" as interchangeable criticism with "I don't like this" weakens the entire medium of games by considering that only something that meets guidelines of taste is allowed to be in the medium at all. This puts a huge burden on designers: Make a thing with this list of features and it must be appealing and good or else you cannot be a game designer at all!

So why have game definitions in the first place? The term *game* means something. When you use it, you are attempting to communicate a concept. If it could mean anything, then the term itself must be empty. Relativism does not help us communicate. We consider the topic so that we can find commonalities that inform all of our work. To the end that a definition works, it is helpful. Otherwise, it is not. An attempt at a definition is not to be exclusionary, but to distill what the magic is that defines the medium in which designers labor and love. Any definition of games that we determine now may become irrelevant by the creation of something new that invalidates that definition. Arguing about that definition is just territorialism.

Make what is in your heart. Let someone else worry about classification.

Summary

- A game designer needs a variety of skills to be the jack-of-all-trades that meets a project's varied needs.
- Nothing that a designer needs is innate. All design skills can be cultivated through practice and a correct attitude.
- Reading about game design can be helpful. That's why you have this book! However, nothing is a substitute for making games. If you wait until you are ready to make games, you'll never make a single one.
- Games are great, but don't only be about games. There is so much to learn in this world in vastly varying domains of knowledge. You never know when you'll be able to connect what you learn to games, so try to learn everything.
- Don't worry about people who waste time arguing about what is or is not a game. It is philosophically interesting, but it does not have much relevance for actually making anything tangible. At worst, it forces design into rigid limitations. If you make something clever and someone calls it "not a game," you have still made something clever, and they have made nothing at all.

2 Problem Statements

A problem clearly stated is a problem half solved.

—DOROTHEA BRANDE

Often designers are working from a completely blank slate. What game do you make? When do you know you are done? How do you know if you have succeeded? One way is to make a problem statement. The *problem statement* is a simple way of asking what the designer or team is trying to do with the game. By identifying the design problem you are looking to solve, you eliminate situations in which you are simply copying the work of others and making something dull and uninspired. One way to formulate a design problem statement is by starting with "What if...?" This allows the design that follows to be an exploration of that question.

Defining the Problem

During the 2000s, Electronic Arts had a concept called "the X." The X was a simple saying or slogan that helped the team "sell" the idea and understand what they were making. It was the problem statement. For instance, *Madden NFL 2005*'s X ended up being the back-of-the-box slogan that marketing used to sell the game: "Defense Wins Championships." This three-word slogan told the team that *Madden NFL 2005* was going to be about improving and polishing the defensive options in the game when compared to previous American football games.

> ◆ **TIP** For a different perspective on the X, see Randy Pausch's "An Academic's Field Guide to Electronic Arts" at www.evl.uic.edu/spiff/class/cs426/Notes/PauschAcademicsFieldGuideToEA.pdf.

Note that problem statements do not explain what the game is when it is finished. That would require prescient future prediction. Often, creative endeavors do not follow a predictable path. Psychologist Dean Keith Simonton found that often a kind of unpredictable search is involved in many successful creative efforts.[1] Having no plan at all is not recommended. Instead, try to distill a game down to a fundamental core for which a new idea can be built. What makes it different? What makes it interesting? All games involve solving problems to some degree. What problems are posed to the player and under what context they appear is the designer's decision. You may have to change that core problem along the way, but that core focus gives you something from which to build.

The following sidebars include example problem statements for some released games with a less effective (bad) version of the statement, a more effective (better) version, and an explanation of why the better statement is indeed better.

---

1   Simonton, D. K. (2010). "Creative thought as blind-variation and selective-retention: Combinatorial models of exceptional creativity." Physics of Life Reviews, 7(2), 156-179.

PROJECT GOTHAM RACING (2001)

BAD PROBLEM STATEMENT: What if a racing game gave out kudos?

BETTER PROBLEM STATEMENT: What if a racing game was determined by style instead of just speed?

WHY: Who cares about kudos? The problem that the game is trying to solve is how to make a new win condition for racing games. The solution was kudos, not the problem! The problem was finding out a different way to "score" a race! One hint is that if you keep asking "Why?" then you probably have not dug deeply enough into the problem. The deeper question here is "Why are kudos interesting?" The answer is "Because they are a different way to score a race." Aha! This digging deeper gets us to the core of the design.

HEAVY RAIN (2010)

BAD PROBLEM STATEMENT: Who is the Origami Killer?

BETTER PROBLEM STATEMENT: What would it be like to "play" a movie?

WHY: The first problem statement here is a question about the story, which is not determined until later in the project and is not the fundamental design motivation to the game. David Cage, founder of Quantic Dream, is an opinionated designer/producer who is largely focused on making interactive narratives. Therefore, in this case, the problem has to be about that influence in some way. Note also that a problem statement does not have to be what makes the game entirely unique. Quantic Dream's earlier games tackled similar design questions.

BRAID (2008)

BAD PROBLEM STATEMENT: What would happen if you could rewind time an infinite number of times, make time relative to a player's position on the screen, and create a shadow character that allowed you to perform multiple actions at the same time?

BETTER PROBLEM STATEMENT: What puzzles could be created if you could manipulate time?

WHY: The first problem is far too specific about the mechanics. It is not likely that the designer started with this specific end goal in mind. It's more likely that the designer thought about ways that time manipulation could create interesting mechanics and puzzles. This leads to the formulation of the better problem statement. The mechanical decisions all come from that fundamental issue of figuring out what happens when a player manipulates time.

SAN JUAN (2004)

BAD PROBLEM STATEMENT: What would a card game version of *Puerto Rico* look like?

BETTER PROBLEM STATEMENT: What mechanics, dynamics, and aesthetics from *Puerto Rico* could be preserved in a card game?

WHY: *San Juan* is a card game version of *Puerto Rico*, and the original design consideration was probably how to make *Puerto Rico: the Card Game*. Yet *Puerto Rico: the Card Game* could be literally any card game with a plantation and shipping theme integrated into the text and art. A better way to start would be to understand what elements of *Puerto Rico* were worth preserving: Selecting roles, piggybacking off the roles of other players, harvesting crops, shipping them, and managing resources are all essential elements that make the transition from *Puerto Rico* to *San Juan*. The better problem statement also yielded another popular game, *Race for the Galaxy*. It was built off the same idea to preserve elements of *Puerto Rico* in a strategy card game.[2]

Poor problem statements don't get at the heart of the game, are overly vague, are overly derivative, are only marketing statements, or don't drive the design. For instance, "How do we make another *Elder Scrolls* game?" is a poor problem statement. It essentially directs the designers to just make a copy of what they have already made.

The *best* problem statements should get down to the concrete design goal so the designer and team can follow up with effective tasks to create a unique and focused design.

Low-Hanging Fruit

After deciding at a high level on what problem you want to solve, the next step is to figure out how to solve that problem. This is usually done by visualizing and describing what the game will look and play like. You can use this high-level sketch of your rules, mechanics, and/or theme in order to start building prototypes.

This process has a few danger areas. Let's look at an example that illustrates these dangers.

. . . .

2   Lehmann, T. (2011, May 11). "Race for the Galaxy Designer Diary #1." Retrieved March 16, 2015, from http://web.archive.org/web/20090227034911/boardgamenews.com/index.php/boardgamenews/comments/game_preview_race_for_the_galaxy_designer_preview_1.

Assume you are tasked to create a game that uses all four of the following elements:

- A standard 17-inch diameter car tire
- Six (three pairs) of calf-height white cotton tube socks
- 5 pounds of Florida navel oranges
- A 10-foot length of thick rope

You do not have to use all of the materials exhaustively (that is, you do not have to use all the oranges, all the socks, or all the rope), but you must use at least a portion of all four elements.

▶ **NOTE** Thanks to Dax Gazaway for the setup for this idea.

Before reading further, write down a one- or two-sentence description of the *first* game you envision. The game should be coherent and feasible, but it does not necessarily need to be fun or strategically fulfilling. Please come up with your idea before reading further... I'll wait.

I have given this exercise to professional game designers, college professors, lay persons with no professional ties to games, and (many) students. Originally, I had planned to keep track of the results as a pseudo-scientific study. However, the first 20 results I received were nearly identical.

The easiest idea, the idea that sticks out the most, is the "low-hanging fruit." This fruit is easy to pick and anyone can reach up and grab it. For the sake of consistency, let's say your idea is like the first ones I received: Create a game where you throw an orange through the tire. This is usually done by putting an orange in the sock and using the sock as a sling. The rope is used to hang the tire from a tree or structure. As I said before, the first 20 people I gave this exercise to did roughly the same thing. There were some variations: Some used the rope to measure distance, some had the tire rolling instead of stationary. Yet the core of the game was the same: Throw oranges through the tire to win. Is this the idea you came up with?

Think of how limiting this is. Think of all the things you can do with an orange. Sure, you can throw oranges, but you can also juggle, balance, eat, squeeze, roll, peel, stack, hide, or catch them, among dozens of other things. A long list of verbs can be created for each of the four elements. Yet each of the first 20 people asked chose a similar set of verbs. These participants had a range of ages and game design experience. They did not choose the same actions because of a similar background; they chose it because it was the easiest solution to imagine.

When solving traditional problems, we often go for the simplest possible solution. But in efforts that require creativity, the simplest solution is the one everyone thinks of first. If an important part of design is the creativity of ideas, then stopping when you think of the first reasonable solution limits you to only the most obvious conclusions.

Although students answered the same as the other participants in this exercise, the difference between them and design professionals is that the design professionals were willing to come back with better answers later. One of the professors I gave this exercise to came back to me the following day with a really innovative game idea for the materials that I had never heard before. Design professionals tend to keep digging away at the idea until they have explored all of its facets. And, as a result, they can choose from a deep list of ideas. Students, however, tend to stop at the first idea that makes sense.

Functional Fixedness

German psychologist Karl Duncker studied a phenomenon related to how the preceding low-hanging fruit exercise produced similar answers from person to person.[3] In a famous test, he asked participants who were given a candle, a box of matches, and a box of thumbtacks to figure out how to attach the candle to the wall so that the candle's wax did not drip onto the table below when lit.

The solution is to use the tacks to affix the box that the tacks came in to the wall and to place the lit candle in the box. However, subjects found it hard to use the box as a tool to solve the problem because they focused on the use of the box as a container for matches. Duncker called this phenomenon *functional fixedness*. To them, the function of the box was fixed as being a container. They could imagine no other function. When designing games, it can be easy to assume that the uses of common objects or mechanics are fixed. In the low-hanging fruit game example, oranges look like baseballs or softballs, so the resulting games largely treated them as such.

Often, the most creative games break fundamental assumptions about genre. *Divekick*, for example, is a fighting game that eschews combos, complex control schemes, blocking, directional movement, and even life bars but still delivers a fun fighting game experience. Its designers took all the elements that most fighting game designers take as being fixed elements and simply threw them out. *Shadow of the Colossus* created a world right out of a *Legend of Zelda*-style adventure game and removed everything but the boss fights.

. . . .
3   Duncker, K., & Lees, L. S. (1945). "On Problem-Solving." Psychological Monographs, 58(5), i.

Brainstorming

One technique studios tend to employ to find creative solutions to problems is *brainstorming*. In classic brainstorming, members from one or many disciplines who are stakeholders in the project get together in the same place to generate ideas. The brainstorm tends to have a theme or purpose; there is some kind of problem the brainstorm session tries to solve. Someone moderates the meeting, and members spout out possible solutions while someone else records the proceedings.

This technique was presented in the 1950s by Alex Osborn in his book *Applied Imagination*.[4] In his book, he coined the term "brainstorming" and its cardinal rules. The rules he created mostly carry over to properly run brainstorming meetings today:

- **QUANTITY, NOT QUALITY.** Worry about "good" ideas later. In brainstorms, just come up with as many ideas as possible.

- **BUILD ON IDEAS.** The reason the brainstorm is a communal activity is that participants use other participant's ideas to spur the creation of new ideas from different perspectives.

- **ENCOURAGE "CRAZY" IDEAS.** Anyone can come up with the obvious ideas. If the obvious ideas worked, the team would not be experiencing the problem that results in the brainstorm session in the first place! Even if the ideas presented are ridiculous, maybe a kernel of that idea will inspire some other better and more feasible idea.

- **NO CRITICISM.** Not only do people self-censor, but when we hear ideas, our critical evaluation centers go active and we try to evaluate why the idea will not work. In corporate environments, there is often a political motive to stamp out competing ideas to develop one's own standing. This is counter to the brainstorm's goals.

Osborn found that when these rules were followed, idea generation was more productive than in a normal meeting situation.

Unfortunately, research on brainstorming versus other techniques in the corporate environment since Alex Osborn created his rules has not been so kind. In fact, research has clearly shown that using the brainstorming rules in an individual setting provides more (and higher quality) ideas per person than the traditional group brainstorming setting.[5]

· · · · · · · · · · · · · · · · · · · ·

4   Osborn, A. (1963). *Applied Imagination: Principles and Procedures of Creative Problem-Solving.* (3rd rev. ed.). New York: Scribner.

5   Mullen, B., Johnson, C., & Salas, E. (1991). "Productivity Loss in Brainstorming Groups: A Meta-analytic Integration." *Basic and Applied Social Psychology*, 12, 3–23.

Researchers took a look at what was holding back group brainstorming and came up with some reasons for the discrepancy:[6]

- **EVALUATION APPREHENSION.** Anyone with any sort of social anxiety understands this at heart. One of the rules of brainstorming is that quality does not matter. Yet in the corporate environment, workers are constantly being judged on the quality of their work. As a result many, even subconsciously, hold back and "test the waters" to see what kind of ideas are being received appropriately. They then use that as a guide for the risk level of other ideas, essentially turning off the "wild idea" center for fear of being judged. Simple body language cues such as frowns or raised eyebrows can turn us off and make us feel uncomfortable about delivering ideas.

- **SOCIAL LOAFING.** If you have ever ridden a tandem bike, the person in front can pedal, steer, and brake. The person in back can only pedal and pray. When you go up hills, you can split the work and pedal equally hard, or the person in the back can enjoy the breeze and let the person in the front do all the work. If your feet are moving around the pedals but not pushing, to any outside observer, it looks like you are working just as hard. This is the concept of *social loafing*. In a brainstorm, you'll usually find that a couple of people will provide the lion's share of ideas. Sometimes these are Type-A personalities who compulsively dominate every meeting. Sometimes these are just naturally prolific idea generators. In practice, everyone else in the meeting sits back and lets these people take the helm. Maybe they don't want to break the flow of ideas. Maybe they just want to be polite. In any case, they reduce the output ideas by not pedaling as hard as other members. Interestingly, when researchers conducted exit interviews in studies of social loafing, the loafers compared themselves to the least producing member of the group, in effect saying: "Well, I didn't do the least" or "I did almost as much as that guy" rather than comparing themselves to the highest producers of the group.[7]

- **PRODUCTION BLOCKING.** This is an unfortunate side effect of the human attention span. When you sit in a room with others and generate ideas, you have to wait for everyone else in the room to be silent before you can chime in and have your ideas heard. This pause is, in essence, limiting individuals from contributing as much as they could. In a brainstorm with only one individual, ideas are recorded as fast as they are generated; there is no pause.

· · · · · · · · · · · · · · · · · ·

6   Diehl, M., & Stroebe, W. (1987). "Productivity Loss in Brainstorming Groups: Toward the Solution of a Riddle." *Journal of Personality and Social Psychology*, 53(3), 497.

7   Paulus, P. B., & Dzindolet, M. T. (1993). "Social Influence Processes in Group Brainstorming." *Journal of Personality and Social Psychology*, 64(4), 575.

Summary

- By being explicit about the design problem your game aims to solve, you can focus early design and development toward achieving a specific goal.

- The first answer you think of to a problem is likely a simple solution, but it isn't often the best. Use brainstorming techniques to power past the low-hanging fruit.

- Functional fixedness causes us to only solve problems in traditional ways, whereas better or more original solutions may be possible.

- The focus of brainstorming is on the quantity of ideas. By using brainstorming rules, you can avoid editing that limits connection-building between ideas.

- Individual brainstorming may be more effective than group brainstorming.

3

Development Structures

Adding manpower to a late software project makes it later.

—BROOKS' LAW

Game development can be a complex endeavor. In many cases, dozens of distinct egos must harmoniously coordinate their efforts to fit moving parts together seamlessly. Needless to say, this can take a lot of organization.

We use models like the *software development life cycle* to wrap our heads around the various processes that go into creating a complex project. This is a model of order: When do we do things and what steps follow what others? These structures are not limited to software development; you can model any product development with these systems. It sometimes only requires modifying the nomenclature.

Production Methodologies

Even though these models were developed with software in mind, they work for many complex creative endeavors. There are many different formulations of the software development life cycle because the needs for various projects and industries differ. However, most break down into one of two general types: waterfall and iterative.

Waterfall

The simplest software development model is the *waterfall* method (**FIGURE 3.1**). Even though it is generally cited as a poor way to organize your software project, the waterfall method's simplicity and predictability, and the fact that many publishers draw up their contracts based on this model, lead many studios to still employ this method. The waterfall method was first mentioned in the 1950s[1] and takes its name from a waterfall in that it is nature's one-way street: Water flows down, never up.

▶ **NOTE** A better allusion might have been to black holes, but that term was not used until the mid-1960s. It's also much more cynical.

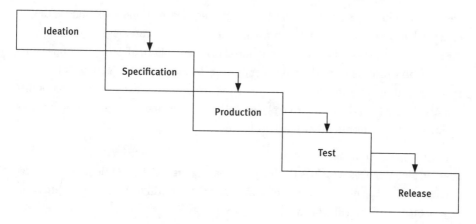

FIGURE 3.1
The waterfall method organizes steps of production that flow in only one direction.

The waterfall method starts with *ideation*, which is, literally, the generation of ideas. This is where the brainstorming, concept art, and sometimes prototyping come together and the team gets an idea of what they are about to build.

In *specification*, the team gets down to the specifics of what they will build. Designers write game design documents (GDDs), engineers write technical design documents (TDDs), and artists start creating base assets or media design documents (MDDs). These first two steps together (ideation and specification) are generally known as *preproduction*.

. . . .
1   Bennington, H. D. (1956, June). "Production of Large Computer Systems." In proceedings during the Symposium on Advanced Programming Methods for Digital Computers at the Office of Naval Research (ONR).

Next, the team enters what is usually the longest phase: *production*. In this phase, the team actually constructs what they laid out in their design documentation. As already mentioned, the key aspect of the waterfall method is that work flows only in one direction. This means that, at this point, the team is strictly making what is on the design documents and is not revising and changing the requirements to adapt to new issues. Production generally splits into self-contained milestones where individual features are completed and then are not touched again. This allows the team to schedule with a great amount of specificity.

The last two steps can require a high percentage of the total work of the project. In *test*, the team works together to eliminate any bugs and rough edges generated during production. This can be laborious since the nature of the waterfall method does not allow the team to go back and make changes that may result in fewer bugs and technical challenges. When the system is sufficiently bug free, the product is *released* and the team starts over with a new project.

Alpha, *beta*, and *gold* are terms for sections of the test phase. Alpha is the state of the project when all the features have been completed and the testing stage begins. Beta is the state when the bug count has been reduced to acceptably small levels, but bugs are still incoming. Gold is when the publisher or team decides the game is sufficiently bug free and sends it to the manufacturer (or releases it to partners) to be printed and/or distributed. These terms can vary from place to place. For instance, Google likes to label its products as beta long after they have been released.

In **FIGURE 3.2**, the number of bugs in the project increases until the features are all complete. In alpha, the team tackles the bugs, decreasing the number (while some bugs are still being added as mistakes are made). In beta, the team still bounces above zero bugs as new bugs are added and tackled.

FIGURE 3.2
Bugs increase as features are implemented and decrease as features lock and the team sets their priority to bug elimination. However, new bugs are constantly found, and it is tough to keep a project at zero bugs.

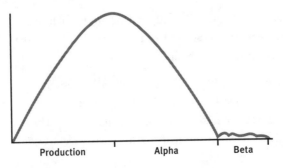

Production   Alpha   Beta

The waterfall method is highly predictable. It can be broken down into tiny, measurable tasks. The financiers can know exactly when the cycle will end and can plan the massive multimillion dollar ad campaign around that release date.

But the drawback is that game development projects are not straightforward and easily predictable. Most software has an easy end state: Did my document print? Did my source compile? Did my photo effect get applied? If yes, you are finished. Games are different. Games involve challenge, mystery, and learning. When you start making a game, you have no idea if your implementation will be fun until it is made. "Fun" is an elusive concept that is highly subjective and personal. It's often the case where what seems like it would be fun on paper simply is not fun in practice, or a system that you created on a spreadsheet has a hidden dominant strategy that you missed during planning. What happens in a waterfall software product? You must forge ahead because there is no turning back. In games, this is deadly. Instead, we need a model where we can test before production and throughout the process and still be able to return to earlier steps. This kind of process is known as an *iterative process*.

Iterative Processes

FIGURE 3.3 shows an iterative process for designing games. The game starts first with an *idea*. That idea causes the team to formulate a *plan*. Often these plans are in the form of design documentation like GDDs, flowcharts, and mockups.

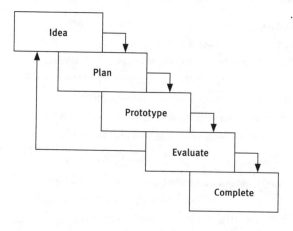

FIGURE 3.3 Iterative processes allow for steps to repeat. Often, they tackle small portions of a project at a time and go through many cycles.

Next the team creates prototypes. A *prototype* is the smallest possible execution of the idea that allows the idea to be tested in a real environment. In board games this is incredibly easy! All a designer has to do is scribble on some paper, assemble some components like dice or playing cards, and go at it! In digital games, this can be a little more difficult because sometimes the technical prerequisites need a substantial amount of groundwork before useful prototyping can happen. This is why some digital game creators start with paper prototypes.

The next step is to *evaluate* the prototype. Here the team figures out what the successes and failures of the prototype are and uses them to formulate new ideas to restart the process. Teams may complete this loop a dozen times or more. Eventually, the creators either run out of time or patience and have to *complete* the project with the best results from previous tests.

Scrum is a popular brand of agile software development. It involves setting up specific roles for various people including the ScrumMaster and the Product Owner, and it focuses on solving problems endemic to the software development process, such as marathon meetings and outside interference.

One of the great metaphors in Scrum literature is the story of the pigs and the chickens. The story goes thus: A pig and a chicken get together and decide to open a restaurant. The chicken suggests serving ham and eggs, but the pig balks. He says that the chicken is only involved, but he, the pig, would be committed. The fable is a parallel to the two types of people involved in a project. Chickens are involved in the project and provide input or consultation, but ultimately it is the pigs that need to make the big decisions because they are the ones fully committed. Respecting the role of the pigs puts the power of the project in the hands of those most instrumental to its success or failure.

This *iterative design method* allows creators to maximize time testing of their ideas. Remember that this is important because you do not know what will be fun or balanced until you see how real, unpredictable players actually interact with it. Many designers resist this model because it forces them to constantly change their ideas. They want to see a fully formed idea go untouched from brain to product. Unfortunately, quite often those products are of inferior quality to ones that were thoroughly tested. Who knows? You may get lucky and get it right on the first try, but do you really want to bet a studio's future on it?

Intuitively agile methods seem to be the way to go, and they anecdotally seem to provide for more organized projects that dovetail with best results. That said, the Game Outcomes Project studied what factors most contributed to the success of game software projects and found only a small effect (if any) on outcomes with regards to project methodology.[2]

. . . .

2   Tozour, P. (2014, December 16). "The Game Outcomes Project, Part 1: The Best and the Rest," Gamasutra: Paul Tozour's Blog. Retrieved April 7, 2015, from www.gamasutra.com/blogs/PaulTozour/20141216/232023/ The_Game_Outcomes_Project_Part_1_The_Best_and_the_Rest.php.

Climbing the Pyramid

The metaphor that I feel most generally covers game development from the smallest board game to the largest software project is a model I call *climbing the pyramid* (**FIGURE 3.4**).

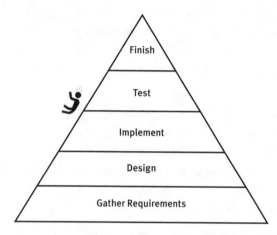

FIGURE 3.4 Climbing the pyramid often involves sliding back down to an earlier step.

Projects start at the bottom of the pyramid. First, they must *gather requirements*. For a board game, this can be as simple as making a list of the features desired and the audience expectations. For a complex software project, requirements gathering can be a long undertaking. In any project, it must include research that supports understanding the needs the project is trying to solve, understanding the competitors in the industry, and understanding how similar projects tackle similar goals. If you have a broad understanding of what techniques are used in the industry, this step can be easier.

Next, the project climbs up the pyramid to *design*. To naive designers, this is where they start and finish. However, for all projects, this is only part of the designer's role. In this phase, the team or designer takes the requirements from the previous phase and translates them into a full set of instructions of what the project will be. In digital games, this can be broken down into game design, technical design, and media design documents (among others). In analog games, this usually starts as a draft of the rules and content.

The third phase often takes the longest and is often confused with being the final phase. To *implement*, the creators put together whatever is needed to make the game playable and complete to the requirements. In digital games, this involves scripting and coding the game, making and placing the art and animations, and tuning and tweaking the aspects of the game that make systems work together. In analog games, this involves creating the materials for the game. This often involves printing and cutting game boards and cards.

The next phase up the pyramid is the most important. To *test*, the teams take what they have made in implementation and put it in front of likely users. This serves multiple purposes. First, it identifies bugs. This may be bugs in the traditional sense—elements that do not work to design—or bugs *in the design* so that elements of the design end up not meeting the requirements. The next purpose is to understand how the implementation works in the real world. Do players like it? What do they do? What do they not do? How does this compare to the game's requirements? Testing is not a static phase. In any development structure, it requires numerous iterations. These iterations continue until the project must be released or it requires no more changes. It is rare for the terminating condition to be the latter.

The final phase, *finishing*, is often ignored wholly in studies of development structure. In finishing, creators take the state of the project resulting from the final test and prepare it for publishing. In digital games, this can be as simple as building an executable and uploading the content to a portal. In analog games, it can be more complicated because parts may need to be sourced and priced.

The essential feature of climbing the pyramid is that during any phase (even during finishing), the project may slide down to a previous step. In fact, the project may slide down multiple steps, requiring a refactoring of the requirements themselves. It is not unheard of for a team to have been working on a digital game for some time when a publisher comes back and asks for it to be tied to a completely different intellectual property (for example, this racing game now needs to take place in the SpongeBob universe instead of Hot Wheels). In this scenario, the team has to go back to requirements gathering. What expectations stay the same and what differ? Some of the work from earlier is preserved, but only that which matches the new requirements and design.

Testing is the slipperiest part of the pyramid. It often requires the team to reimplement features or change the design of old features. It may even require the team to reconsider base assumptions about requirements.

Waterfall projects can fit this model because each is a single case in which a team climbs the pyramid without ever slipping. A pure waterfall project is rare. Teams that intend to use the waterfall method often implicitly go back and revise earlier steps when conditions warrant it.

Regardless of which model is used, creators must have a structure to their project to understand what to do next. Ignoring this structure endangers a game—it might get stuck in constant development with no clear vector toward release and no way for the designers to understand how to proceed.

Scope

Most projects encounter a common problem. It affects new programmers and those who have been producing content for decades. It's so prevalent that an entire job function is to address this one problem—mismanaged *scope*. Most software projects try to fit more into the project than can really fit. The colloquial way of referring to the relationship between the various elements of a software project is the *Project Management Triangle*, which balances features, quality, and cost (**FIGURE 3.5**).

▶ **NOTE** The Project Management Triangle comes in many different formulations. Fast, Good, and Cheap is one. Scope, Cost, and Time is another. Regardless, all versions deal with the reality of limited resources in project environments.

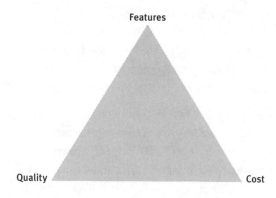

FIGURE 3.5 Projects must balance features, quality, and cost.

Another way to imagine the trade-off between these elements is to imagine three cups that represent features, quality, and resources (cost). You have a set amount of liquid and can distribute that between the three cups in any way you wish (**FIGURE 3.6**).

The amount of liquid in the pitcher is constant. However, you can distribute it in a number of ways. For instance, you can pour a lot of liquid into the Features cup (**FIGURE 3.7**). This allows you to have a ton of features. However, you do not have much liquid left for quality or resources. With low quality, you do not have resources available to apply polish or fix bugs. With low cost (meaning not much liquid is in the Cost cup), you do not have resources to hire a large or particularly skilled team or to spend a long time on the project.

Features   Quality   Cost

Features   Quality   Cost

CUPS SYMBOLS BY RYAN BECK, FROM THENOUNPROJECT.COM COLLECTION.
PITCHER SYMBOLS BY IRENE TRAUTLUFT, FROM THENOUNPROJECT.COM COLLECTION.

FIGURE 3.6 You may focus on any of the three, but each drop you dedicate to one is one drop less for the other two.

FIGURE 3.7 One possible distribution of resources.

You can make a similar trade-off if the team decides to focus on quality, instead. By necessity, when you focus on quality, the team must focus on fewer features at a lower cost. If the team focuses on taking as much time as they need to create a quality product, they scrape resources from producing additional assets. This is one of the reasons that studios perpetually crunch—they try to minimize the Cost cup to increase the Features or Quality cup.

The problem that many professional and student projects encounter is that their costs are fixed. This reduces the number of variables to two. If the team wants to increase the depth or number of features, they must reduce the quality of the rest of the project. Likewise, if they want to increase the quality of the project, they must reduce the number or size of the features. This is why it is recommended for student projects to focus on the smallest number of features necessary to make a playable game. Minimizing features and holding resources constant leads to the highest-quality product.

This is one of the most important lessons to learn in all project development, but it cannot be effectively contained in a document. This is a lesson you have to learn for yourself because it adapts to each new project with each new participant. Always assume that you'll exceed your resources with the proposed features and level of quality. By doing so, you err on the side of caution. It is much easier to add features than it is to cancel them because cancelled features may have dependencies elsewhere. What tends to happen in overscoped projects is that the quality vertex suffers the most. If you care about quality, try to tightly control features and cost.

Many studios attempt to avoid the overscoping problem by including a *fudge factor* in their estimates. For example, take a situation in which a team believes it will take one week to complete each game level and there are 12 game levels to complete. An honest estimate would assume that the game levels would take 12 weeks. However, the team adds a fudge factor multiplier to the estimate to account for bad human planning. A 50-percent fudge factor makes the estimate 18 weeks to do the 12 levels.

An issue with adding fudge factors is that it shifts the responsibility of correctly estimating the project duration from the people making the actual estimates to the people who are deciding what the correct fudge factor should be. A level designer who believes that a level will really take between a week and a week and a half is incentivized to cite "1 week" as the estimate, especially if she knows that her estimate will be padded by 50 percent.

Another danger of fudge factors is that they can compound. In the 12-level game example, the designer for level 3 estimates that it will take her 24 man-hours to implement the level. The producer supervising the level designers adds the fudge factor of 50 percent, so now the estimate is 36 man-hours. The executive producer of the team takes all the estimates, including the 36–man-hour estimate for level 3, and sums them up to 1,500 man-hours. However, because the individual producers already added fudge factors, the real estimate is 1,000 man-hours. The executive producer sees the report of 1,500 man-hours and, knowing that the fudge factor is 50 percent, makes a "real" estimate of 2,250 man-hours. Something that was originally estimated for 1,000 man-hours is now estimated to take 125 percent longer.

Overscoping is tempting because it costs little in the way of resources to come up with an idea. The idea could be great, but unless you also have the resources to implement and iterate it, it risks weighing down the rest of the project. Instead, many successful studios attempt to create what is called an MVP (minimum viable product). This is the smallest game or project that fulfills the game's original problem statement. Perhaps a fighting game is planned to have 12 characters, each with 9 unique moves, but the game would be playable with 2 characters that have 5 moves. The team should plan to make the 2-character/5-move version first and see how long it takes to make that solid and fun; then they will have a better base from which to plan how many remaining characters and moves they can support.

Scope prediction is ridiculously difficult. We are blind to our weaknesses and continually paint ourselves into bad positions due to overscoping. This fells projects from the smallest student work to the largest AAA studios. The best vaccination is constant vigilance against scope increases and active attempts to mitigate their effects.

Summary

- Different production methodologies exist to structure building projects. Waterfall methods generally proceed in a set order, whereas agile methods may not proceed linearly.
- Because they have more than one shot at design, agile methods can plan for changes in requirements based on prototypes and early feedback. That said, agile methods are less predictable.
- Scope measures the amount of effort that can be divided among development activities.
- By focusing on creating new features, a team necessarily gives up on spending time to make existing features better, all else being equal.
- It is tough to make realistic estimates of the time a project will take. Many adjust underestimates by adding a fudge factor. However, care must be taken to make sure this is a realistic determination.

4 Starting Practices

Be great in act as you have been in thought.

—JEAN PAUL

If I can relate only one lesson in this book, it's that the way to become a game designer is not found in the pages of any book, no matter how well-written. The key to becoming a game designer is simply to make games.

When asked about their game ideas, students often answer with riffs on their favorite large AAA games. Their ideas are often about making the next *Skyrim*. That is taking an overly large bite. They subtly ignore the massive complexity of these games, which often have development teams that number in the hundreds.

Making games is a complex affair. Even comparatively simple mobile games can be really complex. Rami Ishmail, cofounder of award-winning developer Vlambeer, is no stranger to complexity: "Even the simplest of games is really complex. When you're starting out you can't see that yet. That's why you need to start simple."[1]

. . . .

1   Ismail, R. (2015, March 17). Twitter Feed. Retrieved March 18, 2015, from https://twitter.com/tha_rami/status/578004339362430976.

Analog Games

Many aspiring game designers do not even consider analog games such as board or card games. Fewer still consider role-playing and storytelling games or sports. Yes, even sports have designers! Games are such a broad medium that limiting yourself to just large, complex games for specialized game consoles is narrow-minded and will lead to only a narrow understanding of the craft. Analog games in particular are a great place to start your design practice because of how analog games typically expose all the inner workings of the game to the player. You may lack exposure to some of these games, so in TABLE 4.1, I have provided a list of some analog games—board games, card games, role-playing games (RPGs), and sports games—along with their level of complexity.

▶ **NOTE** Complexity can be measured by various metrics. For the purposes of this table, I used only an imprecise measurement of the length of the rules.

TABLE 4.1 Example Analog Games and Complexity Levels

Game Type	Simple	Medium	Complex
Board Game	*Loopin' Louie* *Can't Stop*	*Ticket to Ride* *Pandemic: The Cure*	*Power Grid* *Dead of Winter*
Card Game	*Love Letter* *The Other Hat Trick*	*San Juan* *Dominion*	*Race for the Galaxy* *Magic: The Gathering*
RPG	*A Penny For My Thoughts* *Fiasco*	*A Quiet Year* *Microscope*	*Dungeon & Dragons* *Pathfinder*
Sports	Four Square Darts	Badminton Dodgeball	Football (American) Roller Derby

It's important to note that board, card, RPG, and sports are not the only categories of nondigital games. So many examples fit these categories that it makes them salient choices to study. Games are incredibly diverse if you take the time to look. What labels categorize fantasy baseball, *I Love Bees*, Mafia/Werewolf games, or the activities involved in the Jejune Institute?

▶ **NOTE** For an entertaining explanation of the Jejune Institute see the film: The Institute [Motion picture]. (2013). Gravitas Ventures.

To illustrate what I mean by complexity, let me give you an example. I once created a 15-card analog game for a game design contest. I really enjoyed the experience, so I thought I would make a digital version in Unity, which is a popular game engine for digital-game development. What took me only an evening to design, assemble, and test as an analog game took weeks to fully implement digitally. I had so many contingencies I needed to address. Although bugs or vagueness can be reasoned out in a card game, a digital program needs to be explicitly told how to handle all contingencies. Changes are more robustly handled by humans who are OK with ambiguity; programs need clarity.

Another reason to start your game design experience by making analog games is that analog games tend to expose all their workings to the players. Digital games, on the other hand, often hide their mechanisms from both players and designers—they hide their mechanisms from players behind code and from designers by abstracting the game's workings. For instance, in an RPG, you may notice that players have difficulty rolling die to get a certain number, and thus they allow an attack, twice in a row. In an analog game, the reasons should be easy to track down: The players are doing the math themselves, so the inputs and outputs are clear. In a digital game, these calculations are obscured in code somewhere. When you get clear feedback, it allows for quick iteration. However, when you are making digital games, it's often the case that you can't even find out where a problem is hiding!

In the book, *Tabletop: Analog Game Design*, famed designer Greg Costikyan writes: "As many game studies programs have discovered, tabletop games are particularly useful in the study of game design, because their systems are exposed to the player, not hidden in code. It's easy to misunderstand the essential nature of a digital game, if you focus on graphics or narrative without appreciating the way in which system shapes the experience."[2]

Always err on the side of simplicity. With this rule in mind, it makes sense to start by developing board or card games.

Theme and Mechanics

When you are creating games, but most saliently, when you are designing board and card games, it's important to decide whether to focus first on theme or mechanics. By *mechanics*, I mean the rules and procedures of the game. In *7 Wonders*, the main mechanic is clearly drafting cards. In *Terror in Meeple City*, the main mechanisms are flicking, dropping, and blowing on game pieces. *Theme*, in this instance, is the overarching setting or antecedent elements that relate to the game's mechanisms. In *7 Wonders*, the theme is building ancient civilizations. In *Terror in Meeple City*, the theme is monsters destroying metropolitan areas.

If the game's problem statement focuses on thematic concerns, then the game might be too concerned with keeping consistency in that theme at the expense of fun. For instance, if *7 Wonders* was truly interested in taking the theme of building a civilization

· · · · · · · · · · · · · · · · · · · ·
2   Costikyan, G. (2011). *Tabletop: Analog Game Design*. Pittsburgh, PA: ETC Press.

seriously, then some mechanics should manage population, taxation, and land usage. However, additional mechanics about these things would slow the game down and distract from the game's actual problem statement, which focuses on a seven-player drafting experience.

Likewise, if a game's problem statement suggests mechanics, then parts of the game may not make sense in terms of the game's theme. The point of theme is to make the game understandable.

I was once working on a game where players shuffled passengers around an airport. It was an area control game, so it was important to move passengers at the right time to the right spots. Yet playtesters balked at ever moving passengers: "Why would they get on a different flight than the one they came to the airport for?" The mechanics made perfect sense in terms of game operation, but they did not interact well with the theme. Many European board games are criticized for being games about mechanics with a theme "pasted on." This criticism comes only if the game's theme does not assist players in understanding the mechanics and world of the game. For instance, *Dominion* could easily be about any number of themes; this game is about building a deck of cards, and what names the cards have hardly matter. Similarly, the theme of *Chess* does not matter. Trying to "paste on" a theme beyond basic notions of warfare is distracting and not helpful to players.

The proper way to start your design of an analog game is by seeing which way the problem statement points. Some great games have been designed with theme first and some with mechanics first. The two cited examples, *7 Wonders* and *Terror in Meeple City*, come from the same designer (Antoine Bauza) and are clearly mechanically focused and thematically focused in their problem statements, respectively. *7 Wonders*' problem statement asks, "What if a game played well with seven players?"[3] *Terror in Meeple City*'s design started with the intention to make a board game to match the thematic elements of the classic arcade game *Rampage*.

By having a poignant problem statement, you eliminate the need to ask the question of whether the designer should start with theme or with mechanics. The problem statement itself will dictate the direction in which to start. A problem statement is just a guide to help direct your efforts. If the development warrants it, you may change the problem statement. To return to Antoine Bauza's work, his *Spiel des Jahres* winning

. . . .

3   Bauza, A. (2010). "Game Designer Diary: The Genesis of *7 Wonders*, Part 1." Retrieved March 19, 2015, from http://us.asmodee.com/ressources/articles/game-designer-diary-the-genesis-of-7-wonders-part-1.php.

game *Hanabi* is a cooperative imperfect information game about collectively creating a fireworks show. However, it was made from the pieces of another game he designed, *Ikebana*, which was a competitive set-collecting game about arranging flowers that played wholly differently. You never know what direction your ideas and testing will take you, but it is good to have a destination in mind.

Next Steps

The next step is to come up with basic rules. If your problem statement suggests mechanics, this should be easy. If your problem statement suggests theme, then you may want to consider what mechanics may match that theme. It's not important that you get the rules right on your first try, because everything is on the table as far as change goes. In fact, the first version of *7 Wonders* was not about card drafting at all.

Write these rules down on paper or in a digital document, but go only so far as to make a playable game. Do not worry much about the edge cases or complicated matters—the key is to have enough rules to make a playable game. The goal is to build your first prototype.

This prototype is likely to have breakable systems, unnecessary materials, ambiguities, and imbalances. You will have plenty of time to iron these out through playtesting and revision. The key of the first prototype is to get a feel for the game.

The first time that you play your new game, you are quite likely to identify many areas in which the game needs to improve. Perhaps there are not enough interesting decisions for players. Perhaps the rules are unclear about edge conditions. Perhaps the game always plays out in one particular way. Perhaps real players do not do what you expect. These are all areas I'll cover in upcoming sections and chapters, but to apply any of these lessons to your game, you must first have a game on which to test them.

Designing for Others

The 18-to-35-year-old male demographic really, *really* loves first-person shooters. Most students I teach in game design classes are 18-to-35-year-old males. Most pitches that I receive in assignments are for first-person shooters. This is natural. Many game designers want to learn about game design because they want to make games like those that they themselves have enjoyed. Game design can be a long, tedious process. Is it not better to go through all that work for an idea that you love instead of one you don't have a passion for?

If the answer is yes, who is left to make the *SpongeBob* games? They do not hire 8- to 12-year-olds to make games for the 8-to-12-year-old demographic. In fact, much of the industry is making games that do not serve the "core" demographic of 18-to-35-year-old men. It is a gift to be working on games for a living, but it is an extra-rare gift to be working on games that you like for a living. This can be a double-edged sword. Sometimes working on a genre you like can sour you on the genre entirely. For example, I worked on AAA sports games from 2004 to 2009, a genre I really liked. I have not bought a sports simulation game since I left that job. I just played them too much in my day-to-day life, so the magic behind them was lost.

Another issue that arises when you work on the types of games that you already enjoy is that you may find yourself stuck remaking the things that you already enjoy instead of pushing the envelope to make something new and exciting.

The point, however, is that if you are working on a game and you plan on selling 100,000 copies of it, it is quite likely that all 100,000 of those copies will be bought by someone other than you. So you need to be able to step into someone else's shoes to deliver an experience that they will enjoy. And it can be really difficult when what those people enjoy differs from what you enjoy. Yet this is the norm and not the exception. Most designers are designing for people vastly different than themselves. Legendary MUD designer Richard Bartle says, "Designers don't create virtual worlds that they, personally, wish to play; they create virtual worlds that *people* wish to play."[4]

However, some design breakthroughs can be made by considering first how other people react to different elements of games. Independent designer Zach Gage made the hit game *SpellTower* because he did not like the mobile word games that existed and he wanted to make one that would challenge him to understand their appeal.[5] His outside view on the genre allowed him to make an acclaimed and popular title, one that he would not have made if he only made games he enjoyed. The same is true for Michael Brough, who made *Corrypt*. He did not like puzzle-style games, so he made one that was excellent as a puzzle-style game but (because he was not beholden to the norms of the genre) one that also subverted the genre effectively.

. . . .

4   Bateman, C. (2009). *Beyond Game Design: Nine Steps Toward Creating Better Videogames.* Boston, MA: Cengage Learning.

5   Kohler, C. (2012, December 17). "Game Designer Stands at Rowdy Intersection of Entertainment and Art | WIRED." Retrieved April 1, 2015, from www.wired.com/2012/12/worlds-most-wired-zach-gage.

It's easy to say that you should just leave everything to playtesting and that your target audience will direct you on what to make. This is tempting, but also quite dangerous. Playtesters cannot help until they have something to test, which means you must make something with them in mind. Additionally, playtesters reject new ideas as confusing if they are not familiar with them. Sometimes you have to warm them up to a new idea before they embrace it. Also, playtesting is expensive in terms of time. You cannot bring in playtesters every day to make every little decision, nor can you spend the engineering time to A/B test every possible decision. At the end of the day, the designer needs to have an innate understanding of what he is trying to do.

Opening Questions

As an exercise, you can go through a number of key questions about your game to get a good sense of where to begin. These questions are just to help you get started. Most of them will be obsolete by the time you make changes to your first prototype. It is usually a bad idea to keep any of these answers locked down and written in stone:

- *What is your problem statement?*
- *How many players will there be?*
- *What is the object of the game for each player? What are their short-term goals?*
- *Do players work together or alone? Who is their adversary: the game, other players, or something else?*
- *Do you have any key rules in mind?*
- *What resources do the players manage?*
- *What do players do? What decisions do they face?*
- *What information is public, hidden to particular players, or hidden to all players?*
- *What hinders players? What are the trade-offs?*
- *How does the game end? Are there winning conditions?*
- *Explain a turn or two (or equivalent time period) of the game.*

After answering these questions, you can make an attempt to write down the rules for the game.

To use the example of the airport game I mentioned above, earlier in my career, I had a period of about a year when I had to fly somewhere about every month. One evening, I was in New York while a huge blizzard was approaching. It was hammering the Midwest and the flight network was already suffering from delays. As I sat awaiting the fate of my flight, I could feel the tension in the room rise as flight after flight was delayed and announced over the loudspeaker. Periodically, it would be announced that a flight was changing gates. I watched as dozens of stressed travelers grabbed all their belongings and rushed off in unison to another part of the terminal. This happened a half-dozen times as I sat and watched. Having nothing better to do, I started to brainstorm an idea for a board game where passengers rushed through an airport. Here is what I came up with when I worked through the previous checklist of questions:

- *What is your problem statement?*

  What would a board game be like where you had to shuffle weary and stressed passengers through an airport?

- *How many players will there be?*

  I'm going to guess 3 to 5 players. I imagine it will be similar to a Eurogame like *Ticket to Ride*, and those games generally have 3 to 5 players.

- *What is the object of the game for each player? What are their short-term goals?*

  Each player tries to score victory points by getting as many passengers onto correct flights as possible.

- *Do players work together or alone? Who is their adversary: the game, other players, or something else?*

  Players work alone, trying to achieve the best score. Players can out-position other players' passengers to score.

- *Do you have any key rules in mind?*

  Passengers have to make it through security before they can move freely through the airport. Players should be able to move their passengers all at once. When a flight fills up, it leaves, kind of like the boats in *Puerto Rico*. Flights will change gates often.

- *What resources do the players manage?*

  Players will manage the passengers on the board. I want this game to be as minimally random as possible, so no cards or dice.

- *What do players do? What decisions do they face?*

  Players get one action on their turn. They can move people through security, move passengers to gates, or move passengers into club lounges.

- *What information is public, hidden to particular players, or hidden to all players?*

  All information is public. The flight board will show the order of flights.

- *What hinders players? What are the trade-offs?*

  Players hinder players because there will not be enough room on each flight for all passengers. Players must choose to spend their action on getting more passengers, placing them effectively, or changing the flight board.

- *How does the game end? Are there winning conditions?*

  When all the flights are gone from the flight board, the game is over. The player with the most points wins.

- *Explain a turn or two (or equivalent time period) of the game.*

  Each player gets one main action. They choose from a menu of actions. A player may choose to put passengers through security, move their cleared passengers, or move a passenger into a club lounge.

The descriptions from these questions are not enough to write the rules of the game. There is still a lot of work to do. However, it does help to frame the ideas that are nascent. From this, I could start a sketch of what the actual rules look like. Once I have something that can direct play, I could craft a prototype to test where my idea of the rules are broken, fun, or both.

If you do not have answers to all these questions, it's OK. You can still attempt to build a prototype at this point. Playtesting suggests answers. Some of the best games were started by having a broad problem statement that could be built into a functional toy that suggested directions for further development.

Summary

- Analog games such as board and card games offer the interactivity that makes games compelling in a medium that offers easier prototyping and development than digital games.

- A fertile place to start from when considering a game's problem statement is to examine whether you want to start building around a theme or around specific mechanics.

- It is important to try and understand the positive qualities of games you do not like along with the negative qualities of games you do like. You will rarely be making games for an audience that directly aligns with your tastes.

- Whether you start with theme or mechanics, you need to start by determining some basic rules for your game in order to be able to create something that is testable. A great backstory is fine, but it does not help to create something testable.

- By going through a battery of generalized opening questions, you can begin to narrow down your idea into a form that will allow you to construct a prototype that you can use to run playtests.

PART 2

Prototypes and Playtesting

A mirror will not show you yourself,
if you do not wish to see.

—ROGER ZELAZNY, LORD OF LIGHT

After you have a vague hand-wavy understanding of what you plan on building, the next step is to create a prototype. A *prototype* is a quickly assembled sketch of a game. "Quickly assembled," however, is relative. For a game that will be made over the course of years, a prototype may take months to build. For a small card game, a prototype can be assembled in minutes. Prototypes are the single most useful tool for game designers for many reasons:

- Prototypes force the designer to make decisions about non-obvious edge cases.
- Prototypes focus on the core idea without the designer having to spend time on expensive polish elements. Often, digital prototypes prove the core of a game without heavy time investments of art, animation, and code polish.
- Prototypes can be tested by impartial players using playtesting techniques. Playtests allow players to provide feedback without wearing the rose-colored glasses of the designer; feedback includes issues of balance, cognitive load, and edge cases.
- It is comparatively easier to change items in a prototype than it is when you are making something for a shippable version. This is functional because it's quicker to change scribbled note cards than it is to redesign a finished card in Adobe Illustrator, and psychological because it's easier to give up on something when large costs have not been invested.

There is no approved method for creating a prototype. Digital prototypes use whichever languages and libraries are most familiar to those making the prototype. Paper prototypes are often created with whatever materials are available. The most flexible materials for paper prototyping are note cards and dice. Simply leverage the materials that support the basic rules you have envisioned. Whenever a question comes up that the rules and materials do not support, amend your rules and materials so that the game can continue.

If you are prototyping an analog game, it's often OK to prototype the entire experience at once. If the game is a role-playing or storytelling game, it is best to limit your prototype to one scenario.

If the game is digital, return to the question of what it is that the player does. Your prototype can focus on just that interaction. If your game is a platformer, then movement and jumping should be the focus of the prototype. It can later expand to include the mechanics that make the idea unique. If the game is a first-person shooter, then the prototype should focus on movement and shooting.

When building prototypes, failure is an option. The reason prototypes are built as quickly as possible at first is because failure is expected. The prototype shows the designer where the original ideas are unfun or suboptimal. The designer can then refine or change those ideas easily because of the prototype's malleability. Be prepared to throw away ideas you like.

Once you have a prototype, it is necessary to begin *playtesting* as soon as possible. Methods for doing so are explained in later sections. Playtesting is the process of evaluating a prototype against a set of criteria. Playtesting is most often accomplished by getting new players to try your game.

By playtesting as soon as possible, you'll be able to determine if you are meeting your design goals as defined in your problem statement. The later in the project playtesting happens, the more difficult it is to change what you have implemented, and you may have to settle for not meeting parts of your design goals.

Playtesting takes a lot of time. When playtesting is over, you may need to start making the game over again using everything you learned in the prototyping and playtesting process.

5 Paper Prototyping Development Techniques

Finished products are for decadent minds.

—ISSAC ASIMOV, SECOND FOUNDATION

This chapter discusses tools and techniques for developing paper prototypes. This is most useful for analog game development (for example, board and card games), but in some instances, it can be useful for digital game development. For instance, during the development of *Superman Returns* for the Nintendo DS, the design team created numerous playable paper prototypes of the multiplayer aspects of the game.

Digital prototyping requires a lot of specialized knowledge, and the tools for such an activity are not standardized. Any concepts I put forth here as good places to start for digital prototyping would be essentially obsolete by the time this book went to print, and thus, are a waste of space for you, the reader.

No one software package exists that a designer should use over all others to make prototypes. Instead, you must have a mercenary approach—whatever gets the job done is the best idea. First prototypes should be rough. If you spend too much time making your prototype pretty, you'll hesitate to eliminate portions of your game that do not work because the sunk costs of making the change are too high. Pen on note cards is a perfectly acceptable first prototype.

Once you have solidified the games rules, go back and make more elaborate prototypes with better layout and art. Since first prototypes are largely MacGyvered together, I'll assume you are making prototypes after you have established and tested a set of basic rules. Remember, these nicer prototypes will be seen by many playtesters. It helps to have something that looks nice when you are presenting to playtesters because research has shown humans often stick with their split-second, first impressions.[1]

Software and Materials

In other sections of this book, I shy away from specifying that you use particular software packages. Software changes over time, which can easily make obsolete any particular technique I share. However, here I identify ones that illustrate possible ways to solve particular workflow problems when you are making paper prototypes. The paradigm shift that occurs when you realize that you can automate creating paper game materials (**FIGURE 5.1**) is invaluable and vastly timesaving.

FIGURE 5.1 This roguish young designer is paper prototyping a game mode for a very large and expensive project using sticky notes, dice, and candy.

The software I find most helpful for the creating paper prototype materials includes the following:

- Adobe Illustrator is a drawing and layout program that is useful for making game boards and player aids. It's considered one of the more essential programs. However, you can get by with other drawing programs if need be.

----

1   Willis, J., & Todorov, A. (2006). "First Impressions: Making Up Your Mind after a 100-ms Exposure to a Face." *Psychological Science*, 17(7), 592–598.

- Adobe InDesign is a layout program largely for making books and other publications. One of its best features for game designers is its ability to read in data from a spreadsheet and convert that data into individual pages of cards or tokens.

- Adobe Photoshop is a raster graphics editor generally used in conjunction with Illustrator. It is the industry standard for image manipulation and provides many of the tools needed for image manipulation.

- Any word processor can be used to codify the design and rules. Microsoft Word is still a standard because of its bevy of formatting bells and whistles, but Apple's Pages, Google Docs, and others are perfectly acceptable.

- Spreadsheets are useful for defining the features of lists of cards that can then be read in and integrated using InDesign. Microsoft Excel and Google Sheets are industry-leading spreadsheet software.

Here are some hardware and other materials that will be helpful:

- A printer, especially one with cheap ink. Designers tend to go through a lot of ink.

- Copious amounts of blank paper and note cards. This should be self explanatory.

- An X-acto precision knife. This is necessary for precise cutting of game boards, tokens, and cards. Use an abundance of caution while using X-acto knives. They are sharp and can be dangerous.

- A self-healing cutting mat. These are helpful to use under your work when you are using X-acto knives. If you don't use one, you are apt to cut through your work and into the table or material beneath. The self-healing mats take a lot of abuse.

- A guillotine cutter. This will likely not be a weapon in your arsenal at first. Scissors are a vastly cheaper option. However, when you need to cut numerous cards, this saves a massive amount of time.

- A metal ruler with a cork back. This helps you measure and cut cleanly with the X-acto knife. If you use a wood or plastic ruler, it is possible that your X-acto blade will cut into the ruler, making the straight edge no longer straight. Then you have a ruined ruler.

- Full-page labels. Companies such as Avery and DigiOrange make full-page (8.5"×11") labels that you can run through a normal printer. This allows you to print something clearly, carve it out with the X-acto knife, and then stick it to a game board or die. You can also apply these to chipboard to make printed tiles.

- Package of 8.5"×11"chipboard. Along with the labels, you can use this to make heavy tiles or markers.

- Counters such as glass beads, centimeter cubes, pawns, or Meeples. You can purchase glass beads in a variety of colors in most craft stores. Craft stores are often great places for inspiration when it comes to board-game materials.

- Dice, various sides. Blank dice can be purchased online. Usually, you are only apt to need a few dice. Games that rely too heavily on dice often do so at the detriment of meaningful decision-making.

- Card sleeves. When prototyping cards, it's rarely sufficient to use regular printer paper for cards because the paper is too thin to shuffle and manipulate. However, printing on cardboard like you'd use for a finished product is expensive. Instead, it is often easiest to print a prototype card on normal printer paper and pair it with a card in an opaque-backed card sleeve, such as those used for *Magic: The Gathering* (**FIGURE 5.2**). The card backing gives the card the desired thickness and heft, and the sleeve keeps your printed materials on the front.

FIGURE 5.2 Here a printed card prototype is put into an opaque-backed sleeve with a *Magic: The Gathering* card as support.

Art

Some designers are comfortable with art. Others are not. Unless the game requires finished art (games like *Dixit* and *Mysterium* are notable examples of this), then using clear iconography, text, and shapes (**FIGURES 5.3** and **5.4**) is likely better than trying to make a prototype look like it has finished art right away.

When making prototypes that they will share at some point, designers must pay attention to usage rights. Some designers use a Google or DeviantArt image search to find relevant imagery and then cut and paste those images into their game prototypes. This is fine when you just plan on playing among friends. However, if you plan on sharing the game publicly, using the art in this way may be illegal. If you plan on sending the game to a publisher, be aware that they may be wary of even looking at a game that does not respect intellectual property.

FIGURE 5.3 The Portal Games Twitter account posted this prototype snapshot of an *Imperial Settlers* expansion in early prototype form.

FIGURE 5.4 A personal prototype.

Luckily, it is easier than ever for someone with limited art experience to create attractive and clear prototypes. The Noun Project (thenounproject.com) is a massive online iconography library with a variety of flexible usage right options (**FIGURE 5.5**). Most icons are available in multiple formats. Many are freely useable with attribution or are available without attribution for a small price. Other sites, such as game-icons.net, focus on more cultivated collections.

Cards

If your game involves cards, you'll want to design the layout of these cards before figuring out exactly what they do. Your first cards will likely just be note cards that you scribble on. But eventually you'll want to move on to a more readable and professional version.

You can lay out each card individually in Photoshop or a similar program. This is certainly possible for a small game, but if your game has many cards, this can become tedious quickly, especially if you need to make a change that affects multiple cards. Luckily, you can automate this process, but you must understand the proposed design and layout.

First, decide what information must be on the card. As an example, look at the *Magic: The Gathering* cards in Figure 5.5.

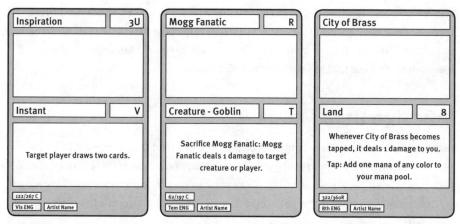

FIGURE 5.5 Three cards with mechanically different effects use similar template elements.

Each of the three cards, which in terms of mechanics are wildly different, can be fully described by a set of replaceable fields:

- Title (upper left)
- Cost (upper right)
- Art (below title and cost)
- Type (center left)
- Set/Rarity Icon (center right)
- Text (below type and set/rarity icon)
- Card #, Set #, and Artist Credit (lower left tiny text)
- Yes/No. Does a power/toughness exist for this card? (lower right in the middle card)
- Power/Toughness (lower right)
- Card color (background)

By breaking down the card elements like this, you can define each card as a row in a spreadsheet, as in **FIGURE 5.6**.

	A	B	C	D	E	F	G	H	
1	Title	Cost	@Art	Type	@Set/Rarity	Text	Card #	Set #	S
2	Act on Impulse	2R	ActOnImpulse.png	Sorcery	2015Uncommon.png	Exile the top thr	126	269	M
3	Phytotitan	4GG	Phytotitan.png	Creature - Plant Elemental	2015Rare.png	When Phytotita	191	269	M
4	Yavimaya Coast		YavamayaCoast.png	Land	2015Rare.png	{T}: Add {1} to y	249	269	M

FIGURE 5.6
Each card is a row. Each field type is a column.

When a new card is added to the game, you add a new row to the spreadsheet; the spreadsheet makes it easy to see if you've missed any of the essential fields. But, more importantly, InDesign (and, more recently, Photoshop) can read in a specific format of spreadsheet and use that to generate cards dynamically.

InDesign Data Merge

Software changes often. It may be that by the time you read this, there will be a new piece of software for easily creating cards from data. Nonetheless, I've provided the InDesign process here to show you one way you can reduce the upfront time investment you need to produce prototype cards and to get you to the important work of testing the game with real players.

InDesign's data merging has a few technical requirements for it to read the spreadsheet. The first is that it must be saved as a CSV (comma-separated value) file. A CSV file is just a text file in which each column is separated by a comma and each row is separated by a line break. This type of file skips all the proprietary cruft that comes with an Excel or other proprietary spreadsheet. It also, however, means that all formatting is stripped out.

▶ **NOTE** In some spreadsheet programs, a cell starting with an @ symbol is a special type of directive. You don't want to do that here. If you get an error, start your cell with an apostrophe (') before the @. This tells the spreadsheet that the cell is text and the apostrophe will disappear.

The first row contains the column headers. In the example in **FIGURE 5.7**, some of the column heads start with the @ symbol, which tells InDesign that the values in that column are not text, but instead are references to outside files. You do this when you want the cell to point to a particular image file. In this example, the @Art and @Set/Rarity fields refer to different images that are swapped out on different cards. All the other fields are text and are just imported as-is.

In my formative years, one of my math classes was given a game named *Twenty Four*. In this game, players turn over a card with four numbers on it. The first player who figures out how to use those four numbers to equal 24 using addition, subtraction, multiplication, and division wins the number of points equal to the number of dots listed on the corners of the card. Players had to use each number once and only once.

As an example, a card shows the numbers 9, 3, 8, and 6. Here are a few ways to solve this:

$9 + 3 = 12$. $12 - 8 = 4$. $4 \times 6 = 24$.

Or:

$6 - (9/3) = 3$. $3 \times 8 = 24$.

Let's make our own cards for this game.

1. Figure out what the data categories are for each card. Here are the items that will change from card to card:

   - First number
   - Second number
   - Third number
   - Fourth number
   - Difficulty

2. In a spreadsheet of your choice, create the columns and rows for the cards using the items/fields you identified in Step 1 (Figure 5.7).

   You must know which columns will be text and which will be images.

3. Treat only Difficulty as an image.

   In actual production, you might treat the numbers as images. For example, in the published versions of the *Twenty Four* game, the designers used a specialized 9 to distinguish it from a 6. However, for simplicity's sake, you'll just use text for this prototype's numbers.

4. Save it as a .CSV file.

5. Open the file in a text editor to ensure it is in CSV form. It should have only the data, commas, and line breaks. If any extraneous markup shows, go back to ensure you are saving the file as a CSV and not as an Excel file or another file type (**FIGURE 5.8**).

   Now you need to design the card.

	A	B	C	D	E
1	FirstNumber	SecondNumber	ThirdNumber	FourthNumber	@Difficulty
2	5	1	5	4	1.png
3	9	3	8	6	2.png
4	3	4	4	4	3.png
5	4	1	4	1	1.png
6	2	7	5	7	2.png
7	9	3	2	2	3.png
8	9	8	1	3	1.png
9	8	5	1	4	2.png
10	4	5	7	1	3.png
11	8	4	1	2	1.png
12	3	3	2	1	2.png
13	1	7	5	9	3.png

FIGURE 5.7 List of the cards in the spreadsheet.

```
FirstNumber,SecondNumber,ThirdNumber,FourthNumber,@Difficulty
5,1,5,4,1.png
9,3,8,6,2.png
3,4,4,4,3.png
4,1,4,1,1.png
2,7,5,7,2.png
9,3,2,2,3.png
9,8,1,3,1.png
8,5,1,4,2.png
4,5,7,1,3.png
8,4,1,2,1.png
3,3,2,1,2.png
1,7,5,9,3.png
```

FIGURE 5.8 The list of the cards as a CSV.

6. Start InDesign and create a new document.

   For this prototype, you want to print standard-sized cards, such as those used in *Magic: The Gathering*, so they fit in standard card sleeves. This will be another divergence from *Magic: The Gathering* since the *Twenty Four* game is printed on square card stock.

▶ **NOTE** A measuring standard used in publishing is known as PostScript picas. An inch has 6 picas.

7. Set the width of the page to 2.5" and the height to 3.5".

   If the intent is set to Print, InDesign renumbers these values to picas: 15p0 and 21p0.

8. Set all margins to 0.

9. On your card, draw whatever design you want to be standard to all cards.

10. Create a text box where you want the first number to go.

11. Tweak the font, alignment, and size until you get it to look how you would like.

    Your placeholder should be the size of your largest text entry. I placed an 8 as a representative number (**FIGURE 5.9**). If your longest card title is "Wand of Nebuchadnezzar," then your card template should support a title of that length. If your title is longer than your placeholder, when you merge your files, those titles will be cut off. If I was supporting cards that had numbers up to 12 on them, then I would make sure 12 fit on every card. Instead, I used 8 since it is the widest number in the font I chose.

12. Copy and paste that field, rotating it for the remaining positions (**FIGURE 5.10**).

    I added an underline as a cheap way to help differentiate between 6s and 9s.

▶ **NOTE** When I was developing an American football game, the names on the jerseys were generated automatically in a similar way. Until that feature was locked down, every player's name was WWWWWWWWW since W was the widest letter.

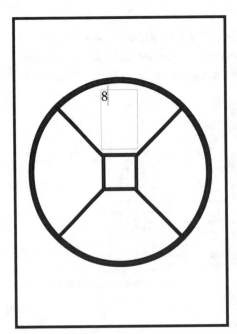

FIGURE 5.9 The first value on an empty card.

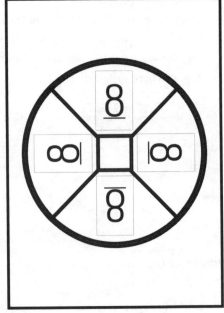

FIGURE 5.10 Using the widest character to measure space.

The last item you need to place is the difficulty. Since the difficulty is an image, you need to first create the images. I found a series of battery icons (**FIGURE 5.11**) from The Noun Project and I have cropped them down to be the right size in Photoshop.

FIGURE 5.11 Difficulty.

BATTERY SYMBOLS BY "HELLO MANY," FROM THENOUNPROJECT.COM COLLECTION.

13. Create the images and save them in your InDesign file.

I saved mine as **1.png**, **2.png**, and **3.png**.

14. Using InDesign's rectangular frame tool, draw a frame that you would like to contain one of the images.

15. Click AutoFit to make sure your source image sizes down to the frame's size.

The Data Merge options are fairly well hidden.

16. Choose Windows > Utilities > Data Merge.

This menu gives you explicit instructions but does not really tell you where the panel menu is. It is the button to the right of the Scripts tab (**FIGURE 5.12**).

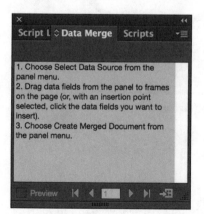

FIGURE 5.12 The Data Merge panel.

17. From the panel menu, choose Select Data Source, and then choose the CSV you created earlier.

    If all went correctly, the window should now show your column headers. Each header should have a T if it is a text field or a little picture frame if it is a linked image field (**FIGURE 5.13**).

18. Delete the 8s you used as placeholders.

19. Drag each of the header labels to the field to which they will go on the card. Do this to the four number fields and the difficulty field. Your template card will look similar to **FIGURE 5.14**.

FIGURE 5.13 Fully linked.

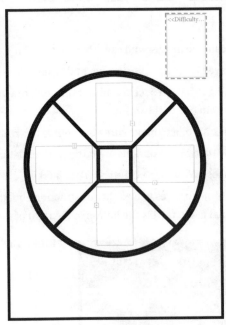

FIGURE 5.14 Our linked template.

20. Click the bottom-right icon (the arrow pointing to a window) in the Data Merge window to create a merged document.

21. Select to merge all records.

    This will create a new InDesign file that has a separate page for each row in your linked file, essentially making a new card on every page.

22. Export this new document as a PDF.

This PDF should have one page for every card in your spreadsheet (**FIGURE 5.15**).

23. Open the PDF in Adobe Reader and choose to print multiple document pages per printer page (**FIGURE 5.16**). If you choose to print 2×3 pages, you can fit six cards on a normal 8.5"×11"page.

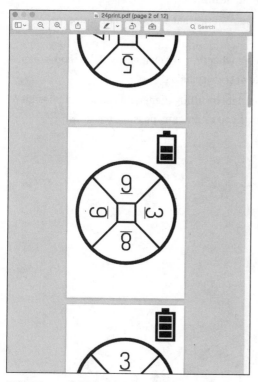

FIGURE 5.15 A PDF with one card per page.

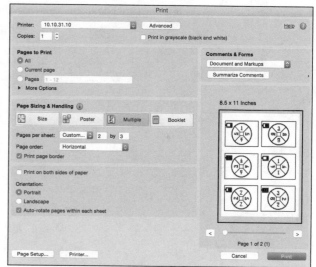

FIGURE 5.16 Adobe Reader print dialog.

Now you have dynamic, customized, and clear cards! Once they are printed, you can put them into card sleeves backed by a normal playing card or *Magic: The Gathering* card for maximum ease of use.

Summary

- Paper prototyping isn't all low-tech. The smart use of software tools can greatly speed up prototyping cycles.
- You should ensure that you have the proper rights to use images publicly. Many sources of royalty-free images are available online.
- InDesign has a powerful tool named Data Merge that allows you to prototype cards quickly.
- To come up with a card template, decide what types of elements will be represented on at least one card. These will be the necessary fields.
- Size up the fields used in the card template by filling them with the widest possible text the card could contain. This allows you to spot any possible overflow.

6 Playtesting

To live a creative life, we must lose our fear of being wrong.

—JOSEPH CHILTON PEARCE

You just spent the last five weeks kicking and screaming to get your game prototype to a playable state. "Yeah," you say, "it still needs some spit and polish, but it works, doesn't it?" You are tempted to release it to the world. This sort of self-lie is incredibly pervasive in game development. Games don't have an easy unit test to determine if they are "done." Getting a game to run or be rules-complete is only the first step. You must make sure it's fun for others. No matter how good you are at "game design," you cannot escape your subjective ties to the state of your game. When you feel you have finished, you have only just begun. Making games is work—the harder the work, the better the game.

To understand how actual players will experience a game, you must put the game in front of actual players. The process of doing so in controlled conditions is known as *playtesting*.

Playtesting Goals

Many methods of playtesting exist, but only a few are discussed here. All playtests share a few common features, with the most important one being that each playtest must have a *goal*. Goals are usually defined in the form of a question.

Playtest goals have two implicit qualities: scope and results. The scope can be specific to a feature or level, or it can be vague so it encompasses a type of play or a range of experiences (**TABLE 6.1**). The goal also needs to generate results that can be either objective or subjective. Generally, the key subjective result is how much fun a player experiences, although you can record many other subjective results.

TABLE 6.1 Playtesting Scope Examples

	Objective Results	**Subjective Results**
Specific Scope	How many coins do players collect on Level 1-1?	Do players enjoy the boss fight at the end of the second dungeon?
Vague Scope	What strategies do players use to beat the puzzles?	Is the game fun?

It is tempting to have playtest goals that are both subjective and vague; however, goals such as these are too ill-defined to have much use. Basically, these playtests usually confirm what you already know about the game. But when you don't know what to test, these playtests stumble upon great insights and can be useful when you do not know what to test. However, given how difficult it is to establish and run effective playtests, you should have more well-considered goals.

The point of playtesting is to conduct scientific inquiry on elements of a game. The point is *not* to confirm your beliefs as the designer about the game. This is known as *confirmation bias*.[1] (I'll discuss confirmation bias in more detail later in this chapter.) You can always generalize or bias a playtest to make it report any finding you desire.

1 Nickerson, R. S. (1998). "Confirmation Bias: A Ubiquitous Phenomenon in Many Guises." *Review of General Psychology*, 2(2), 175.

Playtesters have different backgrounds and experiences, and as a result, they can give conflicting feedback. For instance, Joe thinks that the game is too hard and Jill thinks that the game is too easy. Who is right? Often, you will be tempted to side with the playtester who confirms your beliefs. If you think the game is too easy as is, you'll dismiss Joe's and embrace Jill's opinion. This is a mistake. Jill may be right, but because of Joe's input, you should realize that more testing is needed. The key to playtesting is that it supports your true desire to answer a question; it lets players answer the question. A playtest that tells the designer everything is good is worthless.

Playtesting Benefits

Playtesting is one of the most difficult tasks for a game designer. As designers, we have to sit back and watch people struggle with and fail to enjoy the games we spent blood, sweat, tears, and sleepless nights over. But think of it this way: If you did not playtest the game, you would never have a chance to fix what is wrong with it, and every one of your eventual players would struggle like the playtesters you are watching.

Project postmortems like the ones on Gamasutra.com often highlight strange jumps in insight gleaned from playtesting. For instance, in *Team Fortress 2*, the game's creators noticed that playtesters' in-game players were dying as a result of the same snipers over and over again. Playtesters reported that they had no idea what was going on—they just walked out of the starting area and immediately died. It was extremely frustrating and was something that the designers had not anticipated. However, the designers had experience with the maps that the playtesters lacked. They were never confused about when they would be killed by a sniper because they already knew where the snipers would hide. The players did not have this knowledge. Because of this testing, the developers decided to create the Deathcam. Whenever a player died, this camera zoomed in to show the location of the player's killer. Not only did this new camera inform the losing player of where the sniper was camping (which cut down on camping), but it also allowed the losing player to see the winning player's taunt animation. In this case, the playtest helped identify a problem for which the developers created a solution that added additional operational hooks.

When he was working on the original *Magic: The Gathering*, Richard Garfield had a playtester tell him that he possessed the best card in the game, and that when he cast it, he could guarantee victory on the next turn. Garfield had the player show him the card. The card, "Time Walk," read "Opponent loses next turn." Richard had written it to mean that the opponent skips his next turn, but the playtester understood it to mean that "Opponent loses *game* next turn." Playtesting identified that ambiguity!

Understanding how beneficial a playtest will be before the fact is difficult, if not impossible. A design may have five playtests that yield nothing, only to have the sixth be a bounty of usable feedback. The designer must have the wherewithal to keep testing. Playtesting must continue long after the designer thinks that all the blood has been squeezed from the stone. Once you get a "good" playtest, it can be so tempting to quit and say that the game is done!

Listening to Feedback

Oysters open completely when the moon is full; and when the crab sees one
it throws a piece of stone or seaweed into it and the oyster cannot close
again so that it serves the crab for meat. Such is the fate of him who opens
his mouth too much and thereby puts himself at the mercy of the listener.

—LEONARDO DA VINCI

Playtesting is not easy. It requires finding an appropriate set of players, setting them up to play the game, and conducting a scientific examination of them interacting with what is an incredibly personal artifact.

Fear of Critique

The most common pitfall that keeps novice designers from conducting successful playtests is the *fear of critique*. Even if you are excellent at handling criticism, a layer of your consciousness dismisses it, saying either "Well, she didn't get it. Stupid playtester!" or "That's fine that she didn't have fun. The game isn't done yet." At the other end of the spectrum is the designer who demands that everyone accept his vision at face value. For that designer, the playtest can never yield valuable results except ego stroking. This kind of designer is lampooned in the *Penny Arcade* comic.[2]

In the book *Laws of the Game*, Manfred Eigen tells an anecdote of a particularly over-confident theoretician who, when asked what would happen if experimental facts were inconsistent with his theory, responded, "Well, then so much for the facts!"[3] Do not model yourself after this theoretician.

. . . .

2   Garfield, R. (2004). *The Design Evolution of Magic: The Gathering*. The Game Design Reader.
3   Eigen, M., & Winkler, R. (1981). *Laws of The Game: How the Principles of Nature Govern Chance*.
    New York: Knopf.

Some designers mask this fear of critique with a kind of blasé attitude of superiority to playtesters—they imply that "playtesters only tell you things you already know." During playtests at Electronic Arts of *Superman Returns* for the Nintendo DS, kids would say that the player should be able to go inside every building. That was obviously a technical impossibility, but it did not stop hordes of playtest kids from asking for it. Disgruntled designers then said that playtests were worthless based on this bad feedback and proceeded to ignore all other possible benefits such feedback might have had.

Creative writing has an aphorism: "Murder your darlings." When you create something that you think is clever and beautiful, realizing that it does not serve the story at all is very difficult. In games, this aphorism is sound advice as well. Designers are often blind to what their darlings are, but playtesting can identify them: They find segments or mechanics that are not fun, are odd for the sake of variety, or just do not make sense. Designers then have to let go of ego and remove the segments or mechanics or edit them into a usable state. This is difficult!

Confirmation Bias

Another difficulty with playtesting is that it often gives advice that the creator does not want to hear. As mentioned earlier, humans are susceptible to what is known as *confirmation bias*. Confirmation bias biases us toward accepting information we want to hear and discounting information we don't want to hear. In playtests, confirmation bias is pervasive. It's easy to misread feedback that indicates instructions are too complicated as coming from "stupid playtesters" because you believe your instructions are good. It's easy to ignore comments about deep structural problems with mechanics and favor the feedback for problems you have already identified.

Unfortunately, we are not limited to this bias in playtesting. It creeps into many everyday activities and is particularly visible in political thought. You might think that we buy nonfiction books to further understand the world around us. Valdis Krebs studied Amazon's public sales data leading up to the 2008 US presidential election and found that people who liked Barack Obama largely clustered around buying books that reinforced their preconceived beliefs.[4] People who disliked him clustered around buying books that reinforced *their* preconceived beliefs. Readers spent significant cash just to have someone tell them that they were right. Not only do people spend more *money*,

. . . .

4   Krebs, V. (2008). "Political Polarization During the 2008 US Presidential Campaign." Retrieved May 13, 2015, from www.orgnet.com/divided.html.

but they also spend more *time* reading essays that agree with their preconceived opinions.[5] The political satire show, *The Colbert Report*, looked measurably different to people depending on their political ideology. A 2009 study showed that conservatives who watched the show believed that the show targeted liberals.[6] Liberals who watched the show believed that it was lampooning conservatives. Are the two groups receiving different information when they watch the show, or is it that we are biased to receiving information that confirms our already held beliefs?

Peter Wason, a psychologist in the 1960s, devised a clever test to illustrate how people go about confirming their beliefs.[7] Dr. Wason told participants that he had a rule in mind and asked them to select three numbers; he then told them whether that set of numbers followed the rule. The participants' goal was to determine the rule. To start, he told the participants that 2, 4, 6 met the rule. Participants then picked sets of three numbers and wrote why they chose those numbers. For example, a subject would submit 10, 12, 14 and receive a "yes" or 3, 2, 1 and receive a "no." When participants felt highly confident that they had figured out the rule, they were to write it down and submit it. As subjects tried different combinations, their reasoning was analyzed.

What Wason noticed was that to test their theories, participants continually submitted answers that would receive a "yes." With sufficient "yes" answers, they felt confident that their theory was correct. However, they would not test any combinations of numbers that might break their theory. For example, a common first guess at the rule was that the rule must be "three numbers, with each being two higher than the previous." One subject stated that after guessing 8, 10, 12, then 20, 22, 24, and finally 1, 3, 5 and receiving "yes" to all three, she guessed the rule without ever trying any combination that would violate her rule! A 2, 6, 10 would have received a yes and violated her rule, letting her know that she was on the wrong path, but she did not try it until after she was told her rule was incorrect. In other words, it was only the confirmation of her beliefs that led her to believe her rule was correct, not any attempt to falsify what she thought was true.

The rule was "any three numbers in ascending order."

. . . .

5   Knobloch-Westerwick, S., & Meng, J. (2009). "Looking the Other Way: Selective Exposure to Attitude-Consistent and Counter-Attitudinal Political Information. *Communication Research*, 36(3), 426–448.

6   LaMarre, H. L., Landreville, K. D., & Beam, M. A. (2009). "The Irony of Satire: Political Ideology and the Motivation to See What You Want to See in *The Colbert Report*." *The International Journal of Press/Politics*, 14(2), 212–231.

7   Wason, P. C. (1960). "On the Failure to Eliminate Hypotheses in a Conceptual Task." *Quarterly Journal of Experimental Psychology*, 12(3), 129–140.

Wason would later study this blindness in another way. Let me explain: You have four cards on a table (**FIGURE 6.1**). Each card has one letter and one number on opposite sides. Which of the cards must you turn over to test the truth of this statement: "If a card has a vowel on one side, then it has an odd number on the other"?

FIGURE 6.1
The Wason Selection Task is a great illustration of how we attempt to confirm rather than disprove our beliefs.

In Wason's study, less than 10 percent of participants could get this correct.[8] The only way this rule can be invalidated is if a card has a vowel on one side and does *not* have an odd number on the other side. So the correct answer is to turn over the E and the 2. If either of those does not conform to the rule, then the rule is busted. Subjects often tried to turn over the 3, wanting to confirm that there was a vowel on the other side. But whether it was a vowel or not would tell them nothing about the rule.

This may seem like it has gotten far afield of playtesting. It is easy to protect your ego by only asking questions that confirm what you want to believe: that a mechanism is fun, that an exchange rate is reasonable, that rules are understandable, that an interaction is clear. But that is not the role of the playtest. The playtest should ask the difficult questions and challenge your assumptions.

Remember: Every good novel has edits and rewrites. Every good film has script rewrites and scenes that were shot and dumped. Why should a game be the first thing a designer can think up and implement?

. . . .

8   Johnson-Laird, P. N., & Wason, P. C. (Eds.). (1977). *Thinking: Readings in Cognitive Science*. Cambridge, MA: Cambridge University Press.

Finding Playtesters

Perhaps the most difficult element of playtesting is finding *helpful* playtesters. Designers likely don't have dossiers of individuals who will come and give instructive feedback for you on a moment's notice—for free. The most available people often are not the best individuals for a playtest. For instance, your mom, girlfriend, or boyfriend is often not the best tester. Each of them is likely to want to see you succeed, and each is likely to be overly nice to you, even if only subconsciously. Game designer/enthusiast friends usually are not helpful playtesters either. They find it difficult to play as a normal player would and often want to offer solutions instead of identify problems. They see paths the game could take that the designer has long since dismissed, but they cannot see the process the game has taken. Although these folks can provide useful commentary, they have difficulty being unbiased playtesters.

Instead, try to find people who are the target audience for the game you want to make. If a friend's roommate is available, but she plays only shooters, she may not be the best playtester for a Match-3 game. She may have a helpful outside perspective, but she probably would not buy your game. The best playtesters are strangers who do not owe the game makers anything and have no preconceived notions about the game or the game's makers. The difficulty with these potential playtesters is convincing them to playtest in the first place.

▶ **NOTE** Digital games rarely list playtesters in their credits. However, many analog hobbyist games do.

In all practicality, many constraints limit how many playtests a designer can reasonably do. At some point, the designer needs to decide what feedback to take and what to ignore. There is no reasonable, well-accepted heuristic for this. Only by practice can you learn to glean which playtest events represent significant feedback to accept and use in your game's design.

▶ **NOTE** Even with 261 playtesters, Caverna released with a previously undiscovered infinite combo that had to be fixed as errata.

When it's tempting to pitch or release your game after having exposed it to 10 playtesters, keep in mind that award-winning games like *Caverna* and *Dead of Winter* list 261 and 233 playtesters in their credits at release, respectively.

Iterating

In *Rules of Play: Game Design Fundamentals*,[9] Salen and Zimmerman say:

> A game design education cannot consist of a purely theoretical approach to games. This is true of any design field: designers learn best through the process of design, by directly experiencing the things they make. Therefore, a large part of their training as students of game design must involve the creation of games....
>
> Iterative design is a play-based design process. Emphasizing playtesting and prototyping, iterative design is a method in which design decisions are made based on the experience of playing a game while it is in development.... Iterative design is a cyclic process that alternates between prototyping, play-testing, evaluation, and refinement. ...
>
> Why is iterative design so important for game designers? Because it is not possible to fully anticipate play in advance. It is never possible to completely predict the experience of a game. Is the game accomplishing its design goals? Do the players understand what they are supposed to be doing? Are they having fun? Do they want to play again? These questions can never be answered by writing a design document or crafting a set of game rules and materials. They can only be answered by way of play.

The science of game design is not complete. Because game design is about systems, if the system being created is too complex to view in its entirety, then there is the possibility of interactions that cannot be immediately understood. Try and imagine all the interactions you can do in *Minecraft*; it's impossible to enumerate them all.

Additionally, the game designer is not the entire audience for the game. We are OK at understanding exactly what we like, but we are awful at understanding what other people like. Other people think differently, have different preferences, and have different capabilities. It is a difficult problem.

Since it's impossible to enumerate all the possible interactions and it's difficult to understand if a game will be fun, game designers must guess what to make and then evaluate how well their guess matched their expectations. If the guess was close

· · · · · · · · · · · · · · · · · · ·

9   Salen, K., & Zimmerman, E (2003). *Rules of Play: Game Design Fundamentals*. Cambridge, MA.: MIT Press. (pp. 11-12).

enough, then they are finished. If it was not, though, they must adjust their games to get closer to their expectations. They must do this again and again until the game is at a level of quality that meets their expectations. This process of repeating until finished is known as *iteration* and it is essential to the craft of game design.

Iteration is so important that it's one of the few "absolute truth[s]" designer Jesse Schell mentions in *The Art of Game Design: A Book of Lenses:* "The more times you test and improve your design, the better your game will be."[10]

Many game projects are structured so that a team can make only one attempt at a fun game and then must release it. This rarely results in an excellent game. No matter how successful you are in your career as a designer, you'll never get to the point where your first idea is always your best. I have never met a successful designer who did not believe in iterating as many times as possible before release. The real world has things to say about that, though. Your publisher will have a shipping schedule or your class will have a due date. The key is to be as flexible as possible so you can get as many iterations of the important features done as possible by the end of that cycle.

Summary

- Prototypes are quickly assembled subsets of a game that allow designers to test ideas in conditions approximating those that players will be under when playing the released game.
- Playtesting allows for direct, unbiased, and helpful feedback when the playtest session is run deliberately and playtesters are chosen effectively.
- Designers (and people in general) loathe hearing where they have made mistakes and will interpret data in ways favorable to their own opinions. This makes it all the more important to design playtests to eliminate potential sources of bias.
- Playtesters will not always give useful feedback, but it is important to understand why you accept the feedback you accept and reject the feedback you reject. If a player "doesn't get it," is it her fault or can the game do something better to make the player "get it"?
- Iteration is one of the most important keys to successful game design. Scheduling your activities so that you can maximize useful iteration time is crucial.

. . . .

10 Schell, J. (2008). *The Art of Game Design: A Book of Lenses.* Amsterdam: Elsevier/Morgan Kaufmann.

7 Playtesting Methods

Speech is silver, silence is gold.

—URSULA K. LE GUIN, THE LATHE OF HEAVEN

The best practices for running a playtest are remarkably straight-forward. Success is more about resisting making mistakes than following any particular process.

In the previous chapter, I talked about finding helpful playtesters—folks who give honest feedback without sugar-coating (friends/family) or being hypercritical (hardcore gamers). Now I'm going to talk about how to get the best, most reliable feedback from your playtesters. How do you prepare the environment? How do you prepare your testers? What methods of testing can you use? If you do not manage these elements successfully, you may receive suboptimal feedback from your playtesting sessions. These sessions involve too much work for them to result in bad data that you could have avoided by doing some simple upfront planning.

The Testing Environment

Now that you have your playtesters ready, willing, and able, sit them down in a comfortable place with your game. Get yourself a notebook. If you can, record the session (if the playtesters give you their consent). The playtest is about collecting helpful data. Some expensive and well-equipped testing labs record video of player faces and hands, along with the footage onscreen, so that designers can correlate facial emotions with what the players are trying to accomplish. If you are like most designers, you do not have this kind of luxury, so use what you have available.

Make sure that those conducting the test do nothing that biases the data and the information they receive.

Ask players to play the game as they would at home. They are already in a foreign environment, so do what you can to help them play normally.

Do not tell them what the game is about or exactly what they have to do, unless your game is in such a state that it is impossible to play otherwise. This may bias testers if they have preconceived notions of what the game will be.

During the playtest itself, do not explain anything unless you absolutely must. Remember: The goal of the playtest is not for the playtester to have fun, but for you to gather data. You won't be shipping a copy of yourself with the game, so any information you give the player is beyond what your release players will get. If you need to explain something verbally, then that means it is unclear in the game itself. If a player is struggling or not having fun, resist the urge to fix the issue for the player unless the player has given up.

Keep Playtesters Talking

There is a technique in usability testing, developed in the 1980s at IBM, known as the *Think Aloud Protocol*.[1] Using this technique, the test proctor prompts the user to narrate everything they are doing, thinking, and feeling as they test. This is difficult for people to do while playing a game. They remember for a few seconds, but every time they are faced with a challenge, they focus their attention on the challenge and forget to talk. It's up to the proctor to continually remind them by asking questions such as "How are you solving that puzzle?" "What is your goal here?" Questioning subtly reminds players

---

1   Lewis, C. (1982). "Using the 'thinking-aloud' method in cognitive interface design." IBM TJ Watson Research Center.

to talk about everything they are thinking. This is the closest way we have of getting inside a playtester's thoughts.

Keeping playtesters talking about their ideas and motivations allows you to identify poor assumptions, frustrations, and desires. For instance, if players keep going to a certain area on the map in a first-person shooter, it may be innocuous. But if testers, when thinking aloud, say, "Oh, I thought there would be a treasure there," then you may want to consider what it is about that area of the map that is drawing players to it, and perhaps actually implement treasure there. On the other hand, if a player cannot find a way out of a room and keeps using the "attack" button on a door, when you hear his thoughts—"I want to open the door"—you know that he isn't trying to attack the door and that you may want to consider merging the "use" and "attack" buttons.

Always keep the user talking with as little prompting as possible. Watching a playtester fail again and again can be really frustrating. You'll be tempted to give them the answer so they can continue, but you must wait to see what the tester does next and how they are feeling. The only time you should direct a user should be when your whole playtest will unravel if you do not. In those cases, note where the "give up" point is and direct the user to the next step.

When a tester complains about something that is not finished, it's easy to say, "Yeah, that part is not done yet." or "We know. We are working on it." But you must resist. The proper response to this and most objections or questions is "Why?" Ask the playtester why their complaint bothers them. Remember that the goal is not to make the tester happy but instead to get helpful data.

While the player is playing the game, the proctor should be writing down every observation. What is happening? Where is the tester failing? What did the tester understand right away? How long did it take the tester to achieve [insert objective here]? Capture as much information as possible to analyze later. Also, don't make judgments now.

Always ask, "Why?" You can use Socratic questioning in playtesting to dig out the fundamental issues. However, one of the problems with this method is that players often don't know what the underlying issues are. To deal with this, ask users more specific questions. Ask why they feel the way they do. Ask what evidence they have that supports that feeling and what that feeling means for other elements in the game. For instance, if they try to jump on a ledge that the designer has an invisible wall in front of, ask, "Why are you jumping there?" The user may say, "Because it looks like I can jump there." The facilitator might then ask, "Why do you think you can jump there?" or "Why would you want to jump there?" These types of questions can identify alternative strategies that players might have that have not occurred to the designers. For instance, in this case, perhaps the art should be changed so it does not look like you can jump there. Or maybe the designers should make it so you really can jump there. Regardless, the time to come up with solutions for the problem is well after the playtest. Do *not* try to solve problems during the playtest; only identify and understand the problems.

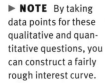

▶ **NOTE** By taking data points for these qualitative and quantitative questions, you can construct a fairly rough interest curve.

At the end of the playtest, have a survey available for the testers that contains a mix of open-ended qualitative questions and quantitative questions. Your qualitative questions should be ones such as "What did you find most fun about the game?" and "What frustrated you about the game?" The most salient issues will come to mind first, so the best and worst elements will be written first. These kinds of questions also serve as a catchall, allowing testers to answer questions the facilitator never even thought to ask. Quantitative questions should be specific so the results can be compared across testers. "On a scale of 1 to 10, how likely would you be to buy this game?" "On a scale of 1 to 10, how fun did you find Level 1? Level 2?" For example, if the team implements a new boss on Level 3, "How did the Level 3 scores change?"

Many teams wait until a product is almost finished to playtest. However, the general consensus among playtesting advocates is that it's never too early to playtest. The most practical time to playtest is as soon as you have a playable build. Some designers go further by playtesting analog versions of their digital game ideas, which is applicable in many situations. Early playtests stop teams from making content or mechanics that don't work. If such content and mechanics are only identified at the end, a team may have to rewrite entire sections of a game. The right idea is to playtest as soon as you can reasonably get useful results, and avoid large amounts of rework or releasing a game that does not mesh well with players.

Hardcore gamers, folks "in-the-know," and game designers often give commentary in the form of solutions. "The champion's attack speed needs to go up." "The level is too long." "The main character isn't tall enough." But these solutions are attempts to solve underlying problems, respectively, "The game feels unresponsive." "There isn't enough to do in the level." "I don't feel powerful." By figuring out the underlying problems beneath the solutions, designers can come up with more creative approaches to solving common problems. So, in a nutshell, always ask why.

One of the most applicable quotes about playtesting is from a writer, Neil Gaiman:

> Remember: when people tell you something's wrong or doesn't work for them, they are almost always right. When they tell you exactly what they think is wrong and how to fix it, they are almost always wrong.

A/B Testing

A particularly advanced form of playtesting is *A/B testing*. A/B testing splits playtesters into two groups and gives each group a different version of the same thing to test. This allows the team to understand the *differences* between two design ideas.

For instance, say a team is working on an online battle game where characters can buy upgrades for their character units in the middle of a game. Earlier playtests show that players are not using the upgrade feature at all. Interviews with playtesters reveal that they figured they could do something like that but were too caught up in the moment-to-moment events to find out how to do it. The design team breaks into two factions: One faction thinks that the game needs better tutorial text instructing players how to upgrade their units; the other faction thinks that the upgrade menu is too difficult to navigate and players won't use it.

In an A/B test, the team implements both ideas. However, they split the playtest group in two. Group A plays the game with the new tutorial text, but the old upgrade menu. Group B plays the game with the old tutorial text, but the new upgrade menu. If the team has the resources, they also create a Group C that has both interventions and a control Group D that has neither.

After the playtest, the team compares statistics. How many purchases did the playtesters in Group A make? How many did Group B make? What did the participants say this time about buying upgrades? A/B testing is extremely informative, but it requires a hefty amount of resources to prepare and evaluate test results.

> ◆ **TIP** Make sure you understand how sampling distributions and the law of large numbers work. An "A" group that has five conversions out of ten is not necessarily better than a "B" group that has four conversions out of ten. Also, it is essential that you understand sampling distributions. This is partially why most A/B testing is done in online games with large user bases.

Self-Playtesting

You, of course, will play your game hundreds or thousands of times before it's released. In most cases, you'll be sick of it by the time you kick it out the door. By the time you are ready to show it off, you already have tons of preconceived notions about where the game succeeds and where it fails. But that does not mean that you cannot playtest your own game. You, after all, will be the most available playtester.

Know that you will not be able to completely playtest your game based on self-playtesting alone. What you must do is attempt to make all your biases conscious and play consciously as if you have no understanding of the game.

You can easily use this technique when designing multiplayer board games. For instance, in testing a card game, you can deal out hands for four players and attempt to play them independently. A known bias is that you have seen the hands of the other players and will have to force yourself to make decisions without that knowledge. You have to imagine four separate personas that are all playing the game independently, often including differing strategies for each. Now naturally, testing in this way does not provide any feedback on how "fun" the game is or on other subjective measures, but the test can measure gameplay states. How often is a particular card used? Is a particular technique broken?

A NOTE ON "GAMEPLAY"

I try to avoid using the word *gameplay*. What is usually meant by the term is the experience of playing a game. However, it is a milquetoast cop-out of a word that keeps the writer or designer from really explaining what he is talking about. When you say a game has "good gameplay," what does that even mean? That it controls fluidly? That it has interesting dynamics? That the rules make sense? That it is fun for its target players? That it meshes with its theme well? These are all more precise and useful descriptions.

You would not explain a painting by saying it has good "artlook." Instead, you would comment on its composition, the painter's brush technique, or its use of color, lighting, figure, symbols, textures, or negative space. All these terms have actual meanings instead of being generic catchalls for an experience.

One positive use of the term *gameplay* is to leverage its lack of meaning. If you ask a playtester about the gameplay of the game that they just played, it allows them a blank page on which to address whatever is their most salient concern.

Giving each player a heuristic or strategy is helpful. To self-playtest *Settlers of Catan*, for instance, play one persona so they focus on building cards, another so they focus on building settlements, another on blocking opponents, and another on making a small cluster of cities. By setting up the playtest in this manner, you reveal how individual strategies react to each other. Perhaps building cards wins every time you try it. Then you know that a single player building cards may be a degenerate dominant technique (Chapter 19). You can then playtest with all personas pursuing that strategy. If no player has an incentive to deviate from the "all cards" strategy, then you know that cards are too powerful and that you either have to increase the cost of cards, lower their effect, or buff other strategies.

Self-playtesting is limited in what results you can glean from it, but it uses a comparatively minimal amount of resources and it can be conducted without you having to face the ego attack that might result from real outside criticism.

GOOD/BAD PLAYTESTING TECHNIQUES

GOOD: Ask questions.

BAD: Answer questions.

GOOD: Recruit your target audience.

BAD: Recruit whoever is available.

GOOD: Create a comfortable environment without distractions for the tester.

BAD: Roll with whatever you have.

GOOD: Ask specific questions, such as "How do you unlock the blue door?"

BAD: Ask vague/personal questions, such as "Did you understand how to use keys?"

GOOD: Collect data, such as how many players fail objectives.

BAD: Use anecdotal evidence, such as "My playtester succeeded. It must be easy."

GOOD: Playtest early and often.

BAD: Playtest when you think the game is looking "ready."

GOOD: Elicit problem statements, such as "I don't understand how to beat the boss."

BAD: Elicit solutions, such as "This gun doesn't fire fast enough."

Summary

- You should take all possible steps to avoid introducing bias. Sometimes this leads to being uncomfortably quiet with your playtesters. However, your job is not to make sure they have fun, but to see where or if they have fun.

- You will not be able to ship a copy of yourself with your game. Therefore any troubles your playtesters have will likely be mirrored by actual players. Don't dismiss them!

- You can't hear your playtesters' thoughts (yet!), so take steps to make sure that they are verbalizing their processes and evaluations of what is going on in the playtest.

- In an A/B test, players see one of two possible treatments and their behavior is recorded. Designers can then compare the behavior of those who saw the "A" treatment to those who saw the "B" treatment to determine which causes different behavioral outputs.

- Self-playtesting allows for quick turnaround times and for testing specialized hypothetical questions, but it does not replace testing with others.

8 Prototypes and Intellectual Property

Don't worry about people stealing your ideas.
If your ideas are any good, you'll have to
ram them down people's throats.

—HOWARD AIKEN

Many designers are reluctant to share their work with others because they are afraid that someone will take their idea, make a fortune on it, and leave them out in the cold. These designers take one of two paths: Either they sit on their idea and try to develop it themselves, with no testing or help, and the idea never becomes marketable; or they spend time and money investing in documents like nondisclosure agreements (NDAs).

Do I Need an NDA?

Here's a fictive conversation with a student, some variation of which I have had dozens of times:

▶ **NOTE** This chapter is the author's opinion based on professional experience and should not be construed as legal advice.

STUDENT: I have a great game idea, but I need to figure out how to get an NDA for it before I can talk about it with you.

ME: Hang on a second. Do you own a bicycle?

STUDENT (CONFUSED): Yes.

ME: How do you lock it up when you take it places?

STUDENT: Oh, I have a little $10 cable lock I bought at Walmart.

ME: Really? You know a simple set of bolt cutters would slice right through that. You can buy a steel u-lock from Kryptonite for $120 that is pretty much impervious to bolt cutters and hacksaws.

STUDENT (LAUGHING): Yeah, but my bike is probably not even worth $120.

ME: You don't care if it gets stolen?

STUDENT: No, I do. I've had that bike since, like, middle school. It's got sentimental value.

ME: If you had a thousand dollar bike, though, you would think about getting a better lock?

STUDENT: Of course. More people would probably want to steal that rather than my beat-up bike.

ME: So the important factor in how much you will spend to protect something is how much it is actually worth?

STUDENT: Yeah....

The student's heart is in the right place. He has an idea with sentimental value, so he does not want to see it stolen. Yet he admits that people will go out of their way to steal only something that has actual worth. An undeveloped idea has little worth beyond to its creator. The hard work lies in developing the idea and the eventual production and marketing of what comes from it. It's ridiculous to want to have an NDA for an undeveloped idea. It is like buying a $120 lock for a $50 bike.

Sometimes students who do not listen as well take the argument further:

STUDENT: You don't seem to understand. That's all well and good for the other guys, but my idea is *amazing*.

ME: I believe you! Let me talk about something unrelated first that definitely will not violate any potential NDA.

STUDENT (WEARILY): OK....

ME: When my grandmother died, she left me a bunch of her old books because she knew I loved to read. She had a lot of books, though, and I just didn't have the room to keep them all just for sentimental reasons. I had to either donate or sell some of them. If I wanted to sell them, how would I figure out a price?

STUDENT: You could go onto eBay or Half.com or Amazon and find out what the books are selling for there.

ME: What if they didn't have the same exact edition of the book I had listed there?

STUDENT: Well, I guess you could guess by seeing what similar books in similar conditions go for.

ME: OK, so if I look at what similar things go for in a marketplace, then I should have an idea of what that is worth?

STUDENT: Makes sense.

ME: Should I be able to do something similar if I wanted to sell a business, or a piece of art, or something like that?

STUDENT: Sure.

ME: So, earlier I said that the amount you should spend to protect your idea is dependent on how much it is worth. Now we've determined that we can figure out how much something is worth by how much it goes for on the market. How much do ideas similar to yours go for on the market?

STUDENT: I... don't know.

ME: There are thousands of indies making games. Pretty much anything that has value is traded on eBay or Craigslist or similar sites. You can buy art assets on TurboSquid. You can hire coders on Elance. Where do you go to buy game ideas?

STUDENT: I don't know.

ME: I don't think such a place exists. I've never seen a listing for game ideas on Craigslist or eBay or anywhere, honestly. If an item has value proportional to how much someone is willing to pay for it, then if you can't find a place to buy or sell it, how much value can it have?

STUDENT: Well, it has value to me. It's a brilliant idea.

ME: Right! Your idea is more valuable to you than to anyone else. That's why others are not willing to pay for it. That means it makes the most sense for you to be the one to develop that idea further. Eventually, when you have a game, you'll have a vehicle for selling that idea to other people. It will have value to others at that point. But right now, it has value only for you.

Ideas and Value

Signing an NDA is not in a publisher's, designer's, or professor's best interest. This is the same reason that many publishers will not even look at unsolicited ideas. Imagine a publisher that has a big pirate game in the works. An unsolicited idea comes in from a stranger who pitches them a similar pirate game. Because of the low-hanging fruit problem from Chapter 2, it is unlikely that you are the first to have any particular idea. The publisher looks at the idea, realizes it is similar to what they are already working on, and politely declines. Then the publisher comes out with the pirate game and the designer thinks that the publisher stole his idea and made it without him! As a professor, I see many game ideas. I also have about a dozen games that are in some stage or another of development from idea-in-a-Google-doc to production testing. If I sign an NDA with you, and then it turns out that your idea is something that I am already working on, I have to throw out that idea to alleviate the risk of a lawsuit. It is not worth it, so I don't sign NDAs to cover undeveloped ideas. Game designers have far more ideas than they have time to implement; there is never a reason to steal one. There is no reason to use an expensive lock on them.

Once a game is created, it certainly has value. If you are working with a team, it makes sense to negotiate what the future ownership rights of the project will be once it is finished. This can take the form of a team charter or a partnership agreement. This, however, is not protecting the idea; instead, it is protecting the time investment that the team members will make in implementing the idea.

Summary

- You should not be fearful about sharing your ideas with others.
- An unimplemented idea gains value when the developer of that idea can test it under real conditions.
- Nondisclosure agreements are important in professional circles when a discussion involves trade secrets that have actual market value.
- It is worth it to spend money on legal protections such as incorporation and contracts only when the entities being protected are worth significantly more than the cost of establishing the protection.
- Many publishers will not receive unsolicited ideas because of the legal issues involved if the publisher is already working on a similar idea.

Meaningful Decisions

A good game is a series of interesting decisions.

—SID MEIER (APOCRYPHAL)

Have you ever played a game and felt that instead of you playing the game, the game was playing you? This is actually quite common, but many players have trouble narrowing down the root cause of their frustration. They just say the game is "boring," which is not really much help to a designer who is looking for feedback and analysis. What players are really saying is that the game just doesn't have anything interesting to do. Making decisions is what the players *do* in a game.

Consider the game *LCR*. It has a score of 1, which is the lowest possible rating, for 354 of its 913 reviews on BoardGameGeek as of November 24, 2014, a site that allows board game players to rate and review board games. In *LCR*, players have a pile of poker chips and some dice with the letters L, C, R, and dots on the faces. For each L the player rolls, he passes a chip to the player on his left. For every R he rolls, he passes a chip to the player to his right. For every C he rolls, he passes a chip into a center pot. The player rolls and then passes the chips according to the rules. When one player amasses all the chips, the game is over.

Each player has no chance in the game to make a decision. Each player is completely at the mercy of the dice. Many players don't find it particularly rewarding to win or lose since they had almost no hand in the results.

The only games that fall below *LCR* on BoardGameGeek's rankings at the time of this writing are *Candy Land*, *War*, *Bingo*, *Tic-Tac-Toe*, and *Snakes and Ladders*. Can you see a commonality between all of these? All these games lack meaningful decision-making. Children's games often lack meaningful decision-making because the players themselves are not cognitively equipped to make decisions that have meaning.

The bread-and-butter of quality game making is crafting *meaningful decisions*. For a game to be interactive, it must let players make at least one decision; otherwise it's just a theme park ride. For a decision to have importance, it must be meaningful.

Just offering players decisions is not good enough. The decisions must also have some meaningful effect on the game state as a whole for current or future play. For instance, on the game show *The Price Is Right*, one of the pricing games is named *Punch a Bunch*. In it, players can win punches. They are provided with a board of 50 holes on which to spend their punches. Each hole contains a random amount of money. A naive examination of this situation would say that the players have 50 options that range in value so the decision has meaning. However, for reasons I'll discuss in more depth later on, the decision of which holes they should spend their punches on is not particularly well crafted.

On the other hand, offering a quantity of decision-making opportunities that affects the game state does not immediately make these decisions meaningful. If I am offered 100 different weapons to choose from and each has an accuracy of between 85.1 percent and 85.2 percent, whatever I choose is largely irrelevant, despite my assortment of options. Meaning is often in the eye of the beholder.

Many video games offer the illusion of choice, which is a way to avoid having to make a real decision. Some games can get away with this if the game is not designed to be replayed, but this works only if other elements of the game make up for the lack of meaningful decision-making. Many narrative-focused games don't offer meaningful decision-making, but in such cases the players draw their enjoyment from the interesting narrative, not the interactive elements themselves. Nothing pierces the veil of choice like replaying, choosing something different, and yet still ending up on the same path.

What about games where you are not making deep, strategic decisions, such as when you are just trying to keep up with a fast song in *Rock Band*? You may not be making these decisions with the conscious effort of the decisions you might make in *Civilization*, but in this case, you are making a different kind of decision. Have you ever played a *Rock Band* song and you could not keep up? Maybe it was on the drums, and notes were flying by too fast, and you decided that "I can't do this hand stuff and feet stuff at the same time; I'll just focus on the four pads and forget the bass pedal." Your score certainly drops, and maybe as you get more comfortable, you can slowly reintroduce the bass pedal a little at a time. Here, you made a decision: Your current approach was not working, and to continue to play, you needed to change your tactics. Is this any different than needing to change your tactics in a shooter when your safe hiding spot is about to be flanked?

The decision-making always takes the form of "I have a goal; how do I achieve it?" Even in a game in which the player just button mashes to succeed, she has options. Does she put the controller on the ground? Does she use multiple fingers? These may not be the most interesting of decisions depending on the audience, but given the right framing and incentives, these kinds of decisions can rival the most brain-burning ones.

9 Flow and the Fundamental Game Design Directive

Boredom is the conviction that you can't change ...
the shriek of unused capacities.

—SAUL BELLOW

Shadow of the Colossus is one of the most critically acclaimed games of all time. In it, you play as a young man who must single-handedly take down massive ancient colossi. The battles are multistaged and intense, which leads you to a real sense of accomplishment and conquest at the end. After each fight, you must travel by horse through a largely barren and unpopulated landscape in search of the next colossus. Why did the designers choose to have these quiet, peaceful rides in between heart-pounding boss fights? The answer requires you to understand how you stay engaged in games. This answer also leads you to a fundamental directive in game design.

One of the universal problems facing game designers is that you are never entirely certain of who your audience will be. If you knew precisely that your audience was Jim from Nebraska, age 31, no kids, introvert, Masters degree in philosophy, then you could base everything you made around Jim's abilities and desires. Jim is not skilled at puzzles, so you keep them easy and to a minimum. Jim has great twitch skills, so you make jumping super difficult in your game.

Of course, the bang for your buck in making a game for one person is quite limited, so you don't do that. Instead, you attempt to deliver enjoyable experiences to as many people as possible. And, in so doing, you are forced to deliver content to people who may have contradictory skills: Jim is bad at puzzles, but Joan is excellent at them. They have to play the same game. If the game is too hard for Jim, he may give up in frustration. If the game is too easy for Joan, she may give up out of boredom. Where that beautiful middle ground exists is known as *flow*.

Game Flow

Psychologist Mihaly Csikszentmihalyi proposed the concept of flow to explain anecdotes of artists and other creative types becoming "lost in their work"—they became so immersed that they lost track of what was going on around them.[1] Flow is a state of focus and concentration on a task that is intrinsically rewarding. Csikszentmihalyi's research suggested that flow transcends cultures and is one of the key components to happiness itself.

The three conditions that must be met for a person to achieve flow are as follows:

- The person must be involved in an activity with a clear set of goals and progress.
- The task must have clear and immediate feedback so the person can adjust his actions as needed.
- The person must balance between the perceived challenges of the task and his perceived skills. He must see the task as neither too easy nor too hard.

Game designer Jenova Chen noticed that Csikszentmihalyi's features of a flow state were similar to what players of video games describe as being the conditions of fun, and he proposed his Master of Fine Arts (MFA) thesis based on trying to elicit the flow state using game design.[2]

. . . .

1   Csikzentmihalyi, M. (1991). *Flow: The Psychology of Optimal Experience* (Vol. 41). New York: HarperPerennial.

2   Chen, J. (2007). "Flow in Games (and Everything Else)." *Communications of the ACM*, 50(4), 31–34.

Chen focused on the relationship between two elements: the *challenge* created by the game and the *abilities* of the player (**FIGURE 9.1**). Flow is a harmonious balance between these elements. As the player's abilities increase, if the game's challenge does not also increase, the player enters a state of *boredom* where the game has become too easy. As the game's challenge increases, if the player's abilities do not correspondingly increase as well, the player experiences *anxiety* or *frustration*. The designer's job is to craft an experience so that the player is always somewhere between anxiety and boredom, and they have to do this beforehand, without knowing what the player's skills will be.

FIGURE 9.1
Being over- or under-challenged relative to skill causes problems.

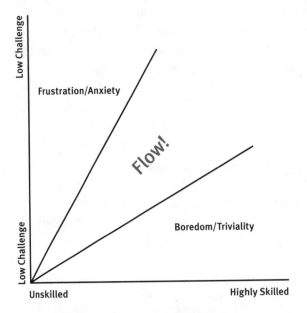

Different audiences find flow in different areas. Hardcore players demand a higher level of challenge per their level of ability and become bored easily, whereas casual players tend to require lower levels of challenge because they become frustrated more easily. As a result, casual games most often err on the side of not providing enough challenge for players, whereas hardcore games err on the side of providing too much challenge for players. The same game can elicit flow at one point and fall out of it at another point. You may have experienced this before: Either you have played a game that took some time to "click" and was woefully frustrating at first, and then you finally settled into a rhythm; or you have played a game that was pleasantly interesting for a while, but it quickly became painfully dull.

Chen's game *flOw* is a result of this research. Its main feature is a system of dynamic difficulty adjustments. It detects how the player's abilities are increasing and adjusts the difficulty to compensate. When the player is failing, the game seamlessly adjusts to provide less challenge. When the player is succeeding, the game subtly increases the challenge. The goal is to always keep players in a state in which their skills are a close match for the level of challenge.

Games have been long structured to take advantage of this phenomenon. Games generally start off with easy introductory levels and then slowly add mechanics that interact with each other to increase difficulty.

Look at World 1-1 in *Super Mario Bros.*, for example. Imagine you are like many children of the 1980s—you have never played a video game before experiencing *Super Mario Brothers*. Thus, World 1-1 requires you to experience a low challenge to match your low skill level. In fact, Level 1-1 has to teach you so many things right off the bat that it requires only a small set of obstacles.

At the start, the game provides you with a relatively safe environment in which you can experiment with the controls. The first screen has no enemies or interactions at all. Here, you just learn how to maneuver Mario. Shortly thereafter, you encounter your first Question Mark Block and your first enemy. You do not have to be told this is an enemy— the menacing eyebrows of the Goomba give it away. You then have to jump on or over the Goomba to pass. For many, especially those who are playing a video game for the first time, this is a challenging maneuver. For players who have been playing games like this for most of their lives, however, this is trivial. The level introduces only three other hazards: a small pit, a turtle (with his shell), and a piranha plant. For some this is too much, but for many, this teaches them the skills they need to adjust to the increasing challenges of the game.

Now take a look at the last levels of the game. By this point, the player has mastered the control dynamics of Mario to an expert level. As a result, the challenge must increase to a correspondingly high level. If every level was as easy as World 1-1, most players would get bored with it by the end. But the designers took this into account. In the later levels, players must bounce off of moving bullets, land on single-block platforms, use springs, and dodge thrown enemies.

Designers use a lot of effort to match the challenges they present to the player's current skill level. Modern AAA studios use sophisticated techniques to find out how to avoid areas that are not conducive to flow. Microsoft's user research arm helped Bungie (the developer of *Halo 3*) produce visualizations when creating *Halo 3* so they could see areas where players were spending more time or were using more ammo.[3] These visualizations help designers see bottlenecks where players are getting stuck and areas where challenges are insufficient. Perhaps a jump or door was not obvious. By measuring player behavior, you can see where players are struggling (or perhaps, not struggling enough).

By measuring player movement over time and using other types of quantitative and qualitative information, designers aim to find out where players are in flow and where they are bored or frustrated. By knowing that the flow state exists and that its boundaries are boredom and anxiety, you are aware of one of simplest tools to generating happiness. Bored? Add more challenge. Frustrated? Remove challenge or increase player skill.

Now I will return to the question of *Shadow of the Colossus* from earlier. Why would the designers follow extremely challenging boss battles with long periods of challenge-free riding? If you are not familiar with that title, you can choose almost any game with a difficult boss encounter, because many share the design pattern of a difficult section immediately followed by an empty or easy section. You'll rarely see a boss fight followed by another difficult section. Why is this? The designers are playing with flow. The *flow channel* is the area on the graph of a player's flow where the player is neither frustrated nor bored. The goal is to get the player to bounce off the edges of her flow channel (**FIGURE 9.2**). After she experiences something difficult, the player needs time to breathe and readjust. Thus, she gets a period of easy play that brings her back down toward the boredom side of the flow channel. Before she gets there, though, the developers reintroduce the challenge again, even harder than before, to deal with the player's increased mastery. It's all flow.

Game designer Richard Lemarchand posed an alternative way to view the ebb and flow of game difficulty. His position is that the amount of attention a player can devote at a specific time is limited; periods of high vigilance must be followed by periods of relative unimportance to restock reserves of attention.

. . . .

3   Thompson, C. (2007, August 21). "Halo 3: How Microsoft Labs Invented a New Science of Play." Retrieved January 8, 2015, from http://archive.wired.com/gaming/virtualworlds/magazine/15-09/ff_halo?currentPage=all.

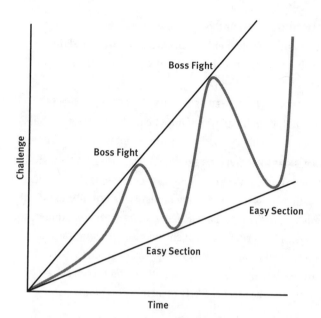

FIGURE 9.2 Oscillating between the boundaries of the flow channel.

Games that do not have an ulterior motive for players besides player satisfaction (for instance, simulations, art games, or games for training all have goals besides simply providing players with fun or satisfaction) should be primarily driven in all decisions toward providing players flow. Most game design heuristics revolve around getting players to a flow state. This principle is so overwhelmingly present under the surface of so much of what we label "game design" that I am willing to call it the *fundamental game design directive*.

Let's consider the "why" behind other commonly held game design heuristics that you'll find in this book and elsewhere:

- **WHY SHOULD YOU PROVIDE PLAYERS WITH MEANINGFUL DECISION-MAKING OPPORTUNITIES?** In absence of these, the players have little to challenge them into a flow state.

- **WHY SHOULD YOU PLAYTEST YOUR GAMES?** You don't have a "flowometer" that you can attach to your games to record the quantitative amount of flow in which a player engages. Instead, you have to test unbiased subjects in a scientific way to see if players are bored or frustrated. Until that flowometer is invented, playtesting is the most reliable way to gain that information.

- **WHY SHOULD THE PLAYER HAVE CLEAR GOALS?** Clear goals allow directing player behavior toward his flow state. Aimless behaviors become boring over time. Behaviors directed toward impossible goals become frustrating.

▶ **NOTE** It fills me with dread to make such a pronouncement. So many wildly "universal" statements about game design have holes easily punched through them. Yet, the more I look, the more this directive holds.

- **WHY ARE RIDDLES GENERALLY POOR PUZZLES?** Most riddles have no way of working toward the answer. Thus the solver either knows it right away and the challenge is trivial, or the solver has no way of determining the answer and the challenge is frustrating.

- **WHY SHOULD YOU CARE ABOUT WHAT THE PLAYER PERCEIVES IS FAIR?** If a player is overly frustrated, justified or not, then the player cannot be in the flow state. What is important is not whether a game is truly fair or not but whether it is perceived as fair.

- **WHY IS THE "NEAR MISS" IN A GAME PERCEIVED AS EXCITING?** Psychologists have studied the effect of the excitement produced by near misses, even when the player does not have control over the result (for example, slot machines).[4] One possible explanation is that a wild miss signals to the player that she must make great adjustments to get to a winning state, but a near miss suggests that she was on the right track. A player who feels she was on the right track is likely to feel an adequate amount of challenge (as opposed to an "easy win" or a miss devastatingly off target, suggesting that a win is impossible), and thus she is more likely to be in a flow state.

All these elements and more can be phrased in terms of providing players with flow. Of course, if there was some simple algorithm for adding flow for players, then I would just spell it out and the book would be complete. Getting players to flow is not easy. Not only are their skills wildly different from player to player, but their desires and perceptions can also interpret the same input in vastly different ways. Thus, we all need to have a deeper understanding for what mechanisms we can apply in what situations to produce flow.

Interest Curves

In the book, *The Art of Game Design*, designer, professor, and juggler Jesse Schell discusses a way to illustrate the concept of a person's engagement over the course of an entertainment experience.[5] He named this concept the *interest curve*. In an interest curve, you relate the amount of engagement you have with a piece of entertainment at various points in time. You then graph the relationship between the amount of interest/engagement/fun on the y-axis and the point in time on the x-axis.

4   Reid, R. L. (1986). "The Psychology of the Near Miss." *Journal of Gambling Behavior*, 2(1), 32-39.

5   Schell, J. (2008). *The Art of Game Design: A Book of Lenses*. Amsterdam: Elsevier/Morgan Kaufmann.

Say the graph in **FIGURE 9.3** represents a session in which I play *League of Legends*. I start out with some level of interest (1), otherwise I wouldn't play. The game becomes more interesting as I ease into the early game and attempt to get my first tower (2). But then something bad happens. I get defeated and my interest plummets (3). I am feeling really bad. In fact, my interest is less than when I started. I have a hard time getting it back. But eventually I catch up and get some great assists, which skyrockets my interest (4). Then my team starts carrying toward victory, which sustains my interest (5). The end of the game serves as a climax, which spikes my interest again (6). At the end, if I am more interested than when I started, I consider starting another session.

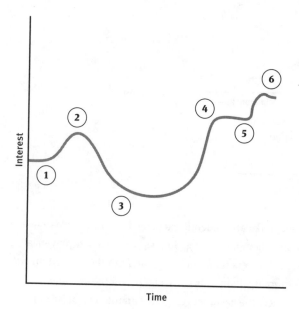

FIGURE 9.3 An interest curve of me playing *League of Legends*.

Along this curve, a number of events affect my interest: the start, attempting to destroy the first tower, defeat, a period of time in which I languish and try to catch up, then a big team fight or two, and then final victory. Mapping my interest over those events creates the interest curve. By examining the interest curve, designers can better understand which events increase engagement, which events decrease engagement, and when these events happen over time.

Each game has an interest floor that, when passed, causes the player to quit the game. Without constant interesting moments to spike up the level on the graph, players will slowly fade down to this quit point. Interest increases when a player is in flow and decreases when a player is bored or frustrated. **FIGURE 9.4** shows the interest curve for a player who cannot figure out the rules of a game. He has some early success, which spikes the graph at one point, but frustration keeps pushing him lower until he finally quits.

FIGURE 9.4
At minimum interest, the player gives up.

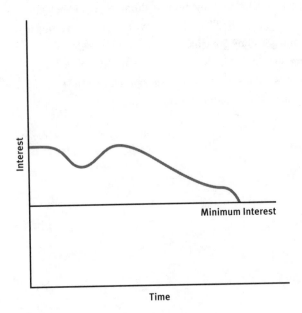

Tracking a player's interest may seem like an academic exercise, but this is actually something that many studios record when playtesting. Some studios survey players at random points in their playtests. The players then rate how much fun they are having *at that given moment* on a scale of 1 to 10. By doing this with a large sample of playtesters at many points in the game experience, the designers can craft an interest curve of how different players are experiencing the level.

By crafting interest curves, designers can identify the weak points in their experiences. Spots where interest wanes are normal (and even necessary—not all moments can be a climax or players would get burnt out), but extended periods of low interest should obviously be avoided. If you notice that interest never peaks again after a certain event, you may wish to save that event for your game's climax. Or if a certain puzzle causes a large drop in interest, it may not be appropriate for the audience.

What does a "good" interest curve look like (**FIGURE 9.5**)? It looks surprisingly like the dramatic structure that Aristotle lectured about over two thousand years ago (**FIGURE 9.6**), explaining the structure of a story.

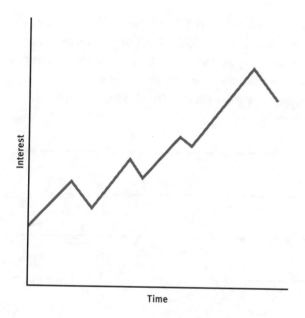

FIGURE 9.5 A good-looking interest curve.

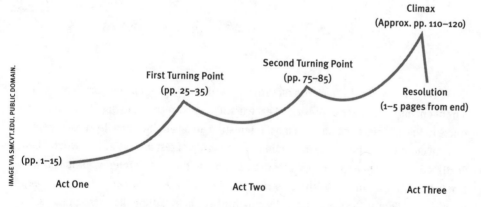

FIGURE 9.6 Aristotelian structure.

In the normal course of a drama, you have an inciting incident that causes some amount of interest, then a series of spikes of rising action. The rising action has a series of conflicts and resolutions that keep upping the ante to the point of climax, where the hero's major problem is resolved in one way or another, which then leads to the catharsis or "new normal." Every well-crafted drama has ups and downs, little victories, and little defeats, that lead up to the pivotal moment. In games, you experience the same structure. For instance, a complicated puzzle has several aha! moments when you discover the mechanics and how they interrelate before the final giant aha! of solving the puzzle.

FIGURE 9.7 shows the number of deaths per map in *Half-Life 2: Episode One* (which Schell also references) taken from Steam's publicly shared data.[6] Each series represents a different set of difficulties. The map that spikes the highest is obviously the hardest difficulty. The maps are listed in sequential order from left (beginning of the game) to right (end of the game). As you can see, the game plays in a linear manner, so players will always encounter the maps in this order.

FIGURE 9.7
One way to interpret this graph is that deaths are related to challenge, and challenge is the interesting aesthetic of the game that regulates flow.

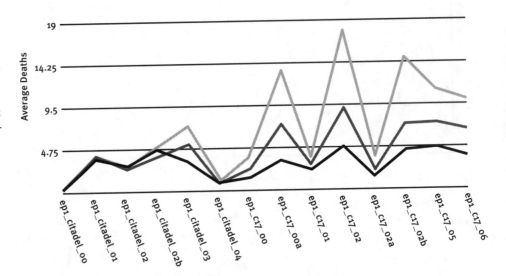

In Figure 9.8, you see the design structure repeated. *Half-Life 2: Episode One* features a number of mini-climaxes at the end of each act. These correspond to high death rates since, in these types of games, the most interesting areas are the ones that provide significant challenge. After these mini-climaxes, a period of rest always occurs where the death rate is low. Then the stakes are raised again and the game's interest jumps back and forth until the climax. With this structure, *Half-Life 2: Episode One*'s designers keep the player in flow as long as possible by matching the actual difficulty to the player's expected difficulty for that point in the game.

. . . .
6   Accessible in summary at www.steampowered.com/status/ep1/ep1_stats.php.

Learning Curves

Another type of graphical representation of player flow is what is commonly known as a *learning curve*. You may have heard of this term before. The popular usage of the term is actually backward. In common parlance, a game with a "steep" learning curve is a game that is difficult to learn early in the experience. However, a learning curve is a graph of learning on the vertical axis over time on the horizontal axis, so a game with a steep learning curve has the player exercise mastery in a short period of time.

The actual use of the learning curve dovetails nicely with the discussion of flow. If a player is constantly learning, then what impact does that have on flow? What if she learns nothing after a certain point? Since a flow diagram relates the amount of challenge needed for the amount of skill, a learning curve tells you how much challenge needs to increase over time. Look at the learning curve in **FIGURE 9.8**. A player learns some initial skills but stops learning after a point. If you know this, you know that to keep the player in flow, you need to increase the difficulty during time range A, while she is learning, and keep the difficulty constant during time range B, when she is not.

FIGURE 9.8 A learning curve.

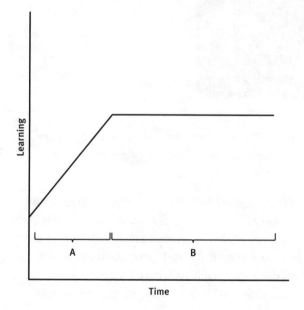

Now relate what you know about the learning curve to the interest curve in Figure 9.6; if you have a game where a lot of learning has to take place before the first climax (the commonly-referred-to *steep learning curve*), then you risk having the player reach her minimum level of interest. Teaching someone is an investment, and if that investment does not pay off in time, the player/learner abandons the activity before the payoff.

For instance, in *Dwarf Fortress*, the player must learn an extraordinarily large number of controls, symbols (**FIGURE 9.9**), and mechanics before he is able to understand how to actively play with the simulation. This amount of learning delays the first big payoff of the game. Not surprisingly, many players never get to that first big payoff. They hit their minimum interest level and quit playing. Because of the large amount of early learning the player experiences, he stays on the frustration side of flow. Players can handle this for a time, but eventually they quit if they cannot break out of that state.

FIGURE 9.9
Interpreting the glyph-based display of *Dwarf Fortress* is just one element of a complex interface.

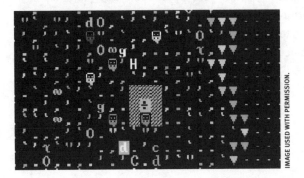

IMAGE USED WITH PERMISSION.

If you have designed a game like *Dwarf Fortress* where the amount the player has to learn before the first payoff is large, what can you do? Using what you've learned from this chapter, you can do one of three things:

- **INCLUDE EARLY MINI-PAYOFFS (MINI-CLIMAXES) SO PLAYERS BECOME INTERESTED WHILE LEARNING THE GAME.** This is difficult to do and requires significant planning and play-testing to see if the events that you intend to be climaxes are satisfying as such. Many games introduce mechanics slowly and let each mechanic pay off before introducing a new one. A particularly excellent use of this technique is the game *Portal*, which methodically teaches new mechanics in a test chamber before the big story payoffs.

- **REDUCE THE AMOUNT THE PLAYER NEEDS TO LEARN FROM THE GAME BEFORE SHE CAN HIT THE FIRST BIG PAYOFF OR CLIMAX** (a subtle difference from the previous strategy). This has limitations in that it changes the dynamics of your game because you are limiting the amount of mechanics you originally intended on having. Many sports games include a "casual mode" that limits the amount of mechanics in play by automating some of the more advanced options. This allows players to get their first wins quickly, yet perhaps with not as much skill as when they are using the default modes.

- **IGNORE THE SITUATION AND CATER ONLY TO PEOPLE WHO TOLERATE LONGER PERIODS WITHOUT MINI-CLIMAXES,** for example, people who have a lower minimum interest level. This obviously limits the reach of your game, since you focus only on the players who have already reached flow with your game as is.

Upward-sloping learning curves mean that at those points, the player is learning while playing. In the book *A Theory of Fun*, designer Raph Koster posits that all fun is based on learning.[7] This would dovetail with flow theory quite nicely. If players are challenged sufficiently, then they are learning how to best utilize their skills, and they are in flow. If players are learning, that is, if the learning curve is trending upward, then the players always have something to challenge them. This is, of course, one-half of the equation. Challenge must exist, but it also must not be too challenging. It's not enough to just provide opportunities for learning; those opportunities must match the skills of the learner. For college-bound students, Introduction to Economics makes sense. Those students have both the theoretic (algebra, geometry) and concrete (real-world experience) tools to understand the lessons. A kindergartner, on the other hand, would have plenty to learn from the class but does not have the tools to do so.

Individual Differences

Remember that individuals have their own personal interest and learning curves. No such thing as "the interest curve" or "the learning curve" exists for a game that is consistent across players and time. Remember that grandma may pick up Facebook games OK, but she will have trouble sustaining her interest in a first-person shooter. Your stereotypical core gamer tires of Facebook games quickly but can play the same shooter for hours and hours.

Designers tend to overestimate player skill in the short run and underestimate it in the long run. Because you have intimate knowledge of your systems, you are likely to find it difficult to imagine what it is like for players who have never seen your systems before. Always underestimate what the player will be able to understand instinctually early in the game.

. . . .
7   Koster, R. (2005). *A Theory of Fun for Game Design*. Scottsdale, AZ: Paraglyph Press.

This reaches an inflection point for your expert players. When you say, "Yeah, the player will always win if he gets six crystals from this lake and takes them the entire way across the world to craft them, which no one would ever do," you are underestimating your expert player's skill, which is also almost always a mistake. On day one of release, you'll be horrified to see videos appearing on YouTube talking about "the crystal trick." Never underestimate how a player will be able to break your systems. Always assume that at least one player will have complete knowledge of everything about your systems and complete skills to maximize that knowledge.

Summary

- Flow is the state in between frustration and boredom that drives player motivation. Generating flow is the fundamental directive of any game designer producing games for player enjoyment.
- Games must be balanced in a way that respects each individual player's level of skill if the designer cares for generating flow in each individual player.
- By mapping player interest over time, designers can get a visual representation of a player's engagement over different sections of a game.
- Learning is integral to the flow process. Complicated games are neither good nor bad; instead, what needs to be managed is how they expose their systems to the player to affect their level of challenge.
- You will always know and understand your own games more than the vast majority of players. Whatever works for you must be toned down for a player who has less understanding of and experience with your systems.

10 Decision-Making

A man without decision can never be said
to belong to himself.

—JOHN FOSTER WATSON

It's not enough to ask players to make decisions—the designer
must frame decision points in a way that is conducive to generating or maintaining flow for the player. This critical component
is where many games fail. To understand how to craft the most
effective decisions, designers must first understand the basics
of decision-making in games and then the basic features that
make those decisions interesting or less interesting.

Interesting decision-making does not necessarily mean
"decision-making that I, the designer, like." Instead, it is
decision-making that keeps the player in a space between
frustrating challenge and tepid boredom.

Player Agency

For players to have a meaningful decision-making experience during play, they must have *agency*. Agency means being able to act on your own behalf. You do not have agency when watching movies because you cannot affect the state of the events. A player who can make only decisions that do not affect the game state does not have agency.

The goal of designers is to give players that agency in areas where they require it and to remove it in areas where they do not need it. Take *SimCity* for example. Running all the operations of a city is a lot of hard work. One responsibility of city planners in some jurisdictions is to determine how and when trash is collected. *SimCity*, however, does not make you do that. Why? *SimCity* is mostly about placing resources in proximity to each other and balancing the budget of a city despite the seemingly random wants and needs of the population. Will Wright, the designer of the original *SimCity* and the designers of subsequent revisions, decided that the player did not need the agency of setting the trash schedules. Perhaps it was not a fun decision to make or perhaps it did not effectively meet the theme of what the designers wanted players to do. And *SimCity* is stronger for it.

Look at two games in contrast: *NBA Street* and *NBA Live*. These are two games made by the same company (and at one point, the same studio) that tackle the same thematic elements (in part) but offer wildly different levels of player agency. In *NBA Live*, computer-controlled players (CPU players) get injured, and teams have to manage their bench, negotiate CPU player contracts, and set up offensive and defensive schemes for the CPU players to execute. *NBA Street* foregoes all this and takes that kind of agency out of players' hands, greatly simplifying the play. The reason is that the two games target different experiences. These are colloquially known as *simulation* and *arcade*, but in reality, the distinction is less binary and more of a spectrum. It is really a question of player agency. In simulation games, players are given much more agency, whereas in arcade-styled games, the focus is squarely on smaller sets of game mechanics and many elements are either abstracted away or handled by the computer.

More agency is not necessarily better. Some players find *NBA Live* frustratingly complex, and others find *NBA Street* boring because it is too simplified. The key is to give the player agency only for decisions he cares about and those that effectively serve the experience that the designers wish to create.

Anatomy of a Choice

Salen and Zimmerman's book, *Rules of Play* (2003), includes a great questionnaire for examining a choice.[1] The following five aspects help you understand the context of a choice:

- **BEFORE:** What happened before the player was given the choice? What is the context of the choice? What is the game state?

- **COMMUNICATION:** How is the possibility of choice conveyed to the player? How does the player know there is a choice or what the options are?

- **ACTION:** How did the player make the choice? What mechanism did the player use to make the choice? Did the player say something aloud, play a card, press a trigger?

- **CONSEQUENCES:** What is the result of the choice? How will it affect future choices? This aspect combines two questions into one—cheating, I know, but they are tightly coupled. For a choice to have meaning, it must affect the game state in some meaningful way.

- **FEEDBACK:** How is the result of the choice conveyed to the player? How does the player know what happens after the fact?

Chess, one of the most studied games in the world, features discrete decisions that make it a comparatively easy game to analyze in this way. Here, I am assuming that you understand the basics of how *Chess* pieces move.

In **FIGURE 10.1**, it's white's move, and the player is faced with the choice of what to move. Let's analyze this *Chess* game with respect to Salen and Zimmerman's five aspects:

- **BEFORE:** What happened before the player was given the choice? Obviously some of the game has been completed. A few pieces are missing from each side, but the game is still fairly even. By looking at the board, you can get some context. Most of the pawns are locked up by being face to face with each other, and thus they can no longer move unless they can capture another piece.

- **COMMUNICATION:** How is the possibility of choice conveyed to the player? Board games like *Chess* make this easy. Since this is a game of perfect information, both players are aware of the whole board state at any time. The white player can see all the available moves. In computer *Chess*, the client will often show all available moves by highlighting squares.

. . . .

1   Zimmerman, E., & Salen, K. (2003). *Rules of Play: Game Design Fundamentals*. Cambridge, MA: MIT Press.

FIGURE 10.1
A possible *Chess* set of positions.

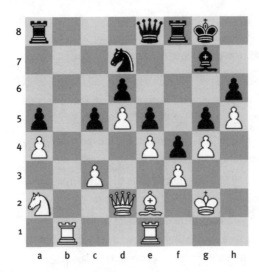

- **ACTION:** How did the player make the choice? The player had to first analyze which white pieces could move and where they could move. White would also have to analyze where black's pieces could move and where they were likely to move. With all this congestion on the board, white feels that knights are more powerful than bishops, so the white bishop is moved to B5 to put black's remaining knight in danger. If black moves the knight out of danger, black puts his queen directly in danger.

- **CONSEQUENCES:** What is the result of the choice? How will it affect future choices? Now black is faced with a problem: give up the knight or the queen? It is a great move for white and will affect future choices by giving her a piece advantage.

- **FEEDBACK:** How is the result of the choice conveyed to the player? Games of perfect information like this are understood by both players and don't have issues communicating the options or results of those options.

> ◆ **TIP** In case you are unfamiliar, it's common Chess notation to list the columns by assigning a letter (A to the leftmost, H to the rightmost) and a number to the row (1 at the bottom and 8 at the top). Thus, the lower-left corner is A1 and the top-right corner is H8.

White has plenty of options here and each has its pros and cons. White did not have to move the bishop. The rook at B1 could have been moved in to threaten the knight. Or white could start maneuvering her remaining knight to jump the blockade of pawns and start picking off the cluster of high-value pieces in the back. This is an interesting decision because many of the options available to white have real consequences for the game state that shift from turn to turn.

By using these questions, you can diagnose where your game is running into problems. For instance, if decisions feel meaningless or arbitrary, it's likely that your answer to the Consequences question is the culprit. If your players are confused, then your answers to the Communication and Feedback questions are likely where you need to look. If players understand what the game is trying to do but still cite frustration at the actual functioning of the game, your answer to the Action question may be the reason.

I've discussed the importance of meaningful decisions in games. A related point is that the act of choosing is highly motivating. Choice itself means control, even when the choice doesn't result in increased control.[2]

Less-Interesting Decision-Making

It is easy for a game designer to add decision-making to the design of her game, but how does she know what an interesting decision is versus a less-interesting decision? Some forms of decision-making are more likely to fall flat than others. They are not always completely inappropriate for use in games, but when bad decision-making needles players in a game, it's often reducible to one of the following categories.

Blind Decisions

This is a type of decision-making seen often in RPGs. As the game begins, you are given a choice: "Would you like to be a Human, a Mole-person, or a Lizard-man?" What information does the player use to determine which is the best choice? Since he has just started the game, he doesn't have a basis for making the decision, except possibly from previous experience with the game or genre. If he has no reason to pick any of the proposed options, then the decision is *blind*; he might as well throw darts at a dartboard to choose (**FIGURE 10.2**).

Blind decision-making can be difficult for designers to root out. Since the designer knows all the under-the-hood mechanics, she has an inside edge and the decision may not be blind for her. But the players are the ones interacting with the system. Even giving them hints, such as "Mole-people can see in the dark!" may not help because the player doesn't know how useful a trait that may be.

. . . .

2   Cordova, D. I., & Lepper, M. R. (1996). "Intrinsic Motivation and the Process of Learning: Beneficial Effects of Contextualization, Personalization, and Choice." *Journal of Educational Psychology*, 88(4), 715.

FIGURE 10.2
Many interesting choices the player is not yet equipped to make.

▶ **NOTE** Creating a tutorial to give the player information to help make decisions is not always the right option. Having a massive tutorial may slow down the player experience too much. Other solutions may be more appropriate.

If a player is allowed to play all three races in a tutorial world that show the pros and cons of each choice, his decision of which to play for the rest of the game is informed. The converse of blind decision-making is *informed* decision-making. When an (American) football coach chooses to call a run play, the decision is an informed decision with information about the opponent's defenses. He believes that, given the personnel on the field and information from previous plays, calling a run play will yield better results than a pass play. He does not pick arbitrarily.

Blind decisions can be acceptable if they lead to information that makes later similar decisions informed. Say you are fighting a boss in *Mega Man 3* and have nine different weapons from which to choose. Your initial decision of what weapon to use is blind. Any weapon is likely as good as any other. But as you cycle through your weapons and see which does the most damage, you can incrementally solve the dilemma of what the optimal play is. The same goes for the role of football coach referenced earlier. If the coach has never seen the opposing team before, the first few play calls may be blind. But as the coach accesses the effectiveness of the different types of play versus the opponent's changing defenses, the decision-making becomes more and more informed. In both of these examples, the decision-making is iterative and the player is not locked in to a blind decision made earlier. If the designer must force the player to make a blind decision, she should make the choice reversible or its effect minimal. For example, the effect of choosing an incorrect weapon for the first few seconds of a battle in *Mega Man 3* is minimal as long as you quickly switch to another weapon.

Obvious Decisions

Another form of ineffective decision-making is the *obvious* decision. An obvious decision is one where every rational player would only ever choose one option. Consider *Tic-Tac-Toe*. If your opponent is one square away from making three in a row, then the choice of where to move is obvious. If you do not block your opponent, the opponent will win. If you are one move away from three in a row, your move is also obvious and a guaranteed win. Since so many of the scenarios involved in *Tic-Tac-Toe* are obvious choices, it gets lumped in with the games that offer no choices at all!

In *Monopoly*, when you land on the Income Tax space, you can pay 10 percent of your assets, or you can pay $200. This is a decision, certainly, but if you know what your assets are worth, the decision is obvious. If you have $2,000 in assets or more, you pay the $200. Otherwise, you pay the 10 percent.

▶ **NOTE** This always rankled me. You don't calculate your income by summing up your net worth!

Consider the folk game *Nim*, a form of which is shown in **FIGURE 10.3**. In this version, the game has three bowls of marbles. Each player takes a turn, taking as many marbles from a single bowl as she wishes, but she must take at least one. The winner is the player who takes the last marble in the game.

FIGURE 10.3 A set of bowls containing marbles for a game of *Nim*.

Adults can play this game with interest, but it is just as solved as *Tic-Tac-Toe*. The difference is that solving the game is less intuitive and requires a bit more math. Nonetheless, the first player can never lose if she plays optimally, much like in *Tic-Tac-Toe*, meaning the decisions are meaningless for players who understand the strategy. Much like a child can play Tic-Tac-Toe with interest before he understands the strategy, adults can play Nim and make meaningful decisions until they know the optimal strategy.

▶ **NOTE** Nim is interesting to play if it is from the perspective of not understanding optimal play. However, once you can see the solution, it's impossible to unsee it, so I'll leave how to solve Nim as an exercise for you... or you could consult Wikipedia.

Another form of obvious decision-making is the *Hobson's Choice*. A Hobson's Choice is a "take it or leave it" choice. Certainly you faced one of these as a child. If you complained about dinner, your mother might say, "You can eat the broccoli or have no dinner at all." The Hobson's Choice is so named because of a 17th-Century livery stable owner. Although Hobson had 40 horses in his stables giving you the illusion of choice about which to borrow, he allowed only the one closest to the door to be rented, leaving his best horses farther back to best preserve their value. Hobson offered the choice: "Take the horse by the door or no horse at all." This is an obvious choice for someone who needs a horse that day. The broken-down horse near the front, although not as good as the young steeds in the back, was certainly better than no horse at all. A choice of the form "Do X or lose the game" is a Hobson's Choice. Although a player could always choose to lose the game, why would he?

Generally speaking, if the action can be automated and the game state is no different for it, then the choice is obvious. Take the evolution of reloading in shooter games, for example. When a player has no bullets loaded in her gun and tries to fire, what happens? What would happen in reality is that the gun would go "click" and not fire. But in games, almost universally now, the gun starts reloading automatically when the player attempts to shoot without bullets loaded. Why? This is an obvious choice. The player wants to shoot but cannot because she has no ammo in the clip. Therefore, she must choose "Do I want to reload?" The answer is obvious and so the digital action is automated.

Meaningless/Misleading Decisions

A decision that is *meaningless* results in no difference to the game state.

Narrative-based games are often forced into meaningless decisions because of the cost of making content to fulfill every possible option. At the beginning of many RPGs, the king asks the protagonist if he will go find the magic MacGuffin in order to save the kingdom/princess/world/universe. The player is then given a "Will you accept the quest?" prompt. If the player chooses "No," he does not engage in a simulation of what the rest of the protagonist's life would be like. Usually, at this point, the king just acts flummoxed and asks the question again and again until the player says "Yes." Then everyone can continue with their assigned roles.

Telltale's *Walking Dead* series of adventure games puts an interesting spin on this principle. Many of the dialogue choices the player makes in the game are meaningless in that they offer no or extremely negligible differences in the game's reaction to those choices. But mixed in with those are similar-looking choices that are extremely meaningful and lead to major changes in cast and plot. By mixing the two together, Telltale makes it so the player never really knows what decisions will come back to haunt her, and thus she has to treat every dialogue choice as meaningful. It's a difficult scheme to reinforce, but Telltale does it by making some of the players' dialogue decisions early on extremely poignant; this approach functions as a tutorial for players so that they can see that the dialogue choices they make have serious effects.

Sometimes, meaningless decision-making is only apparent after the fact. Consider the offensive play caller for a football team. He will make dozens of decisions about what plays to call over the course of the game. Even if the calls are perfect and the team scores four touchdowns, perhaps the defense is poor and allows five touchdowns. The offensive play caller's decision-making was after-the-fact meaningless. Nothing the caller could have done would have changed the result of the game. The offensive play caller's decision-making was meaningless in retrospect, and this incentivizes him to care less about his decision-making in the future.

Blackjack is a game with after-the-fact meaningless decisions. If I am dealt a 16, I can stay or hit (take another card). The next card in the deck is a 10. The dealer has a 20. If I hit, I lose because I go over 21. If I stay, I lose because I have less than 20. Since I do not know what the next card is or what the dealer has, I "play the odds" that my choice will be correct. It has meaning at the time I make the choice, but afterward, it is revealed that the choice had no importance at all. I would have lost either way.

A *misleading decision* is a special case of the meaningless decision. It is when the player chooses to do one thing, but the game or system does another. In the previous "Do you want to save the kingdom?" example, imagine if you said "No, thanks" to saving the kingdom and the game let you. You then go home only to find that the same monster that you would have had to fight to save the kingdom has just broken into your home and stolen your family. Now you must go on the same quest as you would have if you had chosen to save the kingdom. Why have this decision at all if you are just going to mislead the player into making the decision contrary to her desires? This type of decision is often used to force the player into particular narrative situations. If you must force a player into a narrative situation, it is often best to do so without the dishonest illusion of player choice.

Handcuffing Decisions

Designer Daniel Solis pointed out an interesting excerpt on his blog from an interview with Paul Peterson, the designer of the *Guillotine* card game.[3] In the interview, Peterson says his biggest mistake as a game designer is the *Guillotine* card labeled "Callous Guards." The game *Guillotine* is about manipulating a line of nobles on their way to the guillotine during the French Revolution. When a player plays "Callous Guards," it makes other players unable to alter the order of the line of nobles. This eliminates, in one fell swoop, a large portion of the options that players have. Their universe of interesting options shrinks to possibly nothing.

. . . .

3   Solis, D. (2015, July 15). "One Thing to Avoid in Game Design." Retrieved July 18, 2015, from http://danielsolisblog.blogspot.com/2015/07/one-thing-to-avoid-in-game-design.html.

A *handcuffing decision* is one that takes away the ability of players to make further meaningful decisions. The most common way to handcuff players in poor games is to make them freeze or skip a turn. Much like some of the other decision types, handcuffing decisions are not always bad. The value of the handcuffing needs to be weighed against its impact. In *Monopoly*, players are handcuffed (thematically and mechanically) by going to Jail. Jail serves a purpose in that it limits the possibility of someone taking infinite turns by rolling consecutive doubles forever. It also serves the purpose of providing a safe harbor to temporarily prevent the player from landing on high-rent spaces late in the game. Those benefits have to be weighed against the fact that some players will sit in jail, attempting to roll doubles, and make no meaningful decisions for a long stretch of the game.

Handcuffing decisions need to be weighed against the dynamics of the game. Some games are inherently combative and reducing the decision space is part of the normal dynamics of the game. In *Chess*, you would not say that putting someone into check is handcuffing them since it reduces their possible moves to any that get them out of check. Instead, this a normal dynamic for the game, especially considering that an implicit objective of the game is to avoid endangering your king. However, if playtesters are consistently saying, "I don't have anything to do," "There's nothing I can do," "I don't have many options here," or "When am I going to get to take a turn?" then they may be encountering decisions that are serving as handcuffs.

More-Interesting Decision-Making

Whether the actual decision-making in a game is interesting or not is up to the players themselves, but certain types of design patterns help make for interesting decision-making.

Trade-offs

The single most useful technique for making decision interesting, hands down, is introducing a *trade-off*. In a trade-off, the player is given two or more options, each of which has its own unique benefits and drawbacks. For instance, in *Team Fortress 2*, the Pyro can choose as their weapon the flamethrower or the backburner (among others). The flamethrower is the standard weapon. If the player chooses the backburner, she can deal more critical hits than she can with the standard flamethrower, but her secondary attack costs 150 percent more, meaning it can be used less often. The player gets to deal a little bit more damage with her primary attack, but trades that advantage for reducing the effectiveness of her secondary attack.

In the board game *Ticket to Ride*, the players are able to do one of three things on their turns: acquire trains for building, build using those trains, or acquire tickets for additional objectives. Since the player cannot acquire the resources and build on the same turn, the trade-off requires him to choose between acquiring resources and locking in those resources to score points.

For a trade-off to be effective, each option must provide some benefit and some drawback when compared to the other options available. In a trade-off, the players are always giving up something for something else. Otherwise, the choice is dominated (see Chapter 19) or obvious (see the section, "Obvious Decisions," earlier in this chapter). Trade-offs incorporate the concepts of opportunity costs from economics. An *opportunity cost* is the cost of using the next-best alternative. If you choose to go to the movies with your partner instead of going to work, the cost is not only the ticket price, but also the cost of a few hours of lost productivity since you cannot work on developing your game during that time.

In the card game *Dominion*, the players are faced with the choice of purchasing Action cards, which help them during the game but are worth nothing at the end of the game, or buying Victory cards, which are worth points at the end of the game but are useless in the player's deck. When the player chooses to buy a Victory card, his opportunity cost is the benefit he could have received from a similarly valued Action card. Since the game has an endpoint, buying Actions early in the game is best, because the lost benefit from buying Victory cards is huge since that Action card may come up many times. But as the game nears its end, the opportunity cost lessens, since any bought Action card may never come up at all. Note that this change in value is all implicit. The cost in coins written on the card never changes. The cost of each card is 5 (see the lower-left corner of the card), yet on the first turn of the game, almost all players choose Laboratory over Duchy, whereas on the last turn, almost all players choose Duchy over Laboratory (**FIGURE 10.4** and **10.5**).

Trade-offs are not always a wise thing to offer players. In narrative-based games, often the designer would need to make a lot of unique content so the player can have truly meaningful trade-offs. For instance, in another medieval game example, the player can choose to support the king, or kill the king and take the throne for herself. If the game allows that option, it must tailor all the remaining events in the game to the results of that decision. The expectation is that characters will treat the player differently—as someone who committed regicide and stole the throne for herself. Quests that would have made sense for a normal adventurer would no longer make sense for the new queen. Now that is certainly a meaningful trade-off: The player gets the rights and privileges of the ruler of the land, but she has to deal with the responsibilities of being what her subjects see as an unrightfully crowned monarch. The downside for game makers is that the game has a huge swath of content that the player will never see. If the player chooses the "support the king" role, all the interesting post-regicide quests are inaccessible. A game that offers a trade-off like this would seem shorter to a player who only plays through the game once, because she unknowingly misses a large amount of content down the narrative paths she did not choose.

FIGURE 10.4 The Duchy card is useless in the beginning of the game but very useful at the end of the game.

FIGURE 10.5 The Laboratory card is useful during the game but worth nothing at the end of the game.

Trade-offs can backfire in some situations. Have you ever been paralyzed with your choices when a waiter comes by to take your order at a restaurant? The issue of an overabundance of choice was the subject of a popularly cited study.[4] The research group set up a booth at a local supermarket; the booth displayed a number of jams with free samples. Periodically, they would switch from having six jams on display to having 24 jams on display. The researchers found that more customers were drawn to the display when it

· · · · · · · · · · · · · · · · · · ·

4   Iyengar, S., & Lepper, M. (2000). "When Choice Is Demotivating: Can One Desire Too Much of a Good Thing?" *Journal of Personality and Social Psychology*, 995–1006.

had 24 on display (we love choice!), but when the display had only six jams, the display was *ten times* as effective at converting those tasters to sales. The conclusion of the study is that although we may like having options, it doesn't always result in optimal behavior.

Risk/Reward

One of the other surefire ways to make a decision more interesting is to offer options with less certainty and higher payoffs pitted against options of high certainty and low payoffs. This is more commonly called a *risk-reward* choice.

One of the most salient examples of this is the classic game show *Let's Make A Deal*. In it, contestants win prizes and then are asked if they want to keep that prize or trade it for what is behind a curtain, sight unseen. Say the player had just won a $500 television. He could keep that television or trade it for the mystery prize. He does not know whether that mystery prize is worth more than $500 or less than $500. He knows that the show often gives away great prizes on these trades like vacations and cars, but the show often has joke prizes that are worthless as well, such as boxes of bubble wrap. If he knew what was behind the curtain, the choice would be pretty obvious. He would just go with the prize that he valued more. But the fact that the prize is hidden creates risk and makes the decision interesting.

These kinds of risk decisions can be much more subtle. Look at the following diagram of the Elevator level from *Donkey Kong* in **FIGURE 10.6**.

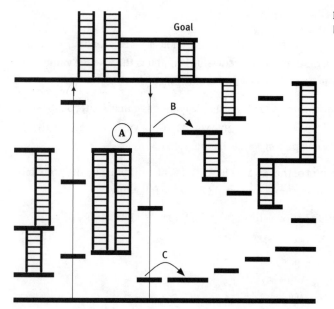

FIGURE 10.6 The Elevator level of *Donkey Kong*.

Mario (or Jumpman) starts in the lower left and has to reach Pauline at the top. Meanwhile, Donkey Kong is throwing these nasty spring things and sentient fires are running around trying to roast our plucky hero. The left elevator cycles platforms up. The right elevator cycles platforms down.

You can tackle this level in at least two ways. Assume that you are at the position marked "A" in **FIGURE 10.6**. The elevator platforms to the right of the "A" position are moving downward. One route is to quickly jump onto the elevator platform and then onto the high platform with the jump labeled "B." The other route is to ride the elevator down to the bottom and take the jump labeled "C."

Taking route B is incredibly risky. It involves a pair of split-second jumps that both need to be executed perfectly. Route C, however, does not require those precision jumps, but you have to deal with the spring things that are constantly raining down. In addition to that, you must make six more jumps than if you had taken route B. Although those jumps are considerably easier than the ones in route B, each is a chance to make a mistake. And, in addition, taking route C involves dealing with a flame monster in the upper-right hand corner (not pictured.)

This is a real risk-reward scenario. A player taking route B is taking a huge risk by taking on the difficult jumps, but the reward is being able to bypass a large section of the level. Many risk-reward scenarios take the form of *time-shifting*: turning short-term risk into the potential for long-term gain versus short-term certainty for short-term gain.

Expected Value

One helpful concept that you can use when analyzing choices is the economic concept of *expected value*. One explanation of expected value is that it is the average value you would receive out of a game if you played it numerous times.

For instance, say I offer you a chance to play a simple coin-toss game. In it, you flip a coin and call it in the air. If you get it right, I give you $3. If you get it wrong, you give me $2. Sounds like a pretty compelling game for you, right? Why?

The expected value is the sum of the rewards for each event multiplied by the probability of each event. In this coin example, you would have the following:

Expected Value = Probability of Correctly Calling the Flip * $3 + Probability of Incorrectly Calling the Flip * −$2.

Expected Value = 0.5 * $3 + 0.5 * −$2

Expected Value = $0.50

Since the expected value for you is to gain $0.50 per game, it makes sense for you to play it because each game, on average, should net you $0.50. If this expected value was negative, it wouldn't make sense for you to play.

Now say that you are trying to balance a monster's treasure drop in an RPG. You want the player to have to beat 100 monsters on average to be able to amass 10,000 gold worth of treasure because the key to the next dungeon costs 10,000 gold. The monster can drop one of three items: a rusty sword worth 10 gold, a necklace worth 200 gold, or a statue worth 1,000 gold. What should the drop rates be?

▶ **NOTE** Drop rate here refers to the probability that a defeated monster will yield a particular item.

If 50 percent of the time defeating a monster gives you a shield, then you would say that the shield has a 50-percent drop rate from that monster. Another way to note this is by using the nomenclature from probability. Here, I use P(Event) to note the probability of an event. I'll discuss probability in greater detail in Chapter 29.

E(X) = P(Sword)*10 + P(Necklace)*200 + P(Statue)*1000

First, you know that you want the expected value to be 100 gold because 10,000 gold/100 monsters = 100 gold/monster. You have two simultaneous equations for three variables, so you know from algebra that you can have many solutions. To make this easier, give P(Statue) the arbitrary value of 1 percent. It's a valuable drop. It makes sense that it should be pretty rare. Now the equation simplifies to one solution:

100 = 10* P(Sword) + 200 * (0.99 – P(Sword)) + (0.01 * 1000)

190 * P(Sword) = 108

P(Sword) = 0.568

P(Necklace) = 0.421

P(Statue) = 0.01

In crafting interesting decisions, the expected value per time or action of your choices must be similar or the choice will be obvious. There is a caveat here that will be better covered when human decision-making is covered later in Chapter 26. We do not always choose what is mathematically "better" for us. Luckily, game designers can use certain observed biases to craft desired behaviors, which will also be covered in Chapter 26. When you craft options for your player with similar expected values over different risk profiles, the choices require the player to make some interesting decisions.

Summary

- Decision-making is crucial to games because good decisions for a player will keep him within his flow channels.

- You can analyze a choice by noting what happens before the choice, how the information about the choice is communicated to the player, what the player chooses, what consequences that choice causes, and how those consequences are communicated to the player.

- Not all decision-making is created equal. There are categories of decision-making offered to players that do nothing for or work against players' need for balanced challenge.

- Two ways to offer more interesting decisions are to frame the consequences of a decision as a trade-off between two resources or as a decision between a high-value reward with low probability and a low-value reward with high probability.

- The concept of expected value allows you to boil down a menu of possibilities to a weighted average result in order to compare complex events.

11 Randomness

> [I]f cause and effect aren't possible, better that there at least be some reward for all the suffering.
>
> —JEFFREY KLUGER

Novice designers' games have a common theme—a heavy focus on *randomness*. Randomness itself is neither good nor bad. Randomness for the game designer is like salt for a chef. Sometimes you want to prepare something a bit salty. Sometimes adding salt only hurts the dish.

Completely Random Games

The "saltiest" games are those that are determined entirely without any intervention from the player. For these games, a combination of die rolls, card draws, or other random processes determine the games' events and winners. *LCR* is a game that is completely determined by dice rolls. You cannot be "good" at *LCR* because no skill is involved in determining the winner.

The card game *War* is another prime example. In *War*, players split a deck of cards and then draw cards from the top and compare the faces. The player with the highest-ranked card collects the lower-ranked card from the opponent. Play continues until one player runs out of cards, or, more likely, until the players get tired of playing. Theoretically, and if a computer knew the decks of both players, it could tell the players who would win before the first card was turned over. In *War*, each player should win with a probability of 0.5, whether the player is a genius or a household pet.

Games with high randomness are usually suited for children with cognitive abilities that make a game with actual decision-making too taxing. *Hi-Ho! Cherry-O*, *Snakes and Ladders*, and *Candy Land* are popular children's board games, and none require decision-making.

However, many high-randomness games are played by adults. One of the highest stakes casino games is *Baccarat*, which is a game that is completely random. The player makes a bet and then cards are drawn. The player and the house each get two cards. The hand value is the ones digit of the sum of the two cards. For instance, if the player draws a 7 and a 5, the hand's value is 2 because 7 + 5 = 12 and the ones digit of 12 is 2. At certain times, the player or house draws a third card, but the algorithm is too needlessly detailed to cover here. At no point after the bet does the player get to make a decision. The player with the highest hand wins.

Famed sociologist Roger Caillois wrote in his book, *Man, Play, and Games*, that in games of pure chance "destiny is the sole artisan of victory, and where there is rivalry, what is meant is that the winner has been more favored by fortune than the loser."[1] It's difficult for adults to feel satisfaction in games of pure chance between human players because the rivalry in the game was not settled by forces they themselves put in motion, but by the chance of a random selection.

Blackjack is similar to *Baccarat*. Both games are dealer-versus-player interactions where the side with the highest hand total wins. However, *Blackjack* allows the simple

. . . .
1   Caillois, R. (1961). *Man, Play, and Games*. Champaign, IL: University of Illinois Press.

decision for the player to press his luck by adding another card that may or may not make the player automatically lose by going over the maximum hand total of 21. This small change allows a player's skill to affect the odds of his winning or losing and thus creates a more popular and meaningful game.

Completely Skill-Based Games

On the other end of the spectrum are games that are completely skill-based. In the purest skill-based games, the player with the higher skill level should always win. The world champion at *Darts* should always beat me. *Chess* is considered a highly skill-based game; however, even it is not deterministically skill-based. The Elo rating system that *Chess* and other games use is a rating of the *probability* that a player will win. You would expect that an expert-level *Chess* player would always beat a novice-level tournament *Chess* player. However, the Elo system predicts that, 3 percent of the time an expert with a rating of 2000 would lose to a novice rated 1400.

◆ **TIP** If you'd rather not do the math yourself, a helpful calculator for computing win probabilities based on USCF Elo scores is available at www.bobnewell. net/nucleus/bnewell. php?itemid=279.

Proponents of European-style strategy board games often favor games that lean heavily toward skill. One of the most popular European-style board games of all time, *Settlers of Catan*, uses the results of dice rolls to distribute resources. Some locations, such as those that pay out on a roll of 2, are probabilistically less likely to give resources, so they are less valuable than ones that pay out on an 8. The player who chooses a position that pays on 2 and gets greater than expected returns because of lucky rolls is often seen as an unfair result because the player is being rewarded not for strategy, but for random chance. This upset so many players that a popular variant uses a deck of cards with die-roll results printed on them in the expected frequencies (that is, one-sixth of cards have a 7 printed on them, while only one of the 36 cards has a 2). This variant mitigates the luck factor of choosing a territory that has a low probability of producing product.

An issue with a game that is entirely skill-based is that if two identical players play again and again, the game plays out the same way every time. The player with the higher skill level should always win. However, if there is no sense of mystery to the game, why play at all? If I play *Magic: The Gathering* with a professional player, I know my probability is low, but I still have a chance. If I competed in a sprint with an Olympian, I know I have no chance of winning. Why go through the motions?

> ▶ **NOTE** In college, I was paired against a professional Magic: The Gathering player at a prerelease tournament. His Elo was 1993. Mine was 1595. I won. It was the talk of the tournament. The Elo scores predicted that I had a 9-percent chance of winning, which makes the win seem less Cinderella-like.

Fairness and Mitigating Randomness

In the book *The Well-Played Game*, Bernie De Koven writes "when the concept of fairness is spoken of in relation to playing games, it is used more as an emergency measure— a semimagical word which, when evoked, gives the utterer the chance to win, too."[2] *Fairness* is key to how players perceive randomness. If they believe that the randomness limits their chances at victory, they can view it as less fair. If they believe that the randomness enhances their chance at victory, they can view it as enforcing fairness.

Sid Meier found that players felt that when they had a 1:3 army disadvantage in *Civilization* (that is, one unit for every three of the opponent's), they should win 25 percent of battles.[3] However, when players had a 3:1 advantage, they felt that their advantage was overwhelming and that they should never lose such a matchup, despite the magnitude of the differences being the same.

One way to design around the limitation of a preconceived victory (or defeat) is by limiting randomization to before the players are exposed to the field. This is the preferred design of many popular European-style games. For instance, the well-regarded game *Agricola* limits randomization to the initial occupation and improvement cards dealt to the players at the start of the game. The game also contains a random element to the order in which the actions of the game appear.

Some players dislike the random dealing of cards at the start of the game, so tournament *Agricola* players often use a *drafting* mechanic in which players take cards from a limited group of cards to smooth out the differences in power at the start of the game. Even if the cards were completely deterministic, the random deal of actions available to players causes games to play out in different ways. Since all players receive the effects of that randomness more or less evenly, it's seen as fair, and no player can gain a large advantage by random chance alone.

FIGURE 11.1 shows two possible distributions for starting cards in *Agricola*. For simplicity, I've assigned a value of 1 to 10 for each card (higher numbers are more valuable), and I limited the number of starting cards to five. In a completely random setup, Zack is dealt cards with a value of 39, while Glo is dealt cards with a value of 20. Zack has a better chance of winning just by the luck of the draw because he has the more powerful cards.

. . . .

2   De Koven, B. (2013). *The Well-Played Game: A Player's Philosophy*. Cambridge, MA: MIT Press.

3   Graft, K. (2010, March 12). "GDC: Sid Meier's Lessons On Gamer Psychology." Retrieved December 8, 2014, from www.gamasutra.com/view/news/118597/GDC_Sid_Meiers_Lessons_On_Gamer_Psychology.php.

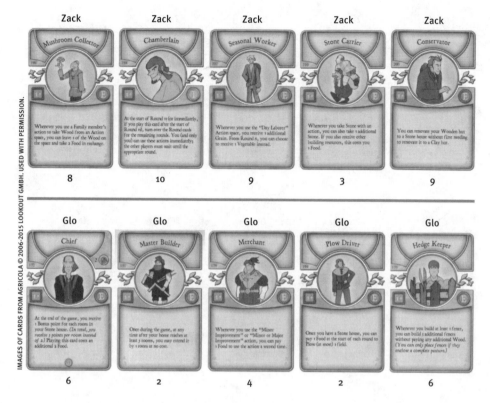

FIGURE 11.1
A randomly dealt start can result in wildly different hands by luck alone.

FIGURE 11.2 shows the card distribution when drafting using the same cards and values. Both players look at the five cards they were each dealt and then each chooses the one with the highest value. The players then each pass the remaining cards from their dealt cards to the other player, who chooses the highest from the remaining four. The players repeat this process until all cards are drafted. The process self-balances and mitigates the randomness of the initial deal. Each player picks the best card from the ones remaining.

At the start, Zack picks the Chamberlain (value 10), and Glo picks the Chief (value 6). Now they switch hands. Zack's highest value choice is now the Hedge Keeper (value 6) and Glo's is either the Seasonal Worker or the Chamberlain (both with value 9). At the end of the draft, Zack has a total value of 30 and Glo has a total value of 29, making the power of their hands nearly identical.

FIGURE 11.2
A more even distribution of cards can be achieved by drafting the cards.

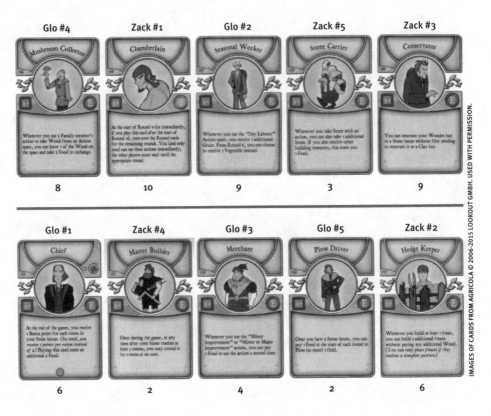

Many popular tabletop games are highly strategic while offering significant randomness. Spiel des Jahres winner, *Dominion*, involves getting a new random hand of five cards every turn. However, the player has a great deal of involvement in which cards go into her deck, so she is often changing the probabilities of what will be in her hand on the next turn.

Out There is a rogue-like space exploration game. Players need certain elements to repair their ship and jump to new sections. Yet, sometimes random events demand elements that the players don't have or cannot get at their location. Thus, players feel as though they are being punished for something for which they could not prepare. *FTL* is a game with similar mechanics that mitigates this by having the difficulty centered on objectives that would be easier if the player had made certain earlier decisions. The difference is in the player's reaction to random elements insofar as their perceived degree of agency. The perceived degree of agency is high in *FTL* and low in *Out There*. This is despite the prevalence of random events within *FTL*.

Summary

- Randomness itself is neither good nor bad. Instead, examine how the randomness in a game affects player choice and, thus, how it affects a player's flow state.

- Although completely luck-based games often fail because complete randomness does not provide enough challenge for the player to enter flow, completely skill-based games can fail if the challenge required by the skill causes too much frustration by either being cognitively overwhelming or not providing any paths to victory.

- Often what matters is not the level of randomness inherent in a game's mechanics, but rather how that randomness is perceived by the players.

- When players lose because of randomness, often they feel as though they had a lack of agency in the result. However, when they win because of randomness, they are less likely to object.

- Drafting is a mechanic that allows players to self-select resources to gain a more even distribution.

12 Goals

When it is obvious that the goals cannot be reached,
don't adjust the goals, adjust the action steps.

—CONFUCIUS

A player needs to make informed decisions if he is to be
interested in the actions of the game system. In Chapter 10,
I discussed decision features that may be interesting to a player,
but I glossed over a fundamental requirement native to all
games that have interesting decision-making—knowing the
player's *goals*. What are they? How does the player find them,
understand them, act on them, and reach them?

How Players Determine Game Goals

The method players use to figure out what their goals are and how to achieve them in a game system is not wildly different from the scientific method (**FIGURE 12.1**).

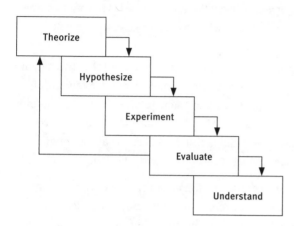

FIGURE 12.1 Astute readers will note the similarities between the scientific method and Agile development.

Imagine a game with no tutorial, no list of rules, no help whatsoever. The player can noodle with elements of the system and see the results of the noodling, but that's it. How does the player determine the rules of the system and the goals that she will set?

Example: *SimCity*

Let's examine how you might determine the game's goals by using *SimCity* as an example:

1. **THEORIZE:** Start by making assumptions about the game and how it works. Sometimes this step is augmented by knowledge you already have: Maybe a friend has summarized how *SimCity* works; maybe you have read a review that goes into some detail about its mechanics; maybe the game contains a helpful tutorial or, if it's indeed a game from the 20TH Century, maybe it contains a helpful manual. From this, or maybe from the screenshots or the splash screen of the game, you establish some sort of theory about how the game works and what its goals are. At this point, maybe you think the point of the game is to have a million residents in the city.

2. **HYPOTHESIZE:** Now that you have some basic understanding, decide what you need to do to reach that initial idea of a goal. Since your protocol is to get a million residents, you decide to spend all the city's initial budget on building residential blocks.

3. **EXPERIMENT:** You navigate the game's interface as best as you currently can and lay down a ton of green residential blocks.

4. **EVALUATE:** But somehow this does not work. The green blocks lie there with the R (for residential) on them, but the population number is fairly stagnant. It looks like no one is moving in. Now you must evaluate these results and come up with a cause-and-effect relationship between your actions and the observed result. If the observed result does not (A) meet your expectations as set forward in your hypothesis and (B) meet the results you expected to achieve your set goal, then you must return to step 1 and start over again.

5. **UNDERSTAND:** Players are experimenters, changing their input until they reach their desired output. Each loop that you make helps you gain greater understanding of how the system works and should lead to more and more informed experimentation. But where games differ from standard science is in the B portion of your observed result from step 4—you may reach the evaluation step and learn that your original goal is not what the game intends or what is best for enjoying the game.

In the *SimCity* example, after a couple of experimentation loops, you may realize that setting a population goal is not the best way to enjoy the game. Maybe you decide that managing the budget and happiness of the Sims is the interesting part of the game. At this point, you take all the knowledge you gleaned from the previous goal's iterations and reexamine it in terms of your new goal. Perhaps while working toward your last goal you learned that residential areas need to be powered, be near transportation, and be near commercial opportunities, but not be too close to industrial producers. You now understand the system—perhaps not completely, but enough to achieve your stated goals. You use this knowledge to work toward achieving your new goal. I'll elaborate on this process further in Chapter 24 when I discuss the concept of constructivist learning.

Example: *Minesweeper*

Let's examine how you might determine a game's goals by using another game that you might have played before anyone taught you how—*Minesweeper* (**FIGURE 12.2**).

WINDOWS® MINESWEEPER IS © 1992-2015 MICROSOFT CORPORATION. USED WITH PERMISSION FROM MICROSOFT.

FIGURE 12.2
How do you play this game?

1. **THEORIZE:** You have a grid of gray squares, two red digital clock-looking numbers, and a smiley face. You don't know what your goal is.

2. **HYPOTHESIZE:** Maybe if you click on some of these elements, something will happen?

3. **EXPERIMENT:** You click, and the gray square disappears, leaving a number behind. One of the digital numbers above starts counting up.

4. **EVALUATE:** The counting-up number must be a clock. Since your click removed a square, maybe your goal is to remove all the squares before a certain time?

   With the information you now have, you cycle back through the steps of the scientific method.

5. **THEORIZE:** Your new goal is to remove all the squares.

6. **HYPOTHESIZE:** You are going to click these squares and remove them all.

7. **EXPERIMENT:** You click on squares and eventually hit one shaped like a mine. It makes an explosion sound effect and your smiley face turns to an ugly dead version. You see the layout of the entire board once the squares are removed. Numbers surround all the mines.

8. **EVALUATE:** Clearly, you need to avoid clicking on the mines. The numbers around them must have some meaning. A quick count is its own mini-loop of the scientific method: The numbers correspond to how many mines are nearby!

By this second iteration, you have a new goal and information that helps you understand the system. Games that feature tutorials or long instruction pages attempt to reduce the number of experimentation loops the player must go through. Although some theorize that players play in order to learn by experimentation, many players have a specific palette when it comes to learning. Some players want to achieve small goals quickly without having to do a lot of tough learning first. These players shy away from tutorials and games with steep learning requirements. Sometimes as the designer, you have to orient your game (through playtesting) to minimize the amount of upfront instruction the player needs before he achieves small goals. In the *Minesweeper* and *SimCity* examples, players can achieve small goals more easily, and thus the need for upfront instruction is limited. More complex games with stiffer penalties for losing, games such as *League of Legends* or *Madden NFL Football*, are incentivized toward teaching the player explicitly, because the rules don't allow for rewarding self-prescribed small goals.

Neither is particularly better or worse, all things being equal, but the designer must understand how much experimentation a player will put up with without achieving goals. If the player's tolerance is low, then more hand-holding or changes in design are necessary. If players ever get to a point where they are unwilling to do another iteration of the theorize/hypothesize/experiment/evaluate process and still have not achieved their goals, the game has failed.

> ▶ **NOTE** Of course, all things are almost never equal. One difference may be in gender. Education research has suggested that an exploratory tutorial style is more effective with males than a cognitive apprenticeship (show-me) style.[1] Females show the opposite preference. This seems to dovetail with the fact that casual social games often have a very hand-holding tutorial methodology while being more inviting to females. As a man, it very well may be that my views on effective game teaching are colored by my physiology.

Criteria for Goals

I observed a playtest of a NASCAR game many years ago. I watched from afar as a middle-aged man sat in front of a television with a controller in his hand. The countdown on the screen went 3–2–1–Go, and yet the car did not accelerate. The man looked at the controller with its 20 buttons, wiggled the joystick a bit, pressed some of the D-pad buttons, and shrugged. He could not get the car to move. After a few seconds, a graphic appeared on the screen: "Press R2 to Accelerate!" Either the man did not read the graphic or did not know the location of the R2 button. He gently placed the controller down, got up, and left.

Now we can sit and laugh at this man's overwhelming lack of skill, or we can try to understand what happened. The man sat down for a NASCAR playtest, so obviously he came to it with some preconceived notions of what happens in a racing video game. When the game actually started, he hypothesized that wiggling the sticks would cause the car to move forward. It did not work. In fact, it gave no feedback at all besides rotating the camera slightly. When he hypothesized that the D-pad had an up button and up meant forward, he experimented with that. He pressed it, and it changed the view of the heads-up display. At that point, it's likely that he was fed up with the game. He did not want to make any more experimentation loops. By the time the "Press R2 to Accelerate!" popup appeared, he was bored. He had not achieved anything. The game did not offer him a way to meet his goals, and so he quit.

I am certainly not insinuating that every mouth-breathing playtester has to be satiated by what the game has to offer. It is likely that the aforementioned man would never play a NASCAR game on his own anyway. But what it does show is that people set their own expectations of how systems work, and although they have some resiliency when those expectations are not met, there is a limit to how forgiving they will be.

. . . .
1   Ray, S. G. (2004). *Gender Inclusive Game Design*. Newton Centre, MA: Charles River Media.

This is the lesson of the story:

- Players must be able to figure out their own goals.
- Players must be able to understand what they can do to reach those goals without overwhelming burden.

Breaking down this lesson further, let me restate with emphasis—players must be able to figure out *their own goals*. Designers can set goals in the game for players, but nothing forces players to accept those goals as their own. If players do not like the goals that the designer sets, they try to play with their own goals instead or, more likely, they quit. *Desert Bus* from *Penn & Teller's Smoke & Mirrors* is a great example here. The game is an exercise in masochism. In it, players are driving a bus through the desert. There are no obstacles or other players, but the bus has a misaligned axle so it veers a little to the right. If the player can stay on the road for eight hours, he earns a single point and starts the drive back. The designers specifically made a boring, frustrating game that the players enjoy *not playing*. Players so loved the novelty of how masochistic it was to play the game that they have set up yearly charity events where players play marathon sessions of *Desert Bus* streamed online. The designers set one purported goal and the players subverted that to their own ends.

Some players eschew the stated goals of games and set goals for themselves solely to annoy and confound other users. This occurs across many genres, such as in massively multiplayer online role-playing games (MMORPGs). If a game does not offer goals worth achieving, these players create their own, to the rest of the community's chagrin. These game changers have a name: *griefers*.

The second part of this lesson is that players need a way to achieve their goals and they must be able to understand how to do so without feeling an overwhelming burden. You may notice that this rule is highly subjective and depends entirely on the individual player. Indeed, that is the lesson: Every player has a different tolerance for how much experimentation she will endure prior to reaching her goals before she quits.

Jesse Schell, in his book *Art of Game Design*, gives three criteria for goals: They must be concrete, achievable, and rewarding.[2]

- *Concrete* means a goal must be specific. But how specific? That's up to the player.
- *Achievable* means the goal must be able to be accomplished. But how difficult should it be? Again, that's up to the player.

. . . .
2   Schell, J. (2008). *The Art of Game Design: A Book of Lenses*. Amsterdam: Elsevier/Morgan Kaufmann.

- And that goal must be *rewarding*, which is the loosest of all the criteria and is certainly up to the individual player.

A great rule of thumb is that a player should always be able to cite what his goal is and be able to act upon it. If he doesn't know what his goal is, he will act aimlessly. If he knows what the goal is but cannot act upon it, then any interaction the player does have will not be in service of the goal. What goals the player sets can be influenced by the designer, but ultimately the goals used and the effectiveness of those goals are up to each individual player; it is largely this that separates a game from being "good" or "bad" on a personal basis. The designer needs to be aware of what goals the players set for themselves and then craft decision-making opportunities that allow different paths to reach these personal goals. Satisfying this objective for the wide variety of people who may play her game is one of the designer's most difficult jobs.

Solving Goal Problems

Players do not necessarily approach your game with the same goals in mind that you have. They read the elements of the game and set their own goals. Take the example of griefers in MMORPGs. These players specifically eschew the goals of the designer in order to satisfy their own goals of causing havoc to other players in the game world. In most games, the problem you set out to address is different than the goal that the player sets for herself.

To best attend to all possibilities, you must anticipate what goals your players will set. The player's goals are fluid and change when the elements in the game change. Often, the goals have various levels based on complexity and timescale. Let's take a look at three types of goals.

- **SHORT-TERM GOALS** are ones that players set for themselves for the immediate future. These are the objectives that the player is looking to complete next. These are things such as "defeat an enemy" or "summon a creature," and are usually simple elements that require only one or a few of the game mechanics.

- **MEDIUM-TERM GOALS** are more complex and usually require the player to complete multiple short-term goals to satisfy the medium-term goal's conditions. These are higher-level goals that may focus on a longer time frame, such as "collect all the sword fragments" or "return the flag to the base." Do not let the *medium-term* nomenclature trick you. These can have a long time frame. However, these are shorter in scope than the object of the game.

- The **OBJECT OF THE GAME** is the longest-term goal. Why is the player working toward the short- and medium-term goals? What is she looking to ultimately accomplish? This is the object of the game.

By figuring out these goals, the designer can then decide what structures need to be created to support these goals (**FIGURE 12.3**).

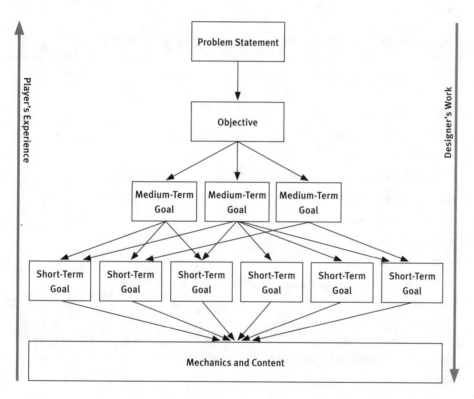

FIGURE 12.3
Nesting of goal structures.

Players experience the game by starting with the mechanics and content, and working their way up to the object of the game. Designers, however, start at the top with the problem statement. They use the problem statement to create an objective for the game. That objective leads to medium-term goals, which leads to short-term goals, which suggest the mechanics and content.

This is not to say that all designers use this process. Some come up with a "fun" mechanic first and then, by experimenting, stumble upon an objective. It's possible to design this way, but it's more effective to use a more structured method to ensure that you have a unique, solvable problem that leads to a unique, interesting game in which the goals are in tune with the heart of the game. Check out the three games in the side-bars and how their designers structured the goals in each.

Also remember Schell's three important qualities of goals: Each goal needs to be concrete, achievable, and rewarding.

PROJECT GOTHAM RACING (2001)

PROBLEM STATEMENT: What if a racing game was determined by style instead of just speed?

SHORT-TERM GOALS:

- Get through the chicane.
- Drift through a turn.
- Finish the kudos streak without hitting the wall.

MEDIUM-TERM GOALS:

- Get first place in the circuit.
- Beat the bonus kudos score.
- Unlock better cars.

OBJECT OF THE GAME: Complete all the objectives with a gold medal.

HEAVY RAIN (2010)

PROBLEM STATEMENT: What would it be like to "play" a movie?

SHORT-TERM GOALS:

- Find Ethan.
- Avoid getting shocked at the power station.
- Scan for footprints at the crime scene.
- Complete the quick time sequence.

MEDIUM-TERM GOALS:

- Collect all the clues by completing the trials.
- Reconcile the stories of the different characters.

OBJECT OF THE GAME: Solve the riddle of the Origami Killer.

BRAID (2008)

PROBLEM STATEMENT: What puzzles can be created if you can manipulate time?

SHORT-TERM GOALS:

- Move player atop ledges.
- Collect the puzzle pieces.
- Cross gaps.
- Unlock doors.

MEDIUM-TERM GOALS:

- Assemble the jigsaw puzzles.
- Complete chapters.

OBJECT OF THE GAME: Complete all levels and rescue the princess.

One mistake that novice designers often make is confusing strategies with goals. For instance, you might say that "Use light to your advantage" is a short-term goal for *Alan Wake*. Although the player certainly does use light to his advantage to succeed, this is not his goal. The player's goal is to reach the end of the level (medium-term). In the short-term, a goal may be "Evade the monster by hiding in the light beam." This is a concrete goal that lists the evaluating conditions.

Likewise, many novice designers also make the mistake of listing goals that are vague. For instance, you may say that a short-term goal for *Guitar Hero* is to "Learn the basics." Although it's certainly true that you must learn the basics to advance, what exactly does this mean? How does the game evaluate that you have learned the basics? What is a concrete way the game can do that? Remember that the designer is not there to help the game make its decisions. Everything must be in code or rules.

Summary

- Players often determine goals through experimentation loops.
- If players don't like the goals the designers have provided, they may create their own that are contrary to the desired play aesthetics.
- Every player has a different tolerance for how much experimentation she'll endure prior to reaching her goals before she simply quits.
- Players should always be able to cite their goal and be able to act upon it in some way.
- Goals should be as explicit and concrete as possible in order for the game to better evaluate whether the goal was achieved.

4 Describing Game Elements

I'm only certain that nothing is forever. No matter how carefully you design a system, it will go bad and die.

—POUL ANDERSON, "TAU ZERO"

In 1994, designer Greg Costikyan penned an article for *Interactive Fantasy*, a British role-playing journal, called "I Have No Words and I Must Design," lamenting the lack of a unified vocabulary for game design." It's now more than 20 years later, and although game studies have come a considerable way, we still lack a unified vocabulary. Many terms, such as "mechanic" or "beta," have different meanings at different organizations.

Although some may see this as an indicator of the medium's immaturity, in practice, it serves only as a momentary speed bump. Chapter 1 suggested that definitions of the word "game" that seek only to exclude certain works as unworthy of study put unnecessary limitations on the expression of craft. The same danger exists with being too dogmatic about other definitions. What's important about terminology is not whether or not the terminology is correct, but if it is useful.

As an example, it's not particularly relevant if we cannot agree on whether gravity's function in *Super Mario Bros.* is a mechanic, a rule, or something else. What *is* important is that we have the theoretical tools to discuss if the mechanisms used to create gravity in the game work to meet design goals. If we know about MDA (mechanics, dynamics, and aesthetics, which Chapter 13 discusses), we can discuss how Mario's ability to change direction in midair allows players to land on narrower platforms, which informs our discussions of both the gravity mechanics and the level design.

Participants in game discussions who are not equipped with a theoretical vocabulary end up arguing over vague concepts instead of sharing ideas. I once received feedback from an executive that a particular feature design was "too interactive." What does that mean? Is the feature too complicated? Does it require too many steps? Are players not interested in the decisions being made within the feature? Are the goals unclear? Are games not, by nature, interactive? That executive thought he was giving clear feedback about how the feature should operate, but by being imprecise with his feedback, he only served to confuse the issue.

13 Mechanics, Dynamics, and Aesthetics (MDA)

This suspense is terrible. I hope it will last.

—OSCAR WILDE

Games have an interesting problem. If you ask someone what a book is about, generally the answer comes in one of two forms: plot and theme. The *plot* in the *Harry Potter* series is about a wizard confronting an evil power from his past. Lots of events happen: He gets his invitation to Hogwarts, he makes friends, he fights a giant snake, and so on. The *theme* of *Harry Potter* is about learning your place in the world and dealing with death. Both of these (plot and theme) are accepted ways to talk about the essence of what a book is. This works with other storytelling media: You can reflect on what a movie is about by talking about its plot and theme. You can describe a play in the same way. But what about games?

What Are Games About?

Games are fundamentally different. Games that use traditional storytelling forms can be shoehorned into the "plot and theme" method of answering what the game is about, but that is only because those games are primarily linear stories before they are games. For instance, *Heavy Rain* uses a game veneer to deliver traditional storytelling devices, so it's easy to reduce the game to plot and theme. So does *Mass Effect*. But what about *Space Invaders?* What is it about? What is *World of Warcraft* about?

For example, everyone experiences *World of Warcraft* differently. For some, the game is highly focused on meeting and interacting with new people. Some may use it to set up an item-trading business. Some may explore a vast new world. Others may never interact with other people on a meaningful level and may just treat it as a virtual rat-slaying simulator. How can you answer what this game is about if everyone can have such a different exposure to it? In this case, the plot is meaningless—while one player went on tours of exotic vistas, another repeated the same dungeon over and over again for hundreds of hours looking for rare items. Not only are the events different, but any thematic interpretation of those events is also meaningless since it differs so vastly from player to player.

Writers have it easy. They use the elements available to them (words) to create structures of meaning (sentences, paragraphs, allusions, similes, and so on) that allow them to easily answer the "what the story is about" question. What game designers need is a framework that uses the elements available to game designers to evaluate *meaning*.

This may seem academic and pedantic, but game designers largely design systems. Systems need to be understood holistically in order to be designed intelligently. When you understand what a game is about holistically, it helps inform you about how to go about making the chosen experience happen.

Resident Evil and *Go* are both games. This is unarguable. But it's easier to answer "What is *Resident Evil* about?" than it is to answer "What is *Go* about?" This is because we fall back to more familiar definitions of meaning based on theme and story. For an abstract game like *Go*, that does not apply.

Designers and researchers have a difficult time reconciling competing philosophies into a coherent vocabulary of games. What some call "mechanics" can mean something completely different within the context of another theory. This makes discussing design theory often a war of defending definitions, which is unfortunate, because it prevents more interesting discussions of depth and importance from happening. You should attempt to avoid arguments on what the "real" definition of a term is—instead, focus on how the underlying theory can be instrumental to your development.

MDA

One of the answers to the question of what a game is about is based on the work of designers Robert Zubek, Robin Hunicke, and Marc LeBlanc.[1] They posit that games have three specific elements:

- *Mechanics* are the elements of the game themselves. These are generally defined as the "rules of the game." These may be formal rules, such as "A player cannot move his king into check," or rules about the features of the game, such as "The properties in *Monopoly* have the names of places in Atlantic City." From the mechanics alone, someone should be able to reconstruct the game.

- *Dynamics* are the "runtime behavior(s)" of the game. When the players interact with the rules, what happens? In *Chess*, you know to sacrifice relatively worthless pawns to capture the powerful opponent's queen, yet nowhere in the rules does it say that a player should do that. This behavior *emerges* from the rules.

- *Aesthetics* are the emotional results generated by the game. When a player says that a game is "fun," that is a generic, emotional response. Players can often be more specific, using terms such as exhilarating, challenging, frightening, tiring, or eye-opening. These are more specific, emotional responses. LeBlanc lists eight kinds of fun that he sees most often but claims it's an incomplete taxonomy: sensation, fantasy, narrative, challenge, fellowship, discovery, expression, and submission. For instance, a game such as *Farmville* may be fun to some because it's an act of submission to a set of systems. *League of Legends* might be fun to some because it's like solving a particularly intense real-time math problem that provides a feeling of accomplishment. To others, it may be fun because it involves playing with friends and the fellowship that comes with team sports. Different features of games generate different aesthetic responses.

Many people have difficulty with the use of the term "aesthetics" in the context of games because it has differing definitions elsewhere. When I say aesthetics in relation to MDA, I mean "play aesthetics," or the emotional values generated by the game states. What I don't mean is the art or sound used in the game. Although those can be aesthetically pleasing, that's a different use of the word: the philosophical study of beauty. Aesthetic is also used sometimes as a noun as a signifier of the look and feel of a game. This is also not the definition I use here. Again, aesthetics here refers to the emotional state generated by the game or, in many cases, the category of fun that the game generates.

. . . .

1   Hunicke, R., LeBlanc, M., & Zubek, R. (2004, July). "MDA: A Formal Approach to Game Design and Game Research." In Proceedings of the AAAI Workshop on Challenges in Game AI (pp. 04-04).

Using these three elements and putting them into a series shows their relationship (**FIGURE 13.1**).

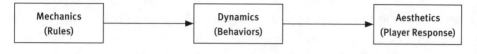

FIGURE 13.1
A designer's view: Aesthetics result from dynamics caused by mechanics.

What is interesting about this relationship is that designers experience their games from left to right, whereas players experience them from right to left. Designers create mechanics, which generate dynamics when players interact with them, which then hopefully generate desired emotional responses. Players, however, experience emotional responses from playing the game, and only through further analysis are they able to determine the source in their own behaviors and the rules that cause them to act.

This leads us to one unfortunate end: The only "knob" that designers get to turn is the mechanics knob. All other elements regarding the dynamics and aesthetics are generated from the designer's choice of mechanics. Designers define what the rules and setup of the game are, but the dynamics and aesthetics are generated by the players in their interactions with those rules. Designers cannot add more "scary" to a horror game. All they can do is add rules that tell the system to place a monster at location X,Y,Z. If X,Y,Z is a corner where the player is particularly vulnerable and this creates a dynamic in which the player can feel particularly frightened, then the designer has met her goal and done her job.

In many of Reiner Knizia's board games, the player must collect all kinds of resources. Knizia wanted this to be an effect that the players pursue, so he wrote the rules of *Ingenious* (and other games) so that the player only counts—for scoring purposes—the resources of which he has the *least*. If a player has three orange tiles, one red tile, and one green tile, then the player is incentivized to no longer go after orange tiles because they don't increase his score. Instead, the player is constantly switching desired tiles to match whatever he has the least of. Once he gets a second green, then he no longer wants green because red is now the least in quantity. This behavior is not written in the rules. Only the rule about the least populous tile being counted is written there. But that rule births a behavior that meets what the designer desires.

▶ **NOTE** This particular mechanic has been used in so many games that board game designers and enthusiasts often simply call counting only what resource you have the least of Knizia scoring.

Because designers can turn only the mechanics knob, game design cannot be simply coming up with "good ideas" if those ideas are limited to settings, characters, or genre. In order to create those ideas, the designer is required to come up with a complete system of rules that generate desired dynamics that lead to targeted emotional responses. It's not as easy as saying, "My idea is a zombie stealth game!" The designer needs to come up with a full topology of rules and conditions that explain every input of the system with its output (this is generally what the game design document explains). Any secondarily generated effects need to be elicited from those rules.

It's important to understand the purpose of a system like MDA. Often, confused students struggle to place their analysis into the three elements. They frequently give me an analysis like, "The game had bugs (mechanics), which caused me to stop playing (dynamics) because it was boring (aesthetic)." Boredom is not an aesthetic just because you do not like the game. That is a bland value judgment. The aesthetics bullet in the previous list contains some of the primary aesthetics that you see in games. "Fun" and "Not Fun" are just far too broad to be useful in analysis. Often "Fun" and "Not Fun" are just synonyms for "I Like" and "I Do Not Like." That kind of analysis could certainly be true, but it misses the point of using MDA. MDA is a *descriptive* system, not a *normative* system. A descriptive system is one that *describes* an element or process. A normative system assigns value judgments. It advises what a person *should* do. Comparing the two, descriptive systems tell us *what is* and normative systems tell us *what should be*.

The point of MDA is not to explain whether a given game or rule set is "good" or not. That is the job of a normative system. What MDA helps you and other designers do is evaluate how the elements of the game work together to create targeted emotional ends.

Example: *Realm of the Mad God*

Realm of the Mad God (**FIGURE 13.2**) is a persistent-world, online, shoot-'em-up game. Like many persistent-world games, it has a ton of different mechanics at play. The game is somewhat social, but the burgeoning of the community only happened when the designers added what they considered a fairly benign feature: dropping items. Once players could drop items, they could effectively trade items by bartering: "OK, you drop that sword, and I'll drop my shield, and we can trade them." Not only did this create the simple behavior of trading, but other behaviors emerged: A currency was created and even complex trading consortiums were established. All this because of a drop feature. The creators never intended for it to be used for anything besides sloughing off excess inventory.

> ▶ **NOTE**   Habbo Hotel discovered this lesson earlier. In it, there was no trading currency, so players used a particular in-game chair as the standard currency.[2]

. . . .

2   Haro. S., (2010). "The Evolution of Habbo Hotel's Virtual Economy." Game Developer's Conference. San Francisco, CA.

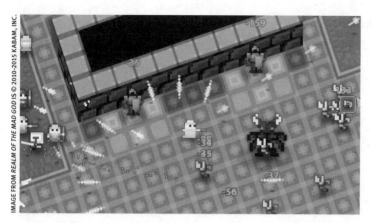

FIGURE 13.2
Realm of the Mad God.

Examine this behavior of the players using MDA. A rule was created: You can drop items, and other people can pick them up (**FIGURE 13.3**). This created a runtime player behavior: You have something I want, and I have something you want; let's use the drop feature to trade! This led to an aesthetic response of fellowship and challenge among many players, so much so that they started their own trading groups.

FIGURE 13.3
Item dropping/trading from an MDA perspective in *Realm of the Mad God.*

Imagine now that you are designing a persistent-world, online game. Your game is lacking in the kinds of community behaviors you want it to have. You want people to feel as if they are part of a larger whole. In short, you want a play aesthetic of fellowship. You just examined one example of a dynamic that would create that aesthetic, but there can be many others. Say you want players to be able to trade. This leads you as the designer to come up with the rules that support that: Players must have items that they value; these items have to be transferrable, and players need to be able to see what items others have available. These mechanics support the desired dynamics that then would support the desired aesthetic. It's not enough for a designer to say that there should be trading. She must come up with all the supporting mechanics that enable that dynamic.

Example: *Monopoly*

You probably play *Monopoly* incorrectly. That's OK, most people do. Answer these two questions about the game: What do you get when you land on Free Parking? What happens if the player who lands on an unpurchased property doesn't buy it?

Most people would answer that you get some amount of money for landing on Free Parking, sometimes $500, sometimes a collection of fees paid into the game from various penalties like the Luxury Tax. But that is incorrect. Players actually are not supposed to do anything when landing on Free Parking. Players do not get bonus money; you just get to park there for free. Hence the name.

Additionally, say I land on St. Charles' Place. It's unpurchased, so I do not have to pay rent to anyone, but my two opponents own the other two maroon properties (one each), so I have no desire to buy it. Most players would just pass the dice at this point, but that is not how the rules are actually written. What you are supposed to do is then auction the property between all players until it is purchased.

People do not play with these rules for a number of reasons, but I bring it up here to show you the impact of rule changes on dynamics. What is the number one complaint about *Monopoly*? It just takes too long to finish! What happens when you inject free money into the system? People are happy in the short-term because, hey, free money. But since every player has an equal chance to hit Free Parking, it takes much longer for players to bankrupt because they have this major cushion of money that can be replenished every trip around the board. The game loses any strategic merit it had and becomes more luck-driven.

The same goes for the auctioning rule. People eschew it because it is complicated and seems "unfair" that someone who did not land on the property can claim it. But this rule makes the portion of the game where people are collecting properties much shorter. You get only one chance! It also serves to decrease the amount of time the game takes before players start going bankrupt because it allows for monopolies to be more easily collected on less than three lucky turns around the board.

Here you see the impact of mechanical changes. Just two rules that seem to be innocuous can lead to huge dynamic and aesthetic changes. Who would not take free money? And that auctioning rule seems complicated, right? However, get rid of them and the game loses any strategic tension. The play aesthetic goes right out the window, and the game becomes only marginally more interesting than *Candy Land*.

Example: *Habitat*

One of the great documented examples of a use for looking at things through the lens of MDA comes from the development of a total commercial failure: A game that would support a "multiplayer online virtual environment." Nowadays, we don't find that feature particularly interesting, but this game was made in 1985 for a system that only had 64 kilobytes of memory. The game was named *Habitat* (**FIGURE 13.4**) and was being developed by LucasArts. Here's a quote from the developers:

> The first goal-directed event planned for *Habitat* was a rather involved treasure hunt called the "D'nalsi Island Adventure." It took us hours to design, weeks to build (including a 100-region island), and days to coordinate the actors involved. It was designed much like the puzzles in an adventure game. We thought it would occupy our players for days. In fact, the puzzle was solved in about 8 hours by a person who had figured out the critical clue in the first 15 minutes. Many of the players hadn't even had a chance to get into the game. The result was that one person had a wonderful experience, dozens of others were left bewildered, and a huge investment in design and set-up time had been consumed in an eyeblink. We expected that there would be a wide range of "adventuring" skills in the *Habitat* audience. What wasn't so obvious until afterward was that this meant that most people didn't have a very good time, if for no other reason than that they never really got to participate. It would clearly be foolish and impractical for us to do things like this on a regular basis.

▶ **NOTE** The development lessons were given in the form of a paper at a conference known as "The First International Conference on Cyberspace." Is there a more 1990s conference name than that?

FIGURE 13.4
Habitat.

IMAGE FROM *HABITAT*, PUBLISHED IN 1986 BY LUCASFILM GAMES.

Massive multiplayer online (MMO) designers continued to make the mistake of ignoring multiplayer dynamics for the next 20+ years. Since designers can only set up mechanics and watch how the dynamics play out, they must understand all the mechanics and dynamics that lead to their particular aesthetic choice. In *Habitat*'s case, they were looking for the same kind of aesthetic as in a modern (at the time) adventure game—the satisfaction and challenge in solving a puzzle. But *Habitat* did not have the same mechanics or dynamics of a single-player adventure game. It had a rich community that shared everything! How could it possibly have the same dynamics? When a player played *Zork*, it did not matter if someone else had solved the puzzle before. In *Habitat*, it did. That was revolutionary at the time. *Habitat*'s designers made a great discovery in making these mistakes that is sound advice even today:

> Again and again we found that activities based on often unconscious assumptions about player behavior had completely unexpected outcomes (when they were not simply outright failures). It was clear that we were not in control. The more people we involved in something, the less in control we were. We could influence things, we could set up interesting situations, we could provide opportunities for things to happen, but we could not predict nor dictate the outcome. Social engineering is, at best, an inexact science, even in proto-cyberspaces. Or, as some wag once said, "in the most carefully constructed experiment under the most carefully controlled conditions, the organism will do whatever it damn well pleases."

Designers can affect the mechanics, but after that, everything is up to the individual player. The impact of game dynamics is unearthed, especially vividly, in the context of making multiuser communities, but it's just as true for a self-contained single-player adventure.

Now, how do we use that today? You must look at your mechanics and try to think one step ahead of the player. Given all the tools available to the player, how do you predict what the player dynamics will be? That is the essential question at the heart of designing game mechanics. One of the modern ways that you determine this is by playtesting and observing the results. I discuss this in Chapter 7. What's important is that you take the time when designing to determine the boundaries of what kinds of behaviors your game will allow and what play aesthetics those dynamics will generate.

More Dynamics

> Its main actions don't involve acting at all, but waiting. Yet that waiting
> contains information essential to play the game well.
>
> —IAN BOGOST, *A SLOW YEAR*

Dynamics are myriad. However, a few dynamics tend to come up with regularity that
are worth mentioning.

Turtling

If a player can gain more by doing nothing than by doing something, then the player is
incentivized to do nothing at all. This is sometimes known as *turtling*. This can be a
dangerous dynamic for a game because it incentivizes players to not interact with the
game's elements and to not move the game forward to its conclusion.

Turtling often occurs in game scenarios where there is a cost or risk to attack but not to
defend. For instance, in a real-time strategy game, each player has a base with some
amount of attack and health that can repel small attacks. Players can either send their
units over to attack or make more units. The first person to break the detente and attack
either defeats the base and wins the game or loses units with respect to the defensive
player. The defensive player now has a unit advantage and can thus repel any attack
from the weaker opponent. He can just sit back and build units until he has enough to
overwhelm the opposition.

In games with three or more players, turtling can be a dangerous dynamic. Say that
each of the three players has 100 units. If Player 1 attacks Player 2 and both risk losing
resources, Player 3 can sit back, watch the carnage, and preserve his power. Player 1
wins the battle, but sustains losses. Now Player 1 has 50 units, Player 2 has 20 units, but
Player 3 still has his 100 units. When the battle is over, if both participating players are
weaker as a result, then the correct strategy would have been to do nothing. Player 3
has an advantage over Players 1 and 2 because he did nothing.

If players realize that the best strategy is to do nothing, then they will sit in stalemate
forever. This is actually a game theoretic reason why countries in the real world do not
go to war, especially in cases where they have multiple enemies. However, in many
non-real-world games, war is preferable because it is exciting and generates desired
aesthetic responses.

A design fix for turtling is to make it advantageous to act. In this battle game example, perhaps implementing an upkeep cost per unit and a glory bonus for winning battles could fix the stalemate. Players would then want to go to war to avoid paying high costs to have units sit around for no potential gain, instead risking the units for the glory bonus.

Camping is another form of turtling where a player's position causes a positive feedback loop. For instance, some first-person shooters have tactically superior spots on the map where a player with a long-range weapon can sit and wait for opponents to come out. Since the position is tactically superior, the player has an advantage where staying still provides benefits over moving. If opponents cannot force the player to move, that player will engage in a positive feedback loop where her superior position will become permanent.

Kingmaking

If players want to win the game, then the players' decisions should have a determining factor on who wins the game; otherwise, the game is blind luck. One dynamic that works against the player's decisions is the determining factor in victory known as *kingmaking*. Kingmaking happens when a player who has no chance to win uses his actions to determine which of the other players will win. This is problematic because the game is not decided by the winning player's decisions or fortune, but by another player's whims.

Methods of fixing this are to build into the game's mechanics ways of isolating potential kingmakers:

- Ensure that actions do not have enough power to determine the winner on a single (or on a few) move(s).
- Ensure that players do not know who is in a position to win, thereby eliminating the possibility of colluding to choose a winner. Games with hidden victory points and hidden roles do this well.
- Isolate the players enough so that their actions cannot affect each other. Some European-style tabletop games take this to an extreme and are derided for being "multiplayer solitaire."
- Add a random aspect to the game, such as dice rolls or card draws, to determine game events that can disrupt kingmaking plans. As always, be careful when adding randomness to ensure it does not disrupt meaningful decision-making.

Button Mashing

Button mashing is seen as a derogatory term in fighting game circles. A button-mashing player plays almost randomly, smashing buttons in frenzied attack. If the game is not designed well, a button-mashing player can have success over a skilled and thoughtful player. If someone randomly pressing buttons can win, then there is no actual decision-making in the game. It's reduced to a game of *War*, and whoever wins the random number generator wins the game.

The key to avoiding button mashing is to give every move a reasonable risk so that playing randomly is discouraged. I'll discuss the game theory behind this more thoroughly in Chapter 19.

Consider two versions of *Rock, Paper, Scissors*. In the first version (**TABLE 13.1**), the equilibrium is for each player to play perfectly randomly with each strategy being chosen one-third of the time. This strategy gives the player the maximum expected value of 0. This encourages button mashing since every button is as good as any other.

TABLE 13.1 *Rock, Paper, Scissors*, Version One

	Angel Throws: Rock	Angel Throws: Paper	Angel Throws: Scissors
Devil Throws: Rock	(0, 0)	(1, −1)	(−1, 1)
Devil Throws: Paper	(−1, 1)	(0, 0)	(1, −1)
Devil Throws: Scissors	(1, −1)	(−1, 1)	(0, 0)

However, if you change the risks involved to make the game more interesting, the strategy changes. Let's make scissors a risky move. If you throw scissors and hit, you get a big reward. If you throw scissors and miss, you get a huge penalty. If you look at rock and paper in isolation, you are tempted toward paper, which tempts your opponent toward scissors, as shown in **TABLE 13.2**.

TABLE 13.2 *Rock, Paper, Scissors*, Version Two

	Angel Throws: Rock	Angel Throws: Paper	Angel Throws: Scissors
Devil Throws: Rock	(−1, −1)	(2, −2)	(−10, 5)
Devil Throws: Paper	(−2, 2)	(1, 1)	(5, −10)
Devil Throws: Scissors	(5, −10)	(−10, 5)	(0, 0)

▶ **NOTE** I discuss this topic more in Chapter 19. Just trust the math for now.

One of the optimal strategies is to play rock with a probability of around 0.59, paper with a probability of around 0.35, and scissors with a probability of 0.06. If that player played against a player who was button mashing by playing all three with equal probability, the player with the more thoughtful strategy would have an expected lead of 0.52 points per game.

This makes sense. If you know a player is going to overplay the risky scissors strategy, then you can sit back and enjoy collecting easy bonuses with more throws of rock. This kind of balance upends the likelihood of button mashing succeeding and directs players to more nuanced strategies. Note also that it employs the risk-reward techniques discussed in Chapter 10.

Grinding

Grinding is repeated play without meaningful decisions. When players grind, they trade time or effort for value such as in-game currency or experience points. Players are playing for those extrinsic motivators instead of for the intrinsic motivators of fun or satisfaction. With this dynamic, players are not directing themselves toward what provides them the most enjoyment.

Grinding happens often because of lack of content. It's easy for a developer to spend most of a development cycle getting two battles to be fun. Knowing that they cannot release with only two battles and still charge a sustainable price, they then require the player to do those same two battles 20 times each. This makes the game the length of a game with 40 battles, but once the player has mastered the two battles, she must still complete the actions many additional times. In these additional battles, the players are just repeating meaningful decisions that they made in the past; they do nothing to formulate new meaningful decisions. Thus, they just follow a recipe.

It's generally recommended to avoid grinding, if possible, in lieu of content that creates original, meaningful decision-making. This, of course, has development costs and is not always wholly possible. Understanding the extent to which players are not making meaningful decisions makes for an unbiased view of the efficacy of the decision-making in the game.

Grinding is not always bad. Sometimes the anticipation of a variable reward is enough to sustain meaningful play, but this is a dangerous element to bank upon. See Chapter 23 for more on this topic.

Press-Your-Luck

Press-your-luck is often cited as a mechanic, because the mechanisms that create it are explicitly called out in the rules of games that use it. However, the behaviors that are created from those rules are what make press-your-luck so interesting.

Can't Stop is a classic game by Sid Sackson that is one of the best examples of the press-your-luck dynamic. In it, players attempt to get three of their pieces to the top of an octagonal board (**FIGURE 13.5**). Players do this by rolling four six-sided dice and grouping them into two pairs of two. For instance, a player who rolls a 1, 3, 4, and 6 could group this into 4 and 10, 5 and 9, or 7 and 7. Whichever grouping the player chooses is in which columns his pawns move up. For instance, if the aforementioned roll was grouped into a 4 and a 10, the player would move his pawns up in the 4 and 10 columns. Players can advance up to three columns per turn. However, if they roll and are unable to advance a column because they have already advanced up three columns or the column has already been completed, then they lose all their progress for the turn, and their turn is over.

FIGURE 13.5 *Can't Stop.*

This dynamic forces players to decide on safely moving only a step or two at a time or attempt to continue rolling to move farther and farther. The farther the player moves in a turn, the more he risks by continuing to roll. Press-your-luck dynamics often focus on regret. Players who push unsuccessfully regret their loss. Players who take the conservative route often regret the possibilities of untaken paths.

This kind of dynamic between pressing for a higher reward or sticking with a safe payoff plays out in many kinds of games. One of the most visible press-your-luck dynamics occurs in football. In it, teams get four downs to legally advance the ball 10 yards. If they do so, they get four new downs. On the last (fourth) down, teams are faced with a decision: They can punt the ball away, which gives away their chance to score but gives the opponent a disadvantage in field position, or they can try for that first down. If they make the distance, then they have successfully pressed their luck and are rewarded with a new set of downs. If they fail, their opponent is rewarded with great field position.

Press-your-luck is generally a positive dynamic to encounter because it means that the mechanics were crafted to allow for interesting trade-offs.

Summary

- To answer what a game is about, you must look beyond the surface details of theme and plot. Many games have no theme or plot at all, so those elements must not be sufficient to explain what a game is about.
- MDA is one theoretical toolset designers can use to understand a game. In it, a game's mechanics lead to runtime player behaviors known as dynamics, which in turn result in player emotions known as aesthetics.
- Designers can directly affect only a game's mechanics when examining a game through the MDA interpretation. To affect other elements, the designer must create mechanics that generate the desired dynamics or aesthetics.
- Examining case studies of dynamic situations can help designers understand both the aesthetics generated by said dynamics but also the mechanics from which those dynamics emerge.
- Dynamics live in support of aesthetics. Dynamics are generally neither good nor bad, except if they support a desired aesthetic response.

14 Milieu

It's not the game that's sacred,
It's the people who are playing.

—BERNIE DE KOVEN

Mechanics are defined by the creators of the game, but the dynamics and aesthetic reactions are defined by the players. This leads to a problem: If the individual player can react to the mechanics in a number of ways, then mechanics do not deterministically lead to dynamics. If dynamics are generated specifically from the mechanics, then the dynamics should be the same if the mechanics are the same. But you often see differences in how the same game is played by different players. Some other factor must influence the game. I call this factor *milieu*.

What Is Milieu?

Milieu is the set of personal, social, and cultural assumptions that players bring to their play experience (**FIGURE 14.1**).

FIGURE 14.1
Milieu adds another dimension to MDA.

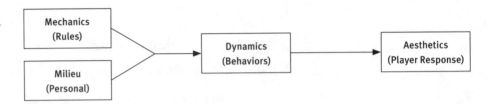

Many "gamers" share a similar milieu, so they act and react to game mechanics in the same way. To help you really understand how milieu affects play aesthetics, it may be helpful for me to use an example of a player from a different milieu. Imagine a grandmother who is playing a first-person shooter. If she is as unacquainted with modern video games and is as squeamish about violence as the stereotypical grandmother, the dynamics that are generated from her interactions with the game system will be different than those of the target player. She'll never reach the targeted aesthetic responses of challenge and sensation because there is little chance that she'll reach the targeted dynamics of using cover and exploiting choke points.

A salient example is from Raph Koster's *Theory of Fun for Game Design*, which he calls Genocide Tetris:[1]

> Let's picture a game wherein there is a gas chamber shaped like a well. You the player are dropping innocent Jews down into the gas chamber, and they come in all shapes and sizes. There are old ones and young ones, fat ones and tall ones. As they fall to the bottom, they grab onto each other and try to form human pyramids to get to the top of the well. Should they manage to get out, the game is over and you lose. But if you pack them in tightly enough, the ones on the bottom succumb to the gas and die.

> I do not want to play this game. Do you? Yet it is Tetris. You could have well-proven, stellar game design mechanics applied toward a quite repugnant premise.

1   Koster, R. (2013). Theory of Fun for Game Design. Newton, MA: O'Reilly Media, Inc.

The mechanics of *Tetris* and Genocide Tetris are similar. The rules are the same, but the display of those rules through play is different. Yet many would react with outrage to the very concept of the latter without qualms about the former. Someone with no knowledge of the referents would probably play this much differently than would a Holocaust survivor, who would likely dismiss it in disgust and walk away. Both players come from different milieux.

Imagine a game with a top-down perspective and sprite-based exploration, where a player walks around a world battling foes using a menu-based fighting system. Hopefully, you are imagining something like the 1990s-era *Final Fantasy* games. Many folks have great nostalgia for these games, and they make many "top games of all time" lists. Now keep the mechanics of the top-down perspective, the sprite-based map exploration, and the menu-based fighting system, but change the artwork and the story.

In 2005, one game-maker did just that, creating *Super Columbine Massacre RPG!*. Although the gameplay tropes are similar to those in 1990s-era Japanese RPGs, the story and the art relates to the horrific massacre of students in the Columbine High School shooting (**FIGURE 14.2**). Mass media picked up on the title and lambasted it as a disgusting exploitation of a tragedy.

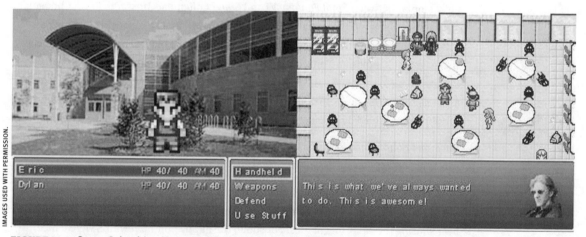

FIGURE 14.2 *Super Columbine Massacre RPG!* was controversial not because of its mechanics, but because of its framing within the milieu of mid-2000s Americans.

SUPER COLUMBINE MASSACRE RPG!

In 2005, on the sixth anniversary of the Columbine High School shooting, independent filmmaker Danny Ledonne released his first and only game, *Super Columbine Massacre RPG!*, which he created using the RPG Maker game engine. In it, players retrace the steps of the 1999 school shooting killers Eric Harris and Dylan Klebold from the morning of the violence to their subsequent death and trip to Hell. It is an odd mélange of journalistic documentary, self-aware parody, and uncategorizable social faux pas.

Because of the RPG Maker engine, many of the tropes used in 1990s console RPGs like *Final Fantasy VI* or *Chrono Trigger* were easy to implement, such as turn-based battles, dialog systems, and sprite-based level map creation. Because of these features, what Ledonne was able to make looked very similar to what a player would see when playing 1990s-era RPGs. Ledonne wasn't a programmer, but he was able to get the necessary work completed with the help of the RPG Maker engine. However, since the subject matter of RPGs at the time was largely limited to pulp fantasy, audiences were not prepared for a game that leveraged an event that was already highly emotional and politicized to challenge their assumptions of the cultural scope of games.

Although the theme gives people the willies, it's only the context of the decisions being made in the game that cause this. The actual options available to the players are strikingly similar between *Final Fantasy VI* and *Super Columbine Massacre RPG!*. Choosing to attack students with a handgun is mechanically identical to choosing to attack a kobold with a sword. But reskinning the game so that the players make the same decisions against kobolds and orcs makes it an entirely different game, even though the options given to the player and the rules governing those options are the same. Players are sensitive to the subject/framing. The massive media reaction of horrified spectators cannot be explained by its mechanics in isolation.

But *Super Columbine Massacre RPG!* is obviously an extreme example. Milieux can have subtle effects on players' behaviors.

At its peak, *Farmville* had over 84 million users in a single day. However, it could not have created the same aesthetic responses for all 84 million of its players, despite every user sharing the same mechanics. For some, the happy pop-up rewards were a nice distraction from their rote day-to-day activities. For others, the game's constant handholding was boring and tedious, but leveling up and sharing that success helped foster their desire for mastery. *Farmville* brought in nongamers from a completely different milieu than traditional games. These players found challenge, sensation, and fellowship from the game's dynamics that many gamers, with their preconceived notions of gameplay, could not duplicate.

In the book *Laws of the Game*, Max Eigen quotes Abraham Moles in saying that the subjective aspect of information "cannot be translated. It does not draw on a universal repertoire but on a repertoire of knowledge that the sender and receiver have in common."[2] Because the receiver of a game's information (the player) is a highly variable entity between players and indeed even over a factor of time within the same player, the milieu activated by a game's systems is a moving target.

Polish

A commonly cited game element is *polish*. However, in many instances saying that a game is "polished" is just another way to say that a game is good. In many cases, polish is a meaningless word like "gameplay." However, Steve Swink, in his book *Game Feel*, provides a fantastic definition for polish: "Polish is any effect that creates [nonessential] cues about the physical properties of objects through interaction."[3]

For instance, in the original *Resident Evil*, when a player chose to use a stairway, the game trigged a loading screen while the upstairs or downstairs level was loaded into memory. This could have been served by a simple black screen that said, "Loading," as many games did at the time. Instead, *Resident Evil* showed a simple first-person perspective animation of a character walking up or down stairs slowly. This masked the loading times and helped preserve the eerie aesthetic of the game. This was polish because it was nonessential to the play experience, but it served to enhance the game's environmental cues. The player was no longer sitting in a living room somewhere waiting for a game to load. He was instead slowly walking up the stairs in a zombie-infested mansion where danger lurked at every step. It was effective polish.

Although Swink was talking about polish in digital games, analog games also have room and expectations for polish. In *Dead of Winter*, for example, each character has a role, and that role thematically and mechanically coincides with that character's ability, which helps players better role-play as the characters. There is no essential reason to include a role for each player. However, knowing that the character Gabriel Diaz is a firefighter helps you understand why he would have an ability that helps him search for survivors. Similarly, if you know that the character Bev Russell is a mother, this partially explains her ability to care for the helpless. These roles provide nonessential cues for players to understand the mechanics of the game.

. . . .

2   Eigen, M., & Winkler, R. (1981). *Laws of the Game: How the Principles of Nature Govern Chance.* New York: Knopf.

3   Swink, S. (2009). *Game Feel: A Game Designer's Guide to Virtual Sensation.* Amsterdam: Morgan Kaufmann /Elsevier.

Polish is not necessarily a determinate of quality, although many polished games are quite popular. Many consider *The Legend of Zelda: Ocarina of Time* to be one of the greatest video games of all time. Yet for some reason, the designers included a few odd quirks that serve as disconnects from the game world. For instance, the designers made the main character able to move up to 50 percent faster by rolling rather than by running and also made it so the character could roll an unlimited number of times in succession.[4] In other words, the player's character never gets tired of rolling. Most players figure this out early and spend the game (which largely consists of traveling long distances by foot) rolling from place to place. This makes no sense in the context of the physical properties of the world.

Polish can be thematic and/or mechanical. In ideal cases, it's both. In any case, polish is an expression of the personal expectations of a player with regard to a world's nonessential elements, which puts it in the category of milieu.

Player Types

For many years, designers and theorists have tried to classify players to help target games for specific types of players. One of the earliest classifications was done by designer Richard Bartle, and his grouping is still used today by many.[5] Bartle was one of the creators of *MUD*, which was a kind of precursor to today's massively multiplayer online (MMO) games. Bartle classified players of *MUD*-like games into four categories, which he named after the suits of the standard playing card deck:

- **HEARTS** (or Socializers)—Hearts play games to share in experiences with other players. The most obvious example is the guild organizer who brings together friends to achieve multiplayer objectives in modern MMOs. But Hearts can be found enjoying single-player games as well; games such as *The Walking Dead* and *Skyrim* that are filled with moments that can be discussed around the water cooler are often compelling to Hearts.

- **DIAMONDS** (or Achievers)—Diamonds play games to beat them. If there are 100 dungeons, the Diamond is not be satisfied until she has defeated all 100 of them. If there is a special badge or a helmet she can display to show that she has completed her tasks, then that is even better. Diamonds need leaderboards or some other representation of their progress to represent their superior achievement.

. . . .

4   "Ocarina of Time—Movement Speeds." (n.d.). Retrieved July 7, 2015, from
     https://www.zeldaspeedruns.com/oot/generalknowledge/movement-speeds.

5   Bartle, R. (1996). "Hearts, Clubs, Diamonds, Spades: Players Who Suit MUDs." *Journal of MUD Research*, 1(1), 19.

- **CLUBS** (or Killers)—Clubs play games to win as well, but they want to show their mastery by defeating opponents or otherwise changing their worlds. This is the player type that is most easily sated. Give them a monster to defeat with their superior skills, and they are quite happy. Given enough boredom or sociopathy, Clubs focus their efforts on denying others a good time just to show their superiority.
- **SPADES** (or Explorers)—Spades want to explore. They want to know everything there is to know about a system. They want to find the secrets and, in extreme examples, create maps and spreadsheets to show that they have completely conquered their world.

Individuals can fall into many categories at once or use different categories for different games. Bartle wants designers to use this taxonomy to look at their features through the lens of these four different types. Do you have something that appeals to Socializers? To Explorers? Why or why not?

In the book *Beyond Game Design*, Bartle recounts the story of the development of *GoPets*.[6] The developers of the game focused almost solely on social gameplay because it was a light, free-to-play, virtual world for children. However, the metrics revealed that a single item in the store (a fruit tree) attracted players who ended up spending money. Fruit tree buyers were 44 times as likely to be profitable players! The difference in that one object was that it had goal-oriented behavior built in; if you looked at the tree for an hour, it would bear fruit. This appealed to the goal-oriented Diamond players and gave them something that the rest of the game did not. As a result of this new information, the design team started developing features for Diamond players, and when they were added to the game, their revenue skyrocketed.

Of course, Bartle's taxonomy is incomplete. Many motivations are not covered or strictly defined in his taxonomy. Dozens of others have followed Bartle (including Bartle himself[7]) in creating more appropriate taxonomies. The important issue is not to have the completely correct taxonomy, but instead to understand what kinds of players appeal to different dynamics.

· · · · · · · · · · · · · · · · ·

6   Bateman, C. (2009). *Beyond Game Design: Nine Steps Toward Creating Better Videogames*. Boston, MA: Cengage Learning.

7   Bartle, R. (2005). "Virtual Worlds: Why People Play." *Massively Multiplayer Game Development*, 2(1).

Motivation

One of the follow-ups to Bartle's taxonomy was proposed by designer Jason Vandenberghe.[8] His model was inspired by the work of psychologists who study motivation (motivation itself is covered in more depth in Chapter 25). Psychologists have done decades of research to narrow down personality to a five-factor model. These five dimensions, they propose, fully explain the personalities of any player you may encounter. The five factors can be remembered by the mnemonic OCEAN:

- **OPENNESS TO EXPERIENCE**—A person who is open to experience is imaginative, independent-minded, and curious about new endeavors. Someone low on this scale would be content with what he already knows.

- **CONSCIENTIOUSNESS**—A person who is conscientious is "on top of it" and can easily control her impulses. She is organized, disciplined, and eschews spontaneity. Someone high on the scale is dependable; someone low on the scale is aloof.

- **EXTROVERSION**—This is one that most people are already familiar with. An extrovert needs stimulation from interaction with others. The opposite, the introvert, seeks solitude.

- **AGREEABLENESS**—A person who is agreeable seeks to avoid personal conflict. An agreeable person is apt to compromise and "play along." Someone low on this scale is not afraid to ruffle a few feathers to get his way.

- **NEUROTICISM**—This is the toughest one. Neuroticism is the tendency with which someone experiences negative emotions. A neurotic person is anxious, worries a lot, and generally is tense. Someone low on this scale wouldn't let any negative experience bother her.

Vandenberghe did qualitative research with many subjects to compare their scores on these five axes along with the games that they enjoy. He was able to make some clear parallels, which he calls "The Five Domains of Play." Here are the parallels along with the OCEAN factor they match up with:

- **NOVELTY** (from Openness to Experience)—Players who score highly on their Openness to Experience like games with highly open and imaginative play (*Minecraft*) versus games where the player aims toward mastery of conventional repetition (*Madden NFL Football*).

---

8 Vandenberghe, J. (2012, March 8). "The Five Domains of Play." Game Developer's Conference. San Francisco, CA.

- **CHALLENGE** (from Conscientiousness)—Players who score highly on their Conscientiousness like challenge (*Dark Souls*), whereas players who score low like less-challenging experiences (*Lego Star Wars*).

- **STIMULATION** (from Extroversion)—Where does the stimulation lie? Is it "in the head" or more physical or social? High-scoring extroverts enjoy more physical and more social experiences (*Just Dance*) whereas low-scoring introverts enjoy more calm and solitary experiences (*Flower*).

- **HARMONY** (from Agreeableness)—Players with a low Agreeableness score enjoy highly combative head-to-head play (*Street Fighter IV*), whereas high scorers look for more cooperative experiences (*LittleBigPlanet*).

- **THREAT** (from Neuroticism)—This is the toughest of the five to relate. Players with high neuroticism let games "get them down," so they avoid games with that possibility. For instance, a highly neurotic player would glom toward *Peggle* before he would try something unforgiving like *League of Legends*.

These set of five dimensions explains the personalities of players better than any model or framework ever studied before it. Your personality trait scores largely stay fixed throughout adulthood.[9] Also, each trait falls on a normally distributed spectrum. For every achievement-seeking Challenge player, there is a potential equal and opposite Anti-Challenge (or Contentment) player who just wants to experience a game without the high skill requirements.

You can take the OCEAN test yourself and find out where you fall on the five spectra. When you do, you'll find that what I have listed is only a small part of the story. Psychologists have broken down the five factors into 30 facets, and these are even more instrumental to understanding player desire. Here are the 30 facets and the particular aesthetic/feature that Vandenberghe believes is affected by that facet of personality:

- Openness to Experience
    - Fact-Orientation versus Imagination (Fantasy)
    - Practical Interests versus Artistic Interests (Artistry)
    - Unemotionality versus Emotionality (Melodrama)
    - Desire for Routine versus Adventurousness (Predictability)
    - People and Things versus Intellect (Abstraction)
    - Traditionalism versus Liberalism (Message)

· · · · · · · · · · · · · · · · · · · ·

9 McCrae, R. R. & Costa, P. T. (1990). *Personality in Adulthood*. New York: The Guildford Press.

- Conscientiousness
    - Un-Self-Efficacy versus Self-Efficacy (Difficulty)
    - Disorganization versus Orderliness (Order)
    - Resistance versus Dutifulness (Obligation)
    - Contentment versus Achievement-Striving (Achievement)
    - Procrastination versus Self-Discipline (Work)
    - Impulsiveness versus Cautiousness (Caution)
- Extroversion
    - Reservedness versus Friendliness (Expression)
    - Nongregariousness versus Gregariousness (Crowds)
    - Receptiveness versus Assertiveness (Role)
    - Low Activity Level versus High Activity Level (Pace)
    - Excitement-Aversion versus Excitement-Seeking (Thrill)
    - Inexpressiveness versus Cheerfulness (Joy)
- Agreeableness
    - Skepticism versus Trust (Trust)
    - Guardedness versus Straightforwardness (Integrity)
    - Non-altruism versus Altruism (Help)
    - Competition versus Accommodation (Competitiveness)
    - Immodesty versus Modesty (Glory)
    - Indifference versus Sympathy (Compassion)
- Neuroticism
    - Fearlessness versus Anxiety (Tension)
    - Calm versus Hostile (Provocation)
    - Resilience versus Depression (Gloom)
    - Lack of Self-Consciousness versus Self-Consciousness (Humiliation)
    - Temperateness versus Immoderation (Addiction)
    - Poise versus Vulnerability (Danger)

This may seem to be an interesting intellectual exercise without application, but Vandenberghe has found it to be otherwise. In his studies of players, they tend to make their play choices similarly to what their personality reflects. For instance, if I am achievement-seeking in the real world, I tend to choose games that let me scratch that itch. We all know counterexamples of folks who are shy introverts until they get onto Xbox Live and unload a series of toxic insults, but the research has shown that this is generally an outlier.

If you are interested in finding out your own scores, you can take two versions: a 120-question version (www.personal.psu.edu/~j5j/IPIP/ipipneo120.htm) and a 300-question version (www.personal.psu.edu/~j5j/IPIP/ipipneo300.htm). The 300-question version should give you more accurate results.

As a game designer, being aware of the players' different motivations lets you pair those motivations with mechanics to create targeted dynamics that produce desirable outcomes. It's not as easy as saying "Players like conflict!" That is true, but only for some players. Just as many potential players eschew direct conflict. Depending on the target aesthetics for your game, you may reach the most audience by trying to accommodate both sides of each personality facet.

Milieu as Design Focus

Let's take a look at a game that uses its players' milieu to its advantage.

Spent puts players in the shoes of someone living at the poverty level and, through a series of decisions, asks them to "make it" when they are given hefty problems and a low amount of resources (**FIGURE 14.3**).

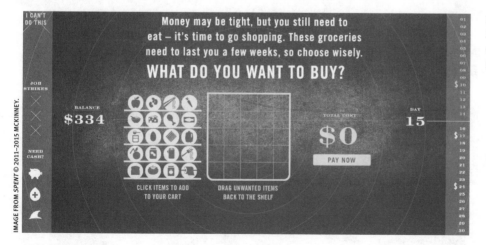

IMAGE FROM *SPENT* © 2011–2015 MCKINNEY.

FIGURE 14.3
Spent offers lessons on poverty through procedural means.

The result is a game that could be seen as mechanically similar to *Lemonade Stand* or any other light economic simulation, but because the decisions offered lead the player to act desperately, the play aesthetic is particularly poignant. The game is an adver-game of sorts. Its purpose is to get you to donate to the Urban Ministries of Durham, a charity that helps those at the poverty level. Players do not just read about poverty, they make the same poor decisions that lead real families to disaster. It's best if you play it for yourself; you can find it at playspent.org.

The mechanics of *Spent* are straightforward: Choose this or that and gain or lose money accordingly. But thanks to the milieu of your own experience with the topic of poverty, this leads you to making more conservative or more morally questionable choices. Only when reflecting on those choices, do you experience the aesthetic that Urban Ministries of Durham is aiming for: that of sympathy with their mission.

Summary

- The personal, social, and cultural assumptions that players bring to games are the player's milieu.
- A game can have different dynamics for different players based on how they act given the preferences generated by their milieu.
- Polish helps "fill in" a world by creating nonessential cues between objects.
- Richard Bartle was one of the first to have a functional taxonomy of gamer types. Others have since elaborated.
- The OCEAN personality traits help explain the domains of human personality. Designers can use those domains to help understand what humans look for in games.

15

Rules and Verbs

The young man knows the rules,
but the old man knows the exceptions.

—OLIVER WENDELL HOLMES SR.

One school of thought takes rules to be the fundamental element
of games. Thus, to explain a game, you need to examine the
rules. For instance, if you used MDA (mechanics, dynamics, and
aesthetics) as your framework for understanding games, the
only element that you can directly affect is the mechanics. The
mechanics, in this case, are just rules of varying scope. But even
if you choose to use some other framework to evaluate your
game, you'll likely need to examine the rules of the game as a
fundamental element of the experience.

Rules

When you are introducing a game to a friend, say *Hearts*, how do you explain the game? Generally, you would say something like this:

> The goal is to get the least number of points. At the start of the round, the dealer deals thirteen cards face-down to each of four players. In the first round, each player passes three cards that they were dealt to the player on their left. The player who has the 2 of clubs goes first and plays the 2 of clubs. Then each player has to play a higher-valued card of the same suit. If a player cannot play a card of the same suit, he may play any card except a heart or the queen of spades on the first round. Play continues until every player has played one card. Then the player who played the highest card of the suit first played wins the hand and collects the cards. That player starts a new hand with any card except a heart, if possible, unless someone has already played a heart or the queen of spades earlier in the game. Once all the cards have been collected, each player receives 1 point for each heart they have collected and 13 points if they collected the queen of spades. There's a special case called shooting the moon. If a player collects all the hearts AND the queen of spades, then every other player is awarded 26 points! It's really hard to do! The game is finished when one player accumulates 100 points. The player with the least number of points wins.

What happened there? You did not explain the story of *Hearts*. You did not explain what a deck of cards was, or why or how the cards are numbered, or what a card looks like. You did not explain why the game was fun or some strategies players could use to win. What you did was enumerate a bunch of rules. Those rules define the game.

▶ **NOTE** For a stellar (if highly philosophical in nature) treatment of rules in games, see Juul, J. (2011). Half-Real: Video Games Between Real Rules and Fictional Worlds. Cambridge, MA: MIT Press.

What are the parts of *Hearts* that you can change and yet still preserve the feel and experience of playing the game? Is it that it is a card game that is important? You can change the cards to tokens drawn from a bag and still *Hearts* would play the same. You could change the ranking of cards from high to low and make the ace of spades the lead card and the 4 of diamonds the big penalty card and the game would remain largely the same. You could play it with a theme, such as *Hearts* is a struggle about trying to rid your nation of pox-laden peasants. Nonetheless, the game would play largely the same. It is the rules that form the essential part of the game.

Qualities of Rules

Salen and Zimmerman's book *Rules of Play* obviously spends a lot of space discussing rules.[1] They define the qualities of rules with the following attributes:

- **RULES LIMIT PLAYER ACTION.** Rules allow you to play games in a meaningful way. *Rules of Play* uses *Yahtzee* as an example. "[T]hink of all the things you could do with the dice in that game: You could light them on fire, eat them, juggle them, or make jewelry out of them. But you don't do any of these things." This is a silly example, but important. By limiting the player's action, rules allow you to set up meaningful choices and conflicts. If play was unlimited, players could always sidestep any situation. Rules are essentially limitations demarcating the line between acceptable behaviors and unacceptable behaviors.

- **RULES ARE EXPLICIT AND UNAMBIGUOUS.** This is perhaps the most important quality of rules for games. If the rules are not complete, then sometimes players find themselves in situations that have no win/lose result and no way to proceed. For example, if you are playing *HORSE* and the ball ends up stuck between the rim and backboard, what do you do? In *HORSE*, you need a rule: "If the ball comes to a complete stop and the called shot was not made, then this counts as a miss and it is the next player's turn." It's of the utmost importance that all conditions are handled! Notice here that the rules do not enumerate every possible way the ball could stop. The rules do not say, "If the ball gets stuck between the rim and backboard, or if it gets stuck in tree branches, or if a tornado carries it into the sky," and so on. This would be pedantic. Instead, you craft rules with parsimony so that they handle all reasonable conditions.

- **RULES ARE SHARED BY ALL PLAYERS.** Players must understand what rules apply in what situations. Have you ever played a game with a friend and that friend conveniently "forgot" to tell you a rule that cost you the game? This does not mean that all players have to play by the same rules. In *Cops and Robbers*, the two roles have different rules for how they should play. But all players share that understanding of the rules. If some robbers think that they can leave jail by counting to 20 and some think they can leave jail only when tagged, then playing the game would result in chaos and turmoil. The game would cease.

- **RULES ARE FIXED.** Imagine that, in the aforementioned *Cops and Robbers*, just as a robber was being tagged, she announces: "No! I'm still free! You have to tag me with

1   Zimmerman, E., & Salen, K. (2003). *Rules of Play: Game Design Fundamentals*. Cambridge, MA: MIT Press.

two hands!" Of course, this new rule would spawn an argument. Rules must be fixed, or the changing of a rule must be governed by a fixed rule. For instance, the card game *Fluxx*'s unique feature is that players change the rules as the game progresses. However, how players change the rules is fixed and understood by all players. Rules can be changed in *Fluxx* only in a specific enumerated way.

- **RULES ARE BINDING.** Whoever said "rules were made to be broken" was not talking about how to design a coherent game. The implicit agreement made in playing a game is that the game will be fair and that the players will be subject to the agreed-upon rules.

- **RULES ARE REPEATABLE.** Say I play *Monopoly* the correct way: When a player lands on Free Parking, that player receives nothing. However, you play with the common house rule variant that when you land on Free Parking you get a bunch of money. If we don't reconcile which rules we are playing with, then when you and I land on Free Parking, we get different results.

Keep in mind that this list is not something that is written in stone. Some games may have as their purpose to break one of these qualities of rules. But these are special cases. In general, coherent rules have the listed qualities.

Types of Rules

Rules of Play also discusses a useful distinction between types of rules that should be understood:

- *Operational rules* are the ones most often thought of when game rules are being discussed. These are the explicit, listed rules that are described in instruction sheets for board games or tutorials for digital games. Nearly all qualities of rules discussed in the previous section are operational rules since they pertain to how to "operate" the game. When designers write design documentation, it is important that they make sure operational rules are complete and enumerated.

- *Constitutive rules* are a little harder to understand. These are the rules that define the game's logic. Designers do not necessarily give these to the player because they are inherent in the game's structure. These rules do not direct the player to action. They instead describe the system. For instance, a constitutive rule of *Hearts* is that there are 13 heart cards in the deck and only 1 queen of spades. A constitutive rule of *Hearts* is that all players start at zero points. These are the basic underlying rules that you would need to explain to a computer for it to re-create the game. This type of rule is needed for play, but it does not need to be spelled out in the operational rules.

- *Implicit rules* are unwritten rules that are tacitly agreed upon by the players. This includes things like expected behaviors of the game and good sportsmanship. What rule in *Hearts* covers marking the cards? How about shouldering your players aside to have a look at their cards? Neither of these things is actually written in the rules, yet players would agree that these behaviors are unacceptable. When writing rules, a designer does not necessarily have to include the implicit rules, but the designer must determine that a rule is so obvious or off-the-wall that it bears including in the implicit category.

When writing tournament or competitive rules, for example, a designer must account for as many degenerate conditions as possible or allow for an arbiter that is empowered by the rules to declare an implicit rule is broken. Football has a rule that the referee can penalize any conduct deemed an unfair act or a mockery of the game. This is a rule that essentially allows the referee to use judgment to disallow any conduct not explicitly covered in the rules, but which violates the spirit of the rules.

Verbs

> What would you say you *do* here?
>
> **—FROM OFFICE SPACE (1999)**

Another common way of examining a game is to examine what the player chooses to do. "Play" is an obvious answer of course, but each game plays differently. Is the type of play the same in soccer as it is in *Backgammon*? Clearly not. What can you use to determine how a player plays? One way is to examine the *verbs* that an observer could use to explain the actions that players take. Each verb must relate to something a player does to affect the state of the game within the game's rules. Actions such as "breathe" or "exist" are not state changes and are not affected specifically by the rules of the game, so you do not consider them as player actions.

For instance, here are some verbs in various games:

- Baseball—run, hit, catch, slide, take a pitch, throw, pitch, steal, jump, tag, tag up, dive
- *Super Mario Bros.*—walk, wait, run, jump, stomp, hit block, grab, bounce, throw
- *Portal*—walk, jump, shoot blue portal, shoot orange portal, pick up, drop
- *War* (card game)—draw, compare

These verbs can (but do not necessarily) create a choice for the player. If these verbs do not create choices, as in the example of *War*, this can clue you into where the players are playing the game and where the game is playing the player!

The classic game *Dragon's Lair* consists mostly of predetermined animated cutscenes interspersed with quick-time events that branch the story to other animated cutscenes. The story involves a young knight on his quest to rescue a princess. However, because the interaction is so limited, it could be said that the verbs of the game are not the things that the protagonist does, such as dodging or using his sword to vanquish evil snakes. The only actions the player can take are to press a direction button or press the sword button. The only verb for the player is "to react" and press the correct button. From the perspective of player verbs, playing *Dragon's Lair* is not much different than playing *Simon*.

A game with no verbs for the player is difficult to defend as a game at all because it's impossible to offer a player a choice when the player has no way to participate in that choice. At the same time, a game with too many verbs becomes cumbersome and unfocused.

In *Super Metroid*, the player is blocked by different-colored doors that lead to new rooms. The designers could have added an additional verb to the game so that the player could open a door. However, that was unnecessary. Instead, they used an already established verb, shoot, to open a door. Creating a new verb was unnecessary because the player has already learned how to use the verb "shoot" and the "open" action would have no connection to any other verbs or mechanics in the game. Designer Anna Anthropy refers to these unconnected actions as *orphaned verbs* and suggests developing in such a way that many interactions are served by just a few verbs.[2]

As an example, look at the wide variety of puzzles served by *Portal*'s parsimonious set of verbs. Players can create a set of portals to move a remote block across a map, drop the block on an enemy turret to disable it, use that portal to traverse a large space, pick up the now dead turret, and use the turret to weigh down a pressure sensor. Complicated interactions are possible with a modest menu of player actions because of the clever design of the verb interactions.

· · · · · · · · · · · · · · · · · ·

2   Anthropy, A., & Clark, N. (2014). *A Game Design Vocabulary: Exploring the Foundational Principles Behind Good Game Design*. Pearson Education.

Summary

- Rules are one of the essential elements of games. It's difficult to discuss play of a game without at least tangentially referring to the game's rules.

- Rules must cover all cases within a game in order to direct player action should that case arise. Analog games can be more lax about this requirement because mentally flexible human beings arbitrate them. Digital games must be complete in their rules because otherwise a computer will not have instructions on how to continue.

- One way to classify rules is to label them as operational, constitutive, or implicit.

- Verbs explain what the player does in the game. These actions relate to state changes in the game itself and are thus an expression of what the player's existence in the game involves.

- Avoid orphaned verbs, verbs that have no connection to other verbs and mechanics in the game.

16

Balance

> The system of nature, of which man is a part,
> tends to be self-balancing, self-adjusting, self-cleansing.
> Not so with technology.
>
> **—E. F. SCHUMACHER**

Is *Chess* a balanced game?

That question is impossible to answer if you do not understand what *balance* means in this context. The concept of balance is a highly "squishy" one—one prone to hand waving instead of definition. A person can mean many things by "balance." One definition is that players have an even chance to win, all else being equal. However, balance can be tricky. If all players have an equal chance to win, does that speak to the game's mechanisms or the player's abilities? What reason does a player ever have to get better at a game if the game's balance always gives him the same chance of winning?

Symmetry

Symmetry is a match between the options of players. In *Chess*, both players have the same number of pieces and those pieces have identical moves. Therefore, *Chess* is mostly symmetrical. The only asymmetry is that the white player moves first. Assuming that the white player does not get a significant advantage or penalty associated with moving first, theoretically, the white player should win approximately 50 percent of the time, and the black player should win approximately 50 percent of the time. If that is true, then is *Chess* balanced?

Try playing against a chess champion if you are a novice. According to the ELO rating system used by the United States Chess Federation, a class E player with an ELO rating of 1000 will have a probability of winning of around 1 in 2500 games when playing against a class A player with a rating of 2000. If you have a 1 in 2500 chance of winning, would you say that *Chess* is balanced?

▶ **NOTE** I determined the calculation of the ELO for the Chess champion versus the novice player by using the ELO winning probability calculator at www.bobnewell.net/nucleus/bnewell.php?itemid=279.

It seems obvious to say that a balanced game is not necessarily one in which each player has an equal probability of winning. For example, *Pandemic* is a popular asymmetric cooperative board game where the players are trying to beat the system so they all win together. Most of the time, the players lose, but every once in a while, they win. The game does not have an exactly 50-percent win rate, yet to many, it still feels as if it is in balance because, among other reasons, it feels fair.

Symmetry is not necessarily balance. Balance is not necessarily symmetry. Why should a game be asymmetric? An asymmetric game can help players get back into flow by using the asymmetries to nudge players back into a competitive or advantageous position. In some cases, having the deck stacked against the player is part of the aesthetic, such as in games like *Dark Souls* and games that attempt to model real-world situations, such as *Pandemic* or sports games. If challenge is the targeted play aesthetic, then failure should be overweighted. In other words, players should lose more often than they win. The game should be balanced in such a way as to achieve these ends.

Following the fundamental game design directive, a single-player or co-op game where a player or players work against the system should be set up so that the players have the ability to win with effort, but not with so much effort that they give up or become frustrated. This usually means toning down the difficulty level at which a true expert (say, the designer) plays the game to adjust it for the differing skill levels of novice players.

Likewise, a game that pits players against one another should signal that players are close to one another in terms of likelihood of winning until the very end in order to keep the players in flow. Some designers attempt to model sports where the higher skilled player may show dominance early. This is fine if the goal is to be fair at the expense of player satisfaction. For instance, if I go up against a professional sumo wrestler at sumo, I expect to lose. That is fair. But a game set up this way is not fun for me to play. If your goal is player satisfaction, all players should feel "in it" until as close to the end as possible in order to provide ample opportunities for flow. This may mean introducing asymmetries.

Self-Balancing Mechanisms

Ancestral Recall is a card in the *Magic: The Gathering* card game. It has what, to the casual or uninitiated player, seems like a simple instruction: draw three cards. The cost is listed in the upper right: one blue mana and the discard of the card itself (which is implied) (**FIGURE 16.1**). The card was quickly cycled out of print because it was vastly too powerful. An updated version, called Inspiration, upped its cost to one blue mana, three(!) other mana, and the discard of the card; in addition, it changed the effect to drawing only two cards. Needless to say, Ancestral Recall is dominant to Inspiration.

> ◆ **TIP** Don't throw away those Magic: The Gathering cards! According to price-tracking site mtggoldfish.com, at the time of this writing, Ancestral Recall sells on the secondary market for $1,700, whereas Inspiration sells for $0.15. I give myself a hard kick every morning for getting rid of my Magic cards in the mid-1990s.

FIGURE 16.1
The original Ancestral Recall card allowed for more card drawing than Inspiration at a much cheaper mana cost.

Balance is a difficult trait to get correct. It may not even be possible to be "correct"; it may be a concept of balance maximization. Often, concerns of balance are framed as an open-ended quantitative question. How much should the sword cost? The designer could arbitrarily decide that the sword costs 100 gold. But what if that is too low? Or what if that is too high? Most of these decisions are done by gut-feel based on understanding the systems of the game and heuristics that provide clues as to what things should cost. What if balance could be determined for individual players based on their skills and values instead of being dictated by a designer?

The question of balance is another way to frame the question of price. Of course, how much something should cost is not a simple answer that you can reveal upon meditation. Different players have different values based on wants and needs. How much something should cost has been solved in a number of ways that you can leverage for games. Let's take a look at two main types and some variations on one of them:

- *Auctions* are the most salient example. *Power Grid* is a board game that uses this mechanic. In it, each player bids on power plants to fuel their energy-production empire. Some power plants are dominant over others; they are clearly out of balance with all things being equal. The #15 power plant powers three cities for 2 coal, but the #25 power plant powers five cities for 2 coal. Why would anyone ever choose to buy the #15 power plant? In *Power Grid*, players bid up individual power plants to the highest bidder. If #15 and #25 cost the same, the first person to have an opportunity to get #25 would clearly have an advantage. But since it goes to the highest bidder, the "balanced" price is whatever a player is willing to pay in that situation. The power plant itself does not need to be balanced; the players do the leg work.

  As a designer, you can use auctions during the playtesting phase to do a kind of price discovery. Find out what prices players are willing to pay for various effects and then, when the time comes for the game to be played in a nonsupervised environment, remove the auction mechanism and hard-code the value into the game. This approach is more accurate than a blind guess, but it has the efficiency of fiat prices.

  Auction mechanisms come in various types:

  - The *English auction*, also known as the *open ascending price auction*, is the type used in the *Power Grid* example. In this auction, all bidders know the current bid and publicly bid higher and higher until only one bidder remains.

  - The *Dutch auction*, also known as the *open descending price auction*, is an alternative. In it, the bidding starts at a high number and then goes down until one bidder accepts the price. In general, Dutch auctions are considerably faster than English auctions, but they also encourage less participation.

- *Vickrey*, also referred to as *second-price auctions*, are a bit more complicated. Each participant secretly bids the highest that they are willing to pay, and the winner (highest bidder) pays what the second-highest bidder bid. eBay uses a form of this type of auction. This is harder to implement in a nonautomated context.

- *Supply and demand* is another method of self-balance. It can be time-consuming to set up an auction for every balanceable interaction. Again in *Power Grid*, resources get more expensive as fewer of them remain in the game. As a result of there being fewer resources, players buy the resource that provides them with the most bang-for-the-buck and balance themselves into buying efficiently.

Remember also that costs do not have to be framed in explicit terms. Money changing hands is only one type of cost. Any limited resource can be a cost. Time, soldiers, units, cards—even information—can all be costs that can be balanced by mechanism.

Progression and Numeric Relationships

The purpose of any progression mechanic is to keep the players in flow. For instance, a player might "level up" in a role-playing game so she can access bigger and scarier monsters that provide additional spectacle and challenge. I use generic role-playing game framing in my examples here, but any game's progression is generally in response to the designer's need to keep a player in flow given her increase in skills and her satiety with content.

Often a designer uses progression because he feels he needs to reward the players explicitly. These rewards then make the game easier for the players because they have some tie to the game's mechanics. As the game gets easier, the players are taken out of flow, and thus the designer needs to establish some measure of progression to push the player back in the direction of challenge.

As an example, say that a sword-fighting fantasy game is fairly challenging to new players when the sword does 1 point of damage and the enemies have 5 points of life. As a reward for killing the tenth enemy, the game gives the player a new sword that does 3 points of damage. Now the enemies only have to be hit twice instead of five times to be defeated. This makes the game a lot easier. Additionally, it is likely that the player's skills have increased. If the difficulty of the enemies does not increase in kind, the player will become bored because the fundamental game design directive was ignored.

So how much should the sword increase in power over time? Many relationships between power and time can be used; but remember that these relationships are applicable to any resource in a game: power, cost, points, and so on.

- **FLAT RELATIONSHIP.** This is easiest relationship to map (**FIGURE 16.2**). In a flat relationship, the output is always the same no matter what the input. This usually occurs in the case of fungible resources, where each additional resource has a set utility. Examples include that 100 coins always gain you an extra life in *Super Mario Bros.*, and every trip around the board gains you $200 in *Monopoly*.

- **LINEAR AND LINEAR INVERSE RELATIONSHIPS.** In a linear relationship (**FIGURE 16.3**), the output scales in a linear manner based on the input. A designer uses a linear relationship if she wants the outputs to scale so that later outputs are more valuable than early ones. For instance, in the board game *Power Grid*, the designers wanted to create a supply-and-demand style economy and to decrease the hoarding of particular materials; they solved this problem by making it so that as players buy materials, the materials become more expensive. The first units of coal are cheap: only 1 Electro each. However, once three have been bought, the cost jumps to 2, then 3, then 4, and so on. Any player who wants to corner the market on a particular resource will have to pay dearly for it.

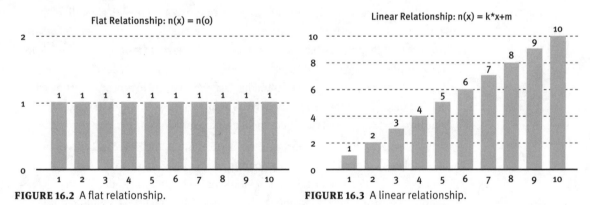

FIGURE 16.2 A flat relationship.

FIGURE 16.3 A linear relationship.

A linear inverse relationship follows a similar principle. However, it starts with a base value and counts down (**FIGURE 16.4**). Each output is worth less than the one before. For instance, the first player to score a monument in *Roll Through the Ages* gets bonus points for getting there before his opponent. Future players score less. In *Le Havre*, the value of boats goes down as more and more players build them.

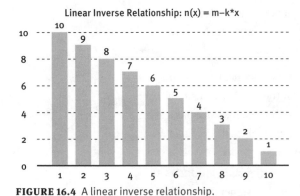

FIGURE 16.4 A linear inverse relationship.

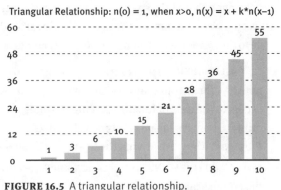

FIGURE 16.5 A triangular relationship.

- **TRIANGULAR RELATIONSHIP.** Often, resources become vastly more valuable the more of them there are. Or similarly, attaining a vast number of resources becomes progressively harder. For these items, a form like the triangular numbers is useful. In the triangular numbers, the gap between the numbers increases with every step. For instance, the fifth step is five higher than the fourth step. The sixth step is six higher than the fifth step (**FIGURE 16.5**).

  One example of a triangular relationship is in the popular board game *Ticket to Ride*. Fulfilling a route with a length of four yields 7 points. A route with a length of five yields 10. A route with a length of six yields 15 points. Since more and more resources are required to build longer and longer routes, the player is rewarded for putting in the additional work to build longer and longer routes. If a player scored only 1 point for each length of route, then it would be easier for players to accrue points by completing the shortest routes rather than triangulating (ha!) between the ease of scoring short routes and the difficulty but high reward of scoring long routes.

  Another popular use of triangular-style relationships is the "level up" curves in most role-playing games. Leveling up from 1 to 2 is easy, much easier than leveling up between 29 and 30. A triangular relationship helps reflect the decreasing marginal utility of power in games, where a little bit more power should require progressively more and more resources, allowing a natural asymptote at some maximum power level.

- **FIBONACCI SEQUENCE.** This is a sequence of numbers similar to the triangular where the first two numbers in the series are 1 and then the next number is the result of the previous two added together: 1, 1, 2, 3, 5, 8, 13, 21, 34, 45, and so on. The Fibonacci Sequence is also a good model for role-playing experience curves, especially if level 1 starts a few steps into the sequence. However, since the distance grows faster with every entry in the series in the Fibonacci Sequence than it does with the triangular numbers, realize that the farther you go in the series, the harder it will be to reach the next step.

- **EXPONENTIAL RELATIONSHIP.** The exponential relationship is another prototypical relationship that is generally used until the designer or team realizes how quickly it can get out of control (**FIGURE 16.6**). For example, would you rather be given $1,000,000 today or be given just a penny today and then be given double the amount every day for 30 days? For instance, a penny today, two tomorrow, and so on. At first glance, the choice seems simple: a million dollars is a lot and a penny is a little. However, because of the power of exponential doubling, the second offer is actually worth a total of $10,737,418.23.

Be very careful when using an exponential relationship because the quick escalation of values involved makes it easy to create a combo that can throw a game out of balance.

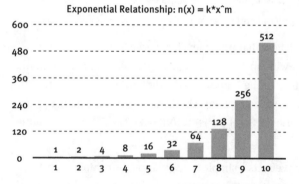

FIGURE 16.6
An exponential relationship.

Situations in which a player's resources grow at a faster than linear rate are generally more appropriate for games in which the player's opponent is a computer that does not care emotionally about balance. In the book *Laws of the Game*, Nobel laureate Manfred Eigen studies relationships within closed systems and determines that "exponential and hyperbolic growth result in a clear selection of one [player] unless stabilizing interactions among different [players] enforce their coexistence."[1]

> ▶ **NOTE** Manfred Eigen also notes that exponential and hyperbolic growth result in player dominance unless there are functional links between the competitors that can mitigate one player dominating the other. Of course, it's the designer's job to establish whether or not the game design cares about preserving game balance between competitors.

. . . .

1   Eigen, M., & Winkler, R. (1981). *Laws of the Game: How the Principles of Nature Govern Chance*. New York: Knopf.

A Triangular Relationship Example

I have worked on a number of games that required experience tables or a list of progressively increasing quantities of challenge to receive rewards. Generally, when you need to complete such a task, you enumerate all the principles that you need to adhere to and then try your best to apply a reasonable numerical relationship that simultaneously meets all the principles.

Here's an example: You are working on a Facebook farming game. The main mechanic is to wait for a crop to grow, and then harvest it successfully without letting it wilt; if he can manage this, the player gains money and experience. The principles are as follows:

- The game will have enough content to unlock 30 player levels.
- A player with perfect coordination will be able to harvest 12 times a day. However, most will harvest on average only 4 times a day.
- The average player should take 28 to 30 days to reach max level.
- The perfect player should take 12 to 14 days to reach max level.
- An average player should be able to level up every 3 days.

◆ **TIP** You can use the function VLOOKUP in Excel to match experience points (XP) with a level.

Your first task is to make a spreadsheet that tracks level, experience points, and the time to reach the maximum level with an average and an expert player. For column A, use the triangular numbers to start. In the columns to the right, track the day versus the level of the average and expert players on that day. On the first pass, for simplicity, make every harvest worth 1 Experience Point (XP) (**FIGURE 16.7**). The XP will determine the player's level.

Now you are able to compare what effects a simple triangular relationship has on an average player and expert player based on the assumptions. Here you see that without any adjustments, the average player hits level 15 after a month (cell G32), and the expert player hits level 17 (cell J16). That is close on many of the requirements. Luckily, it's easy to massage numbers in a spreadsheet. For instance, if you changed the XP per harvest from 1 to 4, you end up with a result where the average player hits level 30 on day 30. However, the expert player is at level 30 far too quickly, hitting it at day 10.

What you want is a slower advancement for the expert player. You can handle this in a number of ways, but the easiest is probably to exploit what makes the expert player different. The average player harvests four times a day and the expert player harvests more. What if the first four harvests were worth a different value than the subsequent ones?

	A	B	C	D	E	F	G	H	I	J
1					Average	Average	Average	Expert	Expert	Expert
2	XP	Level		Day	Harvests	XP	Level	Harvests	XP	Level
3	1	1		1	4	4	2	12	12	4
4	3	2		2	8	8	3	24	24	6
5	6	3		3	12	12	4	36	36	8
6	10	4		4	16	16	5	48	48	9
7	15	5		5	20	20	5	60	60	10
8	21	6		6	24	24	6	72	72	11
9	28	7		7	28	28	7	84	84	12
10	36	8		8	32	32	7	96	96	13
11	45	9		9	36	36	8	108	108	14
12	55	10		10	40	40	8	120	120	15
13	66	11		11	44	44	8	132	132	15
14	78	12		12	48	48	9	144	144	16
15	91	13		13	52	52	9	156	156	17
16	105	14		14	56	56	10	168	168	17
17	120	15		15	60	60	10			
18	136	16		16	64	64	10			
19	153	17		17	68	68	11			
20	171	18		18	72	72	11			
21	190	19		19	76	76	11			
22	210	20		20	80	80	12			
23	231	21		21	84	84	12			
24	253	22		22	88	88	12			
25	276	23		23	92	92	13			
26	300	24		24	96	96	13			
27	325	25		25	100	100	13			
28	351	26		26	104	104	13			
29	378	27		27	108	108	14			
30	406	28		28	112	112	14			
31	435	29		29	116	116	14			
32	465	30		30	120	120	15			

FIGURE 16.7
An experience table spreadsheet structure.

A little spreadsheet magic allows you to change the formula so that the first four harvests point to one cell and all subsequent ones point to another. Keeping the 4 XP per harvest for the first four and making each subsequent harvest 1 XP should not change the average player at all since he harvests only four times a day by the assumption of the average player's behaviors listed above. Therefore, keeping the first four harvests at 4 XP keeps the average player hitting 30 at just the right time. Now you can adjust the subsequent XP to make your expert player hit 30 at the right time.

Using 2.5 XP per subsequent harvest, the table looks like **FIGURE 16.8**.

Decimal points are ugly, though. Although every other directive has been met, the UI designers may not wish to implement decimal points or the design may not call for something as geeky looking as high-precision values. By scaling everything by 10, which is easy in the spreadsheet, you ensure that the game balances on nice whole numbers, and it's not nearly as obvious that the XP table is simply the triangular numbers (**FIGURE 16.9**).

FIGURE 16.8
Staggered values for XP.

| XP per 1st 4 Harvests | 4 |
| XP per Subseq. Harvests | 2.5 |

XP	Level		Day	Average Harvests	Average XP	Average Level	Expert Harvests	Expert XP	Expert Level
1	1		1	4	16	5	12	36	8
3	2		2	8	32	7	24	72	11
6	3		3	12	48	9	36	108	14
10	4		4	16	64	10	48	144	16
15	5		5	20	80	12	60	180	18
21	6		6	24	96	13	72	216	20
28	7		7	28	112	14	84	252	21
36	8		8	32	128	15	96	288	23
45	9		9	36	144	16	108	324	24
55	10		10	40	160	17	120	360	26
66	11		11	44	176	18	132	396	27
78	12		12	48	192	19	144	432	28
91	13		13	52	208	19	156	468	30
105	14		14	56	224	20	168	504	30
120	15		15	60	240	21			
136	16		16	64	256	22			
153	17		17	68	272	22			
171	18		18	72	288	23			
190	19		19	76	304	24			
210	20		20	80	320	24			
231	21		21	84	336	25			
253	22		22	88	352	26			
276	23		23	92	368	26			
300	24		24	96	384	27			
325	25		25	100	400	27			
351	26		26	104	416	28			
378	27		27	108	432	28			
406	28		28	112	448	29			
435	29		29	116	464	29			
465	30		30	120	480	30			

FIGURE 16.9
Experience table spreadsheet with XP scaling. Both players hit Level 30 at around the desired time.

XP Scaling	10
XP per 1st 4 Harvests	40
XP per Subseq. Harvests	25

XP	Level		Day	Average Harvests	Average XP	Average Level	Expert Harvests	Expert XP	Expert Level
10	1		1	4	160	5	12	360	8
30	2		2	8	320	7	24	720	11
60	3		3	12	480	9	36	1080	14
100	4		4	16	640	10	48	1440	16
150	5		5	20	800	12	60	1800	18
210	6		6	24	960	13	72	2160	20
280	7		7	28	1120	14	84	2520	21
360	8		8	32	1280	15	96	2880	23
450	9		9	36	1440	16	108	3240	24
550	10		10	40	1600	17	120	3600	26
660	11		11	44	1760	18	132	3960	27
780	12		12	48	1920	19	144	4320	28
910	13		13	52	2080	19	156	4680	30
1050	14		14	56	2240	20	168	5040	30
1200	15		15	60	2400	21			
1360	16		16	64	2560	22			
1530	17		17	68	2720	22			
1710	18		18	72	2880	23			
1900	19		19	76	3040	24			
2100	20		20	80	3200	24			
2310	21		21	84	3360	25			
2530	22		22	88	3520	26			
2760	23		23	92	3680	26			
3000	24		24	96	3840	27			
3250	25		25	100	4000	27			
3510	26		26	104	4160	28			
3780	27		27	108	4320	28			
4060	28		28	112	4480	29			
4350	29		29	116	4640	29			
4650	30		30	120	4800	30			

Balance Heuristics

When working on game balance, here are a few helpful heuristics to keep in mind:

- **ALWAYS CONSIDER EXTREMES.** What if a player does nothing but one type of action? Is the game out of balance if people are always lucky? What if they are always unlucky; will the game still be in balance? Test all formulas with very high and very low numbers to see if they make sense.

- **FIND "GOOD ENOUGH."** Very rarely is a question of game balance about finding an exact, balanced answer. Most commonly, a balance is sufficient over a range of values. The goal of determining balance is to hit upon the easiest answer that is in balance. For instance, at a damage rate of 10 damage per second (DPS), a gun is too underpowered to include, but a damage rate of 20 DPS would make the gun too overpowered. As a designer, you don't know this innately. You have to make educated guesses supplemented by playtest feedback. Nudging a value a small amount may not result in a difference perceivable by playtesters. This is why many designers believe in a rule of *doubling or halving values* until they find a sufficient answer. Say the value range where most playtesters were happy was between 14 DPS and 16 DPS. If the designer started at 4 DPS and slowly nudged the gun values upward, it would take 10 revisions of 1 DPS to get to a suitable value of 14 DPS. If the designers tested 4, then 8, then 16, they reach the suitable value sooner. If they overshoot, it's easier to determine the edges of the suitable range.

- **KEEP YOUR GOALS IN MIND.** Often it's OK if something is out of balance if it doesn't break the game's aesthetic values. For instance, *Arkham Horror* is not a balanced game. Some elements are wildly more powerful than others, and some scenarios vary in difficulty and complexity. Nonetheless, many players find it enjoyable because they do not expect to win and they do expect to face something where their victory is uncertain.

You can find additional coverage of the topic of balance in Part 5 on game theory and rational decision-making.

Summary

- A symmetric game is not necessarily balanced. A balanced game is not necessarily symmetric.
- You can have players self-balance the values of game items with a few types of mechanics. Auctions are one option. Pricing by supply and demand mechanisms are others.
- Different mathematical relationships can be applied to the amount of resources gathered or lost over time. These relationships are estimates of dynamics to best preserve player flow.
- When testing for balance, always test extreme behaviors. They may not be common in players, but they can identify ways to break the game.
- Balance is rarely about solving an equation. It is more often an exercise in finding "good enough" results.

17 Feedback Loops

If winning isn't everything, then why do they keep score?

—VINCE LOMBARDI

You are playing a game of *Monopoly* with your friends, or at least you were earlier. Now, two of your friends have gone bankrupt and it's just you and one opponent. He has amassed four monopolies and a massive pile of cash. You have no monopolies, and it's just a matter of time before you hit one of his properties and the game ends. The game is a foregone conclusion, so your decisions have become meaningless. Your odds of coming back to win are astronomical, and besides, it would take a couple hours of fruitless rolling. Your opponent does not want you to give up; he wants to earn the victory. It's not a lot of fun. What happened? The game at some point went from competitive and fair to a situation with meaningless decision-making. The rules didn't change, so what caused this?

Any game in which a player's actions affect the game state for later actions has the possibility of entering what is known as a *feedback loop*. In a feedback loop, the players' actions affect the ability for that player to get closer to a goal. In other words, successes or failures early affect the chances of successes or failures late.

Feedback loops come in two flavors: positive and negative.

Positive Feedback Loops

Positive feedback loops in games are mechanics that reinforce the success or failure of the player and make future successes/failures more probable. You will find this type of feedback loop in numerous games, especially in role-playing games. The cliché often used to explain positive feedback loops is that the rich get richer. Having money is often a prerequisite to gaining more money: You need capital to start a business, so the ones making money are the ones who already have money.

In *Risk*, players control armies that are trying to take over the world. They do so by battling other armies. When players win battles and control entire continents, they receive additional armies every turn—this, in turn, "feeds back" into the simple result that having more armies makes you more likely to win battles. So not only does winning a battle give you a direct advantage (the opponent has fewer units), but you also feed back that victory into gaining more units, which should ensure further victories.

Quake II also contains positive feedback loops. The relevant mechanic is that when you die, you restart with guns that are not as powerful as the ones that you can pick up on the battlefield. Therefore, the player with the first kill has an inherent advantage—he'll have better weapons than the newly respawned player and will be more likely to kill her again, given equal skill.

> ▶ **NOTE** Of course, the statement that "the best players lead to the best success on the field" discounts the huge influence of chance on sports results, but folks with sports opinions tend to see results as a more deterministic process.

Professional baseball in America has a somewhat muted positive feedback loop. Major League Baseball (MLB) does not have salary caps, so teams can spend as much money as they have to acquire the best players. The best players lead to the best success on the field. Success on the field leads to more money for the team as people bid up tickets and buy merchandise. That money can then be fed into buying even better players.

The Facebook game *Mafia Wars* originally had a pretty severe positive feedback problem. Players could buy properties that would earn them in-game money over time. Players could dump all their money into buying Mega Casinos, which in turn gave them a lot of additional money in rent, which they could then use to buy additional Mega Casinos (**FIGURE 17.1**). The amount of money players could earn from this dynamic made any other choices in the game irrelevant. Players could log off for months and then come back with enough money to buy any item in the game.

FIGURE 17.1
Positive feedback loops in *Mafia Wars* lead to exponential growth.

During the development of *NCAA Football 08*, its designers implemented a positive reinforcement system named DPR (dynamic player ratings). The idea was to implement the
most straightforward of positive reinforcements. Player events tied to random die rolls
were affected by ability ratings. A player with a 90 catching ability would catch more
often than a player with 70 catching rating. As a player succeeded during the course of
a single game, his ratings would be temporarily boosted, causing more successes.
When a player failed, his ratings would decrease. However, this became a problem.
Player ratings converged to either essential perfection, as successes bred more successes, or complete ineptitude, as failures bred more failures. That system had to be
tweaked; the smallest change could spiral out of control, creating perfect passers or
punters who could not hit the broad side of a barn. In the final product, the feature's
effect was tuned down to look significant to the player, but the probabilities affected
were only slightly nudged. The essential nature of the positive feedback dynamic was
never addressed. This problem is endemic to many sports games, as "stat boosts" seem
to be the only reward structure worth pursuing.

Positive feedback is not always bad. For one, it helps direct player actions. Players want
to become richer and more powerful, so giving them rewards for succeeding makes
sense. It also breaks stalemates. Consider a game such as the card game *War* in which
the player with the highest card value wins. It's entirely random, so on average, each
player should win 50 percent of the time. A series of *War* games will always be in stalemate. No previous game affects the current game. But if the design added a positive
feedback loop that changed this dynamic, the game could progress toward an end state.
Say that players get to turn over an additional card if they won the last hand and can
add that new card to their total. This gives the winning player an advantage that should
cause a positive feedback loop that leads to an end-game state where one player has a
distinct advantage over the other and can be decided the winner. I am not saying that
this will make *War* fun, but it can end the thing.

Always be vigilant to ensure positive feedback loops don't get out of hand.

Negative Feedback Loops

Negative feedback loops in games are mechanics that hinder succeeding players from further success or failing players from further failures. The classic example is *Mario Kart 64*.

Mario Kart 64 is a racing game in which players have weapons that they can use to
speed themselves up or to hinder the progress of their opponents. In this installment of
the *Mario Kart* series, Nintendo added the blue shell weapon. The blue shell is the

ultimate negative feedback loop. It hones in and destroys the player in first place no matter where they are on the race track. There is little the first-place player can do to avoid this. The appearance of the blue shell is almost inevitable—almost every race has one. It's always on the mind of the first-place player. Succeeding players are punished—no one wants to be too far ahead of the pack because the blue shell will knock them back. Instead, it encourages a dynamic where players want to be in second place until the final parts of the race—safe from blue shells but also close enough to take the lead before the finish.

Many sports, such as football and basketball, use negative feedback. You need the ball to score, but after a score, the opponent receives the ball. This allows the opposing team a higher probability of responding with a score of their own, keeping the game close. If the team that just scored receives the ball again, they can score over and over, destabilizing the game.

Negative feedback is dangerous because it sends mixed signals. You direct players to succeed—win the race, kill the bad guys, and so forth—but at the same time, the negative feedback mechanics do not agree with the stated goals if you punish your players for striving toward those goals. The goal of *Mario Kart* players is to outrace their opponents. However, the blue shell punishes those who achieve the goals. This is the type of dissonance that is dangerous when you implement negative feedback.

Some racing games suffer from this problem. Since most racing games are more interesting when you are jockeying for position with other cars, if a player does too well and leaves the pack behind, the artificial intelligence (AI) will cheat and make the opponents go supernaturally fast to catch up with the lead player, which encourages more nail-biting racing. This essentially punishes the player for succeeding, which goes against all the other mechanics in many of these games that are tailored to reward the player for racing well. Players are almost unanimously against this technique—do a search in racing game reviews for "rubber-band AI" and you'll see universal disdain. So designers are faced with a conundrum—have no "rubber banding" and let skilled players race off into the distance (effectively racing time trials), or have the AI cheat to make the race more exciting.

Even relatively simple games can use negative feedback. In the trivia game *Buzz!*, the player in first place never gets to select the trivia category. The player who is selecting should naturally try to pick something that she knows the leader does not know, and thus this should serve as negative reinforcement.

Eight-ball pool is another example of a particularly elegant negative feedback loop. The player who is behind has more balls left on the table to choose from and so has a better chance of having an "easy shot" lined up. The player in the lead is also encumbered by the trailing players' remaining balls; the trailing player does not have to deal with as many of the opponent's obstacles.

Feedback Loops in Action

Feedback loops can come in four forms: two for creating positive feedback and two for creating negative feedback. These can be combined in a number of ways.

Positive Feedback Loop Methods

The first of two methods for creating a positive feedback loop is to reward success. The simulation results in **FIGURE 17.2** shows how this affects the game over time. In the simulation, each player starts with an identical probability of success. Each trial then adjusts the probability of future successes back on the feedback loop method. In this one, the player's probability of success increases whenever he has a success.

Positive Feedback: Reward Success

Score

Time

FIGURE 17.2
A simulation wherein positive feedback is achieved by rewarding success. Early victories cause increasing leads.

In the simulation, the red player gets off to some early successes, which allow her an increased chance of having future successes. The blue player has early failures, however. This allows the red player to pull ahead and have an ever-increasing gap between herself and her opponent. Blue will have a difficult time catching up.

The second way of implementing positive feedback is to punish failure, which shows results similar to rewarding success. In this simulation, if the player has a failure, his odds of success are reduced (**FIGURE 17.3**). Since both players start from a point where they have the same chance of success, they both seem to stay close over time. However, the positive feedback adds up for the blue player, who plateaus earlier than the red player. These plateaus happen because failures eventually push the player's probability of success so low that it becomes very unlikely that he will succeed. Because of earlier victories, that plateau happens later for the red player.

You aren't limited to using one method or the other. Many games both reward success and punish failure. This happens most often in zero-sum games where resources shift from player to player on a success. An example is *Heads Up Poker*. When a player wins a hand, she gains money and her opponent loses money. This means the winning player is rewarded for success and the losing player is punished for failure. This accelerates the differences between the two players (**FIGURE 17.4**).

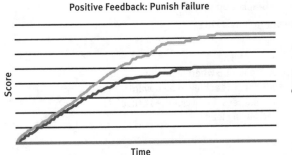

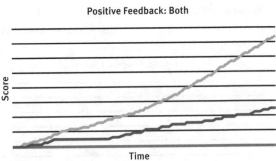

FIGURE 17.3 A simulation wherein positive feedback is achieved by punishing failure. Early failures lead to increasing leads for the player who does not fail.

FIGURE 17.4 A simulation wherein positive feedback is achieved by both rewarding success and punishing failure. Winners of early trials gain a gigantic advantage.

Negative Feedback Loop Methods

Negative feedback loops work to moderate differences between players and can similarly be achieved in two ways: by rewarding failure and punishing success. In both cases, players stay close together, changing leads back and forth. In cases where both methods are employed, as in *Mario Kart 64*, this creates a higher possibility of lead swapping (**FIGURES 17.5–17.7**).

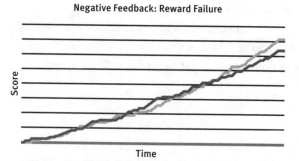

FIGURE 17.5 A simulation wherein negative feedback is achieved by rewarding failure. Scores remain close; however, players are incentivized to not play at their best.

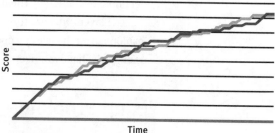

FIGURE 17.6 A simulation wherein negative feedback was achieved by punishing success. A pattern similar to rewarding failure emerges.

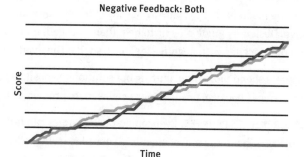

FIGURE 17.7 A simulation using both techniques to achieve negative feedback.

Mixing Feedback Methods

Many games pair positive feedback with negative feedback:

- In the card game *Dominion*, players must collect victory cards to win. But victory cards have no other purpose and thus slow down the player's ability to perform actions with his cards on his turn. Thus, the player has to balance between acquiring cards that give him more power and cards that will eventually allow him to win the game.

- In the board game *The Settlers of Catan*, players who have the most resources can build the most victory-point yielding buildings or cards. But since trading is a large portion of the game, players tend not to trade with players who are clearly in the lead. Thus, players who are not comfortably in the lead have an advantage that the leader does not have.

- In the *Civilization* series, players who attempt a science victory gain access to more technologies that help them advance in the game, including amassing more technologies. Players who are further behind in technology can use less-expensive espionage on the leading civilizations, which gives them a bonus to make up for their early disadvantage.

Fixing Problems

Positive feedback loops occur naturally for a simple reason: Players direct themselves toward actions that make them stronger. In RPGs, they buy swords that let them kill bigger creatures that drop better loot that allow them to buy even better swords. Nothing is inherently wrong with that, but it can cause problems. Negative feedback loops are much harder to come by because they can be simply contradictory and nonintuitive. Designers guide players to help them succeed, and then they sabotage them behind the scenes with negative feedback so that the result of succeeding is bad.

Designers spend more time figuring out solutions to positive feedback situations than negative ones because positive loops cause more problems:

- **POOR INTEREST CURVES.** Even single-player games can fall victim to poor interest curves. What if the player spends all her time trying to level up instead of exploring all the great content you have for her? What if the drops she gets from leveling up make the rest of the game too easy? How can you reward the player with one hand and take it away with the other so that she keeps progressing through the game?

- **PROBLEMS OF BALANCE.** Multiplayer games need to use positive feedback sparingly. If the entire game is decided by the time the first winning move enters the positive feedback loop (such as in the first kill in *Quake II*), then other players may wonder why they should play the rest of the game. In such cases, the loser is continually beaten by the first winner, and without the hope of winning himself, he is probably not having much fun.

- **ENDGAME PROBLEMS.** *World of Warcraft* has a problem. Players get stronger and stronger, but the game can only offer a finite amount of content. Eventually, the player has to reach the strongest sword in the game. At that point, players cannot be directed to kill bigger bad guys for the purpose of better drops that have better stats. The designers have to deal with the problem of "what to give the player who has everything." Naturally, they have done a good job overall because they have a healthy base of players at the maximum level, but this problem exists only because of the positive feedback loops in the game itself.

An additional reason to root out positive feedback loops is that close games are more exciting for both the winners and the losers.[1] In one study, participants bet on simulated horse races and then rated them for personal entertainment value. The close races were rated as more interesting. Even for players who bet on a horse that took an early lead and sustained that lead (thus having a monetary reason to find the race compelling), the close races were more enjoyable.

One technique you can use to fix positive feedback so it does not get out of control is to *decouple* what the reward affects and what the goals require. *FarmVille* and other social games are all about walking up a treadmill to get the next doodad. But, generally, the doodads in these games are not things that help the player succeed. Often they are cosmetic or tangential. For instance, although the harvester in *FarmVille* allows the player to harvest in fewer clicks, it does not make the plants grow faster. The reward is reinforcing the click-to-harvest mechanic and not the XP-gaining growth mechanic. Thus, players can lust over the harvester and harvest like silly without breaking the game. This is a fine technique, but it is not perfect because the player has to desire a reward of something other than what will give him more power to achieve. Thus, it can be applied in only some situations.

Often, if the positive reinforcement is knocking the game out of balance and the designer cannot simply remove the offending mechanic, the best solution is to pair positive reinforcements with negative ones. RPGs do this: When a player levels up, monsters also become tougher. So the player gets stronger, but her enemies do as well, likely at the same rate. The power increase is positive feedback. The enemy's increase is negative feedback. This would be noticeable to players if put that explicitly, so what designers do is allow the player to really beat up on some lower-level thugs after powering up; this gets them feeling more invincible before they are thrown against newly beefed-up baddies in the next level. But this has to be carefully balanced.

In *The Elder Scrolls III: Morrowind*, players could choose to level up and if they did so, stronger baddies and increased player stats would appear instantly. However, a player could stay as a level 1 player for as long as he chose. The quest items that the game gave did not care about the player's level and got better and better as the game progressed, even if the player's level did not increase. If a player chose to stay at level 1, it meant that the game never threw harder enemies at the player while, at the same time, it gave better and better items as the game progressed. After all, why should the player make the game harder for himself? Certainly, it was not what the designers intended, but many players chose that path.

. . . .

1   Reid, R. L. (1986). "The Psychology of the Near Miss." *Journal of Gambling Behavior*, 2(1), 32–39.

"Fixing" positive feedback does not even have to really fix the problem—only the appearance of a problem. The National Football League (NFL) saw the same positive feedback problem that Major League Baseball (MLB) experiences and added negative reinforcements—salary caps (limits on how much a team can spend on personnel) and reverse draft selection (the worst team gets the first chance to choose the best players coming out of the collegiate system.) This is generally seen as more fair. However, from 1967–2014 in MLB, which does not have salary caps and whose draft is less important, the top four teams (Yankees, Cardinals, Athletics, Giants) combined won 39 percent (18/46) of all world championships. In the NFL during the same period, the four winningest Super Bowl teams (Steelers, Cowboys, 49ers, Packers) combine for 43 percent (20/47) of all Super Bowls. Although professional football's system is widely considered to be more egalitarian, the concentration of top teams is not significantly different.

Summary

- Positive feedback loops reward the player for success and/or punish the player for failure. This can cause an imbalance between players.

- Negative feedback loops reward the player for failure and/or punish the player for success. This can be demotivating by directing players away from the behaviors that lead to the goals of the game.

- One of the issues with feedback loops is that it overweighs the importance of earlier successes or failures, thereby making later actions in the game less meaningful with regard to the goal of the game.

- Positive and negative feedback loops can be paired to mitigate some feedback loop problems.

- Additionally, a key way to avoid destabilizing positive feedback loop problems is to decouple the reward from any effects that may influence future success. Finding a decoupled reward that the player still desires can be challenging.

18 Puzzle Design

> It is one of man's curious idiosyncrasies to create difficulties for the pleasure of resolving them.
>
> **—JOSEPH DIE MAISTRE**

Puzzles have been an essential part of games since early in the dawn of play. Much like how in today's video-game market shooters are the *genre du jour*, at one time the best-selling genre was the text adventure. In text adventures, the primary antagonist was a series of puzzles. Many modern games, such as *Portal* or *Tomb Raider*, have environmental puzzles that players are required to solve to continue in the story's progression. The iOS game *The Room* was at the top of the sales charts for a number of weeks in 2012, selling over a million units despite being entirely made up of a series of puzzles.

What Is a Puzzle?

Designer Scott Kim uses this definition of what exactly qualifies as a puzzle:[1]

> A puzzle is fun and it has a right answer.

The two parts of this definition are important. The first part identifies puzzles as play, whereas the second part distinguishes puzzles from other forms of play, such as games and make-believe. "Fun" is subjective, but having a "right answer" is objective. A puzzle does not have to have exactly one right answer. It can have multiple right answers, but it must have at least one.

Scott Kim's definition is attractive for its simplicity, but it suffers as a critical examination because of how wide open to interpretation it can be. Let's take a look at a less succinct but perhaps more instrumental definition.

A puzzle is a type of game that requires the player to use cognitive effort to get from an unsolved state to a solved state, with some limitations:

- **THE PUZZLE CANNOT BE TRIVIAL.** If a puzzle is given as "Turn on the lights," and you can just flip a switch to do so, then it requires no cognitive effort to complete and is thus trivial. In the same way, *Tic-Tac-Toe* is not a puzzle for any adult because the average adult can solve it and tie or win as long as he goes first. This does make the definition of a puzzle subjective for the audience it covers, but making a trivial puzzle and saying it's for toddlers is a cop-out to avoid having to make a puzzle intellectually interesting.

- **THE PUZZLE MUST INVOLVE REASONED EFFORT TO GO FROM UNSOLVED TO SOLVED.** If the only way to solve a puzzle is by brute force, it is not a puzzle. "I am thinking of a number from 1 to 64. What is it?" is not a puzzle if the only feedback given is "yes" or "no." However, if the feedback given allows the player to use reasoned intellectual effort or what Marcel Danesi calls "insight thinking" to figure out the answer, then it may be a puzzle.[2]

- **SOLVING THE PUZZLE MUST BE THE SAME AS WINNING THE GAME.** *Checkers* is a "solved" game mathematically, but solving *Checkers* is a different intellectual exercise than winning the game. The goal of solving *Checkers* is to create a strategy that always wins, but winning *Checkers* is about jumping all the opponent's pieces. In contrast, solving a jigsaw puzzle is the same as completing the jigsaw puzzle.

. . . .

1   Scott Kim attributes this definition to Stan Isaacs: www.scottkim.com.previewc40.carrierzone.com/thinkinggames/whatisapuzzle/index.html.

2   Danesi, M. (2002). *The Puzzle Instinct: The Meaning of Puzzles in Human Life*. Bloomington, IL: Indiana University Press.

- **THE PUZZLE CAN BE GENERATED RANDOMLY, BUT MUST BE DETERMINISTIC ONCE THE PLAYER ENCOUNTERS IT.** A board of *Sudoku* can be generated randomly (with constraints), but once individual players start the puzzle, every player who makes the same series of moves experiences the puzzle in exactly the same way. Puzzles do not require luck or dexterity to solve. If two players encounter the same *Minesweeper* board and uncover the same squares in the same order, those players have identical experiences. However, if two players play tennis against each other and make the exact same movements, those players have a decidedly different game experience.

These four features and Scott Kim's definition help to determine what a puzzle is. Is filing Federal taxes a puzzle? No, because it is not played as a game. Is *Tetris* a puzzle? No, because it is not deterministic. Are riddles puzzles? Yes, most are, as long as they are not trivial and do not require brute force. Is a whodunit mystery a puzzle? It can be if it meets all the criteria.

If you remember the discussion on formalism and defining games from Chapter 1, you may be surprised at the rigid structure given to what constitutes a puzzle. As always, the point of a definition is to ensure that you are applying the correct heuristics to a problem. The point of defining puzzles as I do here is to ensure that we are using the same language to examine the same elements. There very well may be puzzles that do not meet these criteria yet are still commonly understood to be puzzles. That is fine. The criteria I have been discussing here suit us for this examination of the role and design of puzzles.

Puzzles are a particularly transparent use of examining flow and the fundamental game design directive. A puzzle that is too easy ("What is 1+2?") is trivial and leads to boredom. A puzzle that is too difficult ("What is the largest prime number that, when using a Caesar number-to-letter cipher, becomes a single English-language word?") leads to anxiety and frustration. Potential puzzle solvers give up in both cases.

Children often enjoy puzzles and games that are flawed by adult standards because a child's motor skills and ability to reason are limited. Thus, children achieve flow at a lower level of difficulty. Things that are trivial for adults can be frustrating for children.

The key to a great puzzle, like a great game, is to get the solver to experience the flow state. This means that it must not be so hard that the solver does not feel she has the tools available to solve it, and not so easy that it requires no cognitive effort at all. Marcel Danesi, in the book *The Puzzle Instinct* says "[T]he aesthetic index of a puzzle, as it may be called, seems to be inversely proportional to the complexity of its solution or to the obviousness of the pattern, trap, or trick it hides. Simply put, the longer and more complicated the answer to a puzzle, or the more obvious it is, the less appealing the puzzle seems to be." It sounds like he is arguing for flow.

Possibility Space

One of the joys of solving a puzzle is being able to take a problem that has many possible solutions and narrow it down to the one correct solution. The set of possible solutions to a puzzle at a given point in the solving process is known as the *possibility space* of the problem.

As an example, let's look at a logic puzzle:

Zack, Glo, and Rae are about to eat dinner. They can choose from Steak, Salad, and Chicken. But they have the following preferences:

1. Nobody wants the same food.
2. Glo and Rae both want to eat meat.
3. If Rae wants Chicken, then Zack wants Steak.

Who wants which food?"

When you start this problem, the possibility space is large. [Zack→Steak, Glo→Steak, Rae→Steak] is one possible answer, but at this point there are 27 possible solutions.

Now consider the hints. With Hint #1, no one wants the same food. This means the [Zack→Steak, Glo→Steak, Rae→Steak] answer is impossible. It reduces the possibility space to only six:

   [Zack→Steak, Glo→Salad, Rae→Chicken]
   [Zack→Steak, Glo→Chicken, Rae→Salad]
   [Zack→Salad, Glo→Steak, Rae→Chicken]
   [Zack→Salad, Glo→Chicken, Rae→Steak]
   [Zack→Chicken, Glo→Salad, Rae→Steak]
   [Zack→Chicken, Glo→Steak, Rae→Salad]

With Hint #2, you can eliminate any possibility where Glo or Rae wants salad. This reduces the possibility space to two:

   [Zack→Salad, Glo→Steak, Rae→Chicken]
   [Zack→Salad, Glo→Chicken, Rae→Steak]

With Hint #3, you can eliminate the first option in the possibility space. If Rae wants Chicken, then Zack has to want Steak. But you already eliminated any possibility that Zack wanted Steak. Therefore you are down to one, the solution:

[Zack→Salad, Glo→Chicken, Rae→Steak]

This reduction of the possibility space is the process of solving the puzzle. However, it's not always so logically straightforward and transparent.

Breadcrumbs

If the key to making effective puzzles is to get the solver into a flow state, how is that accomplished when different solvers have varied puzzle-solving ability? In the story of "Hansel and Gretel," the protagonists leave a trail of breadcrumbs in the forest in order to find their way back home. This allows them to travel from crumb to crumb (because each is left in visual range of the last) and eventually the trail leads them out of the forest. If they have no breadcrumbs at all, they have to find their way out of the forest on their own. But the task of following the trail still has challenge because they have to find the next breadcrumb. *Puzzle breadcrumbs* are just like that: They are a series of clues that, by logical steps, lead the solver from an unsolved puzzle to a solved puzzle.

These breadcrumbs can be *extrinsic* to the puzzle's structure or they can be *intrinsic*.

Extrinsic Breadcrumbs

Extrinsic breadcrumbs are easier to explain. In the *Professor Layton* series, players are tasked with solving brain teasers. If players get stuck, they can click on a hint button to receive progressively more revealing hints. The first hint is vague, whereas the final hint is generally fairly literal.

In **FIGURE 18.1**, from *Professor Layton and the Unwound Future*, the first hint explains how to use the memo function to make notes on the puzzle itself. This is a pretty light hint, because players of any of the previous games are already aware of this function.

If the player is still stuck, the next hint reminds him that just because the puzzle says the answer is next to a table with a red flower does not mean that the correct answer itself is not a table with a red flower. This hint is an important reminder of logical rules that, at the same time, insinuates that the answer has to do with a red flower.

FIGURE 18.1
Puzzles in the *Professor Layton* series create breadcrumbs using the Hint Coins feature.

The third hint reminds the player that since the tablecloth has to be a different color than those of all the adjacent tables, he can remove from consideration any tables that have adjacent tables with tablecloths of the same color. If the player does this, he will remove every table but one. In fact, the player doesn't even need the hint about needing to be adjacent to a red flower.

The final hint (known as the "super hint" in the *Layton* series) comes right out and says that the answer has a red flower and a red tablecloth.

In this situation, the answer to the puzzle is workable without any hint at all, but each hint gives the player tools to reduce the complexity of the problem.

These extrinsic hints nudge the player in the correct direction and let him reduce the possibility space. Each subsequent hint provides a larger and larger nudge. Someone adept at puzzles may never need a hint, so she stays in flow just by solving the puzzles as is. But someone poor at puzzles may need all the hints to understand the leaps in logic needed to solve them. If only the puzzles with no hints were available, the game may be too frustrating for the poor puzzle-solver. Having the hints progressively reveal more and more brings the player closer and closer to flow. By using all the hints, even the worst puzzle-solvers should be in the realm of understanding the answer.

Intrinsic Breadcrumbs

A different way of providing hints is to make them intrinsic to the puzzle itself. If a puzzle asks for a four-letter word that means "to move around," there can be a number of valid answers (jogs? walk? jump? roll? stir?) or the solver may just be stumped and unable to think of a single valid answer. However, if the design offers the same question as 4-across in the puzzle in **FIGURE 18.2**...

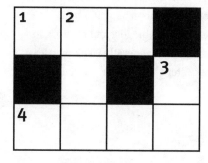

FIGURE 18.2 Crossword puzzles provide breadcrumbs by giving hints in the form of nearby clues the player can solve to unlock letters in other clues.

...then the player can uncover a hint for 4-across by first solving 2-down and 3-down. For instance, say that the answer to 2-down is "Too" and the answer to 3-down is "Am." Since the last letter of 2-down is "O," the solver knows that the second letter of 4-across is "O." Since the last letter of 3-down is "M," she knows the last letter of 4-across is "M." Now instead of being faced with all the possible four-letter words that mean "to move around," she is limited to a four-letter word that means to move around and that fits the scheme "_O_M." Is it possible to solve 4-across now? The player certainly has a better shot than before. The answer for this puzzle is at the end of the section, but the clues to solving it are inside the puzzle itself. This intrinsic hint-giving is used for a number of great puzzles from crosswords, to logic puzzles, to Japanese puzzles such as *Sudoku*, *Kakuro*, and *Nurikabe*.

> ▶ **NOTE** The Japanese magazine, Nikoli, offers well-designed and culturally independent puzzles in a great variety in both print and on its website: www.nikoli.co.jp/en/puzzles. Nikoli helped popularize Sudoku.

The extrinsic method of leaving breadcrumbs is a bit obvious to players and may hurt their pride. In most cases, a breadcrumb system is intrinsic to the puzzle, the player is able to enter flow without having to consciously make any adjustments. The same player who balks at taking a hint in *Layton* likely has no qualms about coming back to a clue after he has revealed some more letters in a crossword.

No Breadcrumbs at All

▶ **NOTE** The answer to the crossword puzzle in Figure 18.2 is "roam."

A type of puzzle that has few or no breadcrumbs is a riddle. In a riddle, the solver generally needs to know the answer to a question that uses a double or hidden meaning. She either knows the answer or does not. The player has no way to work toward the solution in a riddle besides examining the possible hidden meanings on a word-by-word basis. The possibility space is enormous and there are very few cues with which to reduce it. Riddles often require specialized cultural knowledge; as such, riddles rarely cause flow. Either the player knows it, and it becomes trivial, or she cannot reason it, and it becomes impossible. The most effective riddle hides intrinsic breadcrumbs within its wordplay, but most do not offer this affordance and make for generally weak puzzles. Trivia suffers from the same problem. Unless you take steps to mitigate that feature, it can make for a poor puzzle.

Features of Ineffective Puzzles

In 1990, a Stanford researcher did an experiment on a particularly poor puzzle.[3] She had two players and assigned them in pairs as a "tapper" and a "listener." The tapper was to take a well-known song and tap out the rhythm on a table. The listener had to guess the song. Tappers were also asked how often they thought the listener would correctly identify the song. Tappers estimated that 50 percent of listeners would correctly answer. The actual result: 3 successes out of 120 tries or a 2.5 percent success rate!

What went wrong? The tapper served as the designer of the puzzle. She imagined a song and because she imagined it, she had difficulty understanding what it would be like to *not* simultaneously imagine the song along with the tapping. In other words, she had no perspective for the listener's point of view. The tapper could not imagine hearing only the rhythm without the selected tune.

As puzzle designers, we are guilty of being tappers far too often. It is easy for us to envision the solution to the puzzle we created. It is more difficult for players with no perspective to find the solution.

Unfortunately for puzzle designers, there is no formula for the perfect puzzle. However, there are trends that make for bad puzzles that are easy to avoid.

. . . .

3   Newton, E. L. (1990). *The Rocky Road from Actions to Intentions*. Stanford, CA: Stanford University.

Incomplete Critical Information/Missed Assumptions

If the player does not know what his goal is or what he can manipulate in the puzzle, he will ignore any breadcrumb you leave him. If Dorothy does not know that the Wizard is at the end of the Yellow Brick Road and that he is within walking distance, then the road itself is worthless to her. This scenario most often happens in puzzles, not because the designer leaves something out on purpose, but usually because the designer knows exactly what to do because she created the puzzle. By playtesting your puzzles with real players and seeing where they struggle, you can avoid not communicating assumptions. Having playtesters think out their puzzle-solving process aloud also clues you in on areas or cues you have missed that are essential to the player for him to successfully complete the puzzle.

Lack of Ability to Experiment

Famed designer Warren Spector has a great rule of thumb for designing puzzles. He says that a key before a locked door is much less interesting than a locked door before a key. This is because seeing a locked door without having a means to open it poses a puzzle to the player: "How do I get in there? Maybe a guard has a key? Or are there key codes on that computer?" A locked door where the key has already been collected poses no alternative futures at all. The player does not have to form a hypothesis.

To be in flow, players have to be able to receive and use feedback to get them away from states of frustration. If the player cannot manipulate the puzzle itself to see if a solution is correct or not, then she finds it difficult to understand how the puzzle works and is not able to make the cognitive leaps that gets her closer and closer to solving the puzzle.

Games that don't allow players to manipulate their pieces before the games are complete can cause players great frustration. Additionally, puzzles that allow manipulation but don't allow the player to reset the board when he makes a mistake also work against his need to experiment because he fears moving pieces into the wrong positions or not being able to mentally remember all the puzzle's moving parts. Finally, puzzles that penalize the player for experimenting (sending him back to earlier levels or giving him a "time out") also work against getting him into flow.

Brute Force

Consider this puzzle:

> "I'm thinking of a number from 1 to 100.
>
> Is it 1?
>
> No.
>
> Is it 2?
>
> No.
>
> Is it 3?"

This is not fun at all. Instead of using cognitive skills to solve the problem, the player must simply exhaust the whole possibility space. This is the case for many riddles, memory games, and simple children's puzzles. Even word searches allow the player to solve the puzzle with a kind of algorithm rather than having to check every letter from every direction.

Memory games are a special instance of brute-force puzzles. If the player has not uncovered a symbol she has already seen, then the puzzle is completely brute force since she has no way to know which tile she should choose over any other tile. Once the player has uncovered a previously seen symbol, the only puzzle element becomes apparent: "Where did I last see that symbol?" In most instances, this is a trivial question. Remember that in flow, the optimal state needs to be more challenging than trivial, but less challenging than frustrating.

Triviality Surrounded by Complexity

Most mazes fill this criterion. In a maze, what decisions are the players facing? Usually, the player's options are restricted to going left, going forward, or going right. If the player chooses one of those options and ends up at a dead end, he retraces his steps back to his last decision and chooses a different option. Most mazes have many junctions that require decision-making, but that decision-making is almost always blind, and thus it never requires any ingenuity. Although the maze itself looks complicated, it's usually solved by a simple algorithm (**FIGURE 18.3**).

Some game puzzles work in a similar manner, surrounding the player with a lot of red herrings even though he can solve the puzzle in a simple and straightforward way. Adding all the red herrings makes the puzzle look substantial, but it doesn't make the puzzle better.

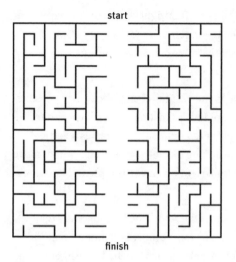

start

finish

FIGURE 18.3 A complex maze with a trivial solution.

Lack of Possibility Space

The absolute worst puzzle is the obvious puzzle. The obvious puzzle may have a lot of features, but it always points to one and only one possible answer (**FIGURE 18.4**). The best puzzles lead players down a path that eventually teaches them that there are different ways to think about the problem.

$$1 + 1 = ???$$

FIGURE 18.4
A puzzle with little possibility space.

Terry Cavanaugh's now-defunct site freeindiegam.es discovered an ingenious Japanese puzzle game named *Jelly no Puzzle* (**FIGURE 18.5**).

▶ **NOTE** Jelly no Puzzle is a free Windows download at http://qrostar.skr.jp/index. cgi?page=jelly&lang=en. There is a partial HTML5 port at http://martine.github.io/jelly.

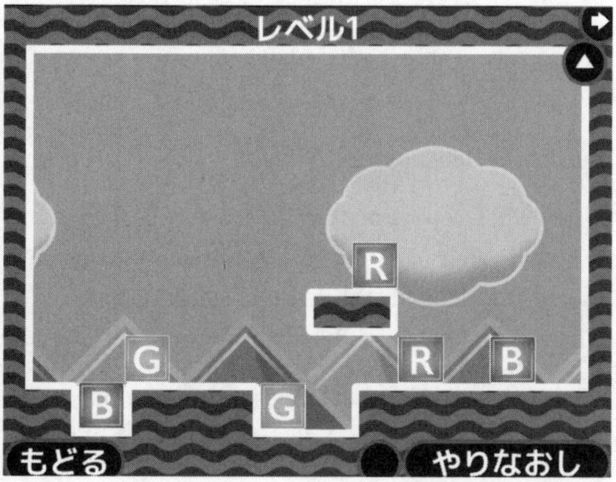

FIGURE 18.5 *Jelly no Puzzle* has some of the finest spatial puzzles ever designed.

レベル1

もどる   やりなおし

In the first level, the objective is to move the blocks left or right so that all blocks of a particular color touch (in Figure 18.5, B = blue, G = green, R = red). Gravity causes any block to fall that is not being held up. Blocks of the same color that touch lock together and become rigid.

What makes *Jelly no Puzzle* fiendishly difficult is the vast number of seemingly possible solutions that turn out to be dead ends. In Figure 18.5 for instance, the player can try moving the top red block down on top of the other red one, but that creates a vertical pillar that forbids her from moving the rightmost blue block. Likewise, she cannot move the leftmost green block to the right or it creates a rigid green vertical pillar, also trapping the blue block to the right.

Eventually, using trial and error and thinking about the setup, the player notices that since the leftmost blue block is locked into place, she must bring the rightmost blue block to it. But this causes new problems! The blue block must get to the left, but a red block and a green block are in the way. Since there is no way to pick up a block, the player must find two "hiding spaces" for those blocks in order to get the blue block free access across the screen. One of those spaces is obvious: the gully in the middle of the screen. Where can the other one be? And what block should she put in the gully? One option is to move the leftmost green block over to the right. This creates a vertical 1×2 green block. However, this prohibits the player from moving the blocks to the right. So should she try to make a horizontal green 1×2 in the gully or put a red with the green down there?

As you can see, this puzzle offers a lot of avenues for thought. Although *Jelly no Puzzle* is inaccessible for a number of reasons (it is quite difficult, offers little in the way of introduction, and is currently only in Japanese), it does show the depth of thought that well-designed puzzles suggest. The possibility space of *Jelly no Puzzle* is large, but the designers achieve that large space with a limited number of pieces and a possibility space that can be whittled down by simple mechanics.

Arbitrariness

> "Yeah, that's a right answer, but not *the* right answer...."

This is a problem novices often run into when coding puzzles. Instead of checking to see if all the logical solutions cause the win state, they check only the solution they first see as being correct. Thus, the player has to get inside the designer's head to find out the "true" solution, even if her original solution was valid. Here's an example:

By clicking on the grid, you can fill in squares. The author here gives you the clue: "18th letter." The 18th letter in the alphabet is R, so the player draws an R. Which of the following is correct (**FIGURE 18.6**)?

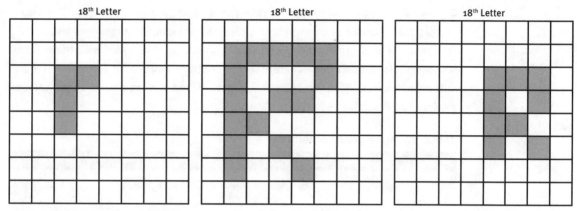

FIGURE 18.6 There are many ways to draw an R with pixels. Which is right?

To the player, all three would be correct. All are representations of the letter R. But if the designer coded for only one possible set of squares to be the "right" R, then any player not able to read the designer's mind would be thinking that he solved the puzzle correctly given the clues, but yet would not able to continue. The player should never have to guess at what the "best" right answer is.

Types of Puzzles

Generally, I avoid taxonomies because they often have arbitrarily declared boundaries and are often incomplete. However, Marcel Danesi's work in *The Puzzle Instinct* provides numerous good examples of puzzles from which game designers can draw inspiration.

Danesi breaks logic puzzles into four types: deduction puzzles, truth puzzles, deception puzzles, and paradoxes.

Deduction Puzzles

Deduction puzzles require the solver to draw conclusions based on a given set of facts. Danesi breaks this type of puzzle into four subtypes: deductions, set-theoretical puzzles, relational puzzles, and inferential puzzles.

Deduction

"Zack, Gloriana, and Christa just finished a three-player board game in which there were no ties. Zack scored one spot higher than his wife. Christa did not come in second. The oldest player came in third. Zack is older than his wife. In what place did each player finish?"

Representing the possibility space of this type of puzzle as a table is helpful; that way you can mark impossible combinations with an X and certain combinations with an O (**TABLE 18.1**). For instance, you know that Zack scored higher than his wife; this means it's impossible for him to have come in third since there would be no lower place for his wife to have scored. Also, you know that Christa did not come in second, so you can put an X in that possibility as well.

TABLE 18.1 Puzzle Deduction Matrix

Player	First Place	Second Place	Third Place
Zack			X
Gloriana			
Christa		X	

Now you do not yet know who Zack's wife is or who the oldest player is (although you know it is not Zack), so you cannot mark those off. What are the remaining possibilities? Zack could have come in first, so call this Case 1. In this case, Gloriana must be Zack's wife because his wife would have to come in second, and you know Christa did not come in second.

The other case (Case 2) is that Zack came in second. In this case, his wife would come in third because she scored one rank lower. In Case 2, you don't know the identity of the wife. However, you do know that the oldest player came in third. Since you know that Zack is older than his wife, his wife cannot be the oldest player, and thus she cannot be the player who came in third, because in Case 2, Zack's wife must have come in third. Thus, you can throw out Case 2. This eliminates the possibility that Zack was second. The answer must be that Zack was first, Gloriana was second, Christa was third, and Gloriana is Zack's wife. No other combination meets all the requirements.

Sudoku puzzles are a type of abstract deduction puzzle.

Set-Theoretical

A *set-theoretical puzzle* focuses on the relationships between groups, often takes a form resembling syllogisms, and can be represented by Venn diagrams. Many probability problems take this form. However, the example Danesi cites from author Lewis Carroll is a perfect example of the form: "What can you conclude from the following statements?"

1. Babies are illogical.

2. Nobody is despised who can manage a crocodile.

3. Illogical persons are despised.

You can draw a Venn diagram to help solve this (**FIGURE 18.7**). First you draw a box for the despised and a box for the not despised. Because of criterion number 3, you know that illogical people are despised, so the set of all illogical people must be contained within the despised box. From criterion 1, you know that the set of all babies must be contained within the set of illogical people, so you draw a circle for babies within the circle for the illogical. Statement 2 makes you draw the set of all croc-managers inside the not-despised box.

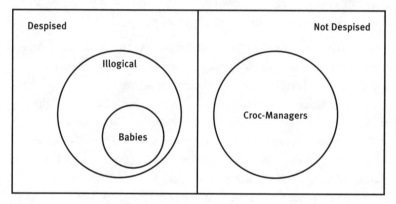

FIGURE 18.7
Carroll's puzzle.

From this, what additional information not clearly laid out in the problem can you conclude? The set of babies does not overlap anywhere with the set of crocodile handlers, thus no baby can manage crocodiles. This was Carroll's answer. Additionally, you could answer that no croc-manager is illogical.

Relational

Relational puzzles are similar to set-theoretical puzzles in that they focus on the relationship of elements within the puzzle. The archetypical example of this is the surgeon puzzle:

A father and son are in a car crash. The father dies instantly. The son is driven to the hospital for emergency surgery. As the son is about to go under the knife, the entering surgeon exclaims "I cannot operate on him; he is my son!" How can this be?

This riddle trips up solvers because the father and son relationship is established earlier in the problem. The answer is, of course, that the surgeon is the boy's mother. Before you decry the problem to be an artifact of cultural gender biases, you should know that a study investigating this very puzzle found that factors like an answerer's education level, exposure to female doctors, or even a battery of tests rating their level of sexism were all irrelevant as to whether that person could solve the riddle.[4]

Inferential

Inferential puzzles require the solver to use inference to figure out the solution. These puzzles can be fairly tricky. In their general form, they require the player to throw out an obvious case, which creates a new obvious case, and so on, until only one case remains. The classic example, which has spawned an entire subfield of puzzle research, is the "prisoners and hats problem" or the "King's Wise Men":

> The King called the three wisest men in the country to his court to decide who would become his new advisor. He placed a hat on each of their heads, such that each wise man could see all the other hats, but none of them could see their own. Each hat was either white or blue. The king gave his word to the wise men that at least one of them was wearing a blue hat—in other words, there could be one, two, or three blue hats, but not zero. The king also announced that the contest would be fair to all three men. The wise men were also forbidden to speak to each other. The king declared that whichever man stood up first and announced (correctly) the color of his own hat would become his new advisor. The wise men sat for a very long time before one stood up and correctly announced the answer. What did he say, and how did he work it out?

Since the king said that there would not be zero blue hats, then the only possible cases are one blue hat, two blue hats, and three blue hats.

If it is the case that there is one blue hat, then there must be two white hats. In this case, whichever person sees two white hats can instantly stand up and say that he has a blue hat. But the other two players do not have that information, each seeing only a white hat and a blue hat, and thus they can make no deductions at all. This scenario goes against the king's assertion that the contest is fair to everyone. Thus, there cannot be only one blue hat, and all three participants should know that.

....

4   Wapman, M. (2014) "Riddle Me This." Retrieved July 24, 2015, from http://mikaelawapman.com/2014/07/03/riddle-me-this/.

If there are two blue hats, then any player who sees a white hat knows that he himself is not wearing a white hat. Why? Because if he sees a white hat, the only way he can be wearing a white hat is if there is only one blue hat. But the previous analysis found that there could not be only one blue hat. However, this scenario gives an advantage to the players who are wearing blue hats. The player wearing the white hat sees only blue hats and cannot know whether his hat is blue or white. Thus, it is unfair to him and it violates the king's rule.

Therefore, the only way for there to be at least one blue hat and for the contest to be fair to all participants is for there to be three blue hats. In this case, each player can stand up and say they have a blue hat.

Truth Puzzles

Truth puzzles require a special kind of deductive reasoning, which concerns the consistency of true or false statements. Danesi breaks these puzzles into two types—one of which is about identifying which statements are true, and one of which is about determining the class of participants—but the distinction is not important for the scope of this writing. These often take the form of detective stories like the following:

> In a distant land, there are two tribes: liars and truth-tellers. Liars always lie and truth-tellers always tell the truth. You meet three people from this land, Mark, Zack, and Glo. Mark says: "All of us are liars." Glo says, "No, only one of us is a truth-teller." Zack says nothing. What are their tribes?

If Mark is telling the truth, then he is violating his own statement. Thus, Mark cannot be telling the truth. Mark is from the liars tribe. So if he is a liar, then there is at least one truth-teller.

If Glo is lying, then there cannot be exactly one truth-teller. But since you have already established that Mark is a liar, if Glo is also a liar, then that leaves Zack as the one and only truth-teller, which is contradictory, because you are assuming Glo is a liar yet is also telling the truth. And all three cannot be liars because that would make Mark's statement true. Since Mark is a liar, this cannot be. Thus, Glo must be a truth-teller.

Since Glo is a truth-teller, there must be exactly one truth-teller. Since that is Glo, you know Zack is a liar.

Deception Puzzles

A *deception puzzle* exploits the ambiguity of language to attempt to direct the solver down a nonproductive path. These puzzles are problematic for game designers because they rely on designers tricking the players. This is dangerous because it risks the player exiting a flow state when he reaches a dead end. Thus, while interesting as thought experiments, I do not see deception puzzles as workable in games.

> ▶ **NOTE** Because of the ambiguity of the riddle, though, there could be multiple answers. Maybe he met the man and his entourage at a fork and joined them on the road? They could have possibly been going to St. Ives; the riddle does not say that they were met in opposing directions.

An example of this would be the classic riddle about the man going to St. Ives:

As I was going to St. Ives,

I met a man with seven wives,

Each wife had seven sacks,

Each sack had seven cats,

Each cat had seven kits:

Kits, cats, sacks, and wives,

How many were there going to St. Ives?

The answer here is one, the narrator. The trick is in deceiving the solver to try to solve a puzzle that is not the puzzle in question.

Paradoxes

Paradoxes are logical puzzles that lead to logical inconsistencies and thus often do not have solutions. An example would be a game designer saying that "all game designers are liars." If that were true, then the statement "all game designers are liars" would both be true (by assumption) and false (by implication).

For game designers, this is clearly problematic because we want the player to succeed enough that she enters a flow state. If we design a puzzle we know has no clear solution, then we are eliminating any possible way for the player to reach flow by design.

Paradoxes are interesting thought experiments, but they have little direct applicability to games. That is not to say paradoxes are just curiosities. Zeno's paradox says that for a runner to finish a race, he must first run half the distance. Then, to finish the second-half, he must run half that distance first. Then, to finish the final quarter, he must first run half that distance, and so on and so on *ad infinitum*. Thus, since there is always another half to run, a runner must never be able to finish a race. This boggled the minds of many great thinkers for centuries until it became one of the inspirational problems behind the invention of modern calculus.

Other Puzzle Types

Of course, myriad other types of puzzles exist outside Danesi's logic puzzles. I'll discuss some examples.

Critical Path Puzzles

Critical path puzzles ask the solver to find a valid path through a process. Mazes, of course, are a kind of critical path puzzle, but they provide flow only to the very young. A better example of a critical path is the river-crossing puzzle in which a farmer needs to cross a river with a wolf, a sheep, and a cabbage but can carry only one item at a time. If he leaves the sheep alone with the cabbage, the cabbage will be eaten. Likewise, if he leaves the sheep alone with the wolf, the sheep will be eaten. The problem can be solved in seven specific steps as I show momentarily, but the difficulty is in understanding that the farmer must bring one of the objects back to the wrong side of the river. This step, which seems to go against the goal, is necessary to solve the problem. Video games often employ this puzzle when they ask players to find a safe route through a maze of enemies.

The River Crossing Puzzle Solution

The farmer (F), the wolf (W), the sheep (S), and the cabbage (C) all start on the wrong side of the river:

FWSC—RIVER

1. The farmer takes the sheep over to the other side of the river. This leaves the wolf with the cabbage, which is OK.

WC—RIVER—FS

2. The farmer returns. This leaves the sheep alone, which is OK.

FWC—RIVER—S

3. The farmer takes one of the other elements over. It doesn't matter which, so in this example, the farmer takes the wolf. This leaves the cabbage alone, which is OK because cabbage is generally shy anyway.

C—RIVER—FWS

4. The farmer cannot leave the wolf and sheep alone, so he must take one back. Since he just brought the wolf over, taking it back would return the puzzle's state back to where it was in step 2. Instead, he takes the sheep back. This leaves the wolf alone.

FSC—RIVER—W

5. If, after returning to the wrong side of the river, the farmer turns around and takes the sheep back, this would return the puzzle to the state it was in step 4. If the farmer takes nothing, the sheep will eat the cabbage. Instead, the farmer takes the cabbage. This leaves the sheep alone.

S—RIVER—FWC

6. The farmer can leave the wolf and the cabbage alone (he already has once before on the wrong shore).

FS—RIVER—WC

7. Now, he can take the sheep across.

RIVER—FWSC

Strategy Puzzles

Strategy puzzles are a class of puzzle in which the player is expected to devise a strategy to solve the problem instead of simply coming up with a specific answer. A particularly clever example is the light bulbs and prisoners problem. In it, a warden tells a group of 100 prisoners that every day he'll take one of them, at random, for questioning in a room that contains a chair and a light bulb. The light bulb will start as turned off and no one other than the prisoners can touch it. At the start of questioning the prisoner can either turn the light bulb on or off and it will remain that way until the next prisoner is questioned. At the end of each questioning session, the prisoner is allowed to ask to leave prison. If every prisoner has already been questioned, when a prisoner asks to leave, then all are released from prison. However, if any prisoners have not yet been questioned, all will be executed. The prisoners are given one day to interact in the general population before the questioning starts; when it begins, all prisoners are isolated so they cannot communicate. What strategy should the prisoners use to guarantee their release?

There are many solutions to this puzzle, but one is that one prisoner should be assigned to be the leader. When any prisoner is questioned, if it is her first time being questioned, she turns on the light. Otherwise, she does nothing. When the leader is questioned, if the light is on, he turns it off and makes a note of it. When he turns the light off 99 times, he knows that every other prisoner has been questioned and he can then ask to be free to go. This works because the light is only on if a new prisoner has been questioned. If a new prisoner has been questioned 99 times, then everyone but the leader has been questioned.

Although this puzzle is more complicated than most found in games, games often dynamically form strategy puzzles for players. The game-design danger in this is that once a strategy is deduced, if it can always work, then the player can apply the solution by rote and will no longer be challenged, which kicks the player out of the flow state.

Algebraic Puzzles

Algebraic puzzles require a careful application of algebra to solve. Although these are easy to create, they must be carefully balanced against a player's symbolic reasoning skills. These problems are difficult for inducing flow, perhaps because even when they are designed well, they remind players of bad school experiences. The best algebraic puzzles still require that shift in perspective that makes the player say, "Aha!" rather than a simple arrangement of variables.

Here's an example:

In ten years, Zack will be twice as old as he was 12 years ago. How old is Zack today?

$Z + 10 = 2 * (Z - 12)$

$Z + 10 = 2Z - 24$

$Z + 34 = 2Z$

$34 = Z$

Physical Manipulation Puzzles

Physical manipulation puzzles are a wide class that includes tangram puzzles, *Rubik's Cubes*, and jigsaw puzzles. They involve spatial reasoning to manipulate a physical structure into a certain form. One example is the class of problems known as matchstick puzzles.

In the matchstick puzzle in **FIGURE 18.8**, move only three matchsticks in the image of the fish swimming to the left to create one of a fish swimming to the right.

The answer to this one is particularly challenging because of the pattern awareness of the solver. The solution requires turning what was once imagined to be the tail of the fish into a new fish's body (**FIGURE 18.9**).

FIGURE 18.8 Goldfish in matchsticks.

FIGURE 18.9 The solution requires you to rethink what makes the body of the fish.

One of the most often-used spatial manipulation puzzles is the *Tower of Hanoi*.[5] In it, a player must move discs on three separate pillars of differing sizes one at a time so that no disc lies on top of a smaller disc, and the end goal is to get all of the discs in the correct order on the last peg. The three-disc, three-peg version is illustrated in **FIGURE 18.10**.

FIGURE 18.10
Tower of Hanoi.

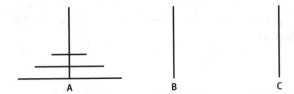

This puzzle can be solved in just seven steps. Let the smallest disc be named 1, the middle disc be named 2, and the largest disc be named 3.

1. Move 1 to C.
2. Move 2 to B.
3. Move 1 to B.

   Now 1 and 2 are on B.

4. Move 3 to C.
5. Move 1 to A.

   Now all three are on different pegs with 3 on the correct spot.

6. Move 2 to C.
7. Move 1 to C.

With three discs, the solution is fairly simple. However, the complexity scales exponentially with the number of discs.[6] With four discs, the minimum number of steps is 15. With five, 31. Perhaps because of its ease of implementation, *Tower of Hanoi* has been seen in many games. The website Giant Bomb lists at least 15 known examples. Since a solved puzzle is generally rote and uninteresting to players, you should be able to bank on a good portion of your audience having seen *Tower of Hanoi* before, making it a poor choice for a puzzle implementation.

. . . .

5   *Tower of Hanoi*. (2013). Retrieved July 24, 2015, from www.giantbomb.com/tower-ofhanoi/3015-5744.

6   Petkovic, M. (2009). *Famous Puzzles of Great Mathematicians*. Providence, RI: American Mathematical Society.

Summary

- Puzzles require a particular devotion to the fundamental game design directive because the different skill levels of players require different approaches to presenting the puzzle.

- The possibility space of a puzzle is the set of all possible answers at a particular step in reasoning.

- Breadcrumbs are hints that may be internal to the puzzle's structure or applied from outside the structure of the puzzle used in order to nudge a solver toward either reducing the possibility space of the puzzle or making the leap in reasoning that will allow them to solve the puzzle.

- Problems in the structure of puzzles largely boil down to either solvers being unable to fairly reduce the possibility space of the puzzle to a single solution or solvers not finding the process of reducing the possibility space engaging.

- Puzzles come in a vast number of forms. Understanding the mental leaps in solving classic puzzles can help when you design your own puzzles.

5 Game Theory and Rational Decision-Making

How little we think about how it is we think.

—NOREEN HERTZ

A field of study known as *game theory* is often confused with game design or game studies. People who have never designed or developed games before often think that you must use game theory because it must be a "theory of how to make games." It is not. Game theory is the specific study of strategic decision-making, often in situations of conflict. Organizationally, it's seen as a field of mathematics.

The "game" in game theory refers to the situations between multiple actors. For instance, game theory treats the real prospect of nuclear war between two countries as a "game." This definition is different from the definition that designers who largely make playable entertainment titles use, as you saw in the multiple definitions of "game" in Chapter 1. Thus, much of game theory has little applicability to the practice of making actual playable games.

What makes game theory useful to game designers? Game theory analyzes what should happen given what players desire. Since designers attempt to create decisions that are meaningful for players, knowing how an ideal player would react to a situation can help a designer better understand the consequences of a decision. Predicting player behaviors can be both instrumental and desirable.

When discussing game theory, I'll be using the mathematical, rather than the cultural or sociological, definition of a game. Here the game must have players, actions, information available to players, and payoffs for each outcome of said actions. Game theory is a deep, and largely opaque rabbit hole for those outside the discipline. But understanding the basics of the field should give you, as a designer, a leg up on predicting possible player strategies and behaviors.

19 Equilibria in Normal Form Games

> There exists everywhere a medium in things,
> determined by equilibrium.
>
> —DMITRI MENDELEEV

First, let's look at what is known as a *normal form* description of a game. Normal form games are good places to start because they are rather simple. In this form, you represent the game as a table or matrix. One player's options are presented by the matrix's rows. The other player (given a two-player game) has options represented by the columns of the matrix. Where each intersects is the *result* of the game with each player receiving a *payoff*.

Where game theory is useful is in determining not what a player *can* do, but what a player *will* do. You need to make a bunch of assumptions in order to determine this, but it can help you to determine whether any options in your game are not logical to ever choose. The result in which players are theorized to end up is the *equilibrium* result.

Equilibria tell us what behaviors are likely to emerge from a particular set of rules.

The Prisoner's Dilemma

The classic example that is always the introduction to game theory anywhere it is taught is called the *Prisoner's Dilemma*. It is set up thusly:

Mister A and Mister B have been apprehended on suspicion of a robbery. Both are isolated and have no opportunity to communicate with each other. The police can already get them both for criminal trespassing and conspiracy, which will result in a two-year sentence. The police give the two the same choice. Become an informant and rat on the partner. In this case, the "rat" would have his charges dropped and the other criminal would get five years in prison for the robbery, criminal trespassing, and conspiracy. However, if both rat, then they will both receive the robbery charge of three years.

What should Mister A and Mister B do? Game theory considers this a game: It has players (Mister A and Mister B), actions (rat or stay quiet), information, and payoffs (sentences). This type of game is usually examined using a table, as in **TABLE 19.1**.

TABLE 19.1 Prisoner's Dilemma

	Mister B Rats	Mister B Stays Quiet
Mister A Rats	Mister A gets 3 years. Mister B gets 3 years.	Mister A gets 0 years. Mister B gets 5 years.
Mister A Stays Quiet	Mister A gets 5 years. Mister B gets 0 years.	Mister A gets 2 years. Mister B gets 2 years.

The payoff cells (sentences) are a bit wordy and redundant, so payoffs are usually listed as a tuple with the payoffs for each player, as shown in **TABLE 19.2**. The sentences are given as (*Mister A's sentence in years, Mister B's sentence in years*).

TABLE 19.2 Prisoner's Dilemma Payoffs

	Mister B Rats	Mister B Stays Quiet
Mister A Rats	(3, 3)	(0, 5)
Mister A Stays Quiet	(5, 0)	(2, 2)

How can someone predict what Mister A and Mister B will do? First, they assume that both criminals are rational, that both understand all the payoffs in the game, and that both players will try to minimize their individual sentences. No weight is given to any loyalty or possible repercussions outside the game. The players are selfish and all rewards are built into the listed payoffs.

Look at Table 19.2 from Mister A's perspective; this shows that ratting is always preferable to staying quiet, **no matter what Mister B does**. If Mister B rats, then by ratting, Mister A gets three years instead of five. If Mister B stays quiet, then by ratting, Mister A gets zero years instead of two. Either way ratting is better for Mister A.

But this game is symmetric. Mister B's incentives are the same as Mister A's. From Mister B's perspective, his results are also always better if he rats. Thus, both should rat.

This is interesting because by acting in their own best interests, they get a worse result than if they cooperate. By following the best strategy, both serve three years, whereas by cooperating, they would have each only served two. The (2,2) result is known as *Pareto optimal*. It is a result where no one can become better off without making someone else worse off.

However, the (3,3) result is the *equilibrium* result. It is the result for which changing a decision in isolation (and with all other players knowing about the switch) would result in a worse outcome for the player choosing to switch.

In game theory terms, you say that "rat" *strictly dominates* "stay quiet" for both players. No matter what the other player chooses, choosing "rat" gives the player a better outcome than choosing "stay quiet." To be strictly dominant, a strategy must produce a better result than any other strategy **no matter what an opponent does**. Any option that is dominated cannot be equilibrium. If an option is *dominated*, it means that something else is always better, so why would the players ever pick it?

A game where the equilibrium is also Pareto optimal is called *deadlock*. In deadlock, both players end on an outcome that is mutually beneficial. It is essentially identical to the Prisoner's Dilemma except that the Pareto optimal result is also the equilibrium.

Solving Games Using Strict Dominance

If you wish to know what the players should do, you must solve for the game's equilibria. When you first look at a matrix of payoffs, any outcome could be an equilibrium outcome. Most games are not as easy to solve as the Prisoner's Dilemma. You can use several techniques to best eliminate results to find the true equilibria. One technique is known as *Iterated Elimination of Dominated Strategies*. That is a mouthful for a way of doing something similar to what we did to solve the Prisoner's Dilemma in the previous section.

Imagine a game, explained by **TABLE 19.3**, in which two players have to choose a character and then each gets points based on how well those characters perform against each other. You can read the table data as "number of points for player 1, number of points for player 2." Which player has the advantage?

TABLE 19.3 Iterated Elimination of Dominated Strategies

	Player 2 Ninja	Player 2 Barbarian	Player 2 Merman
Player 1 Alien	(18, 3)	(1, 4)	(5, 2)
Player 1 Gunner	(5, 4)	(3, 6)	(4, 5)
Player 1 Pirate	(0, 9)	(2, 7)	(8, 6)

A naive strategy would be to take the average points for each player. Here each player has an average result of 5.11 points, so an (incorrect) answer would be that neither player has the advantage.

If you assume that players know all this information, and if players act rationally in their own best interests (all assumptions made in game theory), then you can predict what will happen in this game. You can eliminate any options that are strictly dominated by another option. Remember that an Option A that has strict dominance over Option B means that Option A is better than Option B under every circumstance. If Option A is equal to Option B at any point, this analysis will not necessarily work.

In examining strict dominance, you focus only on one player's perspective at a time. It can often be helpful to remove the other player's payoffs because they can be a distraction. If the player is only trying to maximize his own score, he will not care what score the opponent receives. (A zero-sum game where one player's "plus one" is another player's "minus one" would be different).

Looking from Player 2's perspective, remove the option of Ninja temporarily and look only at the decision between Barbarian and Merman in **TABLE 19.4**.

> ▶ **NOTE** The choice to remove the Ninja option and examine the remaining two options doesn't have any science behind it. You may choose any two options to examine, but these two are worth examining because one ends up strictly dominating the other. That will not always be the case. You may need to try many different combinations before finding a pair that shows strict dominance.

TABLE 19.4 Player 2 Comparing Barbarian and Merman

	Player 2 Barbarian	Player 2 Merman
Player 1 Alien	4	2
Player 1 Gunner	6	5
Player 1 Pirate	7	6

The points for choosing Barbarian are **always** greater than the points for choosing Merman. Thus, both players should know that Player 2 will never choose Merman as long as that player can choose Barbarian. It doesn't matter if you add Ninja back in. If Ninja is better than Merman, that player will not pick Merman. If Ninja is worse than Merman, that player will not pick Merman; as you know, he will pick Barbarian. Now that you know that Merman will not be chosen as long as Barbarian is an option, you can remove it from the game permanently. Bring Ninja back; you were just isolating it for a moment.

This opens a new layer to the analysis. Now that Pirate-Merman has been deleted, there is a dominant relationship between Pirate and Gunner for Player 1. Remove Alien temporarily and look at only Gunner versus Pirate in terms of Player 1's points (**TABLE 19.5**). Remember that the choice between Gunner and Pirate belongs to Player 1, so consider only the payoffs for Player 1. As you can see, Gunner is always preferable to Pirate.

TABLE 19.5 Player 1 Examining Gunner and Pirate

	Player 2 Ninja	Player 2 Barbarian
Player 1 Gunner	5	3
Player 1 Pirate	0	2

This narrows the game further because now you know that Pirate will never be chosen by Player 1, so you can remove it permanently.

You are left with two options for each player. For Player 1, neither Alien nor Gunner is dominant (**TABLE 19.6**). However, looking from Player 2's perspective, Barbarian is always better than Ninja. (4 versus 3 if Player 1 chooses Alien and 6 versus 4 if Player 1 chooses Gunner). This means you know that Player 2 should choose Barbarian.

TABLE 19.6 Player 2 Examining Ninja and Barbarian

	Player 2 Ninja	Player 2 Barbarian
Player 1 Alien	(18, 3)	(1, 4)
Player 1 Gunner	(5, 4)	(3, 6)

You now have a pretty simple game to solve (**TABLE 19.7**). Since 3 is better than 1, Player 1 will choose Gunner over Alien. The equilibrium is that Player 1 should choose Gunner and Player 2 should choose Barbarian. The equilibrium result is (3, 6), thus Player 2 has the advantage.

TABLE 19.7 Player 1 Examining Alien versus Gunner

	Player 2 Barbarian
Player 1 Alien	(1, 4)
Player 1 Gunner	(3, 6)

Using (and Abusing) Dominance

By eliminating dominated options in your games, you are left with only the options that players can weigh for interesting decisions. If a player can reduce a game down to a single pure strategy, then what interesting decision is left? The game submission, shown in **FIGURE 19.1**, that I received in a game design class illustrates this point well.

up + HT, left = MT, down = LT

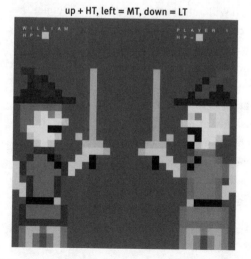

FIGURE 19.1 Swordfighting Game. Used with permission of the author.

It was a swordfighting game where the player simultaneously acted with the AI opponent by pressing one of the arrow keys to choose "high thrust," "mid thrust," or "low thrust." The result would either injure you (Player 1, on the right), injure your opponent (William, in the dashing purple smock to the left), or have no result. After digging through the student's code, I was able to deduce the results in **TABLE 19.8.**

TABLE 19.8 Swordfighting Example

	William High Thrust	William Mid Thrust	William Low Thrust
Player 1 High Thrust	No Result	No Result	William Injured
Player 1 Mid Thrust	No Result	No Result	Player 1 Injured
Player 1 Low Thrust	No Result	William Injured	Player 1 Injured

A cursory glance at this would lead you to say, "There are two scenarios in which William is injured and two scenarios in which Player 1 is injured. This must be fair." But look closer; you'll see the problem. What is Player 1 incentivized to choose? If he chooses high thrust, the possible outcomes are a draw or a point against the opponent. Player 1 can't lose if he chooses high thrust! At worst, he can tie. Now look at if Player 1 chooses mid thrust. The possible outcomes are a draw or a point against the player! Nothing good comes out of choosing mid thrust. Player 1 can never win when choosing this. Low thrust is the most interesting because the player can hit the opponent or the opponent can hit the player. But why would he ever choose that when he has the safety of high thrust?

The student creator of this game chose to code William so that he picked each of the thrusts one-third of the time randomly. But if William was an actual rational human player, what would he do? Mid thrust is as bad for him as it is for the Player 1. High thrust is always a draw for him. Low thrust allows him to score a point as long as the opponent does not pick high thrust, so at first it seems the best choice. But if you assume William knows the rules of the game, he knows that Player 1 will pick high thrust, so he is incentivized to pick high thrust as well. (If he picked mid thrust and Player 1 knew that he would pick mid thrust, Player 1 could always switch to low thrust and score a point, so William has no incentive to ever pick mid thrust). As a result, if both players are playing rationally, they both always pick high thrust against each other and the game is a perpetual draw. Boring, right?

How can you fix this? You need to remove the domination from each player's options. Look at **TABLE 19.9**, where I've made sure that each thrust has one win state, one lose state, and one draw for each player.

TABLE 19.9 Fixed Swordfighting Example

	William High Thrust	William Mid Thrust	William Low Thrust
Player 1 High Thrust	No Result	Player 1 Injured	William Injured
Player 1 Mid Thrust	William Injured	No Result	Player 1 Injured
Player 1 Low Thrust	Player 1 Injured	William Injured	No Result

Or take a look at **TABLE 19.10**, which uses numbers for the data.

TABLE 19.10 Fixed Swordfighting as Payoffs

	William High Thrust	William Mid Thrust	William Low Thrust
Player 1 High Thrust	(0, 0)	(-1, 1)	(1, -1)
Player 1 Mid Thrust	(1, -1)	(0, 0)	(-1, 1)
Player 1 Low Thrust	(-1, 1)	(1, -1)	(0, 0)

With these results, both players are not incentivized to favor any particular technique. The mixed equilibrium is at ⅓ for each type of attack. But does it look familiar?

Rock, Paper, Scissors (**TABLE 19.11**) interests game designers because it is an extremely simple game whose only equilibrium is in *mixed strategies*—throwing one move some times and changing it up often. It does not make for informed choice (since every strategy is as good as any other), but it is certainly better than pure, dominated strategies. In game theory, this "A beats B, B bests C, C beats A" system is known as *intransitive*. Many popular games use intransitive systems as a base, such as *Pokemon*.

TABLE 19.11 *Rock, Paper, Scissors*

	William Rock	William Paper	William Scissors
Player 1 Rock	(0, 0)	(-1, 1)	(1, -1)
Player 1 Paper	(1, -1)	(0, 0)	(-1, 1)
Player 1 Scissors	(-1, 1)	(1, -1)	(0, 0)

If a game's key decisions end up being dominated, some of its options are never played. Not only is this boring from a play perspective, but it means the creators are going to have to create code and assets for situations that should never come up, which is wasted effort. A better design looks for equilibrium only in mixed strategies in which each option has a probability greater than zero of being chosen. This ensures that all options have an opportunity to be played, and the resulting system is more interesting.

Zero-Sum Games

Head-to-head games are often *zero-sum games*. In a zero-sum game, the amount of resources stays the same for all players. For example, a game in which I flip a coin, you give me $20 if it lands Heads, and I give you $5 if it lands Tails is a zero-sum game. Even though it is unfair to you, no matter what happens, the amount of money between us stays the same; we are only transferring resources. *Rock, Paper, Scissors* is a zero-sum game; if a player wins, the opponent loses.

In all two-player zero-sum games, a strategy known as *minimax* solves the game. In minimax, each player forms a strategy that minimizes the pain of their worst-case scenario. In the first "William versus the Player" swordfighting example in Table 19.8, the minimal pain for Player 1 is to choose high thrust. Mid thrust and low thrust each have a worst-case scenario of injury. High thrust's worst case is no result. William's worst-case scenario is no result if he chooses high thrust, but injury if he chooses either of the other two attacks. Thus, the minimax solution is for William to high thrust and Player 1 to high thrust—just what you found earlier. This technique works for all two player zero-sum games.

Since this solution is easily findable by players, most interesting games are either not entirely zero-sum, or they become more interesting when a third player (or more) is added to the game.

As a designer, you can use dominance to guide players away from options that you don't want them to choose. However, the most interesting game decisions often come from solutions with mixed strategies.

Stag Hunt and Coordination

The Prisoner's Dilemma is easy to understand because of its strict dominance. Neither player has to worry about what the other does because there is a better option in all cases. However, in practical application, this is not often the case. Consider this classic example adapted liberally from 18TH Century French philosopher Jean Jacques Rousseau named "The Stag Hunt."[1]

Two hunters (Mario and Luigi) go out to hunt. Each must choose to hunt a stag (a deer) or a hare, and each must choose without knowing what the other hunter chose. If a hunter

. . . .

1   Rousseau, J. J. (1755). *A Discourse on the Origins and Foundations of Inequality Among Men*. Trans. Maurice Cranston (1984) Harmondsworth: Penguin.

chooses the stag, he must have the cooperation of his partner to capture the beast. The stag produces 150 lbs of meat. A day's hunt of hare can produce 20 lbs of meat.

The game can be drawn up as in **TABLE 19.12**, similar to The Prisoner's Dilemma.

TABLE 19.12 The Stag Hunt

	Luigi Stag	Luigi Hare
Mario Stag	(75, 75)	(0, 20)
Mario Hare	(20, 0)	(20, 20)

Examine the game from Mario's perspective. All else being equal, the best result for him is if he chooses Stag and Luigi chooses Stag as well. But if he chooses Stag and Luigi chooses Hare, he and his family go hungry tonight. Luigi is posed with the same dilemma. If Mario chooses Stag, all is well. But if not, he and his go hungry.

This game doesn't have strict dominance. No one option is better for one player than any other option, thus you cannot eliminate Stag or Hare for either player.

Another technique for solving this game is to examine each payoff. If neither player can do better by unilaterally changing her strategy holding the other player's strategy constant, that outcome is a *Nash equilibrium*.

Look first at (Stag, Stag). Mario would not want to change to Hare since that would lower his payoff. Neither would Luigi. This is a Nash equilibrium. This makes sense as an equilibrium because it is also Pareto optimal. It is the best for everyone. Why would anyone want to change?

Look now at (Stag, Hare). If Luigi knew that Mario chose Stag, he would want to change his strategy to Stag as well, because the 20 he gets from Hare is not as good as the 75 he would get for Stag. Thus, this is not a Nash equilibrium. Since this game is symmetric, the same is true for (Hare, Stag). Mario would change if he knew Luigi chose Stag.

Look finally at (Hare, Hare). If Luigi knew that Mario chose Hare, he certainly wouldn't change to Stag. That would get him 0 pounds of meat instead of 20. The same is true for Mario. If he knew Luigi chose Hare, then he would not want to switch either. Since neither wants to switch, this is also a Nash equilibrium.

Both players are better off with the (Stag, Stag) equilibrium, but it's just as rational for players to settle for the (Hare, Hare) equilibrium. If Mario and Luigi ended on (Hare, Hare) or (Stag, Stag), neither has regrets. They chose the best solution given what the other had chosen.

Determining Nash Equilibria in a Larger Matrix

In *The Stag Hunt*, it is easy to find the Nash equilibria because there are only four possible outcomes. With a more complicated game, it is overly tedious to brute force through every outcome.

In *Pokemon*, players select creatures that have an inherent "type" to battle each other. In *Pokemon X/Y*, each attack has one of 18 types, such as Fire, Ground, or Psychic, and each defending Pokemon has a certain inherent type as well. Some types are stronger than others. For instance, a Fire attack is extra effective against an Ice Pokemon, as you would imagine. A Ground attack does not even hit a Flying Pokemon. For 18 Pokemon types and 18 attack types, there is a matrix with 324 outcomes, too tedious to go through one by one.

One technique used to determine Nash equilibria in such cases is to hold each opponent's selection constant and find what the player's best choice is. If that outcome ends up being the best choice for all of the players, then it is a Nash equilibrium.

TABLE 19.13 is a matrix that uses the same game from the previous section, eliminating strongly dominated strategies, but it adds a few new types to the mix.

TABLE 19.13 A More Complex Matrix

	Player B Ninja	Player B Barbarian	Player B Merman	Player B Robot	Player B Fluffball	Player B Dynamo
Player A Alien	(18, 3)	(1, 4)	(5, 2)	(7, 6)	(3, 3)	(4, 5)
Player A Gunner	(5, 4)	(3, 6)	(4, 5)	(4, 8)	(3, 3)	(9, 2)
Player A Pirate	(0, 9)	(2, 7)	(8, 6)	(6, 1)	(3, 3)	(2, 5)
Player A Zombie	(1, 7)	(10, 2)	(4, 4)	(0, 10)	(3, 3)	(1, 8)
Player A Shark	(3, 5)	(9, 1)	(5, 5)	(1, 8)	(3, 3)	(1, 9)
Player A Shadow	(6, 2)	(5, 3)	(3, 3)	(3, 3)	(0, 20)	(3, 1)

Isolate Player A to choose Alien as in **TABLE 19.14**. If Player A chooses Alien, then the best bet for Player B is to choose Robot. Indicate Robot for Player B by circling the result, adding an asterisk, or changing the color. Do something that makes that result stand out. Here, if we know Player A chose Alien, Player B's best bet is to get 6 points by choosing Robot.

TABLE 19.14 Isolating Alien

	Player B Ninja	Player B Barbarian	Player B Merman	Player B Robot	Player B Fluffball	Player B Dynamo
Player A Alien	(18, 3)	(1, 4)	(5, 2)	(7, **6**)	(3, 3)	(4, 5)

Do this for each possible Player A choice. If two choices are equally good, highlight both. For instance, if Player B chooses Fluffball, Player A's best choice is anything other than Shadow. Highlight all the results except for Shadow. After you have highlighted the best choices for B holding A's choices constant, hold Player B's choices constant and find the best option for Player A, highlighting the result for each. After examining all of these, the matrix should look like **TABLE 19.15**.

TABLE 19.15 Best Choices Highlighted

	Player B Ninja	Player B Barbarian	Player B Merman	Player B Robot	Player B Fluffball	Player B Dynamo
Player A Alien	(**18**, 3)	(1, 4)	(5, 2)	(**7**, **6**)	(3, 3)	(4 ,5)
Player A Gunner	(5, 4)	(3, 6)	(4, 5)	(4, **8**)	(3, 3)	(**9**, 2)
Player A Pirate	(0, **9**)	(2, 7)	(**8**, 6)	(6, 1)	(**3**, 3)	(2, 5)
Player A Zombie	(1, 7)	(**10**, 2)	(4, 4)	(0, 10)	(**3**, 3)	(1, 8)
Player A Shark	(3, 5)	(9, 1)	(5, 5)	(1, 8)	(**3**, 3)	(1, **9**)
Player A Shadow	(6, 2)	(5, 3)	(3, 3)	(3, 3)	(0, **20**)	(3, 1)

There is only one result in this game where both results are highlighted: (Alien, Robot). It is this game's only Nash equilibrium. If Player A knows that Player B is choosing Robot, then her best choice is to choose Alien because no other option nets her 7 points or more. If Player B knows that Player A is choosing Alien, then choosing Robot is his best choice because it results in 6 points. Neither player has a reason to switch, so this is a Nash equilibrium.

Mixed Strategies

Imagine a game of *Rock, Paper, Scissors*. You highlight all the best strategies for each player as in **TABLE 19.16**.

TABLE 19.16 *Rock, Paper, Scissors* with Best Results Highlighted

	Lisa Rock	Lisa Paper	Lisa Scissors
Bart Rock	(0, 0)	(**1**, −1)	(−1, **1**)
Bart Paper	(−1, **1**)	(0, 0)	(**1**, −1)
Bart Scissors	(**1**, −1)	(−1, **1**)	(0, 0)

But no result ends up being the best for both players. No pure Nash equilibria exists. This is incredibly common in zero-sum games in which one player directly plays against another, and one's loss is the other's gain. Most sports and multiplayer competitive games are organized this way.

How do you actually play *Rock, Paper, Scissors*? Most of us randomly choose one of the three choices. What if a player weighted one result higher than the others? Say he chose Rock 95 percent of the time. If you knew that, you would play Paper most of the time. If he chose Rock 5 percent of the time and you knew that, you would almost never choose Paper.

Choosing a particular option, no matter what the opponent does, as I have covered before, is known as a *pure strategy*. It is pure because no matter the situation, the strategy is the same. A *mixed strategy* involves assigning probabilities to each pure strategy. An example mixed strategy would be to play Paper 60 percent of the time, Scissors 30 percent of the time, and Rock 10 percent of the time.

You can determine an expected value of each pure strategy based on a mixed strategy. Say that Bart knows that Lisa plays this mixed strategy: p(Paper) = 0.6, p(Scissors) = 0.3, p(Rock) = 0.1) where p(Event) is the probability of an event happening. The expected value (EV) of each of Bart's pure strategies would be as follows:

$$EV(Paper) = (0.6)^*0 + (0.1)^*1 + (0.3)^*{-1} = -0.2$$

$$EV(Rock) = (0.6)^*{-1} + (0.1)^*0 + (0.3)^*1 = -0.3$$

$$EV(Scissors) = 0.6^*(1) + (0.1)^*{-1} + (0.3)^*0 = 0.5$$

This is because the expected value is the sum of each event's payoff times the probability of that event happening. Because this game is zero-sum, Lisa's expected payoff from her strategy is −0.5 since Bart always plays Scissors.

This poses a problem. If it's best for Bart to play Scissors, then Lisa knows that the current strategy is not at equilibrium because she can change it and get a better result. But what should she change it to? With some algebra, you can find out:

EV(Paper) = p(Lisa plays Paper)*0 + p(Lisa plays Rock)*1 + p(Lisa plays Scissors)*−1

EV(Rock) = p(Lisa plays Paper)*−1 + p(Lisa plays Rock)*0 + p(Lisa plays Scissors)*1

EV(Scissors) = p(Lisa plays Paper)*1 + p(Lisa plays Rock)*−1 + p(Lisa plays Scissors)*0

If you are looking for a strategy in which Bart doesn't want to switch to something else, then EV(Paper) = EV(Rock) = EV(Scissors). Also, the probabilities of Lisa playing the three options have to add up to 1, because she has no other options. Reduce the set of equations to the following where P is the probability:

> **NOTE** Also, the probabilities must be between 0 and 1 inclusive.

p(Lisa plays Rock) − p(Lisa plays Scissors) = p(Lisa plays Scissors) −p(Lisa plays Paper)

p(Lisa plays Scissors) − p(Lisa plays Paper) = p(Lisa plays Paper) −p(Lisa plays Rock)

p(Lisa plays Rock) + p(Lisa plays Scissors) + p(Lisa plays Rock) = 1

Since this is three equations with three variables, you can solve it:

p(Lisa plays Rock) = 1/3

p(Lisa plays Scissors) = 1/3

p(Lisa plays Paper) = 1/3

Since the game is symmetric, the same applies to Bart. Thus, the Nash equilibrium is that each player should choose each of the three throws randomly with equal probability. If there are a finite number of players with a finite number of strategies, there will always be at least one Nash equilibrium. It is this finding that earned John Forbes Nash (along with his colleagues John Harsanyi and Reinhard Selten) his Nobel Prize in Economics.

Although *Rock, Paper, Scissors* is a nice real-world example, it can be hard to understand. Try an asymmetric, but smaller example, as in **TABLE 19.17**.

TABLE 19.17 Sonic versus Tails

	Tails Diamond	Tails Club
Sonic Heart	(**3**, 0)	(1, **2**)
Sonic Spade	(0, **4**)	(3, 0)

The best results given an opponent's choice are highlighted to show that there are no pure Nash equilibria.

For Tails, his expected value is as follows:

$$EV(\blacklozenge) = p(\text{Sonic plays } \blacktriangledown)*(0) + p(\text{Sonic plays } \spadesuit)*(4)$$

$$EV(\clubsuit) = p(\text{Sonic plays } \blacktriangledown)*(2) + p(\text{Sonic plays } \spadesuit)*(2)$$

Sonic's strategy, which leaves Tails indifferent, is the one in which Tails' expected value is equal no matter what Sonic chooses to do.

$$EV(\blacklozenge) = EV(\clubsuit)$$

$$p(\text{Sonic plays } \spadesuit)*(4) = p(\text{Sonic plays } \blacktriangledown)*(2) + p(\text{Sonic plays } \spadesuit)*(2)$$

Since $p(\text{Sonic plays } \blacktriangledown) + p(\text{Sonic plays } \spadesuit) = 1$:

$$p(\text{Sonic plays } \spadesuit)*(4) = 2$$

$$p(\text{Sonic plays } \spadesuit) = 0.5$$

$$p(\text{Sonic plays } \blacktriangledown) = 0.5$$

It is a coin flip! If Sonic does a coin flip to choose, then Tails should be indifferent about choosing between Diamonds or Clubs as a strategy. Now calculate the probabilities going the other way.

For Sonic, his expected value for his two possible pure strategies is as follows:

$$EV(\text{Sonic plays } \blacktriangledown) = p(\text{Tails plays } \blacklozenge)*3 + p(\text{Tails plays } \clubsuit)*1$$

$$EV(\text{Sonic plays } \spadesuit) = p(\text{Tails plays } \blacklozenge)*0 + p(\text{Tails plays } \clubsuit)*3$$

Tails' strategy, which leaves Sonic indifferent, is the one in which Sonic's expected value is the same no matter what Tails chooses to do:

$$EV(\text{Sonic plays } \blacktriangledown) = EV(\text{Sonic plays } \spadesuit)$$

$$p(\text{Tails plays } \blacklozenge)*3 + p(\text{Tails plays } \clubsuit)*1 = p(\text{Tails plays } \blacklozenge)*0 + p(\text{Tails plays } \clubsuit)*3$$

Solve this:

$$p(\text{Tails plays } \blacklozenge) = 0.4$$

$$p(\text{Tails plays } \clubsuit) = 0.6$$

To check your results, you just have to see if you can find a better choice for Sonic or Tails given the other's strategy.

Tails will be playing Diamonds/Clubs with a 40 percent/60 percent split.

EV($\heartsuit$) = 0.4 * 3 + 0.6 * 1 = 1.8

EV($\spadesuit$) = 0.6 * 3 = 1.8.

What can Sonic do to get better than 1.8? If he always picks Hearts, he gets 1.8. If he always picks Spades, he gets 1.8. If he picks Hearts 1/3 of the time and Spade 2/3 of the time he gets 1.8. In fact, any combination of the two leads to the same expected payoff. The same is true for Tails. Since neither has a reason to change, this is a Nash equilibrium.

Stag Hunt Redux

Let us go back to the Mario and Luigi Stag Hunt from earlier (**TABLE 19.18**).

TABLE 19.18 Mario and Luigi Stag Hunt

	Luigi Stag	Luigi Hare
Mario Stag	(75, 75)	(0, 20)
Mario Hare	(20, 0)	(20, 20)

You previously found two pure-strategy Nash equilibria. Are there any mixed-strategy equilibria?

EV(Mario chooses Stag) = p(Luigi chooses Stag)*75 + p(Luigi chooses Hare) * 0

EV(Mario chooses Hare) = p(Luigi chooses Stag)*20 + p(Luigi chooses Hare) * 20

For Mario to be indifferent, this is what needs to happen:

p(Luigi chooses Stag) = 20/75 or 4/15

p(Luigi chooses Hare) = 11/15

Since this is symmetric, the same is true for Luigi. Both have a mixed-strategy equilibrium at choosing Stag with a probability of 4 out of 15.

Summary

- When you understand what rational players should do, you can eliminate possibly wasteful options that no player would ever choose.
- An option that is always worse than any other option no matter what the opponent does is known as strictly dominated.
- Players can use a pure strategy in which they always choose a particular option, or they can use a mixed strategy in which they randomly choose between pure strategies.
- A result where no player is better off by choosing to change their strategy is an equilibrium result.
- To find the equilibrium result, each player's expected value for each strategy must be the same across strategies.

20 Sequential and Iterated Games

> I have six locks on my door all in a row.
> When I go out, I lock every other one.
> I figure no matter how long somebody stands there
> picking the locks, they are always locking three.
>
> **—ELAYNE BOOSLER**

Most board and video games are not like the *Prisoner's Dilemma* in which all players make one choice simultaneously and then the game is over. What if a player chooses before another player? What do the results of one game say about the future results of another? If a player is betrayed in one round of the *Prisoner's Dilemma*, how should that affect her if she plays again? In this chapter, I cover games in which players make their choices in order to play games over and over again.

Game Trees

Matrices are insufficient when you are representing sequential games because a second player may behave differently once given the information the first player provides. You need some sort of diagram that shows this contingency. A *game tree* or *decision tree* is one way you can represent these kinds of games. These diagrams show branches for each outcome, such as the one in **FIGURE 20.1** for a sequential game of *The Stag Hunt*.

FIGURE 20.1
Mario/Luigi's
Stag Hunt.

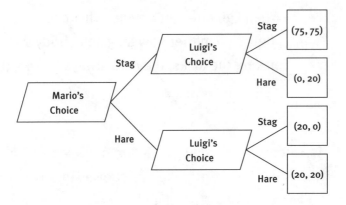

In Figure 20.1, play goes from left to right. The first parallelogram is a choice node in which Mario chooses to hunt Stag or Hare. Then, after he makes his choice, Luigi chooses to hunt Stag or Hare.

Solving these games can be similar to solving simultaneous games. Many of the principles are the same. First, the player making the decision cares only about his payoffs, so those payoffs should be the only criteria he evaluates when making a decision. Second, both players know their situations in the game. The only difference is that to solve this, you need to use a technique known as *backwards induction*.

Start with the rightmost decision. In this example, start with Luigi's decision at the bottom, after he knows that Mario chose Hare. Luigi's choice is between 0 pounds of meat if he chooses Stag, and 20 pounds of meat if he chooses Hare. It is obvious that Luigi will choose Hare. In fact, since Luigi will never choose the (Hare, Stag) node, you can remove it from your analysis.

Next, look at the other rightmost decision. If Luigi knows Mario has chosen Stag, Luigi's choice is between getting 75 pounds of meat for choosing Stag or 20 pounds for choosing Hare. It's again clear what Luigi will choose. He will choose Stag, so you can also remove the (Stag, Hare) node.

This simplifies the decision for Mario to **FIGURE 20.2**.

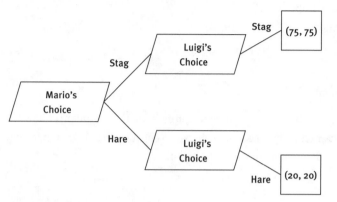

FIGURE 20.2 Removing the decisions Luigi would not make.

Now Mario's decision is the only decision left. Should Mario take Stag or Hare? Since he receives more for Stag, he will take it and the game's outcome will be (Stag, Stag).

Unlike the matrix version of this that had two likely solutions, this version has only one. In any sequential game like the one in Figure 20.1, with no simultaneous moves if each player's payoffs are unique to that player, backwards induction always outputs a unique solution.

Sequential games/decisions allow you to analyze commitment problems. As a university instructor, I am bound by my institution's policies to police academic honesty. If students are cheating, I must act. However, what if I had an option? Let's examine all the options for me and all the options for a student:

- I can actually look for cheating or not.
- I can prosecute cheating if I find it or not.
- A student can choose to cheat or not.

Next, rank the preferences for this game. First, consider students who only care about the amount of work they have to do and not about their long-term educational future. Assume they would rather cheat than not, but only if they will not be caught. I would rather not spend my time looking for cheaters, but if cheaters exist, I would rather catch them than not.

Student's preferences (with 1 being the best):

- Cheat and Don't Get Caught
- Cheat, but Don't Get Punished
- Do Work, Cheat, and Get Caught

Teacher preferences (with 1 being the best):

- Don't Check and No Cheating
- Check and No Cheating
- Prosecute Cheater
- Don't Prosecute Cheater
- Don't Check and Student Cheats

You can depict this as a tree (**FIGURE 20.3**) where the professor lets the students know of the policy and the student has the freedom to choose to cheat or do her work. Assign 4 points for the best result down to 0 points for the worst.

FIGURE 20.3
Cheating student's game tree.

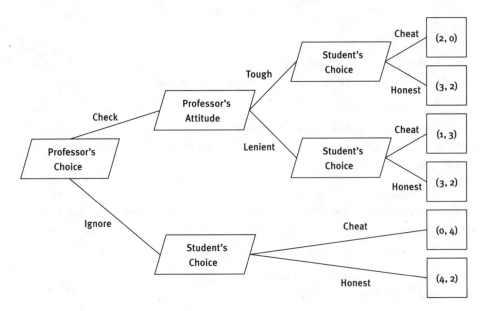

Solve this using backwards induction. First, assume the professor checks and is tough. The student can get 2 points for being honest and doing the work and 0 points for cheating, so if she believes the professor's threat that he is tough is credible, the student will be honest. However, if the student believes the professor will be lenient, cheating will net 3 points to honesty's 2. On the bottom nodes, if it's the professor's policy not to check, then the student's 4 points for cheating is clearly preferable to the 2 points for being honest, so the professor should assume that the students will cheat.

Removing the dominated positions, the professor's tree looks like **FIGURE 20.4**.

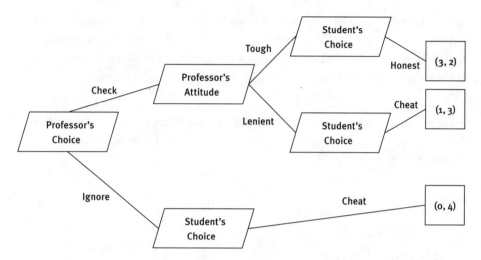

FIGURE 20.4
Reduced cheating
student's game tree.

Using backwards induction for the professor, given the choice between being tough or being lenient, the professor would prefer the students to work, so he must choose to be tough (3 points to 1 point). Next, he must choose between checking or ignoring. He knows he will receive 3 points from checking because he knows that it will follow that he must be tough and that the students will then work. He knows if he does not check, students will want to cheat and he will receive 0 points.

Thus, professors who value students doing their work must follow through on their commitment to enforcing their threats. Otherwise, the threat of punishment will not be credible and the student will cheat. Equilibrium is the professor checking and being tough while the student is honest. This arrangement is not in the short-term interests of either party: The professor has to spend time checking and prosecuting students and students have to spend more time on their work. (3, 2) is not Pareto optimal. The (4, 2) node of the professor not checking and the students doing their work makes one party better off without reducing the utility of the other party. But because of the commitment issues that causes, it's not an equilibrium result. If the (4, 2) node was available, students would just choose to cheat for the easy 4 points.

Promises and Commitment Problems

The double-cross has a long history as a narrative hook. In it, two characters come to an agreement on something that cannot happen at the same time. Party A completes his part of the bargain, but then Party B reneges after getting what she wants. Usually this is framed as a character being evil, but you can see how it can be a perfectly rational play of a game.

Imagine two characters, Lando and Vader. Vader gives Lando the choice of giving up his friend Han in order to keep Vader's forces out of his city. Lando has to make that choice before Vader makes his choice.

Lando's preferences:

- Free Han and No Occupation
- Han to Empire and No Occupation
- Free Han and Occupation
- Han to Empire and Occupation

Vader's Preferences:

- Han to Empire and Occupation
- Han to Empire and No Occupation
- Free Han and Occupation
- Free Han and No Occupation

The game tree looks like **FIGURE 20.5**.

FIGURE 20.5
Lando/Vader
game tree.

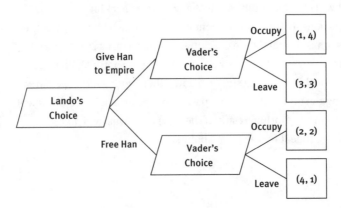

Using backwards induction, if Lando gives up Han, it's better for Vader to occupy (4 versus 3). If Lando does not give up Han, it's still better for Vader to occupy (2 versus 1). So Lando should know that Vader is going to occupy one way or the other and not choose to give up Han (3 versus 2). In other words, if someone made a feature film in which Lando gives up Han, audiences should not be surprised if Vader still occupies.

With this much benefit from a double-cross, why do we all not use this strategy all the time? Luckily, we have created ways to ensure *coordination*. Contracts are one mechanism.

Say you order a car from the factory. It costs you $20,000 to buy and costs the factory $15,000 to make. When you get ready to sell the car to your customer, you value the car at $25,000. In a normal trade situation, you make the transaction and are $5,000 better off and the factory is $5,000 better off. But what if the factory could just take your money and run without giving you the car? Then they could net $20,000 instead of $5,000. You would know that they could do that, though, and so by backwards induction you would never buy a car in the first place. Neither party would gain or lose anything.

Instead, you sign a contract. If the car is not delivered, you get your $20,000 back. Now the decision tree looks different (**FIGURE 20.6**).

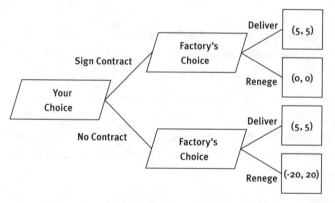

FIGURE 20.6
The contract game tree with payouts in thousands of dollars.

Here the outcome of the game shifts from the no benefit for either (0, 0) of not having the contract to a (5, 5) equilibrium with the concept of the contract. Both players win.

Iterated Games

The *Prisoner's Dilemma* works because the players make their decisions simultaneously without communicating. But most games can be played over and over again. If a player knows there might be repercussions, should he change his strategy?

What should players do if they have to play the *Prisoner's Dilemma* multiple times? As a reminder, **TABLE 20.1** shows what the payoffs look like.

TABLE 20.1 *Prisoner's Dilemma*

	Player B Cooperates (c)	Player B Defects (d)
Player A Cooperates (C)	(2, 2)	(0, 3)
Player A Defects (D)	(3, 0)	(1, 1)

Player A can choose to cooperate or defect. You can represent those strategies with a capital C or capital D, respectively. Player B can do the same, but to differentiate these strategies from those of Player A, use a lowercase c and d. If you want to note the result where both players defect, you can write (Dd). Or, if Player A cooperates and Player B defects, you can write (Cd).

It would stand to reason that if you know you will be playing this game over and over again (and that your opponent/partner knows this as well), you will just agree to cooperate forever, ensuring that you both get 2 points per game.

As an example, what happens if these two players play the game for four iterations and try to use this strategy? Theoretically, you can see (Cc) for the first three games. But in the fourth, both players know that this iteration is the last. They have no reason to keep cooperating, especially if they believe the other player will continue cooperating. So in the last game, both defect: (Dd).

Remember, though, that this information is available to both players. If they know that the fourth iteration will end in (Dd), then by the same logic, the last iteration is actually the third iteration. But the same logic that sabotaged the fourth iteration now sabotages the third. Both players see an advantage in defecting, so the result is (Dd). Now the second iteration is the last iteration. But again the same logic applies. This works backward until all games end with (Dd). By induction, any *n* game of *Prisoner's Dilemma* in which *n* is known to both players ends in (Dd) on each iteration.

This never-ending betrayal, however, makes no sense when you compare it to how individuals play in the real world.

Experimenting with Strategies

Political scientist Robert Axelrod studied the question of what the best strategy for an iterated *Prisoner's Dilemma* would be by posing a contest.[1] He collected diverse strategies of varying complexity from psychologists, economists, political scientists, and mathematicians and used a computer program to pit them against each other to find out organically which was the best. From this, he hoped to glean principles for ensuring success beyond the one point per game that the equilibrium result predicts.

Here are some of the entrants:[2]

- **RANDOM:** Play randomly. Choose C or D by coin flip every round.
- **TIT-FOR-TAT:** In the first round, cooperate. In any other round, do what the opponent did in the previous round.
- **TIT-FOR-TAT PLUS:** In the first round, cooperate. After a defection by the opponent, defect. After a cooperate by the opponent, cooperate with a probability of 9/10.
- **GRIM TRIGGER:** In the first round, cooperate. If the opponent defects, defect and continue defecting for the rest of the game. GRIM TRIGGER never forgives.
- **ESCALATION:** In the first round, cooperate. If the opponent defects, defect once in the next round. If the opponent defects again, defect in the next two rounds. Increase defection by one round each time, punishing the opponent more and more for defection.
- **GROFMAN:** If (Cd) or (cD) happened on the previous round, choose C with a probability of 2/7. Otherwise, choose D.

▶ **NOTE** Spoilers: These listed strategies placed 15th, 1st, 12th, 7th, 5th, and 4th, respectively, out of 15 entries.

Axelrod set up the experiment so that each strategy played every other one, in addition to playing against itself. For example, if TIT-FOR-TAT PLUS played against GRIM TRIGGER, it might look something like **TABLE 20.2**.

TABLE 20.2 TIT-FOR-TAT PLUS versus GRIM TRIGGER

TIT-FOR-TAT PLUS	C	C	C	C	D	C	D	D	D	D	D	D	D	D
	2	2	2	2	3	0	1	1	1	1	1	1	1	1
GRIM TRIGGER	c	c	c	c	c	d	d	d	d	d	d	d	d	d
	2	2	2	2	0	3	1	1	1	1	1	1	1	1

· · · · · · · · · · · · · · · · · ·

1   Axelrod, R. (1984). *The Evolution of Cooperation*. New York: Basic Books.
2   Axelrod, R. (1980). "Effective Choice in the Prisoner's Dilemma." *Journal of Conflict Resolution*, 24(1), 3–25.

In the first rounds, everyone cooperated and did really well, scoring 2 points per round. But eventually, the rule in TIT-FOR-TAT PLUS where 10 percent of the time it chooses to defect after a cooperation caused the player to choose D. Once GRIM TRIGGER saw that, it defected forever and the two became locked into (Dd) for the rest of the iterations, earning only one point per round.

The results at the end of the tournament were surprising. The shortest program (in terms of lines of code) won the entire contest. The winning strategy was TIT-FOR-TAT: In the first round, cooperate. In any other round, do what the opponent did in the previous round. It destroyed much more complicated strategies. For instance, you might think that TIT-FOR-TAT PLUS would be superior because every once in a while it can eke out a couple bonus points by defecting when someone thinks it will cooperate. However, against strategies like GRIM TRIGGER that never forgive a defection, this ends up torpedoing the entire game for both players.

Successful Strategies

Axelrod found three strategic concepts that provided the best results in his tournament. First, the strategy had to be **nice**. This meant that it never defected first. If two nice strategies paired up, they would cooperate forever. Ironically, despite its scary sounding name, GRIM TRIGGER is a nice strategy. If its opponent never defects, neither does GRIM TRIGGER. The top eight strategies in Axelrod's tournament were all nice strategies. There was even a large gap in points between the worst nice strategy and the best non-nice strategy.

Next, what differentiated the nice strategies from one another was how they played against those who were not nice. The second concept that Axelrod determined helped the winning strategies was **forgiveness**. That is, once an opponent defected, he would cooperate again with that same opponent in the future. GRIM TRIGGER is the opposite of a forgiving rule. No matter what, it plays by the maxim "Fool me once, shame on you. Fool me twice, shame on me." It never forgives. ESCALATION forgives after one move the first time, two moves the second time, three moves the third time, and so on. TIT-FOR-TAT, the winner, forgives after only one move no matter what.

Lastly, the strategy had to be **non-envious**. Strategies that look at the opponent's success as a measure of the player's failure lead to poor decisions being made to rectify the inequality. Those strategies can serve to reduce the inequality between players, but they do so by lowering both players' scores. If the goal is to score the most, then envious strategies are not successful. For the resounding success of TIT-FOR-TAT in many different tournaments, Axelrod notes a poignant result: TIT-FOR-TAT *never* received more points than its opponent. It did better than everyone else on average because its design allowed for both players to succeed, whereas other strategies ended up in long strings of mutual defection. This works because the *Prisoner's Dilemma* is not zero-sum. Both players can succeed.

Axelrod says to be careful in extrapolating that TIT-FOR-TAT is the optimal solution for an iterated *Prisoner's Dilemma*. It won the matchup only between the strategies submitted. There are others, in retrospect, that would do better, such as a strategy Axelrod called TIT-FOR-TWO-TATS. It's more forgiving than TIT-FOR-TAT in that it defects only if the opponent defected in the previous two rounds. Taking this to an extreme, would the most forgiving strategy be one that always cooperated no matter what? By pairing overly forgiving strategies with "not nice" strategies, Axelrod shows that a strategy must be retaliatory to some degree, especially against "not nice" strategies. Being nice and forgiving is a great strategy when you are paired up with others with similar strategies, but it does terribly when paired up with strategies that are meant to exploit.

Axelrod cautions that strategies that attempt to be too clever are likely to fail. Strategies that tried to predict the other player's move and defect when they cooperated often failed. These inferences were often complicated and ended up playing pseudorandomly. The best strategy against TIT-FOR-TAT is to simply always cooperate. Yet these predictive strategies that tried to outguess TIT-FOR-TAT ended up defecting at least once, which decreased both players' overall score.

What does this mean for game design? Most online multiplayer videogames are set up so that the players play and then never meet again. In these games, the most successful strategies are the mean ones—to always defect. In games with what Axelrod calls "the shadow of the future," the specter of future games allows players to create strategies that yield better results than what their strategy would yield in a single game by defecting. This has implications for all multiplayer game design. By creating hooks that increase "the shadow of the future," players can essentially be punished for antisocial or anticompetitive behavior and be rewarded for cooperative and goal-aligned behavior. This happens not because of some mystical sense of community, but because of the same incentives that cause players to act antisocial in the first place.

Summary

- You can use game trees to visualize sequential games as a process of decisions and events that read from left to right.

- Sequential games can be solved for their equilibria by a process called backwards induction.

- Games that are played multiple times in succession may have different player behaviors than games played only once.

- In experiments, strategies that were initially cooperative, provocable to punishment and forgiveness, and not concerned with the opponent's payoffs performed the best over iterated *Prisoner's Dilemmas*.

- By increasing the "shadow of the future," you can create an environment in which cooperative behaviors are more likely to endure.

21 Problems with Game Theory

Reality continues to ruin my life.

—BILL WATTERSON

Although game theory is interesting and provides a useful theoretical framework for what rational decision makers should choose, it has its limitations when you're dealing with real-world games. The first limitation is that examples in game theory tend to deal with highly idealized problems where payouts are clear, information is shared, and complexity is mediated to a reasonable level. However, it's difficult to transfer the knowledge from a good game theory problem to action inside a video game as complex as, for example, *Halo*.

However, even if you are able to perfectly model those textbook examples in your game's decisions, you still have reasons to distrust the behavior patterns of human players that game theory predicts.

Rational Actors

The largest problem with applying game theory to real-world situations is the assumption that all players will act completely rationally.

Take this problem, for example:

> A rebellion is rising. The revolutionaries want to bring the evil despot to justice. He is in one of his four castles, situated on a river flowing west to east through the capital city. The revolutionaries can get into one castle before the alarm is sounded and all the castles lock up tight. The despot knows they are coming and can get to the safety of any one of his castles. If they choose the correct castle, they will get the despot. If not, the revolution will fail. Castles 1, 3, and 4 are white. Castle 2, however, is painted a shining gold (**FIGURE 21.1**). Which castle should the revolutionaries storm?

FIGURE 21.1
Which castle should be stormed?

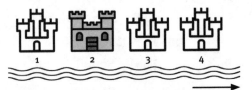

CASTLE SYMBOL BY ANDRÉ RAFAEL, CASTLE SYMBOL BY BUENA BUENA, AND WATER SYMBOL BY ALESSANDRO SURACI, FROM THENOUNPROJECT.COM COLLECTION.

Game theory tells us that all the information about the castle colors, the information about the river, and even the position of the castles relative to each other is not relevant. To the despot, every castle is as good as any other as long as the revolutionaries do not pick it. To the revolutionaries, any castle is as good as any other as long as the despot is there. The equilibrium strategy predicts that both sides would choose each castle with a probability of 0.25. Thus, the despot would lose his head 25 percent of the time (**TABLE 21.1**).

TABLE 21.1 The Despot and the Revolution

	Despot Hide in Castle 1	Despot Hide in Castle 2	Despot Hide in Castle 3	Despot Hide in Castle 4
Revolution Storm Castle 1	(1, 0)	(0, 1)	(0, 1)	(0, 1)
Revolution Storm Castle 2	(0, 1)	(1, 0)	(0, 1)	(0, 1)
Revolution Storm Castle 3	(0, 1)	(0, 1)	(1, 0)	(0, 1)
Revolution Storm Castle 4	(0, 1)	(0, 1)	(0, 1)	(1, 0)

In research that used actual human subjects, however, different results were seen.[1] The expected 25 percent chose to hide in Castle 2. However, 40 percent chose Castle 3! The reasoning likely could have been that an interior palace was preferable, but the gold palace was too obvious. Yet none of those reasons were actual determining factors listed in the problem statement itself. Due to this imbalance, the despot loses his head 30 percent of the time instead of the expected 25 percent of the time if the despot had just chosen randomly.

Human beings are remarkable pattern creators. From even before the time we first looked into the sky and shaped the stars into constellations, we practiced creating stories from data. It is not rational to see points of light in the sky whose sources are billions of miles apart and assign them the qualities of a crab or a bull. The players who choose Castle 3 may be doing the same thing; some may create a story from the problem explanation that biases them toward choosing that castle over any others.

Perhaps the differences between the experimental results and the theoretic prediction in the Despot and Revolution example are just random noise. Maybe over a longer run everything evens out to 25 percent across all four palaces. If that is the case, let's use a different example that hits irrational players where they can feel it: in the wallet.

The Dollar Auction

Game theory sometimes relies on players being able to do difficult feats of math in real time. Earlier problems used induction to solve for the equilibrium. But do actual players use induction?

Imagine that I am going to auction off a $50 bill to a classroom full of students. There is no reserve price, so if the $50 bill goes for $1, so be it. The only catch is that both the winner and the next-highest bidder have to pay me their last bid at auction's end. At the start, the students salivate over getting $50 for cheap, so they start bidding: $1, $2, $5. Soon the bidding is up to $25. Raising to $26 makes sense because the winner would still be up $24. Now look at the decision in **FIGURE 21.2** for the person who has the $25 bid.

· · · · · · · · · · · · · · · · · · · ·

1   Rubinstein, A. (2013, March 27). "How Game Theory Will Solve the Problems of the Euro Bloc and Stop Iranian Nukes." Retrieved March 24, 2015, from www.faz.net/aktuell/feuilleton/debatten/game-theory-how-gametheory-will-solve-the-problems-of-the-euro-bloc-and-stop-iranian-nukes-12130407.html.

FIGURE 21.2
Deep into the dollar auction.

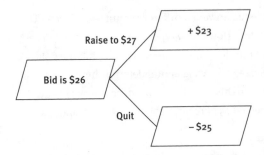

His choice is clear: He should raise the bid. But the person who was just raised faces the same problem. Once the bid is $27, she can choose to raise to $28 for a positive potential payoff or quit and lose her last bid. So she will raise. Once the bid is $50, a raise becomes the possibility of losing only $1 instead of losing $49. This, in theory, could go on forever, netting the auctioneer a tidy bit of money.

An inductive look at the problem shows that bidding is safe only when there can be cooperation. If all the bidders agree that one person will bid $1 and then share the proceeds, then the bidders can win. Otherwise, the auctioneer will bleed the participants dry. In an exercise that demonstrates this with business graduate students at a prestigious business school, the "winner" of the auction (a president of a company) paid $2,000 for a $20 bill. The loser, paid $1,980 for nothing.[2] Although inductive solving processes may make sense for isolated game theory examples, it's questionable whether players use them in practice.

The "Guess Two-Thirds" Game

Another game that shows the limitations of inductive thinking is the "guess two-thirds" game. In this game, a group is asked to have each member choose a number between 0 to 100 so that the person closest to two-thirds of the average of all submitted guesses wins a prize.

What should you choose? Some people assume that every number is as likely a guess as any other number. Under this reasoning, the average guess would be 50, so the two-thirds guess would be 33.33. Some take this a step further. If 33.33 is a likely guess, then two-thirds of that should be 22.22.

. . . .
2   Murnighan, J. K. (2002). "A Very Extreme Case of the Dollar Auction." *Journal of Management Education,*
     26(1), 56–69.

But why would every guess be as likely as any other? Should any player ever pick 100? 100 can win only if every single entry is also 100. In that case, two-thirds of the average would be 66.67, but everyone would be equally close to it. If you believed that to be the case, then you could choose any other number and be closer than everyone else.

No number above 66 and two-thirds can ever be two-thirds of the average because two-thirds of the highest possible guess average is 66 and 2/3. If no number between 66.67 and 100 can ever be the correct answer, then why would anyone ever pick it? Players should reevaluate the problem as one in which the players are trying to get two-thirds of the average between 0 and 66.67. But if this is the case and no rational player would ever pick something above 66.67, then the same logic should hold for the range from 0 to 66.67. If everyone chooses 66.67, then two-thirds of the average is 44.44. Therefore, it's not logical to pick any number above 44.44 because that can never be the right answer for rational players.

This logic repeats itself (**FIGURE 21.3**). If no number above 44.44 can ever be the right answer, then no player should pick a number above 44.44. If that is the case, then two-thirds of the average cannot be higher than 29.63. So a rational actor keeps iterating on this until the only rational choice is to choose 0. A group where everyone chooses 0 has a two-thirds average of 0. Everyone wins and no one has any reason to choose a different number.

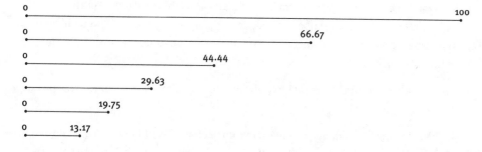

0   100

0   66.67

0   44.44

0   29.63

0   19.75

0   13.17

FIGURE 21.3
Iterated solutions show a narrower and narrower range of rational possibilities.

Experimental results do not show players choosing 0 as a group, even though it is the rational game theoretical result. In one study that tested a similar game with the same expected result, the first time players played this game, not a single player chose 0.[3] In another study, a plurality of players used the reasoning that treats every number as equally likely, resulting in a guess of 33.33, whereas a smaller group of players tried to

. . . .

3   Duffy, J., & Nagel, R. (1997). "On the Robustness of Behaviour in Experimental 'Beauty Contest' Games." *The Economic Journal*, 107(445), 1684–1700.

exploit that likely guess by themselves guessing 22.22.[4] Another study found the same clustering around these numbers while also noting that 10 percent of subjects chose a number that was impossible to be the two-thirds average (greater than 66.67).[5]

It's clear that you cannot always trust real people to give a rational answer.

Second-Price Auctions

Perhaps in the previous examples, the game is just too complicated. What if people are rational up to a point where a problem becomes too complex, and then they give up and use poor heuristics? What if people realize the complexity of the dollar auction only after it is too late? What if you need players to act rationally in a game that does not require infinite iteration such as the "guess two-thirds" game? One example of a simpler common game in which players do not act rationally is the "second price" auction, which I discussed in Chapter 16. You might be more familiar with the concept as similar to the auction system used by eBay.

In a *second-price auction*, participants (players) submit bids in secret for an item. The winner is, of course, the player who bid the highest. However, the winner pays only the amount of the second-highest bidder.

The concept of the second-price auction is popular because the equilibrium strategy is to bid exactly what you think the item is worth, and as such, you cannot "outthink" or "bluff" the other players. No skill is required for a second-price auction. If you bid your actual value for the item, you have no reason to change to a different price. Let's illustrate this with an example.

Say there is a second-price auction for a new pair of headphones. You value these headphones at $50, so you bid $50.

If you have the highest bid, do you have a reason to change your bid if you are allowed to? Say that the second place bid is $40. If you do nothing, you profit $10—the value of the headphones to you minus what you have to pay. Should you increase your bid? If you increase the bid, you still value the headphones at $50 and still only pay $40—you

....

4   Rubinstein, A. (2007). "Instinctive and Cognitive Reasoning: A Study of Response Times." *The Economic Journal*, 117(523), 1243–1259.

5   Nagel, R. (1995). "Unraveling in Guessing Games: An Experimental Study." *The American Economic Review*, 1313–1326.

have the same amount of profit, so you have no reason to do this. Should you decrease your bid? If you decrease it to somewhere in the $40.01–$49.99 range, then this also has no change—you value the headphones at $50 and get them for $40, gaining $10 in profit. If you lower your bid below $40.01, then you do not win the headphones but you also don't pay anything. This is a $0 profit. Since that is less than the $10 you would get for not changing your bid, there is no reason to change your bid if you are winning.

If you do not have the highest bid, do you have a reason to change your bid? Say that you are the second place bid at $50 and the winner bid $59.99. If you do nothing, you profit $0. If you lower your bid, you still lose and so still profit $0. If you raise your bid up to $59.98, you still lose and still profit $0. However, if you raise your bid to $60, you win the auction, but end up paying $60 for a pair of headphones you only value at $50. You end up with a profit of –$10. Thus, even if you are losing, you have no reason to change your bid beyond the maximum you value the item.

If you have ever used eBay, however, you have likely seen or been party to some irrational decision-making. One study compared the value of items on eBay auctions to the "Buy It Now" price for that same item.[6] In the study of one particular item, 42 percent of auctions exceeded the initial "Buy It Now" price. Another study showed that 98.8 percent of eBay prices for media such as books or CDs are higher than the lowest online price found in a 10-minute search.[7] Additionally, in a second-price auction, it makes no sense to ever update your bid based on what the other players have done. Nothing in the previous strategy mentioned when a player should bid. Yet in one study of 240 eBay auctions, 89 had bids placed in the final 60 seconds of a multi-day auction.[8] A variety of providers sell "sniping" software that allows a user to increase their bid at the last possible moment.

▶ **NOTE** An argument can be made that sniping software exists to restrict the flow of information from competitors who do not know their true willingness to pay.

With these examples, it is difficult to justify using game theory alone to determine what players will do when engaged in a game.

6   Malmendier, U., & Lee, Y. H. (2011). The bidder's curse. *The American Economic Review*, 749-787.

7   Ariely, D., & Simonson, I. (2003). "Buying, Bidding, Playing, or Competing? Value Assessment and Decision Dynamics in Online Auctions." *Journal of Consumer Psychology*, 13(1), 113–123.

8   Roth, A. E., & Ockenfels, A. (2002). "Last Minute Bidding and the Rules for Ending Second Price Auctions: Evidence from eBay and Amazon Auctions on the Internet." *American Economic Review*, 92(4), 1093–1103.

Summary

- Game theory provides tools for predicting the behavior of rational players. Unfortunately, the rational player is more of a theoretical construct. Actual player behavior can diverge from the theoretical results.

- Players may be influenced by irrelevant information that has no bearing on their likelihood of success.

- Induction is often not used by real-world players, especially in situations with many iterations of the induction loop.

- Although auctions can provide a way to dig out a player's willingness to pay, auction behavior is not always rational.

- Game theory is a good starting point for beginning to understand player behavior, but it cannot be the only tool you use.

22 Marginal Decision Analysis

A nickel ain't worth a dime anymore.

—YOGI BERRA

One way that economists consider decision behavior is by *marginal analysis*. In marginal analysis, decision makers don't make decisions based on the averages of an action, but rather on the cost and benefit of the next unit.

As an example, say I need three gallons of ice cream for an ice cream party I am throwing to celebrate publishing a book on game design. I can go to my local supermarket and buy a gallon of ice cream for $5. Or I can go to a warehouse club and buy a 5-gallon vat of ice cream for $16. Which should I buy?

The economist would say I should go to the supermarket and buy three 1-gallon containers for $15; a fourth and fifth marginal gallon have no value to me since I only need 3 gallons. But in practice, we consumers often look at prices in different ways. We could look at the average price per gallon at the warehouse club of $3.20 and compare that to the average price per gallon at the supermarket of $5 and think that the warehouse club is the better deal.

In this chapter, we look at a few ways we can use marginal prices to understand decisions.

Marginal Nuggets

On a lunch break one day, I walked into a Manhattan McDonalds for an inexpensive lunch because there are few places you can find an inexpensive lunch in New York City. My head was awash with a spreadsheet of figures for a Facebook game I was working on at the time, so I was keenly conscious of balance and utility. When I looked at the prices for Chicken McNuggets, I found the prices shown in **TABLE 22.1**.

TABLE 22.1 Nugget Prices

Menu	
6-piece	$1.99
10-piece	$3.49
20-piece	$5.99
Value Menu	
4-piece	$1.00

The prices on the regular menu make sense because they are cheaper on a per-nugget basis as you order more. I knew well about the fundamental concept of *decreasing marginal utility*—that is the concept where if you have n items, the next item $(n+1)^{th}$ will provide you less value than the previous n^{th} item. In other words, we get saturated. Or, because I am still thinking about that ice cream party, I think of it in terms of ice cream: The first scoop is really great. The second is pretty good. Three scoops is a bit much. Four scoops? Ugh, maybe. Five? Put it away! Twenty? Are you a villain? You'll pay less and less for that n^{th} scoop as n increases.

Hidden away from the normal prices was that "value menu" listing of four nuggets for a dollar. I started doing the math. I could get 20 nuggets for $6 by ordering the 20-piece, or I could get 20 nuggets for $5 by ordering five 4-pieces from the value menu (**TABLE 22.2**).

TABLE 22.2 Value Menu Prices

Order	Receive	Total Cost	Cost Per Nugget
3×4-piece	12 nuggets	$3.00	$0.25
1×10-piece	10 nuggets	$3.49	$0.35
5×4-piece	20 nuggets	$5.00	$0.25
1×20-piece	20 nuggets	$5.99	$0.30

In fact, no matter how hungry you are, it seems to benefit you to buy only from the value menu (**TABLE 22.3**).

TABLE 22.3 What Are My Savings?

How Hungry?	Value Method	Normal Method	Savings
10	3×4-piece $3.00	10-piece $3.49	$0.49 +2 nuggets
12	3×4-piece $3.00	2×6-piece $3.98	$0.98
16	4×4-piece $4.00	10×6-piece $5.48	$1.48
18	5×4-piece $5.00	3×6-piece $5.97	$0.97 +2 nuggets
20	5×4-piece $5.00	20-piece $5.99	$0.99
26	7×4-piece $7.00	2-piece + 6-piece $7.98	$0.98 +2 nuggets

The smallest denomination (the Value Menu) had the smallest per-unit cost. A 4-piece was only $0.25 per nugget, but the massive 20-piece was $0.30 per nugget. Thus the marginal cost per 4-nuggets was cheapest by buying only value menu nuggets.

This proves that you should scrutinize the menus at fast food joints, but what does it teach about games?

Around the time my studio was getting ready to release our mobile game *Fire and Dice*, we had to decide how much our in-game currency (keys) would cost. Because of the concept of decreasing marginal utility, we knew that the smaller bundles of keys needed to cost more per key than larger bundles of keys. You see this in many games that sell virtual currency. I figured I would do a quick study of the current games out there and see how they implemented discounts.

This was by no means a scientific study, just a brief scan of some popular games at the time. **FIGURE 22.1** shows the results circa December 2011. The x-axis is the cost of a particular bundle in dollars, and the y-axis is the amount of stuff per dollar in terms of how much stuff you get for $1.

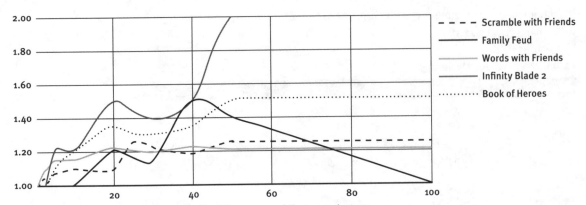

FIGURE 22.1 "Things" per dollar normalized for some mobile games in 2011.

In *Fire and Dice*, for instance (**TABLE 22.4**), our $1 key pack had 7 keys (average cost of 14 cents/key), our $5 pack had 50 keys (average cost of 10 cents/key), our $20 pack had 250 keys (average cost of 8 cents/key) and our $50 pack had 1,000 keys (average cost of 5 cents/key).

TABLE 22.4 *Fire and Dice* Key Prices

Pack	Keys	Marginal Cost for Additional Keys	Stuff Per $ (normalized)
$1	7	$0.14	1 (by definition)
$5	50	$0.09	1.43
$20	250	$0.08	1.79
$50	1,000	$0.04	2.86

The price per key decreases as the bundle price goes up, which means the curve of "stuff per $" goes upward. If we sell 10 keys for $1 and 100 keys for $10, the curve is a flat line because the cost per key is flat.

Additionally, the marginal cost for additional keys always decreases. If the cost for the next key increases, then the player can just buy a cheaper bundle because those keys are cheaper.

Most games have an ever-increasing "stuff per $" curve because they deal with the reality of consumer's decreasing marginal utility for goods. Except for one. Look at the *Family Feud* line in Figure 22.1. It increases until the $40 pack and then decreases. What does this mean? Look at its prices specifically as shown in **TABLE 22.5**.

TABLE 22.5 *Family Feud* Coin Prices

Pack	Coins	Marginal Cost for Additional Coins	Stuff Per $ (normalized)
$2	10	$0.20	1 (by definition)
$5	25	$0.20	1
$20	120	$0.16	1.2
$40	300	$0.11	1.5
$100	500	$0.30	1

There is a problem here! Look at the "moneybags" $100 pack. If I wanted to spend $100 on this game, my option is dominated. There is no way I would buy the $100 pack. Why? The marginal cost for coins increases significantly between the $40 pack and the $100 pack. The $100 pack costs $60 more than the $40 pack, but gives only 200 more coins. This is 30 cents per coin. Why would I spend 30 cents per coin when I could buy $2 packs at 20 cents per coin? It increases to a level *more per additional coin than any other option*. I could buy the $100 pack and get 500 coins, or I could buy two $40 packs and a $20 pack and get 720 coins. That is a significant amount more. That is exactly like buying six 4-piece Chicken McNuggets for $6 instead of the 20-piece for $6.

Ludia, the makers of the *Family Feud* app, noticed this imbalance. Metrics likely told them that people were buying multiple $40 packs, but no one was buying $100 packs. They have since reset their $100 pack to give 1,000 coins, which is 10 coins per dollar.

By examining the marginal cost of resources, you can understand if you are pricing resources in a way that makes sense for players.

Balance on Margins

Balance on margins comes up again and again in games with economic trade-offs, not just in real-money transactions.

As an example, let's say a player can cast two spells as often as he wants: The fireball costs 10 magic points and does 20 damage, and the cone of frost costs 20 magic points and does 30 damage. Which will the player be more likely to use? The game's metrics will likely report an overwhelming preference for the fireball. If he can cast as many spells as he likes, why would he ever cast something that does 1.5 damage per magic point when he could cast something that does 2 damage per magic point? Players will see this mechanic as out of balance. In this particular situation, the only way to balance the two is to give the fireball equal damage per magic point as the cone of frost.

In another example let's say you are making a role-playing game and need to design the stats for three swords for your game's shop. The player can use only one sword at a time, so she must choose carefully. Assigning value to the first two swords is easy: Let's say you have the first do 6 damage and cost 60 coins, and the second do 10 damage and cost 90 coins. You want the third to do 15 damage. What should it cost (**TABLE 22.6**)?

TABLE 22.6 The Cost to Do Damage

	Cost	Damage	Cost/Damage
Wooden Sword	60	6	10
Steel Sword	90	10	9
Master Sword	??	15	??

If you said "less than 135 coins," then you fell into my trap. The first sword costs 10 coins for a point of damage, the second costs 9 coins for a point of damage. Should the third not cost less than 9 coins per point of damage? No. Since the swords are not *fungible*, meaning you cannot interchange them and combine them freely, you do not need to make them ever more effective on a per-coin basis. In fact, that is the kind of design that leads to *power inflation* where the items get better and better at an exponential rate. Since you cannot use two of the wooden swords simultaneously in lieu of the third sword, this kind of transaction is not at all like the *Family Feud* coins example. Coins are fungible. It does not matter what coin you have, only how many you have. In this case, there is not decreasing marginal utility because the class of weapons that do 20 damage are a different product altogether than two swords that each do 10 damage. People will pay an *increasing* marginal cost for goods like these. Why? Because they are also receiving an increasing marginal utility. *As long as marginal utility exceeds marginal cost, the buyer will want that marginal unit.*

Think of cars and horsepower (hp). An engine's horsepower is not fungible: I cannot drop five Honda Civic engines (140hp each) into a car and make it a Lamborghini Aventador (700hp) (**FIGURE 22.2**). When you reach those high horsepower levels, you have to pay a lot of money for just a small amount of additional power. There's *increasing* marginal utility for those at the top. If horsepower were fungible, you would expect the Aventador to cost less than five Civics. However, a Civic costs roughly $20,000, whereas the Aventador costs around $400,000. People pay more and more to get that additional horsepower. Those first few horsepower are cheap. It's comparatively easy to make a 140hp engine. But when your engine is trying to top 500, 600, or 700 horsepower, every drop of additional power requires more and more streamlining and makes the cost more and more expensive. No sports car enthusiast would settle for a weak Civic, so they are willing to pay the ever-increasing price per unit of power.

FIGURE 22.2 Assume similar insurance costs.

CREATIVE COMMONS

What does this mean for your swords? Your third sword could be the Aventador to the first two Civic and Mustang swords. Make it a luxury good: 15 damage and price it at 300 coins, if your mechanics and aesthetics support this.

By examining your players' decision-making from an economic perspective, you can avoid forcing them into obvious decisions. Now they must choose between high damage and inefficient use of their coins or lower damage and more options for how to spend their coins.

Summary

- One way to look at players making decisions about goods is to examine the economic concepts of marginal utility and cost.

- Fungible goods tend toward a decreasing marginal utility. The more a player has of a good, the less he wants the next unit of that good. This is, of course, a guideline. If there is a level-up at 600 of a good and the player has 599, then that 600th good has a high marginal value.

- Rational players should always choose the cheapest way to receive the next good, assuming the goods are identical. This means choosing the good with the least marginal cost.

- Examine the marginal cost of fungible goods to understand if bundle pricing makes sense.

- Putting limits on a good, such as only being able to use one sword or one car at a time, leads to increasing marginal value of that good's performance.

6 Human Behavior in Games

Reason shapes the future,
but superstition infects the present.

—IAIN M. BANKS, THE STATE OF THE ART

When creating models for rational actors, it makes sense to examine an edge case: What would a perfect player do? And the larger your game is, the more looking through the lens of the actions of a perfect player makes sense. A game with a few dozen players can get by with some loopholes. A game with millions of players is likely to have a few players who can ferret out all the possible exploits. Players are still finding exploits in the original *Super Mario Bros.* 30 years after it was published (http://kotaku.com/decades-later-someones-discovered-a-new-super-mario-br-1591884544)

If you assume all your players are perfect robots, your models for how players choose in your games become a whole lot easier, but the challenge of creating an entertaining and challenging game skyrockets. Luckily, you don't have to face this problem. Humans are lazy, but they are massively complex decision makers.

One of the greatest tragedies in games education is that human psychology is not given the same emphasis as programming, art, and project management. Humans play your games and human behavior is delightfully difficult to predict. However, psychology has been asking the same questions of all humans that we game designers have been asking our players since the dawn of the field of psychology itself. How do we choose? Why do we choose what we do? How do we learn? What motivates us? What are our mental limitations? Answers and theories for all these questions have a huge role in game design.

Unfortunately, the answers are not straightforward. The best that you can do is ride on the coattails of powerful peer-reviewed research and try your hardest to not get duped by the charlatans that spout off-the-cuff statements about functional Magnetic Resonance Imaging (fMRIs) (www.theguardian.com/science/2012/may/27/brain-scans-flaws-vaughan-bell) and dopamine in pop-science books, articles, and flashy stage presentations. (For a better look at how complicated a relationship we have with dopamine, see Salamone, J. D., & Correa, M. (2012). "The Mysterious Motivational Functions of Mesolimbic Dopamine." Neuron, 76(3), 470–485). Perhaps this is why game education seems to loathe including psychological findings; too often it's difficult to separate the wheat from the chaff and decide which is the most instrumental truth.

But why should game designers fear learning something only to have it debunked by something else later? We constantly are forced to relearn. When a new game engine or programming language revolutionizes (or simply adds upon) what we know about how we implement games, we do not give up on engines and programming altogether. Being a game designer means constant learning, but it also means constant unlearning. Don't look for truths etched in stone.

Some futurists believe that the time is coming when technology will increase to the point where the human brain can be emulated completely and consciousness itself can be transferred to artificial brains. Inventor Ray Kurzweil believes this can happen by 2045 (Grossman, L. (2011). "2045: The Year Man Becomes Immortal." Time Magazine, 177(7), 42–49). Other studies have projected the full stochastic mapping of the human brain to 2111 (Sandberg, A. and Bostrom, N. (2008). "Whole Brain Emulation: A Roadmap, Technical Report" 2008-3. Tech. Rep., Future of Humanity Institute, Oxford University). It's best to leave this debate to philosophers and speculative fiction authors. Until humanity can fully understand the nature of our own brains, we will only have marginally better and better best guesses as to how that lump of matter in our skulls really works. Once we master the human brain, games will either become entirely irrelevant or the focus of vastly increased leisure time.

In the meantime, let's enjoy the puzzle that is human behavior.

23 Behaviorism and Schedules of Reinforcement

> The way [...] reinforcement is carried out
> is more important than the amount.
>
> —B. F. SKINNER

What do dog trainers, casino owners, and some free-to-play game designers all have in common? They all use schedules of reinforcement to get their users to engage and re-engage repeatedly with what they are trying to teach or sell. To understand what this means and why it is important for the future of games, you need to first learn about a Russian scientist who studied digestion.

Operant Conditioning

Ivan Pavlov (**FIGURE 23.1**) won the Nobel Prize in 1904 for his work on understanding the digestive system. His most popular contribution to science is the concept of the *conditioned reflex*. To simplify Pavlov's research, he fed dogs and coupled the feeding with a stimulus, such as a bell ringing or a buzzer sounding. Quickly, the dogs associated the sound of the stimulus with the act of feeding. When dogs anticipate food, they begin to salivate. Pavlov was able to get dogs to salivate as if they were receiving food even when they only heard a bell ring but were not presented with food.

How this concept could be used to modify behavior was named *classical conditioning*. Later scientists modified this and discovered *operant conditioning*—instead of pairing a neutral stimulus (ringing a bell) with a reward, they paired rewards with whether or not a behavior was successful. B. F. Skinner is the psychologist most closely associated with operant conditioning or its larger school of psychology known as *Behaviorism*. The Skinner box bears his name (**FIGURE 23.2**).

FIGURE 23.1 Ivan Pavlov, the Michael Jordan of measuring saliva.

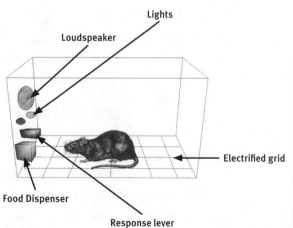

Lights

Loudspeaker

Electrified grid

Food Dispenser

Response lever

FIGURE 23.2 An operant conditioning chamber, or Skinner box.

In a Skinner box, a test subject (the rat in Figure 23.2) is able to press a lever; that action creates some sort of response based on what the researcher is looking for. It may reward the rat with a food pellet, it may cause the floor to be electrified, it may cause an annoying siren to go off, or it may do nothing at all. For our purposes, the details of how and why operant conditioning experiments work is not relevant. What *is* relevant are the results that Skinner and later psychologists were able to discover about how humans and animals act for rewards and punishments. He and others found that certain "schedules of reinforcement," or how the rewards were given out, affected how much the subject subsequently pulled the lever.

For instance, if the rat received a pellet of food every time it pulled the lever, what would you expect it to do? Naturally, it would pull the lever whenever it got hungry, and it would not pull the lever whenever it was not hungry. But what if it got a pellet every tenth time it pulled the lever? What if it received a pellet randomly, but on average, after ten pulls? What if it received a pellet every time it pulled the lever but only after 10 seconds had passed since the last time it received food? What if it received a pellet only after a random amount of time, which averaged to 10 seconds? How would these setups affect the rat's behavior?

Schedules of Reinforcement

All of these setups have names:

- *Fixed ratio* is when the reward is given after *n* responses. For instance, if a player in an RPG levels up after killing every tenth monster, that is reinforcement on a fixed-ratio schedule. *Continuous reinforcement* is a type of fixed-ratio schedule in which the reward is given after every response. Pull the lever, get the food. This is essentially a fixed ratio of 1:1.
- *Variable ratio* is when the reward is given after an average of *n* responses but is unpredictable. If in an RPG each monster had a 10-percent chance of dropping a "level up" gem, this is a variable-ratio schedule. The player may get the gem on the first monster or the twentieth monster. No one knows.
- *Fixed interval* is when the reward is given on the first response after *t* minutes. In an RPG, if the player levels up after killing the first monster once after every hour of play, that is a fixed-interval schedule.
- *Variable interval* is when the reward is given on the first response after a random amount of time that averages to *t* minutes. In an RPG, if the player levels up after killing a monster at random, but on average every 10 minutes, that is a variable-interval schedule.

There are many other types of reward schedules, but these four (fixed ratio, variable ratio, fixed interval, and variable interval) are the most often cited. Which of these four schedules do you think gets the player to kill the most monsters? Why?

If you are a casino owner and you want to develop a new slot machine, how do you design it? Your goal is clearly to get people to spend as much money as possible by providing rewards that keep them inserting coins and pulling levers. Is this not extremely similar to the problem Skinner studied? You have a subject (customer) and you want to understand what it will take for that subject (customer) to want to pull the lever (play the slot machine) as much as possible. This form works for many games in which rewards are important. Which reward schedule should you use?

The results of using a fixed ratio are easiest to understand. In a fixed ratio, the subject slows activity after the reinforcement, but after time, it picks back up. Think of getting food when you are hungry. Generally, you wait until you are hungry to get food. Then after you eat, you do not think about food again until you are hungry again.

The variable ratio is what most slot machine designers use. It causes the greatest amount of activity. When the rats do not know when the food pellet is coming, they push the lever furiously. Players who do not know when the next jackpot is coming furiously insert coins into slot machines in hopes of a reward.

The fixed interval causes a flurry of activity when the deadline approaches, but little activity at other times. Think about eBay auctions. When do you check the auction status? A day before the auction closes you peek in once to see if you are still winning. But as the deadline approaches, you furiously click that refresh button to make sure you are still winning.

> ▶ **NOTE** eBay has changed to an actively updating page simply because too many users were refreshing pages repeatedly near auction ends.

The fixed interval also has a problem with a phenomenon known as *extinction*. Extinction is a melodramatic way of saying that the reward no longer produces the conditioned behavior. Another way of putting it is that the subject just stops pressing the lever. In fixed-interval schedules, once the interval passes, the subject has no reinforcement for pressing the lever for a while, so he quits and may not come back. In games, this is catastrophic! If someone puts your game away, it may be difficult to ever get that player back. Early reinforcement is great for getting someone to do something initially. However, if you do not switch to one of the other schedules, extinction happens quickly.

The variable interval is expected to generate steady activity: The subject is more engaged than with the fixed ratio, the activity is not as furious as it is with the variable ratio, and yet there is no rapid extinction as there is when using the fixed interval. This type still has a higher rate of extinction than the variable ratio (think of how hard it is to pull an engaged player from a slot machine!), and both variable intervals and variable ratios suffer less from extinction than their fixed cousins (perhaps because it takes subjects longer to figure out that a reward is less likely).

You should use the variable interval when you want some steady activity to persist. For instance, say you are a teacher and you want your students to do their homework every night. However, you don't have time to check every student's work every day. But to you, homework is a steady activity that you want the students to do. You don't want students to do a flurry of homework one night and then ignore the homework the next night, so the variable ratio seems inappropriate. How can you use a variable interval to get this steady activity? Perhaps you can say that three homework assignments each month will be checked, but you don't let the students know which ones. The students cannot anticipate which will be checked, so they have to do them all as if they will be checked (that is, until they figure out when no more assignments will be graded).

USING BACKWARDS INDUCTION ON VARIABLE INTERVAL HOMEWORK ASSIGNMENTS

Here is a fun game theory problem. Say you are in a class and the teacher tells you that three homework assignments will be graded. After you turn in the third one, you know no more assignments will be graded, so you can slack off without a grade penalty. The teacher, who is trained in game theory, should know this, however, so he should wait until the last class to take the third homework. This is rational. However, if you, the student, understand this, then you should treat the rest of the class as if you have only two to turn in, as you know the third graded homework will be on the last day. In this case, after you turn the second one in, you know you are safe until the last day of the month. But, the teacher knows this as well, so his best move is to make the second graded homework the next-to-last homework assignment. Extrapolate this and the equilibrium result is that the teacher makes only the last three assignments graded. But you and the other students should know this is the case and feel safe not completing every other assignment, which goes against what the teacher wants! A better system is for the teacher to not let the students know how many assignments will be graded; this does not allow them the visibility they need in order to game the system.

FIGURE 23.3 shows a summary of the schedules. Variable interval is great for slow and steady engagement. Fixed interval is largely effective only for engagement around the interval points. Fixed ratio or continuous reinforcement is great for a burst of engagement. Variable ratio is great for lots of engagement.

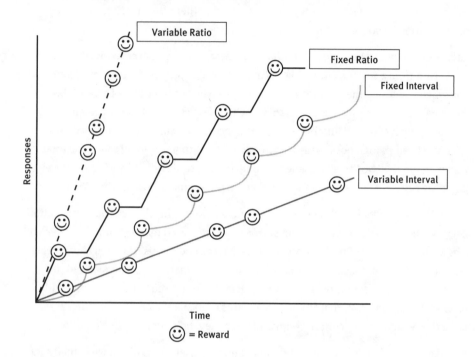

FIGURE 23.3
Responses based on reward schedule.

Anticipation and Uncertainty

What were the dogs in Pavlov's experiments doing when they salivated just because they heard a bell ring? They were not excited about the bell; they were excited about what the bell signified. They were *anticipating* food. Never underestimate the power of anticipation.

It's a stereotype to think of scientists as people in lab coats holding clipboards and watching rats finish a maze, but that is exactly what Dr. Clark Hull did in the 1930s to discover what he named the *goal-gradient effect*.[6] Designers use this effect quite a lot in games. It says that as subjects get closer to a goal, they accelerate their behavior. Hull found that his rats would run faster in his mazes as they neared the end.

· · · · · · · · · · · · · · · · · ·

6   Hull, C. L. (1934). "The Rat's Speed-of-Locomotion Gradient in the Approach to Food." *Journal of Comparative Psychology*, 17(3), 393.

Does this work with humans? Consider this: The Baltimore Marathon had to ask spectators of the marathon not to yell at participants "almost there!" unless they are, in actuality, almost at the end of the marathon.[7] It turns out that even highly trained distance runners who have intimate knowledge of how far along they are in a race can be subtly tricked to exert more energy than they would otherwise choose to do just by being assured by strangers that the end of the race is near!

This does not just work in races for humans and rats. Have you ever received a frequent buyer card from a restaurant? On these cards you get a "punch" for each meal you buy, and when you fill up the card with these punches, you get some sort of award, like a free meal. Ran Kivetz did a study on this in which he gave one group of customers a 10-space punch card and another group a 12-space punch card with two spaces already filled in.[8] Even though both cards required ten more purchases to fill them, the group who received the two "free" punches filled up their cards faster. Why? The 12-space group was already one-sixth of the way there in their minds. "Almost there!"

One of the great behavioral economists, George Loewenstein, showed that anticipation itself can hold value.[9] Another group of psychologists found that a group who received a prize in a condition of uncertainty (such as, "At the end of this trial, you may receive chocolates or one of these other prizes.") were happier than those who received the same prize under a condition of certainty (such as, "At the end of this trial, you will receive chocolates.")[10] In that study, participants even spent more time looking at the prize they won under uncertain conditions than they did under certain conditions.

It is likely that all of us can cite a situation in our experiences in which we gained a lot of pleasure from anticipating something, only to be underwhelmed when we finally had it in our hands. This can be the case for a number of reasons. The most obvious is that the thing we desire just is not any good in the first place. Another is that what we value is less the thing and more the concept of the thing. A third is that we may just be tired.

▶ **NOTE** Psychologists Drèze and Nunes would likely suggest that you have to make the quests for the Mega and Ultra Swords challenging so that the player feels successful through her own self-efficacy upon attaining it.

· · · · · · · · · · · · · · · · · · · ·

7   "Baltimore Marathon Specific about Suggested Cheers." (2014, October 15). Retrieved November 18, 2014, from http://washington.cbslocal.com/2014/10/15/baltimore-marathon-specific-about-suggested-cheers.

8   Kivetz, R., Urminsky, O., & Zheng, Y. (2006). "The Goal-Gradient Hypothesis Resurrected: Purchase Acceleration, Illusionary Goal Progress, and Customer Retention." *Journal of Marketing Research*, 43(1), 39–58.

9   Loewenstein, G. (1987). "Anticipation and the Valuation of Delayed Consumption." *The Economic Journal*, 666–684.

10 Kurtz, J. L., Wilson, T. D., & Gilbert, D. T. (2007). "Quantity versus Uncertainty: When Winning One Prize Is Better Than Winning Two." *Journal of Experimental Social Psychology*, 43(6), 979–985.

Psychologists call this the *post-reward resetting phenomenon*.[11] In a nutshell, after receiving a reward, we tend to care less about receiving subsequent similar rewards. This is a problem in games! After you give a player the Mega Sword, you want him to desire the next step up, the Ultra Sword.

In Games: Coin Pusher

Machines, such as the one in **FIGURE 23.4**, are popular at redemption arcades. They are colloquially known as "coin pushers." The player drops a coin in, and it lands on the upper shelf. The upper shelf moves back and forth so that, with a sufficient mass of coins, the back-and-forth motion pushes a coin, or several, from the upper shelf onto the bottom shelf. The same is true of the bottom shelf. Eventually, a mass of coins causes some coins to fall over the front edge. The player then wins a prize based on the number of coins pushed over.

FIGURE 23.4 A coin pusher.

These coin pushers are an example of a game that masterfully manipulates schedules of reinforcement. Not only is the player reinforced on a variable ratio (he does not know how many coins he will have to drop in to both knock coins off the top shelf and then again knock coins off the bottom shelf), but coin pushers have one advantage over standard slot machines: Slot machines use the gambler's fallacy as a matter of trust. An engaged (or addicted, if you prefer) player may be unwilling to quit because they say a win is "due." In a coin pusher, that estimation is not just based on faith. The player can actually see that a win is about due, yet because of the random (or at least extremely difficult) nature of the game, all he can do is keep playing and anticipate the win.

· · · · · · · · · · · · · · · · · · · ·

11   Drèze, X., & Nunes, J. C. (2011). "Recurring goals and learning: the impact of successful reward attainment on purchase behavior." Journal of Marketing Research, 48(2), 268-281.

Even better, after a win, a slot machine patron can use the same gambler's fallacy logic to quit, saying that a win will not happen again soon. Yet a coin pusher player who just knocked some coins over the ledge can still see areas where coins are cantilevered over the edge. "If I just play one more coin, I bet I could knock that one over too! It is almost there!"

So what does a coin pusher do successfully to get players engaged?

- It offers a variable-ratio reward schedule that keeps players engaged.
- The view through the glass, the tendency of coins to stack upon themselves and cantilever, and the slow methodical action of the movement of the shelf provides anticipation to the player.
- The view through the glass always shows that the player is almost at an award, satisfying the goal-gradient effect.

In Games: *Destiny* Drops

Bungie's *Destiny* uses a particular reward technique that exemplifies what I have been describing. In *Destiny*, killing enemies has a random chance of dropping a piece of loot called an "engram." These engrams are color-coded based on their rarity, so you immediately know when you find something rare.

However, the player cannot know what item the engram will give until she exchanges it later. Sometimes an engram gives her exactly what she wants. But often it gets her something worthless because she is not the correct player class to use the rewarded item. It's all chance.

How is this successful in keeping players slaying bad guys?

- Drops themselves are based on a variable-ratio reward schedule.
- Cashing in the engram reveals another variable-ratio reward schedule.
- There is anticipation gained from the uncertainty of what the engram contains.

The engram system is basically like a slot machine where the player wins tokens to play another slot machine.

Ethical and Practical Concerns

In many instances, principles of Behaviorism work well. It's why you see echoes of it so often in games today. However, Behaviorism fell out of vogue in psychology many decades ago because it has massive limitations. One of the most salient limitations is that it's only concerned with inputs and outputs. What happens within the subject is known as a "black box" and is outside the domain of inquiry. This is problematic for game designers because concepts like "fun" and "value" live inside that black box.

When I discuss the concept of motivation in Chapter 25, I cover the differences between intrinsic and extrinsic motivations. This concept is key because it shows how all behavior is not equal. A game designer's goal is not wholly contained within "get a player to kill a *Destiny* bad guy." There are larger concerns, such as "Is the player having fun?" or "Will the player continue to have fun?" Operant conditioning predicts behavior well in the short term under controlled conditions. However, game designers often don't have that experimental luxury. Many designers want players to be satisfied, not simply engaged in behavior.

Beyond the practical concerns are the ethical concerns. Mike Rose writes in *Gamasutra* about a player addicted to buying keys in *Team Fortress 2* (a mechanic much like the engrams discussed earlier, except that a player spends real money on them) who could not pay his medical bills because of his addiction to the key-crate system.[12] *The New York Times* recounts the story of a *Clash of Clans* player who would take five iPads with him while he showered so that none of his accounts would become inactive.[13] Similar stories regarding these kinds of game mechanics abound. The possibility of addiction alone does not an ethical concern make, but it serves as an illustrative example of what extremes of behavior can surround these game mechanics.

It's just as important for a game designer to examine what a game's mechanics say about what the designer values *as a designer*. The slot machine designer's goal is clear: to get you to pump as many coins into that slot machine as possible. But should a game designer worry about how repetitious a player's behavior is as long as she is having fun? That is a question for each individual designer. Some believe that it's the player's sole responsibility to regulate what she does with a game. Others believe that the designer has an explicit ethical responsibility to make all reasonable attempts to create systems that minimize possible harm to the player.

◆ **TIP** A recommended read on the ethics of game design for gambling is Addiction by Design: Machine Gambling in Las Vegas by Natasha Dow Schüll (2012, Princeton University Press).

. . . .

12 Rose, M. (2013, July 9). "Chasing the Whale: Examining the Ethics of Free-to-Play Games." Retrieved November 19, 2014, from www.gamasutra.com/view/feature/195806/chasing_the_whale_examining_the_.php.

13 Bai, M. (2013, December 21). "Master of His Virtual Domain." Retrieved November 19, 2014, from www.nytimes.com/2013/12/22/technology/master-of-his-virtual-domain.html?pagewanted=all.

Summary

- Behaviorists use experiments to record the effects of stimuli on a subject's observable behaviors.
- A variable-ratio schedule of reinforcement tends to generate the most response.
- Extinction occurs when a reward no longer generates the anticipated behavior.
- The goal-gradient effect suggests that the closer a player is to a goal, the greater the player's effort will be to achieve that goal.
- What do your game mechanics say about what you value? If you respect the player and want him to have fun, is that reflected in your mechanics? Or are your mechanics just a highly complicated Skinner box used to extract money from the player? Neither is *a priori* bad, but be honest about what you value.

24 Learning and Constructivism

Teaching is an act of persuasion.

—DANIEL T. WILLINGHAM

Games are largely about learning. That is not to say that games are essentially *edutainment*, but that most games involve learning new concepts, mechanics, tactics, or strategies. A designer's job is to make new games or update existing games with new parts. To understand how players will play a new game or new parts of a game, you need to understand how players will interact with that new information. Thus, a designer needs to know how people learn.

Edutainment is a marketing portmanteau for educational entertainment. Although games involve learning in general, edutainment games aim to teach the player something that is applicable outside the space of the game itself. Consider a game such as *Oregon Trail* that teaches about frontier life as an example.

Historic Approaches

The behaviorists discussed in Chapter 23 had their own applications of their theories to education. Skinner himself created a "teaching machine."[1] In it, a student would be presented with a question. If the student answered the question correctly, he would be rewarded. If the student answered incorrectly, the question would repeat until the student supplied the correct answer.

Sure, this is boring, rote behavior, but you must remember that the behaviorists were not worried about things like motivation, retention, or fun, because those took place in the "black box." It was only the behavior itself that concerned them. Thus, if they could get the student to answer correctly, it did not really matter if the student had full understanding or was satisfied with his performance. The behavior was enough. Reward success; punish failure.

The dissonance between the behaviorists' experiments and how players learn in games should be clear. Designers *do* care if someone is having fun. Designers *do* care if their players can use knowledge they gain to solve problems. It's not enough for players to know that Mario can bounce off a Koopa. They also need to be able to realize that they can bounce off of multiple Koopas to cross a dangerous chasm.

One response to the behaviorist theories of learning is known as *constructivism*. Constructivism is a school of theories that treats the behaviorists' "black box" as extremely important. The "construct" in constructivism means that each individual learner is constantly constructing new models of knowledge based on what they already know. One of its tenets is that how and what a person learns is influenced by that person's prior experiences. A person learns by taking a concept she already knows and either *assimilating* her new experience to fit her current understanding of a thing or *accommodating* by adapting her understanding of the thing to deal with the new information.[2] Each individual learner is a new challenge for the designer because each player's past experiences are different.

Because of the influence of past experiences, constructivists highly value interaction with learning objects and learning-by-doing. If that sounds familiar, it's because it's largely the primary method that most games use to teach players about the game's mechanics: the tutorial. The players start with some base level of prior knowledge and each step along the way guides the players so they gain experience in a safe way until

1 Skinner, B.F. (1958) "Teaching Machines." *Science*, 128, 969–77.

2 Atherton J. S. (2013) "Learning and Teaching: Assimilation and Accommodation" [On-line: UK] retrieved October 30, 2014, from www.learningandteaching.info/learning/assimacc.htm.

they are proficient with the game. Most games assume a previous level of competency. For instance, most first-person shooters assume that the player is competent using an avatar in 3D space. To someone who has never played a 3D first-person shooter, moving the character around is a skill to be learned and a problem to be solved.

Novices and Experts

Understanding how people solve problems is important. First, there is a bit of an arbitrary distinction between classes of problem solvers. Players fall into one of two groups: *novices* and *experts*.

Experts are able to classify problems based on their structural parts. For instance, if I were to ask what 42×12 is, and then ask how much a book of 12 42-cent stamps cost, an expert would see these two problems as sharing the same structure. Novices would see these problems as an arithmetic problem and a problem about stamps.

Chess is a simple game of enormous possibilities. *Chess* has more valid, possible boards than there are atoms in the known universe.[3] In fact, it's likely that in any long game of *Chess*, any two players will reach some board configuration that has never occurred in the history of the game.[4] Psychologists attempted to study how *Chess* masters were able to play such a massive game in terms of combinatorics at such a consistently high level. What do *Chess* masters do that *Chess* novices do not? Researchers found no difference in the memory abilities of highly skilled *Chess* players; they cannot think much farther ahead than novices; nor is their level of intelligence vastly superior.[5] What is different is their ability to break down *Chess* boards into logical "chunks." The positions of the pieces have meaning as relationships to one another that are organized in a way that only someone who has played thousands of games can understand, and they use this knowledge to identify common positions. They don't think any farther ahead than the novice player, but they do understand a board at a glance by comparing what they see currently to other boards they have seen.

· · · · · · · · · · · · · · · · · · · ·

3 Shannon, C. E. (1950). "XXII. Programming a Computer for Playing Chess." *Philosophical Magazine*, 41(314), 256–275.

4 Silver, N. (2012). *The Signal and the Noise: Why So Many Predictions Fail—But Some Do Not.* New York: Penguin Press.

5 de Groot, A.D. (1946). Het denken van de schaker. [The thought of the chess player.] Amsterdam: North-Holland. (Updated translation published as "Thought and Choice in Chess," Mouton, The Hague, 1965; corrected second edition published in 1978.) Chase, W. G., & Simon, H. A. (1973). "Perception in Chess." *Cognitive Psychology*, 4(1), 55–81

Chess players remember and understand boards much like your average person remembers telephone numbers. You do not remember a telephone number as a disconnected string of ten random digits. Try to remember this number: 4122682323. Tough, right? Instead, you break phone numbers into an area code, an exchange, and the final digits. For instance, the phone number of campus police at my undergraduate college was (412) 268-2323. I still remember this years later. The easiest part for me to remember is the 412. That area code is for all Pittsburgh numbers, and I grew up in Pittsburgh. Next, the 268 exchange is used for most of the university's phone numbers. (The 268 uses the corresponding letters for the digits on the telephone keypad to create the letters of the university: CMU.) The last four digits, 2323, are also an easy to remember since they repeat. By "chunking" the phone number into easier-to-remember parts, you can increase the odds that you will remember it in an emergency.

Imagine explaining the game *Braid* (**FIGURE 24.1**) to someone who has never seen a video game. To expert game players, you explain that it is a platformer and that the triggers serve to rewind and advance time. Further explanation focuses on the time mechanics. But to novices, your explanation glosses over an incredible amount of detail by chunking a lot of discussion down to a single word: platformer.

FIGURE 24.1
Braid is complicated, but less so if you are familiar with plat-former mechanics.

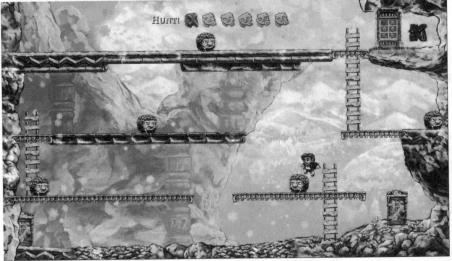

BRAID © 2008 NUMBER-NONE INC.

Here's what the explanation folds up by assumption into that one word:

- You control a single avatar.
- You use the control stick or D-pad to move left or right.
- Gravity pulls down toward the bottom of the screen. You have a side view.
- You have a jump button, which causes the avatar to jump.
- You can climb ladders with up or down movement on the control stick or D-pad.
- You cannot touch enemies from the side. Avoid them.
- You can touch enemies from above and that will kill them.
- Spikes will kill you.
- The screen can sometimes scroll left and right.
- Getting your avatar to some end point by jumping and movement is likely the goal.

Like the *Chess* masters, designers fold huge amounts of experience into more compressed concepts. Giving control of *Braid* to a novice video-game player is likely to result in the player asking "What do I do?" "What am I supposed to do?"

Genre is one way of condensing a lot of information into a particular schema. After mastering a first-person shooter, players do not need to be taught how to manipulate an avatar in a 3D space, reload, switch weapons, or any of the myriad mechanics associated with the genre. Players may have to be taught which buttons correspond to those actions, but they already have the *why* organized when they accept the genre. Novice players do not have those schemata to work from and so they need to be taught all these elements. Experts often forget that this knowledge is not innate. Unfortunately, most game designers are game experts and have difficulty thinking in terms of genre schema ignorance.

Cognitive Load

What happens if you present a player with too many problems to solve at once? How much "new" can someone handle? Psychologists refer to this as *cognitive load*. To discuss cognitive load, I need to really quickly define a couple of other terms central to the psychology of memory.

Long-term memory is generally what we think of when we talk about memories. These memories can last indefinitely. This is in contrast to what is called *working memory*.[6] Working memory is the short-term buffer where we hold information that we have just received. If I pour myself a cup of soda in the kitchen, I use working memory to

. . . .
6   Baddeley, A. (1987). *Working Memory*. Gloucestershire, UK: Clarendon Press.

remember that I left it there so that I remember to pick it up when I return to the living room. Generally, we forget much of what we put into working memory. If I used long-term memory, then I would remember weeks from now where I kept the cup on that day, which is not particularly useful.

When we have to learn and store new elements, we primarily tax our working memory. Unlike our long-term memory, which has a high limit on how much we can store, our working memory space is small and can handle only a few things at a time without forgetting other elements.[7] For many years, researchers believed the amount of information we could keep in working memory was five to nine elements.[8] More recent research has shown that the type of information stored (long words, short words, numbers, nonsense words) also affects how many elements our working memory can remember at a time.[9]

How psychologists define these limits is less important to the game designer than understanding that the limits exist. The five-to-nine estimate probably errs on the high side when you are considering how many concepts players can understand at a given time.

As in the *Braid* example, the number of concepts that have to be in working memory is simplified if you explain new concepts in terms of elements that are already in long-term memory. You don't need to tell the player how to move if you can assume the player has already absorbed that knowledge from other games. This frees up space so you can talk about what mechanics are different in the game, and it is also a good reason for you to forgo complicated story elements early in a game. If the player is trying to remember the names and relationships between the members of the Queen's court, then this gives her less "space" to process how to play the game. The maximum amount of information the player processes at a time is called the *cognitive load*.

An apt analogy to use is the concept of juggling. Beginning jugglers need to start with only two items to juggle at a time. When they've mastered this, they can graduate to three. Then four. Then they can add tricks. If you try to teach someone by starting with how to juggle four balls at once, then the proto-juggler may never understand the concepts. The constructivist method of slowly building to a more advanced understanding is more likely to have success.

. . . .

7   I contend that Darwin would have a hard time coming up with an evolutionary excuse for just how many movie quotes we can recall.

8   Miller, G. A. (1956). "The Magical Number Seven, Plus or Minus Two: Some Limits on Our Capacity for Processing Information." Psychological Review, 63(2), 81.

9   Hulme, C., Roodenrys, S., Brown, G., & Mercer, R. (1995). "The Role of Long-Term Memory Mechanisms in Memory Span." British Journal of Psychology, 86(4), 527–536.

Portal is a game that expertly understands the role of cognitive load. The entire first half of the game is a tutorial, yet the player rarely feels like he is stuck learning instead of playing. This is because each test chamber adds only one or two mechanics or twists on those mechanics. The player slowly constructs his knowledge of the game's systems, and by time the chambers get really complex, the player can juggle a dozen concepts in his head at once.

An opposing example is *League of Legends*. The game has a frustratingly high number of concepts to remember right off the bat.

- The goal is to defeat the opposing team's base.
- There are common mechanics to master such as moving, attacking, and recalling.
- There are four abilities unique to your character in addition to a passive ability.
- There are scores of champions, and each has unique abilities that can affect your character in many ways.

Taken all at once, these concepts are difficult to learn and reconcile. There just is not enough space in working memory to handle it all. It's like starting to juggle by juggling eight balls at once. Once a player is able to commit some of these elements to long-term memory, then it becomes easier to learn and understand more and more new concepts.

Constructivist theorists call the process of providing just as much help as is needed at any given time *scaffolding*. The simile is that scaffolding in construction temporarily holds up a building as it's being created. Learning scaffolding does the same; it supports the learner with effective help until that help is no longer needed. *Portal* has effective scaffolding because it tailors its level of help to the player's estimated skill level based on the player's location in the game. *League of Legends* provides little scaffolding. By comparison, it's attempting to build a building by simultaneously constructing all the pieces in place.

A game that is well-scaffolded has an easier time accommodating new players. It first provides the player with all the help she needs at the time when she needs it. Then it slowly removes that help as the player's skill increases. This is akin to taking off the training wheels when the player has learned to ride the bike. In digital games, the designer can poll game metrics to understand when the player is ready for decreased scaffolding. Thus digital games have a greater opportunity (and, I would say, responsibility) to scaffold the learning experience.

Expertise Reversal Effect

That the player learns and grows in expertise is important to how the game teaches the player. It's understood that new players need well-crafted guidance. However, what happens when an expert player receives the same guidance? Expert players have to reconcile this guidance with what they already know.

Before *Halo* largely standardized how first-person shooters work on consoles, there were many competing control schemes. Some games defaulted to a flight-simulator setup where pressing down on the right control stick caused the camera to pan up. Other games defaulted to a setup where pressing up on the right control stick looked up. Players who had no past experience with either could adjust easily to both. However, players who expected one action and received the other often struggled with the controls. This is because their working memory was being spent trying to reconcile what they already knew with what was being presented. Novice players could outperform expert players in some tasks. This is known as the *expertise reversal effect.*[10]

The implication of the expertise reversal effect in games is that novices and experts need to be treated differently. Novices need guided instruction because they lack the working memory space to absorb large amounts of material at a time. Additionally, novices, if left to their own devices, largely rely on poor problem-solving strategies, such as trial and error.[11] They need the help. Experts, however, find receiving redundant help frustrating. When help does not dovetail with their preconceived concepts, that help can become confusing.

In the *Chess* puzzle game named *One Pawn Army* (**FIGURE 24.2**), players start out with one pawn, and when that pawn captures a piece, it becomes that piece. The opponent never moves. The object is to capture the opponent's king and avoid having your piece threatened by any opposing pieces. The setup leads to some interesting puzzles that are quite different in play than a normal game of chess. However, when the designer had a coworker, who is a *Chess* master, playtest the game, he found that the player had a lot of trouble solving the puzzles. He could not "unsee" the board as an actual *Chess* board. His expertise hindered him.

. . . .

10 Kalyuga, S., Ayres, P., Chandler, P., & Sweller, J. (2003). "The Expertise Reversal Effect." Educational Psychologist, 38(1), 23-31.

11 Kalyuga, S. (2007). "Expertise Reversal Effect and Its Implications for Learner-Tailored Instruction." Educational Psychology Review, 19(4), 509–539.

FIGURE 24.2 One Pawn Army by Mark Diehr.

Novices find it easy to miss contextual clues.[12] If you end up thinking that it is enough to provide a player with the material he needs to learn without examining what the load will be on that player, then you are likely to frustrate that novice player. Tutorials are necessary,[13] but only in the context of effective teaching methods.[14]

Split-Attention Effect

Another useful concept from the study of learning is the *split-attention effect*. This effect was noted in the instructional design of geometry problems. When the geometry problem showed a diagram and then had an explanation under the diagram, students showed poorer results than if the same geometry problem had the instructions integrated into the diagram itself (**FIGURE 24.3**). The theory is that jumping back and forth between the diagram and explanation adds cognitive load that may interfere with solving the problem.

. . . .

12 DiPietro, Meredith. (2009). "Experience, Cognition, and Video Game Play." Handbook of Research on Effective Electronic Gaming in Education (pp.776–790). Information Science Reference, IGI Global Publishing.

13 Glajch, S., Shea, A., & Tyrrell, J. (2006, February 28) "Game Tutorial Analysis." Retrieved from https://www.wpi.edu/Pubs/E-project/Available/E-project-030206-173827/unrestricted/Game_Tutorial_Analysis.pdf.

14 Kalyuga, S. (2008). Managing Cognitive Load in Adaptive Multimedia Learning. Hershey, PA: IGI Global.

FIGURE 24.3
Split-attention and
integrated diagram
designs.

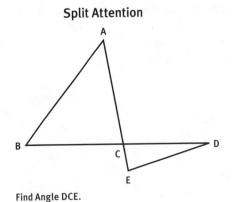

Split Attention

Find Angle DCE.
Angle BAC = 40°
Angle ABC = 75°

Step One:
180° = ABC + BAC + ACB
ACB = 65°

Step Two:
180° = ACB + ACD
ACD = 115°

Step Three:
180° = ACD + DCE
DCE = 65°

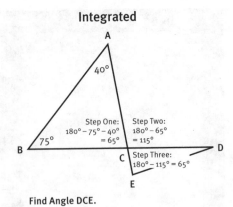

Integrated

Find Angle DCE.

In games, avoiding the split-attention effect has been managed with user-interface elements that combine the game and hint effects. In **FIGURE 24.4**, the *The Elder Scrolls V: Skyrim* chest has its instructions tightly integrated because the player is already looking at the chest. In **FIGURE 24.5**, the instructions for what to do in the *Assassin's Creed* games are away from the action, which requires the player to shift attention from the action to the list of button presses.

FIGURE 24.4 The context-sensitive directions appear on the item the player is looking at in Skyrim.

FIGURE 24.5 The context-sensitive directions are in an upper corner, away from the action in Assassin's Creed.

Tutorials and Learning Design

Tutorials are the broccoli of the game design world. Designers hide them in their napkins if they can by hiding a dedicated tutorial level behind menus or somewhere less accessible. Players also avoid them if possible, demanding to skip them to get to "the game." This is not because tutorial learning is bad. Players want to learn how to be successful. They just want to do it in a fun way. Many tutorials are poorly designed and thus feel like punishment. The best tutorial of all time, in my personal opinion, is World 1-1 in *Super Mario Bros*. Most people had never played a platforming game at the time of its release, so this level served as a perfect teacher of the basic mechanics of what is, honestly, not a very straightforward game. Yet most players consider it just another level of the game and not a tutorial at all.

In the book *Learn to Play*, researcher and educator Matthew White lists a number of principles for what he calls "learning design" instead of tutorials because of the stigma of the term.[15] These principles are based on peer-reviewed psychology research and are distilled for the concept of game design:

- Designers should make sure that all players reach a similar skill level quickly. Thus, the game should follow cognitive principles to offer learning support and inclusive features and feedback for low-skilled players without punishing or holding back higher-skilled players.

. . . .

15 White, M. (2014). Learn to Play: Designing Tutorials for Video Games. Boca Raton, FL: CRC Press.

- Designers should overtly and obviously punish failures and reward success. Reinforcement should be immediate and the punishments and rewards should be large enough to affect behavior. Give big rewards.

- Digital games offer a vast amount of data for the designer to use. Game designers should leverage that data to test the player's skill and offer help, challenge, reward, and punishment dynamically. Teachers do this in the classroom innately. They can use visual cues to understand when a person's attention is waning and change gears to re-engage. A game cannot do that unless it's looking and can adjust itself to address waning interest.

Summary

- Constructivist theories assume that humans learn by building on their experiences and models of their ideas.

- Cognitive load is the measure of how much information a player can manage at once. It is managed by the way that players can effectively chunk information into fewer elements.

- Scaffolding is the process of supporting a player with just the amount of help she needs, removing help as the player no longer needs it.

- The expertise reversal effect suggests that help that is instrumental to novices may actually hinder experts because the experts need to use part of their cognitive load to manage the differences between how they understand the concept and how the help explains the concept.

- The split-attention effect suggests that help should be closely integrated with where the learner interacts with it. Hiding help in a manual is less effective than contextually giving help onscreen.

25 Motivation

> Things need to be worth doing for themselves,
> not just for practice for some future time.
>
> —JO WALTON, AMONG OTHERS

Playing games is a choice; it's voluntary.[1] Any game designer who is forcing people into playing games should seriously reconsider her craft. Given that, you must assume that people volunteer to play games because they want to. Thus, game designers must be intimately familiar with the motivations of players. What makes people want to play? What keeps people playing?

An anthropological discussion of why humans play is beyond the scope of this lesson. For more on that topic, the definitive starting points are Roger Caillois' *Man, Play, and Games* and Johan Huizinga's *Homo Ludens*.[2] Instead, what I want to focus on here is the narrower concern of what motivates individuals to choose one thing over another.

---

1   Caillois, R. (1961). *Man, Play, and Games*. Champaign, IL: University of Illinois Press.
2   Huizinga, J. (1967). *Homo Ludens: A Study of the Play Element in Culture*. Boston, MA: Beacon Press.

Two Types of Motivation

Many psychologists distinguish between two types of motivation: intrinsic and extrinsic.[3] The differences between these two types are important.

Extrinsic motivation is best illustrated by the carrot and the stick. We are extrinsically motivated when we engage in a behavior for a reward distinct from the behavior. Many of us go to work for a paycheck, not simply to do the work. We exercise to look better or to be healthier, not simply because we enjoy the exertion. Sometimes we do homework just for the grade or because we know we have to in order to get the career we desire. In all of these cases, we engage in a behavior for some reason other than the behavior itself.

Intrinsic motivation is when we engage in a behavior simply because we gain fulfillment from that behavior. Mihaly Csikszentmihalyi, the psychologist who popularized the concept of flow, explains intrinsic motivations as *autotelic*. Autotelic comes from Greek and literally means "self-goal."[4] The goal of doing the activity is doing the activity. We play games because we like to play games. We read books because we like the experience. We listen to music because it's enjoyable. In all these cases, the ends are the means. The motivation is intrinsic to the activity.

What's the Problem with Rewards?

Gamification is a popular current trend that can largely be boiled down to putting external motivators such as points, badges, and achievements onto behaviors to encourage people to engage in them. There are gamified programs to read books, work out, even to learn. The idea is that by pairing an activity with a reward, the "players" are motivated to do that activity in the hopes of receiving the reward. Gamification is nothing new; frequent flier miles, "high roller" programs, and even the concept of grades in school are all ways to gamify behavior that were designed well before the term was coined. These external motivators were tested by Skinner and the behaviorists. The rats that push the lever are not pushing the lever as an autotelic activity. They push because they want the food. The push is contingent on the expectation of receiving the food.

In games, the primary goal is generally for the player to have fun. The designer hopes that the player does that through interacting with the game's systems in a particular

. . . .

3   Ryan, R. M., & Deci, E. L. (2000). "Self-Determination Theory and the Facilitation of Intrinsic Motivation, Social Development, and Well-Being." *American Psychologist*, 55(1), 68–78.
4   Csikszentmihalyi, M. (1991). "Flow: The Psychology of Optimal Experience" New York, NY: Harper Perennial.

way. Some designers choose to add external motivators to guide player behavior—for instance, receiving an achievement for finishing the tutorial or a special skin for using all the attacks. At the same time, though, the designer wants the player to be intrinsically motivated in the game itself. What good is the game if it is not fun or rewarding in itself? What could be wrong with that approach?

In 1973, long before gamification was a popular buzzword, Mark Lepper and his colleagues conducted an experiment to find out how external motivators affected internal motivators.[5] They divided some 4- and 5-year-old school students into different classrooms. One classroom was the "expected reward" group. That group was told that if they chose to draw during playtime, they could receive a Good Player Award—a little certificate with their name on it. The students who chose to draw were then given the certificate. A second classroom was the "unexpected reward group." Those students were not told in advance about the reward, but the students who drew during playtime were given the Good Player Award. A third classroom was a control group. They were free to draw or not as they pleased but received no award regardless of what activity they chose. One to two weeks later, the researchers returned and noticed over the next few days how much of the children's free time was devoted to drawing.

The students who received no award regardless of what they did spent 16.7 percent of their free time drawing. The students in the unexpected reward group, those who chose to draw and then were surprised with an award, spent 18 percent of their time drawing, a small boost over the control group. However, the students who were given the expectation of an award spent only 8.6 percent of their free time drawing. It turned out that unless they were being rewarded for it, they no longer wanted to draw!

Similar experiments have been repeated many times over with similar findings. One of the most popular external motivation programs in American schools has been the "Book It!" program. Sponsored by the fast food pizza chain Pizza Hut, the program rewards students for reading by giving them pizzas. However, the program has been criticized because children often read small books and fly through them without being able to answer basic questions about the book that would prove their comprehension. The students just want the point so they can get the pizza. It even *decreased* the amount of reading students did outside of school.[6]

· · · · · · · · · · · · · · · · · ·

5   Lepper, M. R., Greene, D., & Nisbett, R. E. (1973). "Undermining Children's Intrinsic Interest with Extrinsic Reward: A Test of the 'Overjustification' Hypothesis." *Journal of Personality and Social Psychology*, 28(1), 129.

6   Kohn, A. (1999). *Punished by Rewards: The Trouble with Gold Stars, Incentive Plans, A's, Praise, and Other Bribes*. Boston, MA: Houghton Mifflin Harcourt.

Self-Determination Theory and Challenges

So what do people want? Of course, this is a massive question with a wide variety of discourse. One of the most well-respected and well-tested theories is Deci and Ryan's work on *self-determination theory*. Self-determination theory says that there are three needs that humans strive for across time and cultures, and it is these three elements that help explain what makes us intrinsically motivated, assuming our basic needs, like food and shelter, are satisfied.

The first need is *autonomy*. People need to feel control in some measure of who they are and what they do. The second need is *mastery*. People need to feel as though their actions control their life's outcomes. Last is *relatedness*. People have a need to connect with others in some way. Naturally, some needs are more important than others for different individuals.

Games are clearly in the practice of tasking players with activities that challenge their mastery and autonomy. It's part of why games are so widespread in most cultures.

Stimulating the quest for mastery is something that games can do easily. However, when coupled with contingent rewards (as in the Good Player Award example), the reward serves to dampen the desire for mastery and hence the motivation to continue with the behavior. It's not the reward that is the problem, it's the *expectation* of the reward that is the problem. When a person expects a reward, then their motivation shifts to doing the task for the reward. Their inherent need for mastery is no longer served by the task, and so they become disinterested in it when the reward is no longer present. It's why educational psychologist John Nicholls said that the likely result of the aforementioned Book It! program would be "a lot of fat kids who don't like to read."[7] The motivation for reading had become pizza instead of the mastery and autonomy previously associated with reading.

If you want people to keep playing, then you need to stimulate their desire for mastery. However, it's important to note that all games do not need to keep the player playing forever. *Portal* is just as valuable a game as *Dark Souls* even though the former caps mastery around a shorter experience. The designers of *Portal* simply do not care if the player plays for 3 hours or 60.

Remember also the justification for mastery. People need to feel as though their actions control their life's outcomes. If something is too challenging or not challenging enough, then they will not feel that their desire for mastery is being satisfied. *Dark Souls*,

. . . .
7   Kohn, A. (1995). "Newt Gingrich's Reading Plan." *Education Week on the Web*. Retrieved August 31, 2015, from www.alfiekohn.org/teaching/edweek/ngrp.htm.

mentioned earlier, is certainly not a game for everyone. It's simply too brutally hard for many. However, for those who are able to progress in the game, it provides a valuable mastery activity. The game has to be challenging, but not so challenging that the player feels he cannot overcome it. This clearly parallels the fundamental game design directive discussed in Chapter 9.

Competition and Motivation

One of the play aesthetics that comes easiest in game design is competition. Games pit one player against another or one player against an algorithm and assume that the player's inherent desire to win will be enough to be motivating. Sometimes this is true. Sometimes it's not.

Because of competition's origins as a male-dominated pastime, the hobby is seen as a standard play aesthetic. However, although competition is a common motivator for men, women (especially when paired with men in the same competitive space) often show decreased motivation and performance in competitive environments.[8]

Another interesting finding is what psychologists call *the N-effect*. The N-effect is that competitive motivation decreases when the number of competitors increases. To find this out, researchers had students complete a quiz as quickly as possible and told them that the top 20 percent would receive a cash prize.[9] One group was told they were competing against 10 other students; another group was told that they were competing against 100 other students. The group who was told they were competing against 10 students finished their quizzes much faster than those who thought they were competing against 100. The ones who thought they were competing against 100 others were less motivated. They thought they could not possibly win against so many competitors, even though their odds of winning were the same.

Very few games integrate this lesson. One that does, however, is *SpaceChem*, a clever but complicated puzzle game whose puzzles often have multiple solutions. Instead of using a global leaderboard to show the player with the best solutions (as most games would do), the game instead shows where the player ranks as a percentage using histograms (**FIGURE 25.1**).[10]

. . . .

8   Gneezy, U., Niederle, M., & Rustichini, A. (2003). "Performance in Competitive Environments: Gender Differences." *Quarterly Journal of Economics*. Cambridge Massachusetts, 118(3), 1049–1074.

9   Garcia, S. M., & Tor, A. (2009). "The N-Effect More Competitors, Less Competition." *Psychological Science*, 20(7), 871–877.

10 Barth, Z. (2012, June 6). "Postmortem: Zachtronics Industries' *SpaceChem*." Retrieved December 2, 2014, from www.gamasutra.com/view/feature/172250/postmortem_zachtronics_.php?page=2.

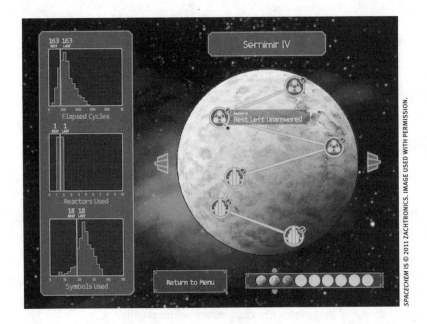

FIGURE 25.1
Histogram-based leaderboards in *SpaceChem*.

This serves to reduce the intimidation of the N-effect. You no longer know you are competing against thousands of others; instead, you know how you compare against the average. As *SpaceChem*'s designer says, "For most players, the only thing a global leaderboard manages to tell you is that you suck (and not even by how much)."

Another example is in the free-to-play card game *WWE SuperCard*. One of the features allows the player to play a season's worth of games against other players for in-game rewards. Many games choose to give the top 100 players in the world every week some reward. What *WWE SuperCard* does instead is limit your competition to 15 other randomly chosen players at around the same power level. This serves to make the challenge of beating players seem manageable and serves to support motivation.

Personality

One of the most difficult aspects of game design is that most often, designers must design for people with different wants, needs, emotions, and mental processes. Psychologists call this collection of traits *personality*. Personality affects so many of the choices we make—both within games and toward which games we are drawn.

Although many psychological concepts are subject to intense debate within the scientific community, the most popular model of personality factors is both widely accepted by the scientific community and verified by many different types of research. This model of personality is known as *The Big Five personality traits*, and it is often referred to by the acronym *OCEAN*. These traits are independent of each other and together they form a complete summary of a person's personality.

This is covered more completely in Chapter 14.

Other Motivation Effects

There are a few other results from the study of motivation that have particular applicability to games.

The *goal-gradient effect* is used in nearly every game with a level-up bar. The goal-gradient effect says that players are more motivated to reach a goal the closer they are to that goal. Think back to the discussion of behaviorist schedules of reinforcement from Chapter 23—a player interacts furiously with a system as he gets closer to the time when he knows the reward is about to appear in fixed schedules.

In games, designers leverage this by showing players a visual representation of how close they are to the next level or objective (**FIGURE 25.2**). When the player knows that he is almost at a reward, it keeps him motivated to continue the behavior that will lead to that reward.

FIGURE 25.2 A bar to fill in *FarmVille 2*.

In many games, players are rewarded with additional XP on big events that cause a level-up to occur and partially fill the next level's XP bar. This gives the player a somewhat illusory sense of progress toward the next level and motivates her to continue the game. This is much like the Kivetz (2006) study from Chapter 23 where customers got free stamps on a dining loyalty card and were motivated more than other customers who needed the same number of stamps to reach a reward.[11]

Another motivation technique common in games is the concept of *scarcity*. It is seen often outside of games in the context of sales. Look at the Amazon image in **FIGURE 25.3**.

FIGURE 25.3
Best hurry.

$6.00 (67% off)
Intex Recreation River Rat Tube, 47-Inch (Colors may Vary)

Add to Cart

95% Claimed
Ends in 01h 47m 50s

Not only does Amazon limit the sale by time (only 1 hour and 47 minutes remaining!), but they also limit it by quantity (95 percent of these pool toys are gone! I have to act now!). Scarcity is highly motivating. In one famous experiment, subjects were asked to test cookies from two different jars.[12] One jar had many cookies in it; the other just a few. The subjects reported that the cookies from the jar with fewer cookies were more delicious, even though both jars contained the same brand of cookie. Scarcity makes us value things more and motivates us to acquire them.

. . . .

11 Kivetz, R., Urminsky, O., & Zheng, Y. (2006). "The Goal-Gradient Hypothesis Resurrected: Purchase Acceleration, Illusionary Goal Progress, and Customer Retention." *Journal of Marketing Research*, 43(1), 39–58.

12 Worchel, S., Lee, J., & Adewole, A. (1975). "Effects of Supply and Demand on Ratings of Object Value." *Journal of Personality and Social Psychology*, 32(5), 906.

Croteam's *The Talos Principle* shows the concept of scarcity in action. By using a found axe, the player can travel to a secret area in each section, use the axe, solve a number of tangram puzzles, and unlock the single-time use of a helper robot to give the player a hint on a puzzle. Only three of these helper robots are in the game and once one is used, it's gone forever. It feels good to unlock that scarce resource, so you spend the time to do it. This is despite the fact that it would take less than a minute to YouTube an answer to each puzzle instead of going through the effort to unlock a hint.

Summary

- There are two kinds of motivation: extrinsic and intrinsic. Intrinsic motivation is the motivation to do something as its own end.

- Extrinsic rewards can dampen the intrinsic motivation for a task.

- The three desires in self-determination theory that help predict human motivation are autonomy, mastery, and relatedness.

- The goal-gradient effect suggests that as players get closer to a goal, they will be more motivated to achieve that goal. Reminding players how close they are can reinforce motivation.

- Scarcity is inherently motivating. Players will value items more if they believe there are in limited supply.

26 Human Decision-Making

> There is no expedient to which a man will not resort to avoid the real labor of thinking.
>
> —JOSHUA REYNOLDS

Humans are often bad at decision-making. We consistently engage in behaviors that are conflict with our stated goals. We misread data and come to bad conclusions. We see things we want to see and hear things we want to hear. We misinterpret odds and act accordingly. The world is a complex and confusing place, and despite our profound ability to change and shape our world in remarkable ways, our ability to understand the world at any given time is limited. Because of this limitation, we take shortcuts. Those shortcuts are called *heuristics* (and their results are called *biases*) and they often result in costly mistakes.

Mental Shortcuts

Take, for instance, the problem of marriage. Say you are an of-age heterosexual man who wants to find a wife. The rational way of maximizing your happiness is to enumerate all the things that would make you happy with a potential wife and then weigh them in accordance with how important they are. Then you would use this scoring system to compare every available woman on the planet and select the best possible woman to court.

Naturally, we cannot do that. Even if we could fairly create that scoring chart, there are nearly 50 million unmarried adult women in the US alone.[1] Instead, we use heuristics to narrow our search. We date a small number of people. Men, on average, have only six relationships before marriage.[2] Six out of 50 million is not an exhaustive search. Even when the stakes are as high as they are when choosing a potential partner for life, humans do not tackle problems in a scientific manner. Instead, we take shortcuts. This chapter is largely about the kinds of shortcuts we take.

These shortcuts are not always conscious and often they do not even make sense. In one study, researchers asked subjects to complete a task in which they had to rearrange words. When they were finished, subjects were asked to walk down the hall to turn in their work. Secretly, the researchers were timing how long it took the subjects to walk down the hall. Researchers found that when the words list included words that reminded people of being old (retirement, elderly, bingo, Florida), subjects walked slower than when those words were not included.[3] The researchers concluded that unconsciously the subjects were primed to walk slowly by the "old" words. This study has been highly controversial and disputed for many reasons, but it is only one of many that shows our decision-making is not necessarily entirely conscious or reasonable.

▶ **NOTE** This, of course, ignores the woman's role in this. What if your best match ranks you as a terrible match?

Attribution Errors

One judgment error is so pervasive that it is named *the "fundamental" attribution error*. The reasons that events happen to people can be split into two categories: *dispositional factors* and *situational* factors. Dispositional factors are factors that happen because of

. . . .

1   DePaulo, B., & Trimberger, E.K. (2008) "Single Women. Sociologists for Women in Society Fact Sheet." Retrieved from http://belladepaulo.com/wp-content/uploads/2013/03/Single-Women-Fact-Sheet-11-1-08.pdf.

2   Daily Mail Reporter. (2014). "No One Said Finding The One Would Be easy." Daily Mail. Retrieved December 3, 2014, from www.dailymail.co.uk/femail/article-2532213/No-one-said-finding-The-One-easy-The-averagewomen-kiss-FIFTEEN-men-enjoy-TWO-long-term-relationships-heart-broken-TWICE.html.

3   Bargh, J. A., Chen, M., & Burrows, L. (1996). "Automaticity of Social Behavior: Direct Effects of Trait Construct and Stereotype Activation on Action." *Journal of Personality and Social Psychology*, 71(2), 230.

the abilities, features, or motives of an actor. When an angry baseball player blows up at an umpire, we call him a "hot head." We attribute his outburst to his disposition. Situational factors happen due to chance or situation. When you become angry with a friend, you often apologize by attributing it to just having a bad day. The bad day is the situation that caused the event, not your disposition.

The fundamental attribution error is the tendency to assign dispositional factors to the actions of others and situational factors to your own actions. When someone cuts you off in traffic, you say that she is a bad driver (dispositional). When you cut someone off in traffic, you rationalize that it just cannot be helped because you are late for work (situational) or the other driver did not give you enough room (situational).

This error is pervasive. Study subjects who are explicitly told that an author's viewpoint was determined by a coin flip still attribute the position to the author.[4] They cannot divorce that author's viewpoint from his disposition. We consistently attribute dispositional factors to others and situational factors to our own behaviors.[5]

Of course, this is not the only way humans fail to attribute success, failure, and causal relationships correctly. A famous study asked subjects to predict coin tosses.[6] Subjects in the study who had early successes believed that their success was attributed to skill, even though the results were clearly random. You are likely to have made the same observation at one point or another. When you win at games, you claim it is because you are skilled. When you lose, it is because the game cheats, the random number generator went against you, or the controller is broken. This is often referred to as the "self-serving bias."[7] When a player loses, the designer should want her to blame herself, not the game or the designer. If the player blames the game, it will cause her to devalue the game experience.

In 1951, Dartmouth and Princeton had a particularly rough football game. Both teams suffered considerable injuries on the field, and both teams racked up penalty after penalty. Princeton fans blamed Dartmouth for the fracas. Dartmouth fans, naturally, blamed Princeton. Luckily, a pair of researchers, one at Princeton and one at Dartmouth found this interesting enough to examine. They recruited a group of students from each school to watch game film and record the number of infractions from each team. Both

· · · · · · · · · · · · · · · · · · · ·

4   Jones, E. E., & Harris, V. A. (1967). "The Attribution of Attitudes." *Journal of Experimental Social Psychology*, 3(1), 1–24.

5   Jones, E. E., & Nisbett, R. E. (1971). "The Actor and the Observer: Divergent Perceptions of the Causes of Behavior" (p. 16). Morristown, NJ: General Learning Press.

6   Langer, E. J. (1975). "The Illusion of Control." *Journal of Personality and Social Psychology*, 32(2), 311.

7   Miller, D. T., & Ross, M. (1975). "Self-Serving Biases in the Attribution of Causality: Fact or Fiction?" *Psychological Bulletin*, 82(2), 213.

groups of students noticed a similar number of infractions for Princeton's players. However, Princeton students saw twice the number of infractions for Dartmouth than the Dartmouth players did.[8] This lead the researchers to postulate that the Dartmouth students were watching different games than the Princeton students, despite all the students seeing the same film. Students' perceptions were such that even given the same images to view, they could not see what the others saw. Their dispositions made them unable to objectively report what was really there. Think about this the next time you blame the officials when your team loses.

THOSE BLIND REFS!

I'm a high school football official. Every week, I am faced with fans, players, and coaches who swear vehemently that they saw something (holding, face masks, a ball hitting the ground) when I did not. At first, I just figured they were lying and trying to lobby for their team. However, now that I've studied psychology for a number of years, I'm convinced that they believe they see what they claim. They are not liars (for this reason, at least); they just are not in a position to be able to view the game fairly. Hence impartial game officials. The awkward effect here is that if coaches get on an official's "bad side," they may involuntarily change an official's disposition and make them "see" a different game.

What is particularly troubling is that even if we know about the bias, we still have a hard time shaking its effects on our own perceptions.

Misunderstanding Randomness

Millions of dollars are spent by professional football teams to eke out additional wins. Yet the distribution of NFL records over a season fits a similar distribution to what would happen if you just had each of the teams flip a coin every week instead of actually play a game.[9] If you assume each team has a 50 percent chance of winning, then you expect a 32-team league to have one 5-0 team and one 0-5 team after the first five games, even though their chances of winning are identical. In 32 trials of coin flips, one of the trials is expected to be HHHHH (all heads) and one should be TTTTT (all tails).

8   Hastorf, A. H., & Cantril, H. (1954). "They Saw a Game: A Case Study." *The Journal of Abnormal and Social Psychology*, 49(1), 129.

9   Hiwiller, Z. (2014, April 24). "ECGC 2014: Design Lessons from Pareto." Retrieved December 8, 2014, from www.hiwiller.com/2014/04/24/ecgc-2014-design-lessons-from-pareto.

Say that you have a fair coin, you have flipped it three times, and it has come up heads each time. You are now offered a fourth flip on which you can place a bet of $50 on the outcome. Do you choose heads or tails? Is tails not due at this point?

Or to put it another way: Say that in a game, you have a 25 percent chance in each session of facing a particularly difficult version of a boss (the MegaBoss). You have 100 playtesters and 50 have already played. Of those 50, 20 have seen the MegaBoss. Of the remaining 50, how many will see the MegaBoss (**FIGURE 26.1**)?

FIGURE 26.1
Already 20 have seen the MegaBoss. How many of the remaining 50 will?

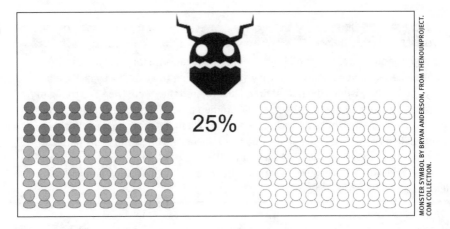

25%

People try to solve this problem in two ways. The first way is that since there is a 25 percent chance of seeing the MegaBoss, then of the 100 playtesters, 25 should see it. Since 20 have already seen it, 5 of the next 50 playtesters should see the MegaBoss.

This method would be committing what is commonly known as the *gambler's fallacy*. The gambler's fallacy is a belief that random processes "remember" what has happened before and adjust accordingly. In this example, saying that 5 of the next 50 playtesters should see the MegaBoss implies that the game knows 20 have already seen it and thus it should make it up to the player by having a lower probability later. This is no different than saying a slot machine is "due" to pay off or that if a couple has two boys then they are "due" a girl.

The second, actual way of solving this problem is by applying the 25 percent for the next 50 players. If the odds of each trial seeing the MegaBoss are 1 in 4, the problem definition says nothing about the MegaBoss knowing how many players saw him before. So ignore the fact that a greater-than-expected number of players saw him before. Going forward, 1 in 4 will continue to see him. The MegaBoss should be expected 12.5 (50/4) more times.

Humans have difficulty understanding randomness.[10] We are loath to attribute variation to randomness; instead we look for hidden patterns and rules.[11] We believe in provably false concepts like streak shooting (or having "a hot hand") in sports.[12] We believe that a pattern of heads and tails coin flips like HTHHTTHTTH looks more random than HHHHHTTTTT, even though they have the same exact probability of happening. This is not just an academic problem. A whole industry revolves around trying to convince people to pay for someone to pick stocks for them, even though people cannot distinguish between real market activity and random patterns.[13]

Sid Meier explained the actual effects that this had on his game design.[14] In *Civilization Revolution*, armies have ratings, and the ratio of those ratings affects how often that army wins. For instance, if an army of rating 3 faces an army with a rating of 1, the 3 army wins 75 percent (3/(3+1)) of the time and the 1 army wins 25 percent of the time (1/(3+1)). Yet players had a hard time understanding this. When they played as the 3-powered army and lost, they complained that they had an overwhelming advantage and should have won. But when they played as the 1-powered army and won, they had no issue understanding that the player with the 1 should win 1 in 4 times.

Also, some players who were OK when they lost on a 3:1 advantage lost their minds when they lost and had a 30:10 advantage, despite these producing the same odds. Their issue was that they claimed 30 was so much bigger than 10 that it should automatically win.

Additionally, players complained that if they lost a 3:1 battle, then they should win the next 3:1 battle. This is just the gambler's fallacy again. These battles are independent events. By probability, one in 16 times, the 3-value army will lose two 3:1 matches in a row. However, when that happened, players freaked out and claimed that the game was being unfair. These reactions prove that many players don't understand probability.

Another time it becomes apparent that players don't understand probability is when compound events are involved. A compound event is made up of a series of simpler

10 Zhao, J., Hahn, U., & Osherson, D. (2014). "Perception and Identification of Random Events." *Human Perception and Performance, 40,* 1358-1371.

11 Schwartz, B. (1982). "Reinforcement-Induced Behavioral Stereotypy: How Not to Teach People to Discover Rules." *Journal of Experimental Psychology*: General, 111(1), 23.

12 Gilovich, T., Vallone, R., & Tversky, A. (1985). "The Hot Hand in Basketball: On the Misperception of Random Sequences." *Cognitive Psychology,* 17(3), 295–314.

13 Hasanhodzic, J., Lo, A. W., & Viola, E. (2010). "Is It Real, or Is It Randomized?: A Financial Turing Test." *arXiv Preprint arXiv:1002.4592.*

14 Graft, K. (2010, March 12). "GDC: Sid Meier's Lessons On Gamer Psychology." Retrieved December 8, 2014, from www.gamasutra.com/view/news/118597/GDC_Sid_Meiers_Lessons_On_Gamer_Psychology.php.

events. For instance, flipping three coins heads in a row is a compound event, and it's made up of three simple coin flip events. It's much easier for us to understand probability in situations with simple events than it is in situations with compound events.[15]

Warren Buffet made news in 2014 when he announced a promotion named the "Billion Dollar Bracket." If a person could correctly pick the winner of all 63 games in the NCAA Men's Basketball Tournament, he would award them a billion dollars. It seems pretty straightforward and millions attempted an entry. However, the odds of picking a perfect bracket are somewhere in the range of 1 in 128 billion to 1 in 9.2 quintillion, depending on your methodology.[16] A player is something along the lines of 100,000 to 10 trillion times more likely to get struck by lightning. In the first year of the Billion Dollar Bracket, none of the 15 million brackets had a perfect score after only the second day of a three-week tournament.[17]

▶ **NOTE** The odds of Streak for the Cash are not as simple as a conjunction of simple probabilities. You can start over after a loss, and odds are not calculated to have 50 percent probability for each side of the bet as they would be in a Vegas line.

ESPN also has a game named *Streak for the Cash*. In it, players have to pick the results of sports events happening that day. To win the cash prize, they must get a large number of these correct in a row. It's easy to visualize 20 wins. But it's harder to visualize 20 wins in a row. If each game has a 50 percent chance of resulting in a win, then the odds of getting 20 in a row right is roughly 1 in a million. Nonetheless, *Streak for the Cash* is popular because people believe the prize is attainable.

Anchoring and Adjustment

One possible explanation for misunderstanding the odds of the Billion Dollar Bracket and *Streak for the Cash* is the concept of *anchoring*. People often get stuck by being exposed to numbers. For instance, in *Streak for the Cash*, players get stuck on the number 20. In the Billion Dollar Bracket contest, players get stuck on 63. However, those are not the numbers players should be thinking about.

Assume you have a sheet of paper that is 0.1 millimeters thick. If you were to fold it on itself 100 times, how thick would the paper be? Think about it for a moment before reading on.

· · · · · · · · · · · · · · · · · · · ·

15 Cohen, J., Chesnick, E. I., & Haran, D. (1971). "Evaluation of Compound Probabilities in Sequential Choice." In Kahneman, D. Slovic, P. & Tversky, A. *Judgement under Uncertainty: Heuristics and Biases*. Cambridge: Cambridge University Press, 1982.

16 Kiersz, A. (2014, March 17). "The Odds Of Filling Out A Perfect NCAA Bracket Are Actually Way Better Than 1 In 9,223,372,036,854,775,808." Retrieved December 8, 2014, from www.businessinsider.com/odds-of-perfect-ncaa-tournament-bracket-2014-3.

17 Kamisar, B. (2014, March 21). "No Perfect March Madness Brackets Left in Warren Buffett's Billion-Dollar Contest." Retrieved December 8, 2014, from http://thescoopblog.dallasnews.com/2014/03/just-16-brackets-still-in-running-for-warren-buffetts-billion.html.

Common answers range from centimeters to a few meters. The actual answer is 1.27×10^{23} kilometers—a distance trillions of times farther than the distance between the Earth and the Sun.[18] Most people think about the first few folds, saying "OK, after one fold it is 0.2 mm thick. Then after two folds it is 0.4 mm thick. Then after three it is 0.8 mm thick." They anchor on these small values and ignore the latter stages of the problem.

This is replicated in a famous study where students estimated that $8 \times 7 \times 6 \times 5 \times 4 \times 3 \times 2 \times 1$ would be a number four times larger than $1 \times 2 \times 3 \times 4 \times 5 \times 6 \times 7 \times 8$. Students anchor on the first few numbers and ignore the rest.[19]

Anchors don't even have to be coherently related to the problem at hand. Researchers found that writing down the last two numbers in one's Social Security number affected how much subjects bid for items in an auction.[20] If subjects wrote down a high number, they bid more!

This is unfortunately used nefariously quite often in games. Say you are trying to sell your virtual currency in your game. You have four bundles to choose from. A small bundle is 99 cents, a medium bundle is $1.99, a large bundle is $4.99, and an extra-large bundle is $9.99. The principle of anchoring suggests that you show the player the $9.99 bundle first. This will force the player into weighing everything else by the concept of spending $9.99. None of the bundles seem expensive when presented this way. However, if you start with the 99-cent bundle, then the $9.99 bundle looks really expensive.

Even including a bundle that you do not expect anyone to buy can cause anchoring to occur. Add a $99.99 bundle to the list first and every player will be locked into a higher number. Ridiculous anchors like these can have an effect. Researchers asked subjects questions with entirely implausible anchors, such as "Is a whale larger or smaller than 0.2 m? How long is a whale?" or "Was Aristotle born after 1832? When was Aristotle born?" and even those anchors affected subject's answers.[21] High anchors resulted in higher guesses. Lower anchors resulted in lower guesses.

. . . .

18 Plous, S. (1993). *The Psychology of Judgment and Decision Making.* Philadelphia: Temple University Press.

19 Tversky, A., & Kahneman, D. (1974). "Judgment Under Uncertainty: Heuristics and Biases." *Science,* 185(4157), 1124–1131.

20 Ariely, D., Loewenstein, G., & Prelec, D. (2006). "Tom Sawyer and the Construction of Value." *Journal of Economic Behavior & Organization,* 60(1), 1–10.

21 Strack, F., & Mussweiler, T. (1997). "Explaining the Enigmatic Anchoring Effect: Mechanisms of Selective Accessibility." *Journal of Personality and Social Psychology,* 73(3), 437.

Understanding Value in Uncertain Situations

Games are often about making choices in situations of uncertainty. Should I take the pistols or the sniper rifle? That depends on the type of battle and terrain that I expect. Should I choose a pass defense or a run defense? That depends on what type of play I expect to come up. Should I spend skill points on archery or diplomacy? That depends on the payoffs between increases in each of the skills. In all these cases, the decision is contingent on what will happen in the future.

One of the easiest models for understanding how people make decisions in these cases is the use of expected value. When using this, you multiply each probability of each world state by the value of that world state happening. Then you sum all those and get the "value" for that branch.

Let's use a simplified version of American football as an example. You, the player, are choosing a play for the defense. You can choose to line up in a run defense or a pass defense. Your opponent can choose either a run play or a pass play (**FIGURE 26.2**). In any case, you are trying to minimize the amount of yards the opponent gains.

FIGURE 26.2
Simplified game tree
for playcalling.

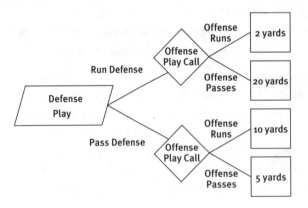

▶ **NOTE** A little algebra work shows that given these payoffs, you should choose pass defense until you are 15/23 or around 65 percent sure that the opponent will run.

Which type of defense you should choose depends wholly on what you believe your opponent will do. If you believe 100 percent that the opponent will pass, then the 5 yards they gain from choosing a pass defense is better than the 20 yards they gain from the run defense. But if you are 50/50 on what your opponent will choose, then you must use probability. The expected value of each of your options is the sum of the payoff for each event times the probability of that event. The expected value of choosing a run defense would be $0.5 \times 2 + 0.5 \times 20$, or 11 yards, whereas the expected value of the pass defense would be $0.5 \times 10 + 0.5 \times 5$, or 7.5 yards. Since 7.5 yards is less than 11 yards, in this case, you should choose the pass defense.

Expected value is really flexible and works in many situations. It's easy to apply and easy to understand. However, it doesn't always work. Mathematician Nicolas Bernoulli identified this problem in the 18th Century, since dubbed the *St. Petersburg Paradox*.

Say you have a game in which you flip a coin and you get $1 if it comes up heads and nothing if it comes up tails. What would you pay to play that game? Expected value tells you that the value of the game is $1 \times 0.5 + 0 \times 0.5$ or 0.50. So you would theoretically pay up to 50 cents to play that game.

Consider a different game. In this game you flip a coin until it comes up tails. Then you receive $2 if the game ends on the first toss, $4 if it comes up tails on the second toss, $8 if it comes up tails on the third toss and so on, doubling the payoff for each consecutive heads. What would you pay to play that game?

We can try to evaluate this by calculating the expected value as we did in our first game. The odds that the game ends on the first toss are 0.5. The odds that the game ends on the second toss are 0.5×0.5 or 0.25. HT is the only combination that would end the game on the second flip. HH continues the game on to the third toss. TH and TT cannot happen since the game would have already ended. Thus, 1 in 4. Odds that the game ends on the third toss are $0.5 \times 0.5 \times 0.5$ or 0.125. Using the same logic as you did earlier, HHT is the only combination that can end the game on the third toss. Since that is one of eight possible results for three coin tosses, the probability is 0.125. And so on. So the expected value of the game should be $(0.5 \times 2) + (0.25 \times 4) + (0.125 \times 8)$ and so on infinitely. The expected value is infinite, $1 + 1 + 1$, forever repeating.

But if you ask people what they would pay to play the game, they will not pledge to pay infinite money. Hence the paradox. A resolution, provided by another mathematician— Nicholas Bernoulli's cousin Daniel 25 years later—is that people do not value all gains equally.[22] A poor, starving man will gain more from a 100 dollar bill than a billionaire will. Thus, those extreme examples late in the series are discounted when compared to the rewards of early losses in the series.

This is the concept of *diminishing marginal utility*. Your first donut is delicious. Your second is OK. By the time you get to your sixth donut, you never want to see a donut again. How much you value a thing is based on how much of that thing you already have. In games, this is pervasive. As you gain experience points, for example, you gain skills that make gaining more experience easier. Thus, for the same benefit, you need more and more experience. Each individual experience point is marginally worth less.

. . . .

22 Bernoulli, D. (1954). "Exposition of a New Theory on the Measurement of Risk." *Econometrica: Journal of the Econometric Society*, 23–36. (Original work published 1738).

One additional concept to analyze when discussing decision-making under uncertainty is how a decision maker treats risk. If people truly acted as expected value maximizers, then no one would ever play the lottery or buy insurance because both of those activities have a negative expected value. Expected value maximizers are called *risk-neutral*—they don't care about risk; they seek only to maximize some value.

Yet in some situations, we are clearly *risk-averse*. As a society, we pay billions of dollars in premiums to insurance companies to mitigate risk. Consider life insurance. Say you have a 1 percent chance of dying over the insurance period and you want to maximize the amount of money your family will receive. If you work your whole life, you will make $1,000,000. You want to buy an insurance policy to replace that income if you were to die, so you buy a policy that costs of $100,000 (**FIGURE 26.3**).

FIGURE 26.3
Game tree for insurance.

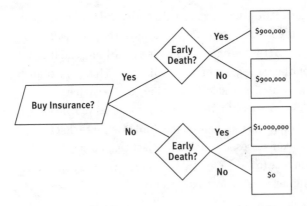

According to expected value, this is irrational. The "buy insurance" option has an expected value of $900,000. The "No insurance" option has an expected value of $990,000. We buy insurance for safety. We are risk-averse. We don't want our family to end up in the $0 outcome, so we pay a premium to ensure that.

▶ **NOTE** This analysis ignores the smaller prizes for simplicity.

However, sometimes we are *risk-loving*. Consider the Powerball jackpot. Odds are roughly 1 in 175 million that you'll win the jackpot. As of today, the Powerball jackpot is listed as $60 million (**FIGURE 26.4**).

Here, the expected value of buying a ticket is −$1.65 and the expected value of not buying a ticket is $0. A risk-neutral person would not buy the ticket. Yet millions buy Powerball tickets every day. They pay a premium for a chance at a big payout.

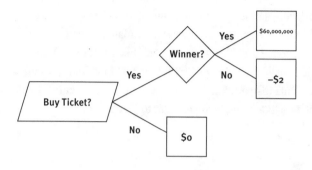

FIGURE 26.4 Game tree for the lottery.

Loss

When I was buying my first new car out of college, I felt a real dilemma. I was torn between getting a reliable, cost-effective Honda Civic, and a fun, yet more expensive Mini Cooper convertible. I had test-driven both and kept going back and forth to the dealerships. The salespeople were likely sick of me. One day at the Honda dealership, the salesperson hands me the keys and says "Take it home for a couple days and see how you feel." That was odd to me. They would let me test drive it without someone there? What if I took it cross-country and returned it after? What if I got into an accident?

I didn't realize at the time, but the dealership was using a classic psychological trick called the *endowment effect*. It states that you value something more that is in your possession.[23] I would feel the loss of giving the car back greater than the gain I received by getting to take the car home. Behavioral economists Daniel Kahneman and Amos Tversky found that people lose more satisfaction from losing x dollars than they gain satisfaction from winning x dollars.[24] This is called *loss aversion*.

This is a simple manipulation that is often done in games. In *Metroid Prime*, you are given all the weapons in the game at the beginning and then they are taken away. That loss hurts more than never having the weapons in the first place, and it motivates you to seek them out. If you choose to not check in on your *FarmVille* farm, your crops wither away. There is a minor loss due to withering when compared to never having planted at all, but there is a large loss compared to harvesting them at the right time. Thus players continually come back to avoid the "loss" of spoiled crops.

· · · · · · · · · · · · · · · · · ·

23 Kahneman, D., Knetsch, J. L., & Thaler, R. H. (1991). "Anomalies: The Endowment Effect, Loss Aversion, and Status Quo Bias." *The Journal of Economic Perspectives*, 5, 193–206.

24 Kahneman, D., & Tversky, A. (1984). "Choices, Values, and Frames." *American Psychologist*, 39(4), 341.

Game designer Ray Mazza recommends that you (the designer) always keep players as happy as possible to avoid their pain of loss. "[Mechanics that punish a player] may be fun for everyone else, but they are lousy for at least one player. They're often used to insert randomness into [a] game to even out chances for those less skilled, but that can be accomplished with positive events instead. Rather than lose a turn, try to gain a turn. [...] The happier everyone is, the less likely they'll never want to play again."[25]

Framing Decisions

How a designer presents a decision can affect how a player evaluates it. A classic poll showed that when a survey asked if the United States should *forbid* public speeches against democracy, 46 percent of those polled agreed.[26] But when the poll asked if the United States should *allow* public speeches against democracy, 62 percent said no despite the fact that a "no" answer to allowing the speeches is logically the same as a "yes" answer to forbidding them. The only difference here is in framing. "Allowing" something feels better than "forbidding" something. As in the examples of loss aversion earlier, people don't want to lose something.

Students and researchers registering for a conference were split into groups where one group was offered a $50 discount for registering early. The other group had a $50 charge if they registered late. Both groups paid the same price on the same day; the only difference was the wording of the fees. Of the registrants, 93 percent of the junior researchers involved registered early when it was framed as a penalty for not registering early, while only 67 percent registered when it was framed as a discount for registering early.[27] And these students and researchers were economists! They should have been well educated regarding *framing effects*.

Here's another example: Experimenters showed subjects video of a traffic accident and then asked them how fast the car was going at the time of the accident.[28] However, different groups received different verbs when they were asked about the accident. Some groups were asked how fast the car was going when it "bumped" the other car. Some were asked how fast it was going when it "smashed" the other car. When researchers used words such as "smashed," subjects thought the car had been going faster. The verb used affected how fast the subjects remembered the car to be going!

· · · · · · · · · · · · · · · · · · ·

25 Costikyan, G. (Ed.) (2011), *Tabletop: Analog Game Design*. Pittsburgh, PA: ETC Press.

26 Rugg, D. (1941). "Experiments in Wording Questions: II." *Public Opinion Quarterly*. 5, 91-92.

27 Gächter, S., Orzen, H., Renner, E., & Starmer, C. (2009). "Are Experimental Economists Prone to Framing Effects? A Natural Field Experiment." *Journal of Economic Behavior & Organization*, 70(3), 443–446.

28 Loftus, E. F., & Palmer, J. C. (1974). "Reconstruction of Automobile Destruction: An Example of the Interaction between Language and Memory." *Journal of Verbal Learning and Verbal Behavior*, 13(5), 585–589.

Another way of framing is by putting a decision in context. People are bad at estimating how much something is worth, but they have an easier time understanding how much things are worth relative to something else. For instance, you may not know how much a one-carat diamond should cost, but you can be reasonably sure that it costs more than a half-carat diamond. Economist and author Dan Ariely writes in *Predictably Irrational* about the *Economist* magazine's subscription model.[29] The print subscription is offered for $59, the digital subscription for $125, or the print-and-digital subscription for $125. Given the choice of the digital-only subscription, the print-and-digital looks like a no-brainer value, and so customers are driven to this more expensive product.

We do the same thing when we shop at stores and see price tags that say that an item's regular price has been slashed. In one study, an item priced at $40 sold better than the same item priced at $39 because the $40 tag was marked down from $48.[30]

When you quit a *Steam* game, you are dropped back to the *Steam* application that shows you how much time you spent on that game (**FIGURE 26.5**). You might think that is a bad idea, allowing a player to feel guilty for the amount of time they spent playing.

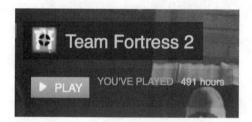

FIGURE 26.5 The number shown here for play time is just on this *Steam* account.

Research contradicts this, however. It turns out that when you are asked about the time you have spent with an experience, it makes you rate the experience more favorably than if you are primed with questions about how much money you spent or if you are not primed at all.[31]

By framing your game's decisions correctly, you can subtly direct players toward options of your choice.

29 Ariely, D. (2008). *Predictably Irrational: The Hidden Forces That Shape Our Decisions*. New York: HarperCollins.

30 Anderson, E. T., & Simester, D. I. (2003). "Effects of $9 Price Endings on Retail Sales: Evidence from Field Experiments." *Quantitative Marketing and Economics*, 1(1), 93–110.

31 Mogilner, C., & Aaker, J. (2009). "'The Time vs. Money Effect': Shifting Product Attitudes and Decisions through Personal Connection." *Journal of Consumer Research*, 36(2), 277–291.

Summary

- The fundamental attribution error is a tendency to explain the behavior of others using dispositional factors while explaining your own behavior with situational factors.

- People value risk differently. The risk-averse accept a negative expected value to avoid risk. The risk-loving accept a negative expected value to engage with risk.

- People are more sensitive to losses. Losing something is more emotionally powerful than gaining something of equal value.

- The endowment effect illustrates that once someone has something, they cite its value as higher than if they did not have it at all.

- How a decision is framed greatly affects the behavior of those making the decision. Simply by changing the words used to describe it or the cues placed around the decision, you can affect the behavior of the decision makers.

27 Attention and Memory

I have a memory like an elephant.
I remember every elephant I've ever met.

—HERB CAEN

When we drive, we are assaulted by hundreds of stimuli: other cars on the road, signs on the side of the road, the radio, other passengers in the car, and so on. Some of these stimuli require little processing—the tree on the side of the road requires little. Some require more—a car merging at a high speed requires a good deal of processing. The act of focusing on one element is known as *attention*. Attention allows us to process an item by putting it in conscious awareness.

We are not limited to processing only items to which we consciously pay attention. For instance, we are often unaware of tasks we perform automatically. Perhaps you drive home while daydreaming, and all of a sudden, you are in your driveway. This is because the highly processing-heavy act of driving has been made automatic by repetition, which leaves your attention to be (dangerously) diverted elsewhere.

Attention

Many elements affect what items humans pay attention to.[1] Differences in color, orientation, size, and motion affect our ability to guide our attention.

In **FIGURE 27.1**, SPR, the ad makers for the firm GSR exploit our tendency to let our attention be drawn toward salient elements rather than dangerous elements. Because the Sikh plumber looks different than the mustachioed plumbers, our attention is drawn to him first, despite the fact that one of the mustachioed plumbers on the bottom row has the dangerous item.

FIGURE 27.1
Advertisement.

1   Wolfe, J. M., & Horowitz, T. S. (2004). "What Attributes Guide the Deployment of Visual Attention and How Do They Do It?" *Nature Reviews Neuroscience*, 5(6), 495–501.

One of the most invasive myths about attention is that humans have the ability to multi-task. As modern men and women, we are used to checking our phones, Twitter, and Facebook while walking, cooking, catching up on Netflix, and reading something for work or school. This leads many of us to the conclusion that we have mastered multi-tasking by necessity. The problem is that this is not true. The brain can focus on only one thing at a time. What humans are doing when they are "multitasking" is switching their attention between all these tasks. This *task-switching* has a cost—namely, we are worse at tasks that involve task switching.[2] We take longer to complete such tasks and make more mistakes than we do when we perform the same work in sequence. Some studies have posited that the task-switching involved when a driver makes a cellphone call behind the wheel makes him more dangerous than an undistracted but legally intoxicated driver.[3]

What is most important to games, however, is that this task-switching decreases a player's ability to learn effectively. People who task-switch frequently are more susceptible to interference from other stimuli, making them less able to focus on any particular task[4] and take longer to complete similar tasks.[5] In terms of flow, these players drop out more frequently.

Attention Misdirection

Horror games are the most fertile grounds in which to abuse human attention. One tactic these games use is the *jump scare*. The jump scare directs the player's attention elsewhere and then quickly introduces a threatening element. The juxtaposition of safety/danger causes the player to be frightened.

Take a look at an example from *BioShock* at www.youtube.com/watch?v=xlwFe-qNxqI (Warning: video contains explicit language and violence).

In the *BioShock* YouTube video, the player's attention is focused on a reward: the tonic. The designers know the player must be facing the desk because that is what triggers the sequence. When the player is in position, fog is introduced surrounding the player. Since the player assumes that the fog is going to be used to introduce enemies, she

. . . .

2   Rubinstein, J. S., Meyer, D. E., & Evans, J. E. (2001). "Executive Control of Cognitive Processes in Task Switching." *Journal of Experimental Psychology: Human Perception and Performance*, 27(4), 763.

3   Strayer, D. L., Drews, F. A., & Crouch, D. J. (2006). "A Comparison of the Cell Phone Driver and the Drunk Driver." *The Journal of the Human Factors and Ergonomics Society*, 48(2), 381–391.

4   Ophir, E., Nass, C., & Wagner, A. D. (2009). "Cognitive Control in Media Multitaskers." Proceedings of the National Academy of Sciences, 106(37), 15583–15587.

5   Fox, A. B., Rosen, J., & Crawford, M. (2009). "Distractions, Distractions: Does Instant Messaging Affect College Students' Performance on a Concurrent Reading Comprehension Task?." *CyberPsychology & Behavior*, 12(1), 51–53.

spins around to face the danger because she knows it is not going to come from the direction of the wall. Her attention is then focused on distant threats because the entrance to the room is far away. Instead, the fog clears to reveal a mad dentist in dangerously close proximity. This startles many players because they expected a far danger yet received a near danger.

Haunted houses abuse this tendency as well. When a participant enters a room, the designers of the house generally know where his attention will be drawn.

FIGURE 27.2 shows the schematic of a haunted house room at Universal Studios Florida from 2011. The participants enter the room and see a woman in skimpy clothing sawing a man in half on a table. As the participants keep walking forward, their gaze is directed toward the girl and the saw. This is a "look here!" element because this is the only lit area in the scene and because the sound effects blast in the room directing the participants' attention toward this area. The designers correctly assume that the vast majority of participants will have their attention drawn to the lit area.

FIGURE 27.2
Attention
misdirection.

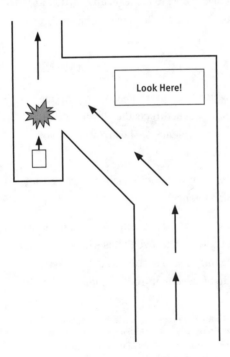

As the participants round the corner and are looking toward the distracting scene, from the opposite direction, a performer in a menacing giant tree costume jumps out at them. This works because the participants' attention is drawn away from where the tree emerges. If the girl was not there, participants would have a chance to see the tree coming. If a designer knows where a participant is looking, then she also knows where the participant is *not* looking.

Games often use this concept to draw attention away from some elements and toward others. Using lighting is a common way to direct attention. Areas that are lit draw players toward them. Players don't often choose to walk into dark areas when lit areas are available.

Attention Direction

The original *Halo* was constrained by its development schedule, which forced the developers to craft levels from similar repeating elements. Instead of repeating the same room over and over again, the level designers created variations on the same room to increase variety. However, they were concerned that this "sameness" would cause players to assume that the entrances and exits were always identical, even though the level designers changed them up for variety's sake. To solve this, the level designers used a simple trick: They drew arrows on the floor that lit the direction in which the players should go (**FIGURE 27.3**).

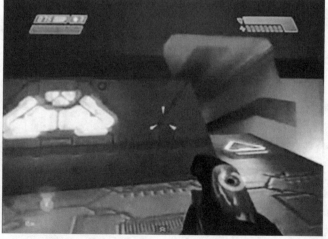

FIGURE 27.3 The floor directs attention.

Paths, lighting, color, arrows, sound effects, and orientation decisions can all help designers subtly affect where a player will choose to focus his attention. In the book *Art of Game Design*, Jesse Schell relates a story in which a designer drew a simple line on the ground; this line caused players to follow it instead of exploring the open environment.[6] *The Stanley Parable* is a dark comedy game that is largely about game design, and it makes a number of jokes at the expense of these techniques (**FIGURE 27.4** and **27.5**).

FIGURE 27.4
The Stanley Parable lampoons choice in games...

FIGURE 27.5
...by highlighting the ways in which game designers direct attention.

6   Schell, J. (2008). *The Art of Game Design: A Book of Lenses*. Amsterdam: Elsevier/Morgan Kaufmann.

Memory

Another human deficiency relevant to games is our extremely limited memory. The common rule of thumb that is cited for human short-term (or working) memory is seven plus or minus two elements.[7] This rule is widely used but not scientifically accurate. Its origin is actually from a psychologist's notes from a professional meeting, not from actual research. Since the original estimate of "seven plus or minus" two, copious research has been done on the limitations of working memory, and this research has found that the number of items most subjects can keep in short-term memory is actually four.[8]

These four items do not have to be discrete; often, they are grouped together in items called chunks. So a person can hold four chunks of information in short-term memory. For instance, if I told you to remember the letters GAMEDESIGNLIFE, you would likely easily remember them as GAME, DESIGN, and LIFE, which should make it easy for you to recall the entire string later. However, if I gave you the letters HKNLZAMDKJPQBXL to remember, you would likely have difficulty, despite this string and the original being the same length.

This fact is extremely important to remember when you are teaching players complex games. Fighting games tend to have dozens of moves players need to memorize. These are difficult to remember as a massive list, so many novice players just punch buttons and hope for the best. League of Legends, for instance, has an incredibly difficult number of concepts to master. Luckily for newer players, the makers of League of Legends decided that most game characters would have only four unique abilities that may be activated, keeping them easily in line with the number of elements able to be held by working memory at one time.

Other elements (shown on the in-game display in **FIGURE 27.6**), such as the summoner spells, recall, and the health and mana bars, are more universal across the game's characters. When a player needs to learn a new character, she often only has to juggle four new concepts in memory.

▶ **NOTE** Assuming that a player has only four new concepts to learn can be problematic if that the player has not reached automaticity with all the other concepts in the game. As an example, learning the four abilities for a new character will be tough if the player also has to learn the game's basic rules and mechanics simultaneously.

FIGURE 27.6 There are a lot of elements to take in here.

7   Miller, G. A. (1956). "The Magical Number Seven, Plus or Minus Two: Some Limits on Our Capacity for Processing Information." *Psychological Review*, 63(2), 81.

8   Cowan, N. (2001). "Metatheory of Storage Capacity Limits." *Behavioral and Brain Sciences*, 24(01), 154–176.

Helping with Memory Limitations

Designers can employ a few techniques to help players avoid the natural limitations of memory:

- **ORGANIZATION.** By better organizing elements that need to be remembered, designers can make it so players have an easier time remembering a list as a whole. Humans understand the relationships of elements in a list and can use those relationships to aid memory. In one study, subjects remembered words presented in a hierarchical order three-and-a-half times better than random words.[9]

- **MEANING.** Items that are well-understood are easier to remember, even when they are assembled into new concepts. Using established nomenclature and symbols saves precious processing ability. A recent study found that participants learned new Chinese phrases much more effectively when they were taught using symbols that the participant already knew and could, thus, easily turn into chunks.[10]

- **ORDER.** In some situations there is a primacy effect. The primacy effect is when an early element in a sequential list is remembered more strongly than other elements in the list. In other situations, there is a recency effect, where elements presented later have more impact. Which is correct? Is early or late information more important? Research seems to suggest that if a person is asked to make a decision about the information in a short amount of time, primacy effects are stronger.[11] That is, if you are given a list of items and are then asked to choose one, the first items listed will have the strongest weight. However, in situations in which a person has time between when he is exposed to the list and when he needs to make a decision based on the information, then recency effects seem to have weight. Since most game tutorials emphasize playing immediately after learning how to play, it seems to make sense to put the most important information first to make use of the primacy effect.

- **ENVIRONMENT.** In what must be a Guinness World Record example of getting a grant foundation to support a ridiculous-sounding study, Godden & Baddeley tested people's recall of words based on whether they learned those words while in a wetsuit

. . . .

9   Bower, G. H., Clark, M. C., Lesgold, A. M., & Winzenz, D. (1969). "Hierarchical Retrieval Schemes in Recall of Categorized Word Lists." *Journal of Verbal Learning and Verbal Behavior*, 8(3), 323–343.

10 Reder, L. M., Liu, X. L., Keinath, A., & Popov, V. (2015). "Building Knowledge Requires Bricks, Not Sand: The Critical Role of Familiar Constituents in Learning." *Psychonomic Bulletin & Review*, 2015 Jul 3. 1–7. doi: 10.3758/s13423-015-0889-1

11 Hogarth, R. M., & Einhorn, H. J. (1992). "Order Effects in Belief Updating: The Belief-Adjustment Model." *Cognitive psychology*, 24(1), 1–55.

underwater or while in a wetsuit on dry land.[12] They found that people who learned the list of words while underwater were better able to recall the list while underwater and that the people who learned the list on dry land were better able to recall the list on dry land. This implies that where a person learns has some effect on how she learns. In games, this suggests that lessons should be taught in an environment similar to the one in which they will be used.

- **REPETITION AND USE.** One of the goals of learning is to move information from the constantly rewritten short-term memory to the relatively more stable long-term memory. By repeating and using information, the odds of long-term retention of that information increases.[13] By having players perform the actions that you want them to remember, you increase the odds that they will remember those actions.

- **EMOTION.** We tend to remember events that pull at our emotions better than neutral events. Commercials are keen to manipulate using this tactic. In the 2015 Super Bowl, insurance company Nationwide ran an emotionally charged ad in which a child narrated the things he would not be able to do because an accident killed him. This ad was the number one most-talked-about ad the following day despite the hundreds of millions other advertisers spent on the event. The USA Today headline summed it up: "Nationwide ad provokes; little else in Super Bowl does."[14]

Perception

Game designers can help in the cognitive load of learning and playing their games by understanding more of the mechanisms of human perception.

Colorblindness

An often forgotten limitation is the inability of a large percentage of the population to distinguish between colors. One in 200 women are colorblind. One in 12 men are colorblind.[15] Red-green colorblindness is the most common form. Blue-yellow colorblindness and complete colorblindness are possible, but rare.

. . . .

12 Godden, D. R., & Baddeley, A. D. (1975). "Context-Dependent Memory in Two Natural Environments: On Land and Underwater." *British Journal of Psychology*, 66(3), 325–331.

13 Medina, J. (2008). *Brain Rules: 12 Principles for Surviving and Thriving at Work, Home, and School.* Seattle, WA: Pear Press.

14 Horovitz, B. (2015, February 3). "Nationwide Ad Provokes; Little Else in Super Bowl Does." Retrieved February 4, 2015, from www.usatoday.com/story/money/2015/02/02/nationwide-super-bowl-advertisingmarketing/22749245/.

15 Colblindor (n.d.). Retrieved February 4, 2015, from www.colorblindness.com/2006/04/28/colorblind-population/.

Games can use color to distinguish elements, but their designers must be careful to also use additional channels to distinguish differences. The board game Ticket to Ride uses both colors and symbols to differentiate between the train cards, so even when the player's ability to differentiate color is removed, the cards look unique. The routes on the game's board each have a color and a symbol. These symbols correspond to the symbols on the corners of the cards, which allows colorblind players a way to distinguish between the routes (**FIGURE 27.7**).

FIGURE 27.7
Routes use both colors and symbols to help visually impaired players.

Ticket to Ride has sold over 3,000,000 copies.[16] If you assume, modestly, that each copy of the game was played by only two people, then the game has a reach of 6,000,000 players. Assuming colorblind people play the game in proportion to the general public, then 480,000 colorblind players have played the game. This illustrates how including considerations for the colorblind can be worth considering.

Colorblindness is, of course, not the only disability of which game designers need to be aware. A good source of information on designing for accessibility is the IGDA Accessibility SIG, an international special interest group that focuses on awareness of accessibility issues for disabled players.

Text Might as Well Be Invisible

The easiest way to solve the problem of playtesters being confused with a mechanic or puzzle is to provide hint text on the screen. It generally takes only a few lines of code to make this happen and designers assume that directly telling players what to do is an

16 Duffy, O. (2014, October 27). "All Aboard–How *Ticket To Ride* Helped Save Table-Top Gaming." Retrieved February 4, 2015, from www.theguardian.com/technology/blog/2014/oct/27/all-aboard-how-ticket-to-ride-helped-save-table-top-gaming.

efficient way to teach players. The trouble is that players generally don't read what is onscreen. The more text that is onscreen, the less it will be read. Where is the player's attention? If their attention is in the game world, players cannot simultaneously focus on the action and the text and are loath to switch attention. The solution to this is difficult, but effective. Tutorials that introduce elements by having the player learn as he plays instead of being dictated to will increase the player's agency in learning and will avoid having him shift his attention to poorly retained text.

Humans generally retain concepts related through pictures better than concepts expressed through words alone.[17] Although psychologists have had trouble defining why this is true, they have replicated the effects in numerous studies. In one study, the subjects remembered pictorial information decades later.[18] In the book Brain Rules, John Medina references a study in which after 72 hours, subjects only remembered 10 percent of oral information, but when the material was presented both orally and with pictures, the retention rate jumped to 65 percent.[19]

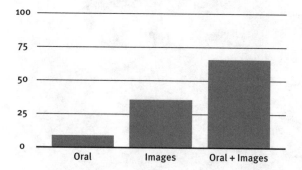

FIGURE 27.8 Use images and words for the best retention.

Additionally, we just don't spend that much time searching for answers to our questions. According to internal Google research that used eye-tracking, in 47 percent of searches, users didn't even look at items lower than the first two results.[20] This can be explained as users trusting that the first two Google results are relevant, but a likely alternate explanation is that users just do not want to read much, even if doing so will give them a helpful answer.

. . . .

17 Nelson, D. L., Reed, V. S., & Walling, J. R. (1976). "Pictorial Superiority Effect." *Journal of Experimental Psychology: Human Learning and Memory*, 2(5), 523.

18 Read, J. D., & Barnsley, R. H. (1977). "Remember Dick and Jane? Memory for Elementary School Readers." *Canadian Journal of Behavioural Science/Revue Canadienne des Sciences Du Comportement*, 9(4), 361.

19 Ibid.

20 Ronson, J. (2015). *So You've Been Publicly Shamed*. New York, NY: Riverhead Books.

Gestalt Grouping

We tend to perceive things with expectations based on their representation. Things that look alike should act alike. There should be contrast between interactive and noninteractive elements. L.A. Noire presents players with a vast cityscape. Every home and storefront has a door. Naturally, it was out of scope to make every door open to a fully realized interior; yet some doors had to open to an interior. The player needs to know which doors open and which do not. In L.A. Noire, the designers achieved this by coloring the doorknobs that open doors a vibrant gold.

FIGURE 27.9 shows a scene from the Resident Evil series, which has always featured complex environments in which players can interact with only a small fraction of the items. The designers alert the player to objects she can take by adding a visible sparkle to them. The difference between these objects and other objects in the scene lets the player know that the interactive objects are different in some way.

FIGURE 27.9
The sparkle directs attention in an otherwise visually busy scene.

IMAGE FROM *RESIDENT EVIL* © 2002 CAPCOM.

First Impressions

An ironic concept to end this chapter with is the importance of beginnings. Humans make impressions of people after less than a tenth of a second.[21] Once we have made these split-second impressions, we tend to stick with them.[22]

Researchers formed groups of students and had them solve math problems collaboratively while on camera.[23] The researchers wanted to know how the groups determined their leaders. What they found was that in 94 percent of the math problems, the group's first answer was their final answer. The key was not to be the smartest at math problems or the most persuasive voice in the group; it was simply to speak first. That is how powerful the first impression can be.

Summary

- Despite how you may feel, you cannot multitask. You can quickly task-switch, but this is at a detriment to the performance of any individual task. This penalty is reduced when the tasks have become automatic and do not need your attention.

- In general, a person can hold a small number of "chunks" of information in working memory at a time. The more closely related and the stronger the chunks, the more of them can be held.

- You can direct a player's actions by using light, color, motion, or other attention-grabbing effects.

- Use already understood pieces to teach new concepts.

- Text alone is one of the worst mediums for retention. That makes it ironic reading it here, no?

. . . .

21 Willis, J., & Todorov, A. (2006). "First Impressions: Making Up Your Mind After a 100-ms Exposure to a Face." *Psychological Science*, 17(7), 592–598.

22 Tetlock, P. E. (1983). "Accountability and the Perseverance of First Impressions." *Social Psychology Quarterly*, [Au: Issue/Vol? RR]285–292.

23 Anderson, C., & Kilduff, G. J. (2009). "Why Do Dominant Personalities Attain Influence in Face-to-Face Groups? The Competence-Signaling Effects of Trait Dominance." *Journal of Personality and Social Psychology*, 96(2), 491.

7 Game Design Tools

> Do not wait; the time will never be "just right."
> Start where you stand, and work with whatever tools
> you may have at your command, and better tools will be
> found as you go along.
>
> —GEORGE HERBERT

A game designer has to work with a variety of tools, both theoretical and practical, to get the job done successfully. However, the task of learning to use those tools seems particularly challenging in the field of game design for a number of reasons.

First, especially in the field of digital games, tools change quickly and drastically over time. When you learn to use a specific tool, this knowledge comes with the implicit guarantee that the tool's shelf life is limited and that something new may take its place in a short time. There was a time when Adobe's (and previously Macromedia's) Flash was *the* software tool for designers to use to prototype digital games. Designers rushed to learn ActionScript, Flash's proprietary language. Fast forward a decade and few designers use ActionScript or Flash to prototype. Currently, Unity is one of the top digital prototyping tools. A decade hence, designers will likely use another tool with another set of practices.

Next, the tools that a designer uses are often not consistent from studio to studio. When I was at Electronic Arts, we used an entirely proprietary solution for game design documents. No lesson from a book or lecture could have prepared me to use it because it was used only inside that studio. When I became employed by another studio, we used a wiki to keep design documentation; this used a completely different model and workflow.

Also, since game designers must be conversant in a large number of subjects, so too must they be comfortable with the basic use of tools in those subject areas. In the same day, it would not be strange for a designer to have to use the following: Microsoft Project to adjust a schedule, Jira to track bugs and issues, Microsoft Word to update design documentation, Cacoo to make diagrams, and Slack to share new information with the team. With varied skills and responsibilities comes a learning curve of many new tools.

Because of all these difficulties, you should treat tool-based knowledge as disposable. Instead, focus on the function that the tool provides. Whether you use Microsoft Excel, Google Sheets, Apple Numbers, or OpenOffice Calc to run spreadsheets is less important than the concepts of tracking and evaluating the data that spreadsheet tools provide. The concepts themselves have a longer shelf life, and thus they provide more bang for the learning buck.

As a designer, you should know how to complete a number of tasks with the tools at hand. One task is being able to communicate using the written word to create many different forms of documentation. You should also be able to communicate ideas and concepts through visual and spoken presentations. The designer should be able to use tools to answer complex questions about a game's structure, which often requires a deep understanding of probability, data analysis, and simulation. All of these topics are covered in this section.

28 Documentation and Written Communication

A design document never survives contact with the enemy.

—DAMION SCHUBERT

Game designer roles come in all shapes and sizes. The "traditional" game designer role is the one you see at big video-game studios: Designers manage and communicate the vision for a large team, often crafting levels and features themselves, but just as often they delegate to engineers and artists. Designers at small video-game studios also have to rely on documentation to solidify what are often ephemeral design ideas taken from conversations and playtesting. Analog game designers need documentation most of all: Almost all analog games ship with written rules.

One thing is certain: A designer cannot rely solely on verbal communication. Documentation is key to ensure that ideas and issues are communicated without signal loss. What good is a designer whose contributions get lost in the shuffle? Every designer thinks they communicate clearly, but not everyone can be above average. Only by study, reflection, and work can you become better at the skills that are the bread and butter of successful designers.

The Game Design Document

One of the game designer's most useful tools in digital games can be (when used effectively) the *game design document* (GDD). Naive outsiders believe that the GDD is the beginning and end of what the game designer does. It's one of the most useful tools in a designer's toolbox for communication, but it's also one of the most misunderstood. Nearly every professional video-game designer deals with GDDs. But what are they? Why are they so ubiquitous?

When a game development team is only three people (say a designer, an artist, and a programmer), the team has only three channels of communication they need to keep open: designer-artist, designer-programmer, and artist-programmer (**FIGURE 28.1**).

But add just one more programmer, and lines of communication don't increase by just one; they jump to six (**FIGURE 28.2**).

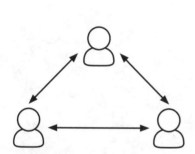

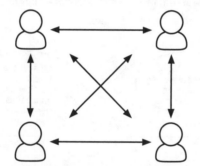

FIGURE 28.1 Communication lines between three parties.

FIGURE 28.2 Communication lines between four parties.

Now you might see why professional game development can be a mammoth undertaking, especially with team sizes in the hundreds. If everyone on a team of 100 had to connect with every other team member, it would require 4,950 interpersonal connections. Ubisoft has teams of up to 600 people.[1] If you take such a team as an example, 179,700 connections would need to be maintained between the team members if every team member needed to directly talk with every other member.[2]

· · · · · · · · · · · · · · · · · · · ·

1   Weber, R. (2013, February 28). "On Reflections: First Interview with the Ubisoft Studio's New MD." Retrieved March 5, 2015, from www.gamesindustry.biz/ articles/2014-02-26-on-reflections-first-interview-with-the-ubisoft-studios-new-md.

2   Dantzig, G. B. (1960). "On the Shortest Route through a Network." *Management Science*, 6(2), 187–190.

As you might have guessed, this is too unwieldy. Real-world teams are not structured so every team member has access to every other team member. Instead, larger teams are subdivided into groups by either discipline or project area. For instance, the artists may all talk with each other, but they route their communication with other disciplines through a producer. Or all team members working on the multiplayer portion work together, whereas the single player teammates communicate only with their own group members.

This causes another problem: Instead of team members being able to directly communicate with each other freely, communication has to be routed through gatekeepers, such as producers or leads. If you have ever played the childhood game *Telephone*, you know how multiple rebroadcasts can add noise to a channel.

A fluid and, at times, highly vague concept like game design cannot be faithfully communicated in such a manner. Teams devise artifacts that can be digitally replicated to eliminate the signal loss of the "telephone" method in **FIGURE 28.3**. The GDD (or GDDs) is a tool used to solve this problem.

FIGURE 28.3
Additional communication steps add noise.

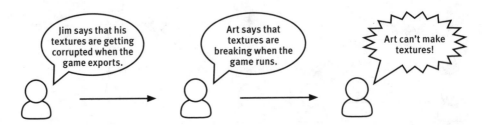

Jim says that his textures are getting corrupted when the game exports.

Art says that textures are breaking when the game runs.

Art can't make textures!

A GDD is any method of documentation that gives sufficient specifications for building a game or feature. From team to team, and from studio to studio, GDDs can take wildly different forms and be constructed using widely different methods. There are also common misconceptions about the form and purpose of a GDD.

Common Misconceptions

There are a number of misconceptions about GDDs. This is largely because so many sites—just a Google search away—claim to show you how to make a GDD. The problem with these sites is that often the author has worked in only one organization and is basing her conception of GDDs on a narrow definition of what she uses them for. Documentation is used in many different ways in a game development organization; any one unified way of creating them in general is bound to be incorrect.

Common Misconception 1:
The GDD Is a Repository of All Information About a Game or Feature

Game design documents are there to serve a primary purpose—to inform team members about what they are to build. To this end, there are a number of stakeholders:

- **PROGRAMMERS.** Because they need to build the thing.
- **ARTISTS.** Because they need context to know what they are creating.
- **PRODUCERS.** Because they need to be able to gauge how long a feature will take to develop.
- **QA.** Because they need to know what a feature looks like when it's working.
- **OTHER DESIGNERS.** Because their systems need to work with the feature.
- **LICENSORS.** Because they need to OK use of their intellectual property.

To look like they are producing a lot of content, many designers fill a GDD in with explanations of all the influences behind a system—the backstory, the design discussions, or other ephemera. Unless it directly instructs a programmer or artist on what exactly to make, leave such material out of the GDD proper. You may relegate it to an appendix (see the "Appendix" section in this chapter) or to another document.

In some cases, it's necessary to keep a second pseudo-GDD in cases in which you have external licensors or overly involved executives. They often want to get their hands on what the team is making. In these cases, the GDD will likely be too technical for what they need. For these situations, Design Overviews or Executive Summaries are sometimes useful.

Common Misconception 2:
The Word in the GDD Is Law.

Aspiring designers who are just entering the field often hold this misconception. Game design is an iterative process. It requires experimentation and often copious trials and errors. Yet many GDDs are written and attitudes hardened as if the GDD will never change. In the worst-case scenarios, programmers print the GDDs and build from a static conception of what a feature is.

The GDD is the formulation of an idea at a given time. The GDD's function is to foster communication throughout a team, not to be a dictate.

Often, I have heard from programmers that they don't read GDDs. A little later, I'll get into the cardinal sins that cause this attitude, but one of the reasons for this attitude is that GDDs are not kept up-to-date. If a programmer reads a GDD and is then told to make something contrary to what she read, she'll wait to be told what to do in the future rather than trusting what the GDD says. It's the designer's job to keep documents as up-to-date as possible, no matter how tedious a job that may be.

Remember the purpose of the GDD: Unless you personally want to communicate a change in design to every member of the team, you must keep the GDD aligned to the most current design.

Common Misconception 3:
There Is a Template to How All Studios Create Design Documentation

Often, students ask to see sample design documentation. I can show them a made-up example, but it won't look much like whatever the first game design document they see in industry looks like. Why I hesitate to show them anything at all is that every studio has its own documentation processes. Each studio uses its documentation to solve different problems so each studio's documentation is bound to look different. The reason a student asks me for a sample is so he can copy the formatting. Students think that a game design document becomes "legit" if it's formatted correctly. But the formatting is actually the least important part!

The design documentation is written specifically for a particular audience. Blizzard's design documentation for MMOs is going to look quite different from Quantic Dream's narrative-heavy design process. Who are your programmers? What do they know implicitly? Remember, you are writing your documentation for a particular audience.

You can leave implicit knowledge out of a GDD's instructions. The team behind the *Madden NFL Football* series does not have to spell out that ending a down past the line-to-gain results in a first down or that a first down resets the down counter and results in a new line-to-gain. That knowledge is implicit since the team knows they are making a football game and they do not change the rules of the game every year.

Some studios do, in fact, have massive templates for game design documentation. This can be a useful practice if needed sections are commonly left out. The danger with templates, however, is that they are often not updated as the team and the project change, and are thus prone to overloading documentation with wasteful, empty categories. If programmers and other stakeholders have to scroll through empty sections, this makes it more difficult for them to find the information they need. This is anathema to having a formal GDD at all.

Given all the other things you have to deal with when writing your design document, keep clarity as the most important goal.

The GDD Creation Process

> Whatever can be said at all can be said clearly, and whatever cannot be said clearly should not be said at all.
>
> —LUDWIG WITTGENSTEIN

Let's go through an example of creating a short, concise design document. Assume you are on a small team that is putting together a fantasy RPG for Facebook. The lead designer comes to you and says you need to design a crafting system for the game. How would you go about creating the documentation?

Step One: Determine Purpose/Desired Scope/Connected Systems

Designers often have lead designers or creative directors above them. The goal of the design you are working on will likely be tied to a larger design goal held by designers at higher levels.

If you don't know the purpose of the system, all you can do is copy a similar crafting system from another game. So determine the purpose first. Start by interviewing stakeholders. Ask probing questions. Find out which systems need to interface with your design and what the developers of those systems expect and need. Make sure you really understand the motivations behind the assignment before you begin writing or prototyping.

Designers have an awful tendency to overdesign. It's simply easier to come up with ideas than it is to spend the man-hours evaluating and testing them. What this means is that given an assignment, designers often come up with nuanced, complex systems. In isolation, this is not a problem. But in aggregate, no project can sustain complexity in every system and still expect to ship on time and be understood by users. Great designers know which systems benefit from complexity and which benefit from simplicity. By identifying the scope of the feature, designers get an idea of the depth of the system they need to create (**TABLE 28.1**).

TABLE 28.1 Levels of Innovation and Risk

	Description	Risk	Example
Innovative (Level 1)	The design is beyond the level of functionality of other games in the market.	Highest Risk	Creature Creator in *Spore*
Market-Leading (Level 2)	The design is similar in functionality to the best example currently in the market.	High Risk	Progression System in *Destiny*
Market-Standard (Level 3)	The design matches similar functionality as is expected in the genre.	Low Risk	Destructible terrain in *The Last of Us*
Present (Level 4)	The design is as bare-bones as it can be while still satisfying the basic functionality of the design.	Lowest Risk	In-Game Store in *Assassin's Creed*

If the lead designer tells me this, "We have a lot of art time for this, so you can make it broad, but the entire game is pretty casual, so keep the complexity low." I would probably choose to go with the "Market Standard" complexity as described in Table 28.1.

What systems does the design need to interface with? What if you need to give a player items, but the inventory system doesn't support this? What if there is no inventory system? What designer is in charge of the economy so you do not flood your game's market with free goods? Who do you need to contact? When you are formulating your GDD, make sure that none of these statements are contradictory. For instance, if the purpose of the design is to have a fully customizable character generator while the scope of the design is to be simple, then you need to meet with your lead designer to find out what must give.

Step Two: Research

The scope level you come to in Step One will help you decide how much and what type of research you need to do. Having a wide breadth of exposure to other titles in the industry helps here. How will you know about features that may eventually creep into your genre if you have not been exposed to other similar games? For instance, what is going on in matchmaking for leagues in sports games may be relevant for multiplayer online battle arena (MOBA) games. One of the best ways to grow as a designer is to play bad games and endeavor to understand why they are bad. By identifying features that are unsuccessful, you can design around the pitfalls and mistakes your industry brethren have made.

Of course, your research is not just limited to games. **TABLE 28.2** includes a few ideas for expanded research outside of games.

TABLE 28.2 Research Methods Suggestions

	Description
Innovative (Level 1)	Since, by definition, you are attempting to create something that has never been done before, you cannot take features from other games and apply them to yours. However, you do still need to know the best practices for similar features to determine whether yours exceeds the quality of the market leader.
Market-Leading (Level 2)	This step requires influences from beyond the world of games. You do read outside your design work, correct? From what fiction and nonfiction works can you pull inspiration? From what non-game interactive systems (ATMs, toys, events) can you draw inspiration? Be thorough.
Market-Standard (Level 3)	Play games that implement similar features. Which are the best implementations? Why are they the best? How can you adapt their systems to your game's requirements?
Present (Level 4)	Play games that implement similar features and try to find what they have in common. Can you take anything else away while still preserving the purpose of the feature? This requires design by subtraction. What is the simplest possible version of this feature?

Step Three: Idea Generation

After the research you completed in Step Two, you should be well-equipped to envision a number of possible solutions to your design problem. Come up with as many ways as possible to solve this problem. You will quickly exhaust the low-hanging fruit (Chapter 2). If you can push past that, you may be able to come up with unique perspectives on how to implement your design goals. You can record these ideas using any method you wish, just remember that you are apt to discard most of your ideas eventually. If you are doing this exercise with others, it may help to use some collaborative tool such as Google Docs. At this time, this recording is not for the game design document; it is only for your own use.

Step Four: Murder Your Darlings

You'll have a lot of possible directions you can pursue at this point. It's best to sleep on them, come back to the possible ideas, and eliminate ideas that

- Are not in line with the chosen scope
- Are impossible to create
- Are not effective in researched titles

- Do not meet the purpose of the design (be honest with yourself)
- Conflict with another design in the project

Step Five: Fully Detail the Best Answer

You learned about how other games tackle problems in Step Two and how to generate a large number of ideas in Step Three. It would be easy to put your voluminous knowledge down on paper. Stop!

Remember your audience.

If you are writing for programmers (and it's likely that you are if you are working on a digital game), remember that programmers will transform your words into logical code. The closer the form of your document is to how they think, the easier it will be for them to translate it into code that works for their system. Generally, programmers prefer hierarchically formatted lists like this:

- Player chooses a race (see RaceList.doc).
  - If player chooses elf, +2 speed.
  - If player chooses dwarf, + 2 strength.
  - If player chooses cow, +2 mooing.
- Player then chooses a class (see ClassList.doc).
  - If player chooses priest, starting skill is heal (see Skills.doc).
  - If player chooses paladin, starting skill is smite. If player chooses paladin, he cannot choose evil alignment later.
  - If player chooses critic, starting skill is annoy. If player chooses critic, he cannot choose good alignment later.

This, of course, is a generalization. There are many types of programmers and each may prefer a different style. As a heuristic, simple bulleted lists are more successful for getting programmers to understand your system than are walls of text. When in doubt, ask the programmers what they like to see. They are just as afraid of you as you are of them. Generally, they will tell you, "Something short and easy to read." No one has ever said, "Something 30 pages long with lots of details."

Err on the side of brevity. Remember that it's your duty to keep the design documents up-to-date. Which do you think is easier to update? Short hierarchical bulleted lists? Or vast walls of text? Always ask yourself: What can I do to make this document clearer and shorter?

Step Six: Edit and Find Edge Cases

You have already written down the most salient feature idea and condensed that idea down to a logical list form. Now you must perform two more tasks, and it helps to do them simultaneously. The first task is sending the design out to your fellow designers and folks who are implementing the feature. Ask them the following questions: Is this clear? Are there mistakes? Where does it break down?

An *edge case* is a problem that occurs only under extreme conditions. While others are reviewing your documentation, try to perform the second task—find edge cases in your own design. Test the extremes to see if your system breaks down.

For instance, here's a simple design:

> "The player's jumping height is equal to her strength divided by the weight of items in her backpack."

Sounds reasonable. What if the weight of items in her backpack is zero? 18/0 means the player can jump an undefined height!

Here's another:

> "Players can put items in the "bag" item, which has 20 storage slots."

Neat. What happens if a player puts a bag in a bag? What happens when a player tries to put a 21st item in a bag? What happens to the in-bag items when the player tries to sell the bag itself? These are all questions that you need to answer. Since the bag-in-a-bag question is a little awkward, it is an edge case. The others should have been thought out in the draft.

It's difficult to identify edge cases sometimes—at least it's more difficult than my simple examples let on. The easiest way to check for edge cases is to make extreme examples of your players. What if a player has zero of something? What if he has everything? What if the maximum number of players all try to stand on the same spot? What if a player does this action 20,000 times? What is the most illogical way the player can access the features in this design?

FIGURE 28.4 is a screenshot from a game of *Dead Rising 2*. Having explosions that can cause chain reactions is a valid design idea. But what happens if the player piles up 100 propane containers and something ignites them? Should there be a maximum velocity of objects? Or should there be a limit to the number of explosive objects in a scene?

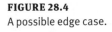

FIGURE 28.4
A possible edge case.

References

Did you notice the "see RaceList.doc" mentions in the sample hierarchical list for the programmers? Those are references and implementing them is the most helpful technique for keep your document size small. If you find yourself copying and pasting information into multiple designs, consider separating that information out into a reference and just adding a hyperlink. In the example, I could have spelled out all the races, and their designs, attributes, and locations in the character creation design, but is it relevant to that particular design?

Another benefit to using references is that it makes editing easier. If the orc's strength bonus changes, it has to change everywhere it shows up in the GDDs. If you use references, you will only have to make the change one place instead of many.

Appendices

What if you have some background information that is necessary or helpful to include? We do not just throw that out, right? Absolutely not. Jesse Schell points out in the book *The Art of Game Design* that game documentation is a cure for the frailty of human knowledge.[3] But since the programmers will not be using that background information to scheme up how to create the feature, you don't want it cluttering up the design document proper. Therefore, put all the "bonus" material at the end of the document in an appendix section or in a linked FAQ document in which you have few restrictions on brevity. You can add anything that needs to be remembered (design battles, reasoning for certain choices, sketches, and so on) to the appendix section/document. If you find it painful to be brief in the design document, you can let loose in this section.

. . . .
3   Schell, J. (2008). *The Art of Game Design: A Book of Lenses.* Amsterdam: Elsevier/Morgan Kaufmann.

Documentation for Tabletop Games

GDDs for tabletop games are very different from ones for digital games. The documentation for a tabletop game consists of the rules of play and an appendix that describes what all the materials in the game do, such as card or tile effects. In contrast to digital games, the purpose of the documentation is to explain the current state of development rather than to guide the development itself. This is due to the comparative ease of implementing tabletop games compared to digital games. To make a significant change in a digital game, a team may have to plan exactly what the change will look like and architect a plan to get there. In a tabletop game, usually a designer can easily make a change and then document it when the change is evaluated.

The documentation for tabletop games is generally considered "the rules." However, this is a misnomer of sorts because "the rules" can contain a lot of helpful information that is not the actual rules but rather strategy tips, diagrams, the backstory, and more.

Unlike documentation for digital games, these rules are generally read by the players themselves. Players either read the rules before playing the game or someone who already has a concept of the rules summarizes them. Some players will have learned the rules directly from the designer. However, most players' first experience with a game will be through either the written explanation of the rules or a verbal summary.

Because the rules are usually read before they are used as a reference, the order and presentation matters. It's important that the information about the player's objective in the game (Chapter 4) occurs very early and is clearly stated. The object of the game creates a mental framework for understanding everything else that follows. As players read the rules, they will be reconciling how the rules will affect their ability to meet the game's objective.

Unless the designer can ship himself with the game, the rules must cover every case that may arise, within reason. No case can remain uncovered by the rules or else the game will grind to a halt and will not be able to be completed.

At the same time, the rules must be succinct enough that the player can understand enough at one time to play effectively (remember the human memory limits from Chapter 27). Thus, the tabletop rules designer must balance between succinct readability and painting a complete topography. This can be a difficult balancing act.

One way to test a game's rules is to implement a *blind playtest*. In the blind playtest, players who have never seen the game before must attempt to learn and play the game using only the rules. The designer speaks or steps in only if the playtest is in risk of failing or going so far off track that the rest of the playtest results would be invalid. A blind playtest is the closest to the reality of players opening the box for the first time. It's difficult to arrange and emotionally draining to complete, but a blind playtest will highlight where rules are making little sense for players.

Another way to evaluate your rules is to consider (or even record) how you explain your game to playtesters. After many playtests, designers tend to settle into a rhythm that prioritizes the important parts of the game before the game starts and then eschews finer points until the game actually begins. By sorting items into these bins, you can figure out the order in which these topics should appear in the rules: important items first, then more contextual items in specific areas related to that topic.

A helpful element that tends to be removed before a tabletop game is published is a complete list of the cards and effects of every element of the game. It is helpful to have all information about the game in one place during development. However, if cards are self-explanatory, then you do not need this in the rules and including it can overwhelm the player.

States and Flowcharts

Games exist in a number of *states*.

In a platform game, such as *Super Mario Bros.*, the player is in a number of states simultaneously. First, the game itself is in the play state, the animation state (when player inputs are ignored, such as at the end of each level), or the game over state. Mario can be in the small, large, fire flower, or invincible states. Mario can also be standing still, walking, running, jumping, falling, swimming, or climbing. Mario is not the only object of the game with states. A block can be standard, question mark, broken, spawning an item, or solid.

More importantly, games transition between states. When Mario in the falling state collides with the top of a turtle in its walking state, that turtle changes to the shell state. When Mario in the small state touches an enemy fireball, the game transitions to the death animation state.

If games can be seen as formalized *transitions* between states based on definitions, then you can draw the game as a flowchart diagram. This can be helpful for many games because it allows abstract concepts to be viewed in a visual form. In digital games, this can be particularly helpful because the formalized documentation of states is an aid in architecting the algorithms that will make up the systems. In my own practice, not only have I found creating flowcharts to be helpful in scripting systems, but programmers I have worked with have thanked me for including flowcharts in game design documentation. In analog games, flowcharts can help you analyze how to teach the game through the rules, and they can also help point out ambiguities in the rules.

First, it is helpful to point out that while the forms of flowcharts are similar between places, many designers disagree about how to use the particular shapes and functions of flowcharts. Although the basics are generally the same everywhere, specifics can differ. As with any communication tool, the point is not to use it in some universally "correct" way, but instead to use it in the way that best communicates. If that means a completely different paradigm than what I use in this book, then that is what you will have to do!

FIGURE 28.5 is a flowchart for a simplified single hand of *Blackjack*. This version ignores the mechanics of splitting, doubling down, and automatic payoffs on a two-card blackjack for simplicity. The basic concept of a flowchart is that a user can begin at the starting location (nearly always in the top left) and step through the game step by step until she reaches an end space. For this to happen, there must be one starting point and at least one ending point. There must be no dead-ends except for the defined end states. Additionally, the user is only at one location in the flowchart at any given time. The user cannot follow multiple paths at a time.

▶ **NOTE** Practitioners disagree on the shapes and functions of the elements in a flowchart, even in documented standards, such as UML (unified modeling language), which is used in other facets of software design.

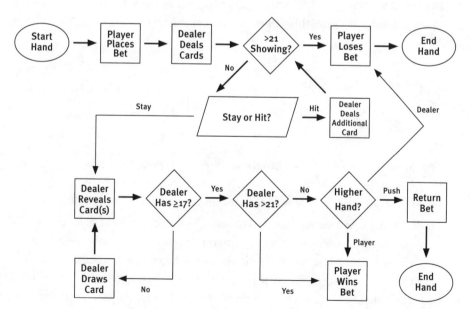

FIGURE 28.5
Blackjack flowchart.

Now let's go through each of the elements of a flowchart, highlighting the uses and needs of each:

- **OVALS** are used to start or end the flowchart (**FIGURE 28.6**). Every flowchart must start with a well-labeled starting point. Generally, flowcharts are read from left-to-right and top-to-bottom. Thus, a starting oval should be in the top left of the flowchart. There may be multiple ending conditions. However, ovals are the only shapes that may be missing an arrow pointing to it or away from it. Every other shape must have at least one of each.

FIGURE 28.6
Ovals in flowcharts.

- **ARROWS** are used to connect shapes. The arrow indicates how to leave one step of the flowchart and enter another. If multiple arrows exit a shape because there may be multiple events that result from that shape, then each arrow must be labeled so that the user knows which arrow to use. For example, in the diagram in **FIGURE 28.7**, the game checks if the player has busted. If the player has busted, then the flow uses the "Yes" labeled arrow. If not, it uses the "No" labeled arrow. The two arrows pointing to this check do not need to be labeled. Only the ones leaving the shape must be labeled. Since "Yes" and "No" are the only two possible answers, the flow must leave this shape and must leave through one of the defined directions.

FIGURE 28.7
Every out arrow from
a diamond or paral-
lelogram needs to be
labeled with an
exclusive case.

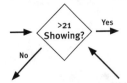

Additionally, arrows must point in only one direction to avoid confusion. If the flow of the game causes something to immediately feedback into the step from which it came, this should be represented by two separate arrows: one pointing in each direction.

- **DIAMONDS** are used for conditional statements evaluated by the game. If event X happens, do this. If event Y happens, do that. This is not for player decisions, which are covered momentarily. An arrow must leave the diamond that represents each possible result of the conditional. If any are missing, then the flowchart can stall. For instance, if the player makes it to the point where she compares hands with the dealer, there are a few possibilities. The player could have the higher hand. In that case, the player wins what she bet. The dealer could have the higher hand. In that case, the dealer takes what the player bet. But there is a third possibility. The player and the dealer could have the same valued hand. If this was ignored in the flowchart, then when both the dealer and player have hands of 20 (as an example), the flowchart stalls and no one knows where to go. Since the game can only end at one of the end ovals, this is obviously wrong. Diamonds must have at least two outputs, and all outputs must represent the universe of possibilities for that element.

- **PARALLELOGRAMS** are used for player decisions. Parallelograms are related to diamonds. Both have multiple, labeled outputs. The difference, however, is that it is the player's action that decides which arrow is used continue flow, not the game rules. The parallelogram reflects any input that comes from outside the system. In flowcharts outside the scope of games, this usually means some action a user performs that is not a choice (such as receiving information from another system), and thus it generally only has one arrow leaving the element. However, because of the interactivity inherent to games, the vast majority of player decisions result in multiple outputs depending on the consequences of the decision.

In the hand of *Blackjack*, there is only one player decision: to hit or stay (**FIGURE 28.8**). If the player chooses to hit, she receives an additional card, the game checks if she busted and, if not, she is given the same choice again. Note that the game loop for the dealer is defined by rules, not player decisions, so that section of the chart is driven by a diamond whereas the player's loop is driven by a parallelogram indicating player decision. Simply counting the number of parallelograms in a game's flowchart can help you identify whether the player has enough interactivity because every other shape ends up being "played" by the game itself. The game for the player lies in the parallelograms.

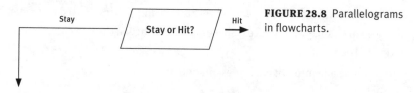

FIGURE 28.8 Parallelograms in flowcharts.

- **RECTANGLES** explain game processes. These are elements that happen in the game that must be noted, since they do not involve player choice with regard to the scope of the flowchart; they result in only one possible outcome. For instance, we could describe how the dealer deals cards with some sort of algorithm corresponding to this description (**FIGURE 28.9**). However, in each case, the result is the same: The player receives two random cards from the deck.

FIGURE 28.9 Squares in flowcharts.

Notice in the schematic in Figure 28.5 that the player choosing a bet is noted within a rectangle. This is because the game reacts the same whether the player bets $1 or $100. In each case, the flow of the game remains the same. Thus, even though this is a player choice, no meaningful branching occurs from this point, so a rectangle is most appropriate shape.

- **CIRCLES** are used as distant connectors. This shape does not appear in the *Blackjack* diagram. Circles are used to connect to other flowcharts and they act as a kind of special ending point. As an example, in the tabletop game *Flick 'em Up*, players play as Old West lawmen or gangs by flicking discs around a table. A special case happens when two discs belonging to opponents enter a building. In this case, they have to duel. However, dueling has its own set of rules and occurs physically away from the main game. If you were flowcharting the states of this game, instead of crowding the flow of dueling into the main diagram, you could simply place a circle in the flowchart labeled "Go to Duel." This would shift the flow to another page with a "Duel" diagram with its own start and end states.

Summary

- The purpose of game design documentation in digital games is to clearly and succinctly describe the features to be created in a form that the person or people doing the implementation prefer.
- The game design documentation should be consistently updated as design decisions about the game change the scope or function of the features.
- Not all features should be of the same level of innovation. Some features will almost necessarily need to be cut. Plan for this by limiting the level of complexity early.
- Creating external references is preferable over cutting and pasting reused elements, since one design change would necessitate only one change in the game design documentation to keep it up-to-date.
- A flowchart can be a helpful visual representation of a system.

29 Probability

> "Probability is the bane of the age," said Moreland, now warming up. "Every Tom, Dick, and Harry thinks he knows what is probable. The fact is most people have not the smallest idea what is going on round them. Their conclusions about life are based on utterly irrelevant—and usually inaccurate—premises."
>
> **—ANTHONY POWELL, A DANCE TO THE MUSIC OF TIME**

One of my favorite probability stories comes from Nobel laureate Manfred Eigen's *Laws of the Game*.[1] A man is about to take a long plane trip, but he is concerned about all the bomb threats and hijackings he sees on the news. He calls his insurance agent, who tells him that the risk of a bomb being on the plane is very small. Undeterred, the man asks the agent what the odds are of there being two bombs on his plane. The agent, flustered, says that the probability should be astronomically small. If the odds of one bomb were 1 in 10,000, then the odds of two bombs should be 1 in a 100 million. The man seems calmed by this. A few weeks later, the agent sees on the news that a bomb was seized from a local passenger's suitcase. At trial, the man claims that he only took the bomb on board to lower the risk of another bomb being on board.

---

1   Eigen, M., & Winkler, R. (1981). *Laws of the Game: How the Principles of Nature Govern Chance.* New York: Knopf.

A skill that is perhaps one of the most important in order to be a successful game designer is a strong understanding of the concept of *probability*. From simple card games to sprawling massively multiplayer online (MMO) games, all use probability as core to their game experience. An innate understanding of probability is essential to making wise gut reactions.

Probability Is Fancy Counting

The reason probability scares a lot of new designers is that they think it's math. Something happened in schools across the world to make people get gun-shy about math. Probability calculations can get hairy and complicated, but at its basest level, probability is nothing more than counting.

Probability = Count of Specific Event / Count of All Events

As an example, you want to know how many times a player will be dealt an ace as his hole card in a game of *Baccarat*. There are four aces in a deck of 52 cards. The item you want the probability of is "Drawing an Ace." All events would be "Drawing a Card." So here you would have to count the number of aces and the number of unique cards. So the probability of drawing an ace is as follows:

Count of Aces / Count of Number of Unique Cards = 4 / 52 = 7.7%

Joint Probability

▶ **NOTE** When I mention a "fair" coin or a "fair" die, I mean a coin or die where each side has the expected equal probability. A fair coin has a 50 percent chance of landing heads and a 50 percent chance of landing tails.

The most common probability operation you'll likely perform is finding a *joint probability*. Joint probability is the odds of multiple events occurring at the same time. Before I cover the mathematical way of finding joint probability, I'll start with an easier example that mostly involves counting.

You have three fair coins: a penny, a nickel, and a dime. If you flip all of them, what are the odds that they all land heads? What are the odds that you get exactly two heads? Since there are only three coins, this is easy to count.

These three coins can land in eight different configurations (**FIGURE 29.1**). How many of these configurations have all three as heads? Since only one does and the odds of every coin are fair, the probability of getting all three heads is ⅛. How many have exactly two heads? If you look at the table in Figure 29.1, you see that there are three: HTH, HHT, THH. Therefore the probability of getting exactly two heads is ⅜.

FIGURE 29.1 Flipping three fair coins.

This was just counting, but if you have larger permutations, the counting can get massive. Luckily, there is an easier way.

First, here are some principles you need to understand:

- Probability will always be a number between 0 and 1 inclusively. A 0 means the event never happens; 1 means the event always happens. Any number larger than 1 does not make sense because how can something happen more than always? Likewise, less than 0 makes no sense. How can something happen less often than never?

- Probability is represented in a number of ways. Sometimes it's in fractional form. Sometimes it's in decimal form. Sometimes it's in percentage form. The value ½ is equivalent to 0.5 is equivalent to 50 percent. These all say the same thing.

- Shorthand for the probability of an event is generally represented by P(Event) where "Event" is some notation for when you want the probability to be counted. So P(Heads) is another way of saying "the probability of getting heads."

The probability of all disjoint events (mutually exclusive) adds up to 1. *Disjoint* means that no occurrence can happen in more than one event. For instance, a person can be 64 years old or 65 years old, but not both. So the event of "being 64" and the event of "being 65" are disjoint. However, "likes pancakes" and "is American" are not disjoint since both can happen simultaneously. When you have disjoint events, you can add up their probability to get the probability of at least one of the events happening. "Is a registered Republican," "Is a registered Democrat," and "Is neither a registered Republican or Democrat" are disjoint events that reflect all Americans who are registered to vote. Therefore if you add up these three probabilities, you are guaranteed to get 1.

What are the odds of flipping the penny and getting heads? There are two faces, each with equal probability, so just by counting, we know that the odds of getting heads is 1 in 2 or ½ or 0.50. The odds of getting heads on the nickel and dime are the same.

When events are *independent*, meaning that what happens in the event doesn't affect the probability of another event, you can find the joint probability of all those things happening together by multiplying the probabilities together. Another way of explaining joint probability is by thinking of it as ANDs. The probability of all three being heads can be written as follows:

Probability of (Penny being heads AND Nickel being heads AND Dime being heads)

P of (Penny being heads) * P of (Nickel being heads) * P of (Dime being heads)

(1/2) * (1/2) * (1/2) = 1/8

This is a little more complicated for finding out the probability of the three coin flips resulting in exactly two heads. What are all the disjoint ways you can get exactly two heads results?

P(Penny=H AND Nickel=H AND Dime=T)

P(Penny=T AND Nickel=H AND Dime=H)

P(Penny=H AND Nickel=T AND Dime=H)

Since these coin flips are independent, you can find the probability by multiplying the probabilities of these coin flips:

P(Penny=H AND Nickel=H AND Dime=T) = (1/2)*(1/2)*(1/2) = 1/8

P(Penny=T AND Nickel=H AND Dime=H) = (1/2)*(1/2)*(1/2) = 1/8

P(Penny=H AND Nickel=T AND Dime=H) = (1/2)*(1/2)*(1/2) = 1/8

P(Getting exactly two heads) = 1/8 + 1/8 + 1/8 = 3/8

This is easy when you are using even ($\frac{1}{2}$ and $\frac{1}{2}$) probabilities. However, change the exercise so the coin is a trick coin that is no longer fair and lands heads 70 percent of the time instead of 50 percent of the time. Now, the counting exercise cannot be used because a heads landing does not happen with the same weight as a tails landing. Here you must use the following math:

P(Penny=H AND Nickel=H AND Dime=T) = (0.7)*(0.7)*(0.3) = 0.147

P(Penny=T AND Nickel=H AND Dime=H) = (0.3)*(0.7)*(0.7) = 0.147

P(Penny=H AND Nickel=T AND Dime=H) = (0.7)*(0.3)*(0.3) = 0.147

P(Getting exactly two heads) = 0.147 + 0.147 + 0.147 = 0.441

Go back to the *Baccarat* example of drawing an ace. The probability of drawing an ace is $\frac{1}{13}$. If the *Baccarat* deck is a standard deck of cards, what are the odds of the next card being an ace as well? Since the odds of getting one ace are $\frac{1}{13}$, then the odds of getting two aces should be $\frac{1}{13} * \frac{1}{13} = \frac{1}{169}$ or 0.006 or 0.6 percent, right? Not quite.

Remember that you can multiply probabilities *only* if the events are independent. These events are not independent because once you have drawn the first ace out of the deck, fewer aces are left in the deck to draw. Just by counting, you knew that the odds of the first card being an ace are 4 in 52 or 0.077. If the first card is an ace, then the odds of getting the next card to be an ace as well are 3 in 51 or 0.059 (or 4 aces minus the one already drawn, and 52 cards minus the one already drawn). Drawing that first ace changes the odds from 7.7 percent to 5.9 percent. Thus, the actual probability of drawing two aces is as follows:

P(Drawing two aces) = P(Drawing first ace) * P(Drawing second ace)

P(Drawing two aces) = (4/52) * (3/51)

P(Drawing two aces) = 12/2652 or 0.0045 or 0.45%

Note that this is much less likely than our original estimate of 0.6 percent!

Conditional Probability

When dealing with events that are dependent on others, it can be helpful to use what is called *conditional probability*. In conditional probability, you use the fact that some other event has occurred to change the probability of another event. As an example, say that you are doing market research for a children's game and you need to choose between ponies and spaceships for your theme. You do a survey of ten kids to ask them what they prefer (**FIGURE 29.2**)

FIGURE 29.2
What themes the kids want.

To find the probability that a kid would prefer ponies or spaceships is just simple counting:

P(Ponies) = 4/10 or 40%

P(Spaceships) = 6/10 or 60%

Also, our demographics can be found just by counting:

P(Boy) = 7/10 or 70%

P(Girl) = 3/10 or 30%

Now you have to be careful about how you ask your questions. If you have a boy gamer, what is the probability that he will choose spaceships? This is a different question than what is the probability that a gamer is both a boy and chooses spaceships. For the latter, you count the five boys who said "spaceships" and divide by the ten total kids to get 5/10 or 50 percent. You cannot just multiply the 70-percent chance of picking a boy and the 60-percent chance of picking someone who said "spaceships" and multiply them together, because they are not independent.

The former question already assumes that you have a boy gamer, so why count the three girl gamers? The answer to the former question is 5/7 or 71.4 percent.

The question of "what is the probability that a gamer is both a boy and chose spaceships?" is notated like this:

P(Boy and Spaceships)

The former question of "given a boy, what is the probability that he will choose spaceships?" is notated like this:

P(Spaceships|Boy)

The vertical pipe means "given," so you read this as "Probability of Spaceships given Boy."

A helpful formula is this:

P(A and B) = P(B|A) * P(A)

Which is better illustrated by the classic Venn diagram in **FIGURE 29.3**.

The value of P(B|A) is represented by the proportion of the P(A) circle that is also P(A and B). This is because you know A is true because you are given A. Therefore, you can ignore all things that are not A. This may be easier to see if you use something countable (remember that overlapping squares count twice, once for A and once for B) as in **FIGURE 29.4**.

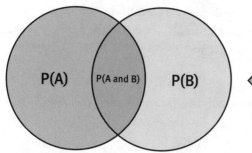

FIGURE 29.3 Venn diagram.

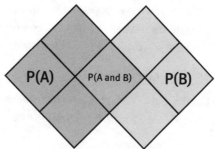

FIGURE 29.4 Countable Venn diagram.

You have eight total squares. If you know A is true, then you only need to look at the diamonds that count toward P(A). So when you ask for P(B|A), you look only at those four diamonds and count the ones that are also counted in P(B). In this case, there are four squares that are "given" as A. So given those four squares, what is the probability of B being in them? There is one square in those four that is also B, so the answer is 1/4.

P(A and B) = P(B|A) * P(A)

(1/8) = (1/4) * (4/8)

Back to the survey:

P(Spaceships | Boy) = P(Boy) / P(Boy and Spaceships)

P(Spaceships | Boy) = (7/10 / (5/10)

P(Spaceships | Boy) = 5/7

Because the example is so simple, you can just count all three quantities, but this is not always the case.

Let's say you are playing in an online gauntlet match in which the winner stays alive and gains more loot and the loser is knocked out. The probability of any player staying alive for X games or P(X) is as follows:

P(1) = 1.00

P(2) = 0.50

P(3) = 0.24

P(4) = 0.10

P(5) = 0.06

P(6) = 0.02

Let's say you have successfully won your fourth game. What is the probability that you will win the next game? This is a conditional probability. Given that you have won four, what is the probability that you will win at least five?

$$P(4 \text{ and } 5) = P(5|4) / P(4)$$

But P(4 and 5) = P(5) because if someone has survived their fifth game, then they have survived their fourth by definition. So:

$$P(5|4) = P(5) / P(4)$$
$$P(5|4) = 0.06 / 0.1 = 60\%$$

Not bad odds!

Adding Die Rolls

A common frustration in learning probability can be easily demonstrated by the common mistakes that surround the probability events with multiple die rolls.

To start, what are the odds of rolling a 4 or higher on a six-sided die? This is easily calculated since the events are simple:

$$P(\text{Getting a 4 or higher}) = P(4) + P(5) + P(6)$$
$$P(\text{Getting a 4 or higher}) = 1/6 + 1/6 + 1/6$$
$$P(\text{Getting a 4 or higher}) = 3/6 \text{ or } 0.50 \text{ or } 50\%$$

> ▶ **NOTE** This is popularly recognized shorthand for saying the result of a die roll. XdY refers to rolling X individual dice all with Y sides and summing up the total. So rolling two four-sided dice and summing the total would be 2d4. Rolling a four-sided die and a six-sided die and summing the total would be 1d4+1d6.

To create the stats for a *Dungeons & Dragons* character, one method is to roll three six-sided dice and add up the results.[2] Thus, a character's score can be anywhere from 3 and 18. This is written in shorthand notion to be 3d6 (or three die rolls of six-sided dice). What are the odds of getting a 16 or higher?

The naive way to calculate this is to say that there are 16 possible outcomes that are disjoint between getting a 3 and getting an 18, and three of those (16, 17, 18) are 16 or higher, so the odds must be 3/16.

$$P(\text{Getting a 16 or higher}) = P(16) + P(17) + P(18)$$
$$P(\text{Getting a 16 or higher}) = 1/16 + 1/16 + 1/16$$
$$P(\text{Getting a 16 or higher}) = 3/16 \text{ or } 0.1875 \text{ or } 18.75\%$$

. . . .

2   Cook, D. (1989). *Advanced Dungeons & Dragons, 2nd Edition, Player's Handbook*. Lake Geneva, Wisconsin: TSR.

This is, unfortunately, incorrect. It assumes that it's equally likely that you will get a 16 as often as an 18 because you have three dice where every side comes up as often as every other side.

You can solve this by counting, but it could be a bit tedious. What do the individual die rolls have to be to get a 16 or higher? There are 216 possible results for rolling three six-sided die. There is only one event in which you can get an 18: If all dice come up 6. But there are three ways the dice can sum up to 17: If the first two dice come up 6 and the third comes up 5, if the last two dice come up 6 and the first comes up 5, or if the first and third dice come up 6 and the middle comes up 5. Likewise, there are six ways the dice can sum up to 16 (**FIGURE 29.5**).

FIGURE 29.5 Ways to roll >= 16 with 3d6.

So just by counting, you can see that there are ten ways that the dice can add up to at least 16. The answer, 10/216 is 0.046 or 4.6 percent, is vastly different than our original guess of 18.75 percent. Why is this? This is because as you get closer to the middle of all the possible results, there are more and more ways to combine the dice together to add up to that number. The numbers 3 and 18 are extreme; there is only one way each to get them with three dice. But 10 or 11 each have 27 different ways. Thus, rolling a 10 is 27 times as likely than rolling an 18 (**FIGURE 29.6**).

FIGURE 29.6
Probability distribution for 3d6.

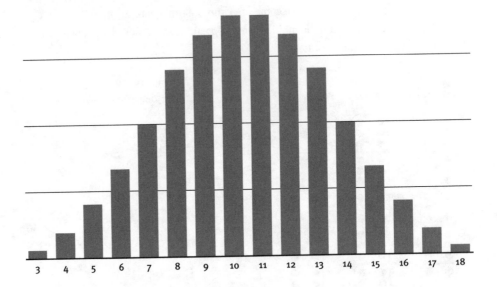

This shows you that you cannot simply add dice rolls together and have the result be the same as a die of that many sides. For instance, as shown in **FIGURE 29.7**, 19d2 gives a result between 19 and 38, and also 1d20 + 18 gives a result between 19 and 38. However, 1d20 has a flat distribution. Any result happens just as often as any other. But 19d2 has a sharp curve with a high probability in the middle and low probabilities at the edges. The more independent die rolls you sum together, the steeper that curve will be. In 1d20 + 18, 19 happens 5 percent of the time because rolling a 1 on one die happens 5 percent of the time. But to get a 19 with 19d2 requires rolling a 1 nineteen times in a row or 0.0002 percent of the time:

▶ **NOTE** Much like flipping heads on 19 of 19 coin flips, rolling 19 1s in a row would happen with a probability of (Probability of rolling a 1 on a two-sided die)^{19} or 0.5^{19}.

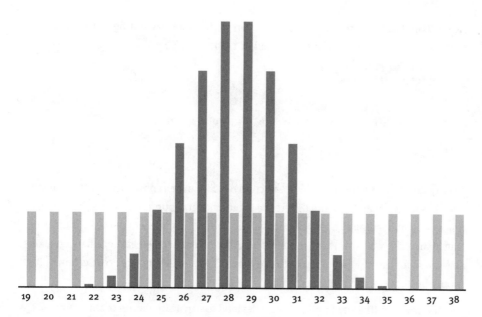

FIGURE 29.7
Although 19d2 and 1d20+18 have the same range, they have vastly different probability distributions.

Example: The H/T Game

Probability is often difficult to understand intuitively.

As an experiment, look at a simple game I call the H/T game. In its basic form, the H/T game has two players. One of the players has a coin and flips it. If a player's coin lands heads, he receives a point. If a player's coin lands tails, the opponent receives a point. Players play for 1,000 rounds. Yikes!

It would not be an interesting game to play, but its simplicity allows you to show how probability can fool us. The H/T game is probably the fairest game you can imagine. Each player has a 50-percent chance of winning each round. How often should the lead change from one player to the other?

Most people envision a series of coin flips like this:

THHTT HTHHT HTTHT THHHT

That looks pretty random. In 20 flips, it has 10 heads and 10 tails.

If this string represents the first 20 flips of the H/T game, Tails would start winning on turn 1. Heads would start winning on turn 3. Tails would start winning again on turn 5.

Heads would start winning on turn 9. On turn 13, Tails starts winning again and keeps that lead until turn 19. This is represented in **TABLE 29.1**.

TABLE 29.1 Lead changes in a run of the H/T game.

Flips	T	H	H	T	T	H	T	H	H	T	H	T	T	H	T	T	H	H	H	T
Score Difference	-1	0	1	0	-1	0	-1	0	1	0	1	0	-1	0	-1	-2	-1	0	1	0
Last Winner	T	T	H	H	T	T	T	T	H	H	H	H	T	T	T	T	T	T	H	H

Twenty flips in this game have five lead changes. Since the probability of getting heads and tails is identical, the score difference should hover around 0 no matter how many times you flip, leading to a lot of lead changes. Twenty-five percent of the flips have a lead change. If you extrapolate to the 1,000 flips you established earlier, then a reasonable guess for the number of lead changes should be something like 250. Certainly, it should be above 15 at a minimum, right?

Because my coin-flipping hand is slow, I decided to run a simulation of this game in Microsoft Excel. I had my computer play the H/T game 1,000 times and count the number of lead changes (that is a 1,000,000 flips!). **FIGURE 29.8** shows the results.

FIGURE 29.8
Simulation of lead changes in the H/T game with a 1,000 flips per game.

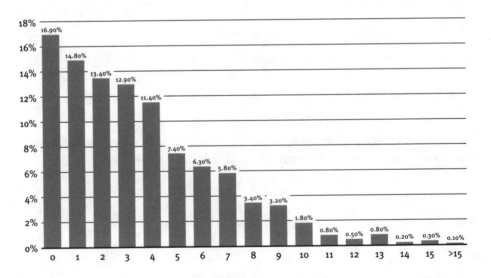

One in a 1,000 games had more than 15 lead changes. Nothing ever even got remotely close to 250 lead changes. The most common number of lead changes was 0!

If you played the H/T game as the Tails player and Heads started winning and remained winning for all 1,000 flips, you would likely get upset and assume that the coin was fixed. After all, with a fair coin, the number of flips should be even between heads and tails!

This is counterintuitive! This game has no feedback loops (Chapter 17). Having flipped a head previously does not increase or decrease the player's odds of flipping another head. Yet in more than one in six games, a player takes the lead and never relinquishes it, even in an extremely long game.

This is just one example of how our instincts about probability can fool us. Be careful.

> ▶ **NOTE** In another spreadsheet, I decided to try to add a negative feedback loop. I added a factor that "nudged" the probability of getting heads by the amount the player was winning. So if Player 1 had a lead of 4 flips, her probability of flipping heads would be, say 0.5 − (4 * 0.05) or 0.3, and her opponent would have a probability of 0.5 + (0.4 * 0.05) or 0.7, where 0.05 is the "fudge factor." Theoretically, this should keep differences closer to 0 because as the lead grows, it becomes harder and harder to flip heads to sustain it. What surprised me, however, is that when I bumped the fudge factor up to its maximum value (that is, if you could not throw a heads and your opponent would always throw heads if you were winning), even then I could get a game of 1,000 throws to have only 40 lead changes.

▶ **NOTE** Although there is an advantage for the leading player in terms of determining when a lead change happens, the actual odds of flipping a point are still always 50-50.

Being Careful

Probability can be tricky, as I'll show with some additional examples. One of the ways to not be tricked is to be deliberate with your use of events and conditions, writing them down and charting them out rather than making assumptions. The first two problems that follow will show you how quick, "obvious" answers are nothing but.

Problem #1: The Boy-Girl Problem

"I have two children. At least one of them is a boy. What is the probability that both are boys?"

Most people instinctively say that the probability is one-half. It's irrelevant what gender the other boy is and that the question is only asking what the gender of other child is. Since you assume a 50/50 split between boys and girls, the odds that Child #2 is a boy is 1/2. Some will answer that since there are four possible permutations of gender in two children and only one of them is boy-boy, that the answer must be 1/4.

This is a situation where it helps to slow down and be deliberate. There are four possible birth combinations: boy-boy, boy-girl, girl-boy, and girl-girl. However, we were told that one of these combinations is impossible. Girl-girl cannot be the result since we know that I have at least one boy (**FIGURE 29.9**).

FIGURE 29.9
The Boy-Girl
problem.

This leaves us with three possibilities: girl-boy, boy-boy, and boy-girl. In those, only one meets the criteria that both are boys. So the answer is actually 1/3.

Problem #2: The Weirder Boy-Girl Problem

▶ **NOTE** Thanks to Jesper Juul for first turning me on to this problem through his blog.

This version of the problem was posed by puzzle designer Gary Foshee. It looks roughly the same as the previous problem:

"I have two children. One is a boy born on a Tuesday. What is the probability that I have two boys?"

At first, it seems an absurd reduction of the first problem, so a knee-jerk answer would be "Also 1/3." What would being born on a Tuesday have to do with gender probabilities?

The first thing to note is that our enumeration of all the possibilities is a lot more difficult than in the first problem. In that one, we had only four options. Now each of the four options has 49 sub-parts: 7 possibilities for Child 1's birthday and 7 possibilities for Child 2's birthday. This leads us to 7 * 7 * 4 or 196 possibilities (**FIGURE 29.10**).

Each of the squares represents a possibility. For instance, if the first child is a girl, the second child is a boy and they are both born on a Friday, then the result is represented by the top-left table with the square that intersects F and F.

Now, you must be careful about understanding what the question is asking. We know that one child is a boy born on a Tuesday. Given that, what is the probability that the other child is a boy? The question is asking for P(Other child is a boy | One child is a boy born on a Tuesday). When we found conditional probabilities earlier, we first highlighted the set from which we were counting. In this case, since we are given that one child is a boy born on a Tuesday, we first limit our counting to those squares. In the diagram, we can do this by highlighting them as in **FIGURE 29.11**.

FIGURE 29.10 Setting up the weirder Boy-Girl problem.

FIGURE 29.11 A step in the weirder Boy-Girl problem.

This is a total of 27 squares: 7 in the top-left table, 0 in the top-right table, 7 in the bottom-right table, and 13 in the bottom-left table. From these 27 squares, you want to know in which cases are both children boys? This part is easy. Only the squares in the bottom-left table. Since there are 13 squares there the answer is 13/27.

You may be upset at this and ready to throw out the entire concept of probability, but wait. This problem does not say that having a boy on a Tuesday somehow changes the probability of having another boy. All it's doing is giving you a fairly complicated statement of facts: I already have two children and here is a partial set of information about them. If I were to have a third child, the probability of that child being a boy or a girl would still be essentially 50/50.

It should also be noted that there are reasonable arguments to discount this as the only solution, due to ambiguity of concepts.[3]

Problem #3: Isner-Mahut at Wimbledon

Wimbledon is a tournament of spectacle in the tennis world. However, it's not often that a first-round match between a 23rd ranked player and an unranked qualifier player gets any immediate or subsequent attention. The 2010 Wimbledon first-round match between American John Isner and Frenchman Nicholas Mahut bucked that trend, setting records that will not easily be broken.

In major tennis tournaments, close matches are decided by tie-breaking games, except in the final set. In the final set, after playing a number of games and remaining tied, players must play until one player scores six games or more *and* wins two games in a row. Thus, a final set can be infinitely long in theory. Before 2010, the longest tie-breaking final set (in terms of games) went to a final score of 21–19 for a set of 40 games and a match length of 5 hours. Isner and Mahut's match was played over three days because of lighting conditions, ending in a final score of Isner 70, Mahut 68 for a final set with 138 games. The match lasted a total of 11 hours and 5 minutes, nearly doubling the duration of the previous longest match in history (**FIGURE 29.12**).

3   Khovanova, T. (2011). In *Martin Gardner's mistake. Martin Gardner in the Twenty-First Century*, (p. 257). Washington, DC: Mathematical Association of America.

FIGURE 29.12 Isner and Mahut pose after their record-breaking match.

IMAGE VIA FLICKR USER "VOO DE MAR". USAGE UNDER CREATIVE COMMONS ATTRIBUTION-SHAREALIKE 2.0 GENERIC LICENSE. IMAGE WAS CROPPED FOR FORMATTING.

If you wanted to model the probability of another match that rivaled the length of the Isner-Mahut match, you might start by assuming that the match lasted so long because the players were so evenly matched that each had a 50-percent chance of winning any game. Many commentators, such as those at *The Daily Mail* and the *New York Times* (among others) made such an observation. [4,5]

Looking back at the H/T game, though, you know that flipping a series that perfectly alternates HTHTHTHT is very improbable. If it was as simple as Isner and Mahut being evenly matched, then by chance alone, one or the other would have lucked into a couple of "Heads" coin flips in a row and ended the match. A series of 138 tosses that ended HTHTHT... or THTHTH... is so unlikely as to be impossible.

One element that a 50–50 assumption makes is that every game plays like every other. However, if you understand tennis, you know this is not true. The player who serves each game has an enormous advantage. This advantage is mitigated by alternating who serves on each game. To win two games in a row, the player has to win a game where he serves, but he also has to win a game where he does not. Winning a game in which you do not serve is called "breaking serve" in tennis.

Making the assumption that the probability that Isner or Mahut wins any particular game is 50 percent assumes that the probability of either player breaking serve is also 50 percent. In a simulation of over 1,000 matches that go to tiebreakers, if you assume a 50-precent break chance, no match exceed 25 games, let alone approached 138 games.

. . . .

4   Harris, P. (2010, June 24). "Game, Sweat, Match! After 11 Hours, We Finally Have a Winner of the Longest Match." Retrieved June 10, 2015, from www.dailymail.co.uk/news/article-1289130/WIMBLEDON-2010-John-Isner-Nicolas-Mahut-longest-tennis-match-ever.html.

5   Drape, J. (2010, June 23). "The Odds on How the Match Will Play Out." Retrieved October 20, 2015, from www.nytimes.com/2010/06/24/sports/tennis/24betting.html.

▶ **NOTE** We cover simulation in Chapter 31, so I am leaving out the details of the simulation and focusing only on the results.

However, if the simulation is changed so that each player has a 25-percent chance of breaking serve, then the longest match jumps to 39 games. If each player has a 0-percent chance of breaking serve, no match would ever end because the serving player would always win and no player would ever break.

If you change the odds of breaking serve to 5 percent for each player, simulation results determine that one match in a 1,000 reaches 138 games. With those odds, 31 percent of matches that go to tiebreakers still end before the 20th game. So even if Isner and Mahut were able to keep a huge 95-percent service win rate, they could play each other again and again and never see the marathon of Wimbledon 2010 happen again. I am sure they would be relieved to hear that.

The point of this example is that you need to be careful when you make assumptions about probability. Here, an assumption that a marathon game between two highly skilled opponents must mean that each has equal odds of winning each game shows a flaw in analysis that can ruin further assumptions about how the game will play out. A more careful analysis uncovers that it was not that Isner and Mahut were evenly matched, but that each was extremely highly skilled at keeping serve against the other on that day. Choosing the correct items to model leads to more valid projections and simulations.

> ▶ **NOTE** Some may object and say that their high-service win rates were what made them evenly matched. You can massage the inputs such that Isner has a 97-percent service win rate and Mahut has a 90-percent service win rate and see similar results. In this, there is an asymmetry between the players, yet the observable statistics remain largely unchanged.

Summary

- Probability is an essential mathematical tool for game designers. Those who shy away from math should be comforted in knowing that probability is just advanced counting.
- Joint probability can be found by multiplying the probability of two independent events.
- Conditional probability can be determined by dividing the joint probability by the probability of the given condition.
- Adding the probabilities of two random events can be challenging when they do not have a uniform distribution.
- Slowing down to enumerate the cases in a probability problem allows you to use simple methods to reach your conclusions.

30 Spreadsheets for Simulation

> Get your facts first. Then you can distort them as you please.
>
> —MARK TWAIN

A system designer's weapon of choice is the *spreadsheet*. A spreadsheet allows a designer to organize data visually and calculate changes on the fly. A full description of the features of a spreadsheet application is beyond the scope of this book, but this chapter does focus on some basic elements of spreadsheet programs, like Google Sheets and Microsoft Excel, that are fairly evergreen and are compulsory for effective use as a game designer. Even though I don't spend much time describing spreadsheet programs, a vast number of other books, videos, and websites cover the intricacies of spreadsheet software more fully and these are easily available.

Why Use Spreadsheets?

Spreadsheets provide a user-friendly solution for ordering and manipulating data. Designers constantly need to analyze and adapt values of various features in their game for balance, bug-fixing, and playtesting reasons, among others. Game designers (and producers) often use spreadsheets as a visual way to keep track of tasks, schedules, and dependencies. For productivity reasons, this tracking is essential.

But perhaps the most useful "magic" that spreadsheets allow is the ability to crunch many numbers quickly to simulate random results. This is called *Monte Carlo simulation* or sometimes less accurately as just *simulation*. The process gives a quick answer to complex and time-consuming questions like "What is the average amount of treasure players will collect in an hour?" or "How many players will go through a quest without receiving a rare item?" These questions seem like minutiae but can end up being make-or-break elements in terms of the player's enjoyment. (This will be covered fully in Chapter 31.) First, I'll discuss some useful elements of spreadsheets to get you started.

Basics

In this section, I'll cover basic nomenclature and use. If you are well-versed in Excel, you should skim the rest of the chapter.

Each rectangle in Excel is known as a *cell*, and each cell holds a discrete piece of data, such as a name or a number. By placing like cells next to each other, you can relate cells together. Generally, a row of cells describes some instance (such as a task, customer, or feature) and columns describe elements of that instance. **FIGURE 30.1** is part of an Excel table of customers. One row is a customer. Each column is a feature of that customer.

FIGURE 30.1
One row of data.

LastName	FirstName	Address	City	OrderTotal
Doe	Alphonse	123 Fake Street	Springfield	$21.13

Often, you don't have a unique identifier for every row, as in Figure 30.1. Sometimes you have to supply that yourself. In database language, this is known as a *primary key*. It's an identifier for every row that is unique. For instance, names are considered poor candidates for primary keys because two people can have the same name (for example, which John Smith did you mean?), so it's common to assign a unique number to every row.

Say you just pasted a thousand values from some other source into your spreadsheet. **FIGURE 30.2** is a database of the GameRankings.com critical average for every console game up until early 2011.

	A	B	C	D	E	F
1	Date	Studio	Game	Platform	Rating	NumReviews
2	1/1/2011	BioWare	Mass Effect 2	PS3	92.97%	31
3	1/1/2011	Media Molecule	LittleBigPlanet 2	PS3	92.26%	51
4	1/1/2011	Visceral Games	Dead Space 2	X360	89.40%	43
5	1/1/2011	Visceral Games	Dead Space 2	PS3	89.24%	42
6	1/1/2011	Capcom	Ghost Trick: Phantom Detective	DS	84.77%	30
7	1/1/2011	Southend Interactive	ilomilo	X360	81.52%	26
8	1/1/2011	Hudson Soft	Lost in Shadow	WII	69.88%	25
9	1/1/2011	Square Enix	Kingdom Hearts Re:coded	DS	69.64%	29
10	1/1/2011	Reality Pump	Two Worlds II	X360	69.16%	22
11	1/1/2011	Atomic Games	Breach	X360	60.38%	24
12	1/1/2010	Nintendo	Super Mario Galaxy 2	WII	97.12%	54
13	1/1/2010	BioWare	Mass Effect 2	X360	95.66%	73
14	1/1/2010	Rockstar San Diego	Red Dead Redemption	PS3	94.76%	50
15	1/1/2010	BioWare	Mass Effect 2	PC	94.48%	30
16	1/1/2010	Rockstar San Diego	Red Dead Redemption	X360	94.18%	71
17	1/1/2010	Harmonix Music Systems	Rock Band 3	X360	92.38%	46
18	1/1/2010	Blizzard Entertainment	Starcraft II: Wings of Liberty	PC	92.34%	53
19	1/1/2010	Namco Bandai Games America	Pac-Man Championship Edition DX	X360	92.17%	29
20	1/1/2010	SCE Santa Monica	God of War III	PS3	92.04%	71
21	1/1/2010	Bungie Software	Halo: Reach	X360	91.59%	68

FIGURE 30.2
Spreadsheet of every console game's GameRankings result up to 2011.

You cannot just assume every game has a unique title and leave it at that because you would be wrong. If you quickly look through the data in Figure 30.2, you see that it shows that remakes and different editions have the same title despite being different games. *Max Payne* for the PC from 2001 is a different game than *Max Payne* for the Game Boy Advance from 2003. Now you can see why you must add a unique number to each row to differentiate identically named games.

Problem: The database has over 5,000 rows. Adding these numbers by hand is likely to be tedious, time-consuming, and prone to mistakes. But using Excel, there is a better way.

First, you need to add an empty column in which to insert the primary key.

1. Right-click the "A" above the first column, and select Insert Column.

   You now have a place for unique numbers for your primary key.

2. Type 1 in the first row, 2 in the second row, and 3 in the third row (**FIGURE 30.3**).

FIGURE 30.3

Adding a primary key.

	A	B	C	D	E	F	G
1	Key	Date	Studio	Game	Platform	Rating	NumReviews
2	1	1/1/2011	BioWare	Mass Effect 2	PS3	92.97%	31
3	2	1/1/2011	Media Molecule	LittleBigPlanet 2	PS3	92.26%	51
4	3	1/1/2011	Visceral Games	Dead Space 2	X360	89.40%	43
5		1/1/2011	Visceral Games	Dead Space 2	PS3	89.24%	42
6		1/1/2011	Capcom	Ghost Trick: Phantom Detective	DS	84.77%	30
7		1/1/2011	Southend Interactive	ilomilo	X360	81.52%	26
8		1/1/2011	Hudson Soft	Lost in Shadow	WII	69.88%	25
		1/1/2011	Square Enix	Kingdom Hearts Re:coded	DS	69.64%	29

You can direct the software to figure out the pattern you are aiming for and fill in all the appropriate spaces until the neighboring column runs out of data. When your series is 1, 2, 3, this is pretty easy. But Excel can also do 2011, 2010, 2009 or 3, 6, 9. It's not a remarkably detailed solution generator, but for a simple series like this, it does its job.

3. Select the cells holding the series elements you have already filled in (not just the last cell), and hover over the bottom-right portion of the last cell you filled in.

   There should be a small dot in this corner of the selected cell. Your cursor will change to a plus (+) sign when you hover over it.

4. If you have a short list, drag this plus down to the place you want the series to fill (**FIGURE 30.4**).

   If you have a long list like I do, double-click the plus (+) to have Excel fill in where it thinks everything should go, which should be down to the last row in the spreadsheet.

FIGURE 30.4

Dragging a row to fill in a series.

	A	B	C	D	E	F	G
1	Key	Date	Studio	Game	Platform	Rating	NumReviews
2	1	1/1/2011	BioWare	Mass Effect 2	PS3	92.97%	31
3	2	1/1/2011	Media Molecule	LittleBigPlanet 2	PS3	92.26%	51
4	3	1/1/2011	Visceral Games	Dead Space 2	X360	89.40%	43
5	4	1/1/2011	Visceral Games	Dead Space 2	PS3	89.24%	42
6	5	1/1/2011	Capcom	Ghost Trick: Phantom Detective	DS	84.77%	30
7	6	1/1/2011	Southend Interactive	ilomilo	X360	81.52%	26
8	7	1/1/2011	Hudson Soft	Lost in Shadow	WII	69.88%	25
9	8	1/1/2011	Square Enix	Kingdom Hearts Re:coded	DS	69.64%	29
10	9	1/1/2011	Reality Pump	Two Worlds II	X360	69.16%	22
11	10	1/1/2011	Atomic Games	Breach	X360	60.38%	24
12	11	1/1/2010	Nintendo	Super Mario Galaxy 2	WII	97.12%	54
13	12	1/1/2010	BioWare	Mass Effect 2	X360	95.66%	73
14	13	1/1/2010	Rockstar San Diego	Red Dead Redemption	PS3	94.76%	50

Formulas

Formulas are the most powerful aspect of spreadsheets. Formulas allow you to ask the software to evaluate a statement: What is the average of all these items? How many times does this statement show up? What is a random number between 1 and 100?

Most formulas refer to a cell by name. For instance, the upper left-most cell is A1. Columns to the right are alphabetic, whereas rows below are numeric. So the second row and the second column meet at cell B2. This is elementary, but important to understand when talking about cells.

The formulas in the following sections are generally similar between software packages and should work for both the latest versions of Microsoft Excel, Apple Numbers, and Google Sheets. However, if there are discrepancies, a quick web search of the function name and the name of the software you are using should give you results with the correct syntax and name.

Formula Operator

Let's take a look at the simplest possible formula—one that echoes the value of a cell.

1. Open a new Excel workbook.
2. In cell A1, type the number 14.
3. In cell B1 type =A1.

   The equals sign (=) is the flag that tells the software this is a formula. What follows the equals sign is what is to be evaluated. In this example, you are telling the software, "In this cell, put whatever is in cell A1."

4. Press Enter to complete the formula.

   B1 changes to 14. If you change the value in A1, B1 will reflect that change.

Basic Math

Let's take a look at some basic math formulas.

1. Clear all the cells by highlighting them and then pressing the Delete key.
2. Type three numbers in cells A1, A2, and A3.
3. In cell A4, type =A1+A2+A3.
4. Press Enter.

   The software evaluates the function, summing the values of all three cells. You can even chain these together.

5. Change A3 to =A1+A2.

   A4 still sums all the cells above it! This chaining is part of what makes simulating in Excel so simple and powerful.

SUM, PRODUCT

You can use any of the basic operators in functions: + – * / ^. You can use parentheses to control the order of operations. If, however, you have a list of items you want to add or multiply that is large, you don't want to spend time typing =A1+A2+A3+A4+A5…. Instead, you can use the SUM function over a range.

A range is a collection of cells and is defined by a starting point followed by a colon (:) followed by the ending point. This will include all cells in that range. If you want to sum cells A1, A2, and A3 down to A100, you can type =SUM(A1:A100). Easy.

Likewise, if you want to multiply those cells, just change the function name.

=PRODUCT(A1:A100)

Additionally, you can add cells not adjacent to the range to the SUM or PRODUCT by separating them with a comma.

=SUM(A1:A100,B7)

MAX, MIN

Other operations are particularly useful when discussing ranges. The MAX function returns the largest number in a range. The MIN function returns the smallest number in a range. Say you had a spreadsheet with 100 student grades in cells B2 to B101. To find the best grade, you would use the formula =MAX(B2:B101). To find the worst, you would use the formula =MIN(B2:B101).

AVERAGE, MEDIAN, MODE

Statistical functions are available. If you want the average grade in the list of 100 student's grades, you would use the formula =AVERAGE(B2:B101). These are simple. MEDIAN provides the middle element when the list is sorted numerically. MODE provides the most common element in the list.

RANK, PERCENTRANK, PERCENTILE

Now we are getting into the more interesting functions. In **FIGURE 30.5**, in each cell next to a student's grade, I want to put that student's rank in the class. In this case, I need to supply two arguments to the function separated by a comma. The first is the number

I'm examining. In the example of the student's grades, when I'm inserting the formula in C2, the number I'm examining is in B2. The second argument is the array of numbers I am using to calculate my rank: =RANK(*cell being examined, first cell in range:last cell in range*). In this case =RANK(*B2,$B$2:$B$21*). The returned value is a number from 1 to the total number of students (here, 20) where cell B2 falls in the ranking of all the rows. If it was the highest grade, the function would return a 1.

	A	B	C	D
1	Name	Grade	Rank	PercentRank
2	Murray	52%	19	5%
3	Frankie	98%	1	100%
4	Nick	70%	15	26%
5	Alphonso	95%	2	95%
6	Buford	63%	16	21%
7	Hilton	71%	13	32%
8	Moses	50%	20	0%
9	Sang	87%	5	68%
10	Joesph	75%	12	42%
11	Randolph	86%	8	63%
12	Van	79%	11	47%
13	Grady	94%	3	89%
14	Kenton	87%	5	68%
15	Jae	58%	17	11%
16	Columbus	84%	9	53%
17	Alden	71%	13	32%
18	Elijah	89%	4	84%
19	Bud	58%	17	11%
20	Tuan	84%	9	53%
21	Ike	87%	5	68%

FIGURE 30.5 Grades list.

Absolute ranking is sometimes useful, but if you want to see a cell's rank as a percentage of the population, use PERCENTRANK. For some reason, PERCENTRANK wants the array first and then the number being examined, completely reversed from the RANK function: =PERCENTRANK(*first cell in range:last cell in range, cell being examined*). So, =PERCENTRANK($B$2:$B$21,B2) would give a number 0 to 1 where the cell B2 is ranked as a percentage. If the cell fell right in the middle, the function would return a 0.5.

PERCENTILE is the inverse of PERCENTRANK. You can give it a number, and it will tell you where it would fall as a PERCENTRANK in that array. For instance, say that B2:B502 was a list of all SAT scores for a particular school. You want to know what score would put a student in the top 10 percent. This is the same as saying that score is in the 90th percentile. So, =PERCENTILE(B2:B502,0.9) would tell you that.

ROUND, TRUNC

Often the spreadsheet will return a function with too much precision for what you are looking for. Returning to the grade example, perhaps your institution accepts only integer grades. A 69.9 should be reported as a 70. But you don't want to manually nudge all the results to their proper place. You can use the ROUND function to round to the nearest integer or TRUNC to truncate the number (removing the decimal place part).

Another element that makes Excel statements so powerful is that you can nest statements together. This means that in one cell, you can put multiple statements and functions inside each other.

Take the PERCENTRANK from the previous example. It will give you a number between 0 and 1 for the student's class rank when unformatted. Say you want this in integer form. Perhaps the class is curved, and the worst performing student gets a zero and the best gets a 100. First, you have to multiply the PERCENTRANK by 100 to get the number to fall in the 0 to 100 range. But then you are left with pesky decimal places, so you can wrap a function around the PERCENTRANK function. Functions are evaluated from inside to outside so the PERCENTRANK happens first. Here's what it would look like:

```
=ROUND(100*PERCENTRANK($B$2:$B$21,B2))
```

Both functions need opening and closing parentheses. This is why the statement ends with two end parentheses.

RAND, RANDBETWEEN

The random number generator is the most important function in creating Monte Carlo-style simulations in spreadsheets.

RAND takes no arguments. It simply returns a random number between 0 and 1.

There is an important note about Excel to bring up at this point. Every time you change a cell, Excel recalculates all the functions in every cell. This means that every time you change a cell, Excel generates a different random number for each randomizer function in your workbook. This is the default behavior. If you want to change the functionality so that functions calculate only when you say to, go to Excel's preferences, and look for the Calculation options where you can switch this to Manual. If you do so, it recalculates only when you press F9 (or Cmd+= on Macs).

RAND gives a decimal with many significant figures, but that is not often useful. Random numbers are great for generating die rolls, but when you roll a normal die, you don't get 0.20351 as a result. You get some integer between 1 and 6. There are two ways to fix this. In most programming languages, you must multiply the random 0–1 number by the largest number in your range and then add one. Then you truncate the result. I have already gone over the tools to do this in Excel. A die roll from 1 to 6 would look like this:

```
=TRUNC(6*RAND())+1
```

That is ugly though, so Excel gives you a function to simplify the process called RANDBETWEEN. It requires two arguments, a lower bound and an upper bound. Your 1 to 6 die roll becomes:

```
=RANDBETWEEN(1,6)
```

CONCATENATE

CONCATENATE is a string function because it evaluates text that programmers call "strings." CONCATENATE takes two strings (bits of text) and shoves them together. If you have last names in column A and first names in column B and want to put them together in column C with a space between them, you would do this:

```
=CONCATENATE(A1, " ", B1)
```

CONCATENATE can take as many strings as you wish to supply it. You may be wondering what the second argument is in the example code. It's telling Excel to put a single space between the first and last name. If you used =CONCATENATE(A1,A2), you would get results like JohnDoe, JaneDoe instead of John Doe, Jane Doe.

VLOOKUP, HLOOKUP

When you use a function like MAX, often you want to know more about the row from which the return comes. If I'm using my game reviews database from earlier (Figure 30.2), maybe I want to know what the highest rated game is. If I use =MAX(F2:F5027), this tells me only the highest rating, not which game that rating belongs to. With lookup functions, you can find out more.

VLOOKUP and its brother HLOOKUP are a little complicated, so let me break them down step by step.

The form of a VLOOKUP statement is

```
=VLOOKUP(Value, Range, Column, Approximate)
```

The first argument VLOOKUP needs is the value it's looking for. Remember that you can nest functions, meaning you can put functions inside of functions. So in this example, you are looking for the max value cell. The first argument is a function in itself. One common error to note here is that the lookup value must be the leftmost column in the table array. You may have to do some rejiggering of how your table is formatted to get this to work. In this example, I am copying the scores into the A column.

The next argument tells VLOOKUP where it's looking. Here you have to input the top left-most cell and the bottom rightmost cell to let the function know the bounds of where it should search.

The next to last argument tells VLOOKUP what you want to return. In this last argument, you put a column number. In the range of cells, which column do you want back? Using the database of values from Figure 30.2, you want to return the fourth column, the name.

The last argument is whether or not you want an approximate or exact match. Since you want an exact match, set this to FALSE.

Using actual values, to find the highest rated game in the database you would use:

```
=VLOOKUP(MAX(A2:A5027), A2:G5027, 4, FALSE)
```

This asks the spreadsheet program to look for the maximum value in the "A" column in the range of all values in the spreadsheet and return the fourth column in the row it finds. It returns The Legend of Zelda: Ocarina of Time.

HLOOKUP works the same, only it searches rows for a value instead of columns and then returns values from the column instead of the row.

IF

I have buried this a bit under the scads of other functions, but IF is the most important function of all. It's a logical function that can evaluate between true and false statements.

The form of the IF statement is simple and contains three parts. The first part is the logical test itself, which must always return true or false. What are you evaluating? Perhaps you want to know if the cell is greater than the cell below it. In this case, your logical test would be something like A2>B2. If the logical test returns true, then the whole IF function returns the second argument. If it returns false, it returns the third argument. These arguments can just be text strings like so:

```
=IF(A2>B2, "Greater", "Not Greater")
```

Thus if A2 is greater than B2, this cell will have the word "Greater" as its data. Otherwise, it will have "Not Greater" as its data. Until you experiment with this, you may not realize how powerful this function actually is.

COUNTIF, SUMIF

COUNTIF is a clever function that counts the number of cells that meet a logical test. For instance, in the game reviews database, how many of the reviews are above 70 percent?

```
=COUNTIF(F2:F5027, ">70%")
```

This returns 3,497.

Note that the logical operation is only the second half of the equation. COUNTIF fills each cell in the range with the cell reference, so you need to supply only the comparison. You must include the quotation marks.

As a bonus, let me tell you about the COUNT function, which is limited in that it returns the number of cells that have numeric values in them. (COUNTA is the name of the function that counts whether anything is in the cell.) But when you combine it with COUNTIF or other functions, it becomes useful. Knowing that 3,497 reviews are above 70 percent does not help us. Out of how many is this?

```
=COUNTIF(F2:F5027, ">70%")/COUNT(F2:F5027)
```

This returns 69.57 percent. This means that approximately 70 percent of games are a 7.0 (70 percent) or higher. If you create gaps in the data, deleting rows at will, this statement still reflects the right proportion, even with the gaps.

There is also a COUNTIFS function that allows you to chain COUNTIFs together in a single function.

SUMIF is similar to COUNTIF except that instead of identifying cells, it takes whatever is in a cell and adds it to every other cell it identifies.

Say you want to count the number of reviews in that database for each individual platform. The platform is in column D and the number of reviews is in column G. If you want to count the number of reviews for the PS2, you could use this formula:

```
=SUMIF(D2:D5027, "=PS2", G2:G5027)
```

The first argument is the range you are checking, the second argument is the criteria you are checking, and the third argument is what you are looking to sum if the second argument is true. You can omit this third argument if the first and third arguments are the same.

OR, AND

The Boolean functions check for a number of true or false statements and then return either true or false. OR returns true if any of the statements inside it are true. AND returns true if all the statements inside it are true.

```
=AND(Coin 1 landed Heads, Coin 2 Landed Heads, Coin 3 Landed Heads)
```

This statement returns true if all three coins landed heads. If any of the coins landed tails, it returns false.

This can be combined with IF statements, which expect a true/false as the first argument:

```
=IF(AND(Coin 1 landed Heads, Coin 2 Landed Heads, Coin 3 Landed Heads),
"All Heads", "Not All Heads")
```

Common Formula Errors

A number of common mistakes are made by novice and expert users alike when using formulas in spreadsheets. The following errors can appear in Excel spreadsheets; similar errors are reported in other packages:

- #NAME—This is one of the most common errors. It means that Excel cannot find the function you are trying to use. What most likely happened is that you misspelled the function name. Maybe you typed CONUTIF instead of COUNTIF. Or you have a syntax error somewhere else. Are you missing quotes? A comma? A colon? (Better get that checked out.) Another reason this can show up is if you are referring to an advanced function that is not loaded in your version of Excel. This happens with older versions of Excel and functions from Add-In packs.

- #DIV/0—Despite your desires, Excel will not divide by zero. Somewhere you have two cells dividing (sounds like Biology), and one of them can be a zero. The quickest way to sniff this one out is to look for division symbols and then find the denominator cells. Once you have done this, try to figure out under what conditions those can be zeros.

- #VALUE—Something is wrong with your arguments. Maybe a function expects a logical operation, and you used a string. Or it expects numbers, and you used strings. Or perhaps you left out a required argument in a function.

- #NUM—This is usually an easy fix. A formula expects a number, but it is getting text that is not a number. Or you are returning a number that is larger than what Excel can handle. If you are using a function like IRR that guesses and checks values recursively until it finds a solution, you'll get this error if the function goes for too long without finding an answer. To fix this particular problem, check to make sure your problem has an answer, and assuming it does, provide a better starting guess.

- #REF—This one is annoying. Excel is trying to find a cell that does not exist.

- #N/A—This one is the most annoying of all because it's a "catch-all" error message that does not narrow down a cause. It's likely you are using a function in the wrong way, supplying bad arguments, or violating some assumption of the function (such as how VLOOKUP assumes the lookup column is the leftmost column.) It's also returned when you are using a searching function that cannot zero in on a value.

- ########—If you see a cell full of pound symbols, don't despair! This just means that your cell is not wide enough to display the proper value. This is not actually an error at all. Just drag the cell width larger, and you should eventually see the correct value.

Anchors

Say you have a table in a spreadsheet as in **FIGURE 30.6**.

	A	B	C	D	E	F
1					Fudge Factor	1.25
2						
3			Points Given	Cumulative Point	Time for Action	Time Elapsed
4		User Clicks a Cow	1	1	0:01	0:01
5		User Invites a User	100		1:22	
6		User Opens a Treasure Ch	23		0:54	
7		User Stomps a Monster	17		0:32	
8		User Scores a Touchdown	7		1:29	
9		User Clicks Another Cow	1		0:02	

FIGURE 30.6
Sample spreadsheet.

You have a list of tasks the player will do in a run-through along with experience points they will gain from each action. This is an extremely simplified version of the kind of analysis designers commonly do to determine when a player will hit certain game states.

You can go through each of the cells in the cumulative experience column and input the formula = Above Cell + Left Cell in each, but there is an easier way. Remember how you can drag a series and have Excel fill in the blanks? You can do this with formulas as well. Excel is smart enough to know that when the cell moves down one row, it needs to change the formulas so that the inputs also go down one row.

1. Create the first cell at D5 and fill it with the formula =D4+E5.

   This will add whatever is above it (the cumulative before this row) to what is beside it (the entry for this row).

2. Highlight the lower-right corner of D4, and drag down to D9 or just double-click the bottom of D9 (**FIGURE 30.7**).

Notice how Excel does the work for you! This is nice with large spreadsheets with tons of rows or columns.

Now try it for the time estimate column (column E). A common practice in time estimates is to include a "fudge factor" or a margin of error to factor in unforeseen events. Here, we will use 25 percent as a fudge factor. That is the function of the cell at F1.

3. In cell F5, enter =(F1*E5)+F4.

This multiplies the fudge factor by the value to the left and then adds the value above (**FIGURE 30.8**).

4. Now try dragging this down.

You end up with some not-great results, as in **FIGURE 30.9**.

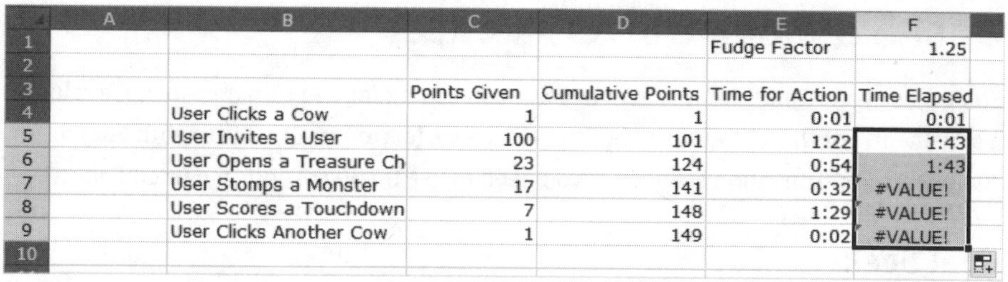

FIGURE 30.9
...leads to confusing results.

This is because when you drag it down, Excel is not only moving the reference to the left-hand cell but also the fudge factor cell.

5. Click cell F6.

   The formula should be =(F2*E6)+F5, but F2 is empty.

   What you need is a way to tell Excel which cell references should hold still and which should move when you drag formulas around. Excel has a simple solution for identifying which cells should hold still—it's called an *anchor*.

   If you place a dollar sign ($) before either the row number, the column name, or both, it will anchor them in place so that they never move when the cell containing the formula moves.

6. Remove the incorrect entries.

7. In cell F5, type the correct formula: =(F$1*E5)+F4.

   This anchors the row number of F1 in place. No matter where you drag the cell, the row number referenced here will be 1. If you want a little more security, you can anchor the column too.

8. Change cell F5 to =($F$1*E5)+F4.

   Now the referenced cell will always be F1.

9. Drag down the formula (**FIGURE 30.10**).

   Success! Toy with the fudge factor to see how it affects the total.

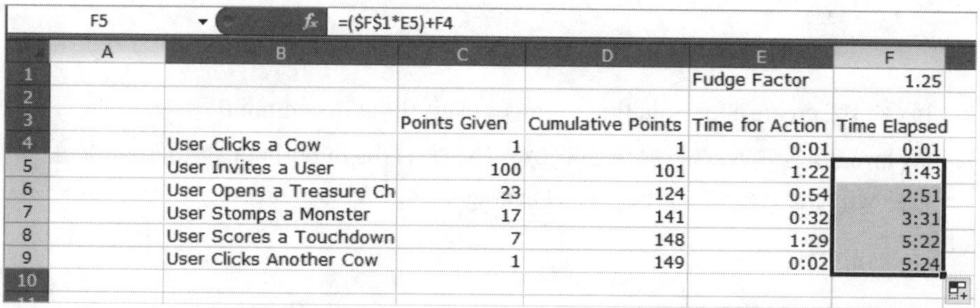

FIGURE 30.10
Corrected with anchors.

Goal Seek and Solver in Excel

Sometimes you want a spreadsheet to solve something for you rather than just evaluate a statement. For these times, the built-in *Goal Seek* feature in Excel is useful. For more complicated optimization scenarios, you need to use the Excel add-in named *Solver*.

Goal Seek

Goal Seek is an automated "guess and check" system. You choose one cell to change and one cell with a target value. Excel then keeps guessing and checking until your target cell reaches the target value.

For a simple example, say you have a set of lap times from some playtesters for a racing game track. As the designer for that track, you have a target time in mind. You want the average lap time for the average player on their first try to be 2:00 minutes.

Here are the results of nine playtests: 1:59, 2:11, 1:58, 1:50, 2:20, 2:04, 1:45, 2:05, 2:33. What does the tenth playtest time need to be to average 2:00? If you can set up the spreadsheet for this, you can always know what result you need no matter how many times you run the playtest.

1. Open a new spreadsheet.

2. Enter the times in column B from **FIGURE 30.11**.

   I entered the times in seconds because it's easier to read, and because it's more difficult to make simple math errors this way.

FIGURE 30.11
Sample times.

Run #	Time
1	119
2	131
3	118
4	110
5	140
6	124
7	105
8	125
9	153

3. In cell D2, create a formula that averages everything in column B.

   My formula is =AVERAGE(B2:B1000,D3). The D3 is the hypothetical run that Goal Seek will change to find the correct average.

4. Under the Data tab (**FIGURE 30.12**), find the What-If Analysis button, and choose Goal Seek.

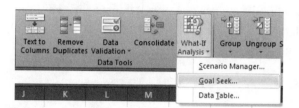

FIGURE 30.12 Finding Goal Seek.

Goal Seek consists of three values. First, the "Set cell" needs to point to the cell that you want to reach a specific value. "To value" is the value you want the first cell to be. "By changing cell" is pretty obvious; this is the cell you will be changing to try to get the "Set cell" to the "To value."

5. Enter D2, 120, D3 in the three fields, as in **FIGURE 30.13**.

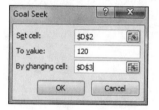

FIGURE 30.13 Selecting a cell to change and a cell to compare to.

▶ **NOTE** Remember: We are using seconds as the units.

6. Click OK and watch Excel do its instant magic.

Your answer is 75 seconds. As long as the next tester does the lap in 75 seconds or less, the average will be 2 minutes or less. Now you can run Goal Seek a number of times with either the same observations or new ones. Say you don't want the lap times to go above 2:10 minutes. Run a new Goal Seek and you find the new answer is 165 seconds, or 2:45 minutes.

Solver

Goal Seek can be really useful, especially when compared to doing the guessing and checking on your own, but what if you need to answer a question that is a little more complicated? Solver is an optimization tool you can use to find maximums or minimums under constraints. If you have taken an introduction to calculus course, you may be familiar with some of the math behind it.

Solver is an add-in that needs to be installed. It does not come enabled with every distribution of Excel.

In earlier versions of Excel, the add-ins dialog could be accessed through the Tools menu. In Excel 2010, you access it through the File tab. Here are the general steps you use to execute an example game in Solver.

1. Select File tab.
2. Select Options (**FIGURE 30.14**).
3. Select Add-Ins.
4. Select Solver Add-In, and click Go.
5. Click the checkmark beside Solver Add-In and click OK.

   Once installed, Solver is located in the Data tab under the Analysis section.

FIGURE 30.14
Adding in Solver.

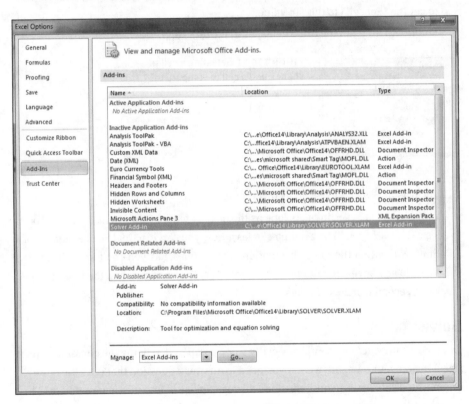

6. Fire Solver up, and you'll see the dialog shown in **FIGURE 30.15**.

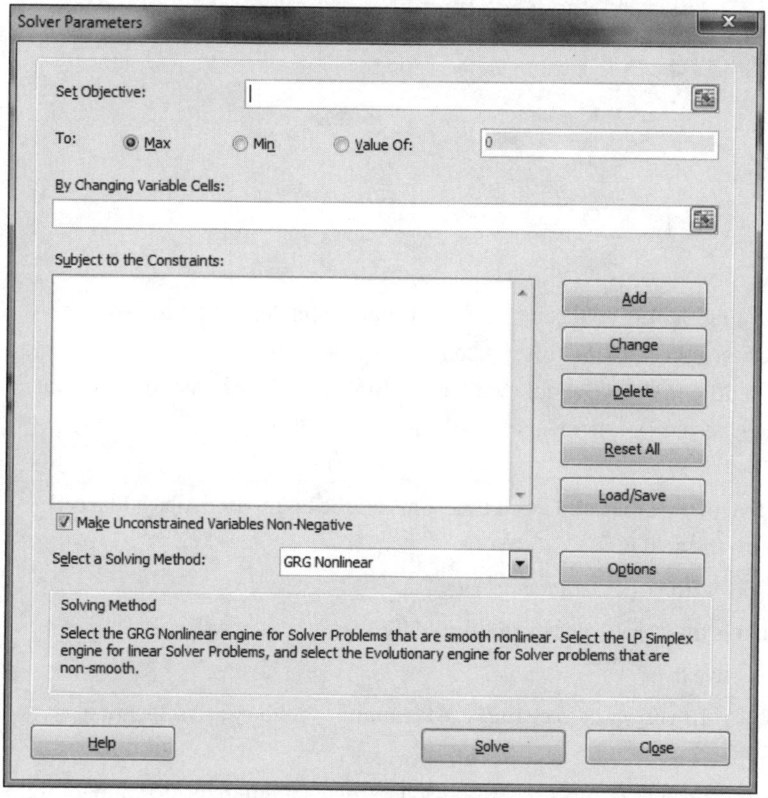

FIGURE 30.15 Solver dialog.

In Solver, you first select the cell that you are looking to maximize or minimize. Then you select the cells you wish to change and the *constraints* you wish this to be under.

Say you have a number of sources of money in your game and each one takes a certain amount of time (**FIGURE 30.16**).

A player can spend time hunting and selling skins, but that gives her a weak 15 gold per hour. Or a player can go to the archery game. That starts out being lucrative, but then it drops off, and as the player gets tired of the game, she starts losing money. She makes 20 gold the first hour, 40 the second, 20 the third, breaks even the fourth, and loses 20 the fifth. Or she can do the quest, which results in a treasure chest. She gets 50 gold and the quest takes one hour, but she can do it only once. How much can a player make in five hours?

How do you model this in Solver?

▶ **NOTE** "Value of" is similar to Goal Seek, except it allows the user to add constraints.

7. Create a 3×3 table in a spreadsheet. The first column is labels, the second is hour spent, and the third is how much gold the activity yielded.

FIGURE 30.16
Starting to figure out
how a player can
maximize value.

	A	B	C
1	Activity	Hours	Gold
2	Hunting & Selling	0	0
3	Archery Game	0	0
4	Treasure Hunting	0	0
5	Total	0	0
6			

8. For the Hunting/Selling gold cell (C2), the formula is simple: 25 * hours. For the Treasure Chest gold cell (C4), this is also simple: 50 * hours. The archery game gold cell (C3) is a little trickier. Get out your algebra/statistics skills to model this or just create a long nested IF statement along the lines of IF(Hours < 3, Hours*20, 20 - 20*(Hours-3)).

9. At the bottom of the table, add a cell that sums all the hours (B5). Also add a cell that sums all the gold (C5).

10. Now run Solver from the Data menu.

    The cell that is the objective is the total gold (C6).

11. Set the objective to C6.

12. The variable cells you want to change are the number of hours, so select that range (B2:B5).

    Now work on the constraints. Constraints tell Excel what numbers are valid for this calculation. You add a constraint by clicking the Add button (**FIGURE 30.17**). First, the total number of hours spent must be between 0 and 5. Select the hours summation cell and add that constraint. Also remember that you can only do the Treasure Hunt task once, so limit that to one hour.

FIGURE 30.17
Adding a constraint.

Also, remember that none of the tasks can be done for fewer than zero hours and, for the sake of our example, all of them must be integers. **FIGURE 30.18** shows all the constraints (phew!).

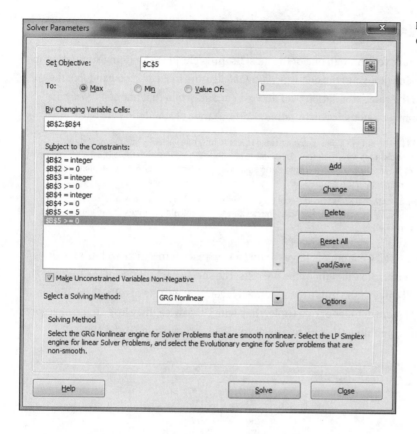

FIGURE 30.18 All the constraints.

Look at the constraints. Hopefully, they all make sense. If you are following along with the book, enter in all the constraints listed in Figure 30.18.

13. Click the Solve button.

FIGURE 30.19 shows the results: one hour treasure hunting, two hours playing the archery game, and two hours hunting and selling. Awesome! Change the variables and try it again. What if you have six hours? What if you double the value of hunting and selling?

Solver can be an extremely valuable tool. Be creative with it.

	A	B	C
1	**Activity**	**Hours**	**Gold**
2	Hunting & Selling	2	30
3	Archery Game	2	40
4	Treasure Hunting	1	50
5	*Total*	5	120

FIGURE 30.19 Solved!

One-Way Data Tables

Finally, I'll talk you through one of the most useful techniques for doing simulation in Excel. By using (abusing) the *one-way data table* feature in Excel, you can force the software to run the same simulation over and over again. When that happens, you can generate summary statistics on hundreds or thousands of simulations at once.

▶ **NOTE** The data in a one-way data table refers to only one variable. In a normal table, this value changes with each row. An example of a normal one-way data table is a list of times of players in a race. In a Monte Carlo simulation, each row is a different roll of all random numbers in the simulation.

A two-way data table has two variables change with each cell. For example, a two-way data table would be the table of Body Mass Index values. That calculation takes in two variables: height and weight.

In the **FIGURE 30.20** example, I have created a spreadsheet in which each trial is three six-sided die rolls. To the right of the die rolls, the sheet checks if two of the rolls are the same or if all three of the rolls are the same. Players get five sets of rolls. If the player gets three or more doubles or one triple, they win. Otherwise, they lose. You can accomplish this by combining the functions as explained earlier using IF and AND.

FIGURE 30.20
A simple simulation.

	A	B	C	D	E	F
1	Trial #	Die Roll #1	Die Roll #2	Die Roll #3	Doubles	Triples
2	1	6	1	4	Lose	Lose
3	2	1	1	6	Win	Lose
4	3	2	6	4	Lose	Lose
5	4	6	2	4	Lose	Lose
6	5	1	1	4	Win	Lose
7						
8					2	0
9						
10					Game Result:	Lose Game

But to answer questions about this game that spans multiple games, such as "How often does the player win?" or "How often do players win because of doubles and how often because of triples?" an observer would need to recalculate and count wins and losses by hand. This is not necessary.

To do this automatically, you would start with a table like **FIGURE 30.21**.

FIGURE 30.21
Recording individual games.

H	I
Game #	Result
	Win Game
1	
2	
3	
4	
5	

One of the odd things you must do to have a successful data table is make the first row of that table a reference to the element that you want to simulate. Here the cell in this row says either "Win Game" or "Lose Game," so I2 is a reference to F10 in Figure 30.20. Column H is just an incrementing series. Next, highlight everything except the header in the data table (here H2:I101) and select the Data Table feature in Excel. You'll see the dialog shown in **FIGURE 30.22**.

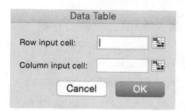

FIGURE 30.22 Data Table dialog.

This is a more meaningful menu if your data table needs to rely on some external input. However, in this case, you want identical trials (**FIGURE 30.23**). Select the Column Input Cell field, and enter the cell, or choose any empty cell from the spreadsheet by clicking the spreadsheet icon. This empty cell is a placeholder for Excel to use as an input. It must be an empty cell. Click OK, and you should have a list of trials on which you can then use other functions like COUNTIF or AVERAGE.

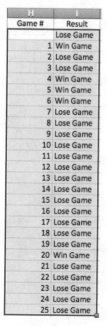

H	I
Game #	Result
	Lose Game
1	Win Game
2	Lose Game
3	Lose Game
4	Win Game
5	Win Game
6	Win Game
7	Lose Game
8	Lose Game
9	Lose Game
10	Lose Game
11	Lose Game
12	Lose Game
13	Lose Game
14	Lose Game
15	Lose Game
16	Lose Game
17	Lose Game
18	Lose Game
19	Lose Game
20	Win Game
21	Lose Game
22	Lose Game
23	Lose Game
24	Lose Game
25	Lose Game

FIGURE 30.23 You must have the correct rows selected for the data table to function correctly.

If your results throw an error or don't make sense, make sure that you have highlighted the entire table except for the headers, but also that you have included your reference cell at top. Also make sure you have selected an empty cell for your column input cell.

Summary

- Spreadsheets allow designers to simulate and record data effectively.
- Functions are largely similar across spreadsheet packages. These functions can be nested to create complex evaluations.
- You can use random number seeds to simulate random and/or uncertain elements. Each time you change a cell in a sheet, all random elements are rerolled by default.
- Goal Seek and Solver allow you to solve for a particular value or for a maximum or minimum value in a spreadsheet.
- One-way data tables are necessary for Monte Carlo simulations, and they require an empty cell as a placeholder.

31 Monte Carlo Simulation

All generalizations are false, including this one.

—MARK TWAIN

Games often rely on random number generation to determine the events of the game. The *Monte Carlo simulation* is a method in mathematics in which results are gleaned from trials generated by random numbers. By using the random number generation and manipulation within spreadsheet software, you can use the Monte Carlo simulation to answer fairly complex questions about how a game will behave.

It is often cited that the Monte Carlo simulation is named after the roulette wheels of the Casino de Monte Carlo in Monaco. However, this is not entirely true. During World War II, scientists working on the atomic bomb needed to figure out a way to simulate neutron penetration for shielding purposes. Because it was a secret project, John von Neumann chose the loosely related name "Monte Carlo" for this method since it used random numbers; the name has persisted.

In this chapter, I'll show some examples of how you can use the immense computational power of spreadsheets on modern computers, including how to simulate random elements in games in order to further answer questions about the effects of various game design decisions.

Answering Design Questions

The primary way game designers use Monte Carlo simulation is to quickly test how complex random events will act over time. Here is an example:

> If a player hits the opponent with an attack four times in a row successfully, the fourth hit and each consecutive hit after is a *super attack*. The player can make 100 attacks per round. If the attacks hit or miss randomly at 50 percent and the designer wants to see 10 super attacks in a round, are there enough super attacks?

Creating a probability tree can solve this problem, but due to the size of the tree, it should be easier to solve this problem with a simple Monte Carlo simulation. To do this, you first need to understand what elements you need to track.

1. Make a list of the elements in the game.
   - What is the number of attacks (it must be less than 100, since we established that there is a maximum of 100 per round)?
   - Does each attack hit?
   - How many attacks in a row have hit?
   - Is this attack is a super attack?

2. Create a spreadsheet, and make a column for each item in the list, labeling them in row 1 as in **FIGURE 31.1**.

   In the example here, I use two columns to answer the question about whether the attack hits. Column B rolls a random number, and Column C evaluates that number, translating it into a hit or miss.

FIGURE 31.1
Simulating super attacks.

	A	B	C	D	E
1	Flip #	Rand	Heads?	Heads in a Row	Super?
2	1	0.20169643	Hit	1	
3	2	0.17086596	Hit	2	
4	3	0.05551776	Hit	3	
5	4	0.13798832	Hit	4	Super
6	5	0.91183648	Miss	0	
7	6	0.90425971	Miss	0	
8	7	0.6914306	Miss	0	

3. Add the following data and formulas to the spreadsheet in row 2:
   - Column A is a sequential number that just indicates when I have reached 100 attacks. I called these "flips" in the header of the sheet just as a reminder that these are random events, like coin flips.
   - Column B is a randomly generated number. In B2, enter the formula =RAND().

- Column C answers whether that random number is good enough for a hit. It checks cell H1 (**FIGURE 31.2**) which is labeled "Hit Rate" and is set to 0.5 because the player hits 50 percent of attacks. In C2, enter the formula `=IF(RAND()<$H$1,"Hit","Miss")`.

- Column D is the trickiest one here. It checks column C to see if it is a hit. If it is, it adds 1 to the number above it to come up with its own entry. Otherwise, it sets itself back to 0. However, the first attack doesn't have a previous attack to look at, so its formula cannot be the same as all the subsequent attacks. In D2, enter the formula `=IF(C2="Hit",1,0)`. In D3, enter the formula `=IF(C3="Hit",D2+1,0)`.

- Column E just prints out "Super" if the attack is a super attack. Otherwise, it leaves the cell empty. In E2, enter the formula `=IF(C2="Hit","Super","")`.

4. With all these in place, you can drag the contents down to repeat for 100 attacks.

5. Column F is empty, just for readability. In column G, label a cell as **Hit Rate** and another as **Super Count** as in **FIGURE 31.2**.

G	H
Hit Rate	0.5
Super Count	6

FIGURE 31.2
How many?

6. In H1, enter **0.5** for the hit rate.

   This is a constant value for each attack.

7. In H2, enter the formula `=COUNTIF(E2:E101,"Super")` that counts the number of times "Super" appears in Column E.

   This will give the answer to how many super attacks happened in that simulation.

   Figure 31.2 shows that the simulation ended with 6 super attacks, so it is way under schedule. However, this is really sensitive to fluctuation. By changing a cell somewhere else or by using the recalculate shortcut in Excel, you can have the simulation run again and get drastically different results, as shown in **FIGURE 31.3**.

   The problem is that 100 attacks are not enough to eliminate the variability of a 50-percent hit rate. One possible solution is to create a one-way data table that runs these 100 attacks over and over again.

G	H
Hit Rate	0.5
Super Count	13

FIGURE 31.3
Rerun the simulation, and you may get a very different result.

8. Create a reference in a new column (here I use K1, see **FIGURE 31.4**) to the Super Count value in H2, and list a trial number in column J up to 1000 trials. Remember from Chapter 30 that you need a dummy element that references what you want to reflect from each trial. Since you are looking for the number of super attacks in each trial, your dummy element in K1 simply points to the Super Count in H2.

G	H	I	J	K
Hit Rate	0.5			4
Super Count	4		1	
			2	
			3	
			4	
			5	
			6	
			7	

FIGURE 31.4 Setting up for a Monte Carlo simulation.

FIGURE 31.5
Highlighting for the
data table.

G	H
Hit Rate	0.5
Super Count	3
Below 10	82.8%
Exactly 10	4.9%
Above 10	12.3%

FIGURE 31.6
Using COUNTIF.

G	H
Hit Rate	0.575
Super Count	19
Below 10	46.5%
Exactly 10	7.1%
Above 10	46.4%
Min	0
Max	29

FIGURE 31.7
Using MIN and MAX.

9. Highlight the entire table of trials (in this example, it is from J1:K1001, see **FIGURE 31.5**), and in Excel, choose to make a Data Table, selecting any empty cell as the Column Input.

   This should give you a varying list of results for 1,000 different 100-flip games. How many of these are above 10, and how many are below 10? By doing a COUNTIF on the results, you can determine that.

10. To determine the proportion of games that are below 10, enter the formula =COUNTIF($K$2:$K$1001,"<10")/COUNT($K$2:$K$1001). You can do this to calculate exactly 10 and above 10, similarly as in **FIGURE 31.6**.

Most of the time, there are fewer than 10 super attacks. Now that you have done all the leg work, you can change the Hit Rate cell (H1 in Figure 31.6) and try to find a hit rate where the number of super attacks above and below 10 are equal. A more robust solution is to make a two-way data table from the start where the hit rate fluctuates.

However, if you use a two-way data table, you must be sure to pick the hit rates to try carefully. As you will see, if you play with these numbers, the rate at which super attacks are above or below 10 is really sensitive. Fifty percent is far too low, but 60 percent is far too high. It turns out that when you nudge the hit rate from 0.5 to 0.575, the game sees the number of super attacks the designer desires. If you make a two-way data table and test only 10 percent, 20 percent, and 30 percent, and all the way up to 100 percent, you miss all the detail in the critical range between 50 percent and 60 percent.

The variability, however, remains high. By looking at the minimum value in the list of game results and the maximum value, you can see a range as in **FIGURE 31.7**.

It may be that the design itself needs to be changed to address this variability if 0 or 29 are too low or high to be acceptable to the designer.

Hot Hand

In basketball, a player is said to have a "hot hand" if he has made some number of baskets in a row. The concept of the hot hand is that the player is *more likely* to make his next basket because he is hot. Similarly, a "cold hand" is when misses indicate that the player is likely to continue to miss.

You want to implement this feature in a basketball game you are making. Consider a player who has a base shot success rate of 50 percent. Every time the player makes three shots in a row, increase his percentage 10 percent (up to a maximum of 90 percent because you never want shots to be automatic). Every time the player misses three in a row, his percentage drops by 10 percent (down to a minimum 10 percent because you never want shots to be impossible).

You can spend the time to code this into your game or you can run a simple Excel simulation. Draw a random number for each shot, determine if it is made or missed, and decide to adjust the probability for the next shot up or down (**FIGURE 31.8**).

FIGURE 31.8 Hot-hand simulation.

Shot #	Percentage	Shot Is	Adjust
1	50%	Missed	-
2	50%	Missed	-
3	50%	Missed	40%
4	40%	Missed	30%
5	30%	Made	30%
6	30%	Missed	30%
7	30%	Missed	30%
8	30%	Missed	20%
9	20%	Missed	10%
10	10%	Missed	10%
11	10%	Missed	10%
12	10%	Missed	10%
13	10%	Made	10%
14	10%	Missed	10%
15	10%	Missed	10%
16	10%	Missed	10%
17	10%	Missed	10%
18	10%	Missed	10%
19	10%	Missed	10%
20	10%	Missed	10%
21	10%	Missed	10%

After 200 trials of 100 shots each, you can see a clustering of results (**FIGURE 31.9**).

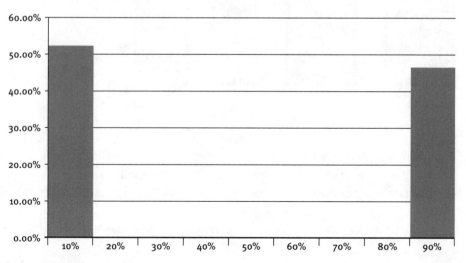

FIGURE 31.9
Hot-hand simulation
end-value results.

After a while, the players converge to the hottest and coldest values. Once the player gets up to 90 percent, it's unlikely he'll ever miss three in a row to get colder. Conversely, once a player gets down to 10 percent, it's unlikely he'll ever hit three in a row to boost his percentage. With a couple minutes of work, you can see that either you need to change your numbers or drastically rethink the feature.

By the way, researchers have shown that the "hot hand" phenomenon does not exist in basketball and that it is just an artifact of people misunderstanding randomness.[1]

Monty Hall

Marilyn vos Savant writes a column for *Parade* magazine in which she solves puzzles and other questions. A September 1990 edition of her column caused an uproar when she was posed what is called "The Monty Hall Problem":

> Suppose you're on a game show, and you're given the choice of three doors: Behind one door is a car; behind the others, goats. You pick a door, say No. 1, and the host, who knows what is behind the other doors, opens another door, say No. 3, which has a goat (**FIGURE 31.10**). He then says to you, "Do you want to pick door No. 2?" Is it to your advantage to take the switch?

FIGURE 31.10
Monty Hall problem.

PUBLIC DOMAIN IMAGE.

Marilyn answered that the correct strategy is to switch, because a switch provides a win 66 percent of the time. Thousands of angry letters flooded her and the *Parade* offices including many letters from readers with Ph.D.'s from prestigious mathematics

. . . .
1   Gilovich, T., Vallone, R., & Tversky, A. (1985). "The Hot Hand in Basketball: On the Misperception of Random Sequences." *Cognitive Psychology*, 17(3), 295–314.

departments who insisted that switching or not switching should each have a 50-percent chance of winning.[2] This makes initial sense. The prize is between one of two remaining doors, so the odds of winning when switching must be 50 percent. Who is right?

You don't need to be a mathematics Ph.D. to solve this. You need only a spreadsheet and some ability to perform a simulation (**FIGURE 31.11**).

	A	B	C	D	E
1	Game #	Where is the Prize?	Player Chooses	Host Opens	If Switch
2	1	2	1	???	Win
3	2	1	3	???	Win
4	3	2	2	???	Lose
5	4	3	3	???	Lose
6	5	2	1	???	Win
7	6	3	1	???	Win
8	7	1	2	???	Win
9	8	2	2	???	Lose
10	9	1	1	???	Lose
11	10	2	3	???	Win
12	11	3	1	???	Win
13	12	1	2	???	Win
14	13	3	3	???	Lose
15	14	3	3	???	Lose
16	15	1	1	???	Lose
17	16	1	1	???	Lose

FIGURE 31.11 Setting up Monty Hall.

In Column B, a simple formula =RANDBETWEEN(1,3) chooses a random door for the prize. The same formula works for the player choosing a random door.

The only difficult part here is understanding which door Monty will reveal (**FIGURE 31.12**).

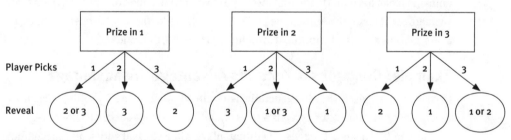

FIGURE 31.12 Diagramming the logic helps visualize the problem.

. . . .

2 Tierney, J. (1991, July 20). "Behind Monty Hall's Doors: Puzzle, Debate and Answer?" Retrieved March 3, 2015, from www.nytimes.com/1991/07/21/us/behind-monty-hall-s-doors-puzzle-debate-and-answer.html.

You do not actually need to understand which door Monty will open, though! Does it matter what door the player sees? Column E uses an IF statement to output "Win" if Columns B and C are the same. All that's left to do is count the frequency of Wins: It should be around 0.66.

Marilyn's naysayers would say that it does matter what door you are shown, so I should probably go through with the exercise.

Which door will be opened? If you know two of the door numbers and know that they are different, then the third door must be neither of those since there are only three doors. You don't need a complicated formula for this. The three door numbers sum up to 6 no matter in what order they are placed. If you know two of the door numbers, then you can calculate the number of the remaining door as 6 – DoorOne – DoorTwo. If the randomly chosen door and the randomly assigned prize door are the same, then it doesn't matter which of the remaining doors the host reveals.

To check if switching results in a win, see if 6 – ChosenDoor – RevealedDoor equals the door number where the prize is (**FIGURE 31.13**).

FIGURE 31.13
Runs of Monty Hall.

A	B	C	D	E	F
Game #	Where is the Prize?	Player Chooses	Host Opens	Final Choice if Switch	Win Result If Switch
1	3	3	2	1	Lose
2	1	1	3	2	Lose

▶ **NOTE** The sum of the door numbers always contains a single 1, a single 2, and a single 3. 1+2+3=6 in any order.

Now drag the cells down to create more runs of the game. (In this example, I chose to use 5,000 trials.) Next, create a cell that does a COUNTIF on the Win Result If Switch column and looks for Win. Divide that by the number of trials, and you have the odds that switching will result in winning the prize. In this example, the spreadsheet calculated a 66.7 percent chance of winning if switching, just as Marilyn said!

Example: *Dungeons & Dragons* Advantage/Disadvantage

Players of *Dungeons & Dragons* generally determine random events by rolling dice. If the number rolled meets or exceeds a target number, then they succeed. Otherwise, they fail. In *Dungeons & Dragons* 5TH Edition, players have to deal with a new mechanic named "Advantage and Disadvantage."[3] With this mechanic, if the player is in a

. . . .

3   Wizard's RPG Team. (2014). *Dungeons and Dragons Player's Handbook* (5th ed.). Renton, Washington: Wizards of the Coast.

situation in which the character has a higher-than-normal likelihood of succeeding, she rolls two dice and takes the higher number. This is "advantage." If the player is in a situation where the character should have a lower-than-normal chance of succeeding, she rolls two dice and takes the lower number.

Game designers can use simulation to determine the effect of this mechanic on successes and failures. Before *Dungeons & Dragons* used the Advantage/Disadvantage system, a way to increase or decrease difficulty was to have a bonus or penalty based on a roll. For instance, if something was difficult, the player may have had to subtract 3 from her roll. Does "advantage" give too much advantage? How much does it give when compared to the old system? This is something that can be easily modeled in a spreadsheet.

1. Open your spreadsheet of choice, and create headings to organize the data, as in **FIGURE 31.14**.

   I have created headings to track die rolls (two are needed because the Advantage/ Disadvantage mechanic uses two rolls), and the results. A d20 roll is a 20-sided dice. This can be done by taking a random number between 0 and 1 and multiplying by 20 and then rounding up to the nearest integer. This gives a random number between 1 and 20. However, most spreadsheets have a RANDBETWEEN function, so it is easier to use that.

   The "straight" result would be to just take the first die roll.

2. In column C, enter the formula =$A2.

   The "advantage" result would be to take the higher result.

3. In column D, enter the formula =MAX($A2,$B2).

   Likewise, the "disadvantage" result takes the lower result.

4. In column E, enter the formula =MIN($A2,$B2).

	A	B	C	D	E
1	d20 Roll #1	d20Roll #2	Result (Straight)	Result (Advantage)	Result (Disadvantage)
2	18	13	18	18	13

FIGURE 31.14
One set of rolls using all three systems.

5. Highlight the cells with the formulas you just entered, and drag down to copy them to 1000 repetitions.

   Now, by using the =AVERAGE function, you can calculate the average result for straight, advantage, and disadvantage.

▶ **NOTE** The more repetitions you use, the less variability you will have in your results.

6. Use columns G and H to label and calculate the straight, advantage, and disadvantage averages (**FIGURE 31.15**):

Label	Formula
Average Straight Result	`=AVERAGE(C:C)`
Average Advantage Result	`=AVERAGE(D:D)`
Average Disadvantage Result	`=AVERAGE(D:D)`

The average result for a straight roll is easy to visualize. Since every side on a 20-sided die should come up with even frequency, the average should be (1+2+3+...+20)/20 or 10.5. If your average is much different than that (below 10 or above 11), keep rolling dice or check your math.

FIGURE 31.15
Summary statistics. It makes sense for the average straight result to be 10.5.

G	H	I
		Difference
Average Straight Result	10.51	
Average Adv. Result	13.86	3.34
Average Dis. Result	7.21	3.30

In the trial, the straight result's average was 10.51, which was expected. The average "advantage" roll resulted in a 13.86 or a 3.34 difference to the straight result. The average "disadvantage" roll resulted in a 3.30 difference to the straight roll. Thus, you can say that the "advantage" system is somewhat equivalent to the old system of adding 3.3 to a d20 roll and the "disadvantage" system is somewhat equivalent to subtracting 3.3 from a roll.

To go further, you can check each row against success of a target value to generate a win or loss for each value. Then, by counting wins versus losses, you can generate a table of probabilities for each technique for each target value (**FIGURE 31.16**).

FIGURE 31.16
Checking against a target value in F$1.

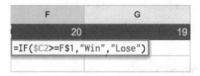

F	G
20	19
`=IF($C2>=F$1,"Win","Lose")`	

Most spreadsheets recalculate all cells every time a cell changes. Thus, large spreadsheets with many calculations (as in this exercise) can result in a slowly running spreadsheet, so be careful to change a cell only when you can wait for the recalculations. Excel allows users to change a sheet's preferences so it recalculates only on a particular key press, which lets a user decide when the sheet should crank out the calculations. Google Sheets, at the time of this writing, does not have this setting.

Check the results in **FIGURE 31.17** of simulating every difficulty under the three conditions. You know that each step on the "Straight" column should increase the probability by 5 percent, since each side has an even 5-percent chance of showing up. Since this is a simulation, there will be some variability. But more or less, it meets expectations.

Difficulty	Straight	Advantage	Disadvantage
20	4.6%	9.7%	0.4%
19	9.8%	18.3%	1.0%
18	14.7%	27.6%	2.2%
17	20.1%	35.8%	4.2%
16	25.1%	43.8%	6.3%
15	29.8%	50.9%	9.3%
14	34.6%	57.2%	12.5%
13	39.7%	63.5%	16.4%
12	44.1%	69.1%	20.4%
11	49.6%	74.9%	25.4%
10	54.5%	80.0%	30.5%
9	59.4%	84.2%	35.9%
8	64.3%	87.4%	42.1%
7	69.5%	90.8%	48.9%
6	74.6%	93.4%	56.2%
5	79.9%	95.6%	64.1%
4	85.0%	97.5%	72.2%
3	89.9%	98.9%	80.9%
2	94.8%	99.8%	90.1%
1	100.0%	100.0%	100.0%

FIGURE 31.17 Probabilities of winning against stated difficulties in all three systems.

This is a better way of evaluating the Advantage/Disadvantage system because it answers more questions than the previous evaluation. Now you can see exactly how different the probabilities are under each condition for each difficulty level.

For instance, a difficulty of 15 has a 50-percent chance of a successful attempt under an Advantage roll, but has less than a 10-percent chance when rolling Disadvantage. The previous +or – 3 is a good rule-of-thumb analysis for the difficulties near the middle of the spectrum, but as you can see, when you chart the probabilities (**FIGURE 31.18**), all types converge at the top and bottom and diverge toward the middle. You can even see that Advantage's... uh... advantage is more prominent when you examine only the high-probability rolls.

FIGURE 31.18
The same probabilities graphed.

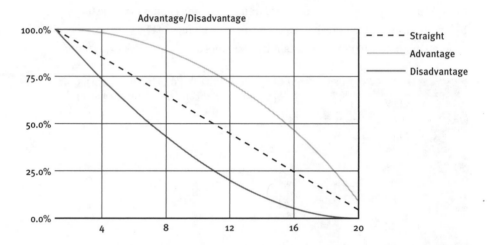

All of this can be done using spreadsheets on just a simple mechanic.

Once Around the Board

The ABC television network aired a *Monopoly* game show for a short time in 1990. It followed the traditions of normal game shows while being somewhat *Monopoly*-themed. One of the contestants would win the main part of the episode, and then get a chance to win additional prize money in the bonus round called "Once Around the Board."

In the bonus round, the goal was to start the player's pawn at Go and make an entire lap around the *Monopoly* board. But before the round began, the contestant had to choose four spaces on the board to transform into "Go to Jail" spaces. One space had to be placed in the Maroon/Orange properties, one on the Red/Yellow properties and two on the Green/Blue properties. In addition to the traditional "Go to Jail" space, there were five spaces on the board where the player would automatically lose.

The player had five rolls to complete the circuit but would get a bonus roll if he rolled doubles. If the player quit or ran out of turns without hitting a "Go To Jail" space, then he would win $100 per space cleared. If he passed Go, he would win $25,000. If he landed on Go, he would win $50,000.

Assuming the player never chooses to quit early, and assuming that the properties in each block where the player must choose to place an extra "Go to Jail" occur with the same probability, what are the probabilities of winning? Say you are working for the producers of this show, and they can only afford to give away an average of $12,000 per episode. Is this a good design for that limitation?

> ▶ **NOTE** Assuming that the properties in each block occur with the same probability is not strictly true. See: Collins, T. (1997, May 4). "Probabilities in the Game of Monopoly." Retrieved May 21, 2015, from www.tkcs-collins.com/truman/monopoly/monopoly.shtml. However, if the probabilities are close enough to each other, you can still make that assumption. The special effects of Jail and Community Chest/Chance cards that Collins makes in his analysis do not apply here since those cards are not drawn in this game mode, which should mediate differences.

First, I created a list of all the locations in the game in the order they appear on the board. Since I assume that each location that can receive a "Go to Jail" space happens with the same probability, I can choose any four that meet the requirements and call them "Go to Jail" as in **FIGURE 31.19**. The names are not a requirement for this to work, but it can help with readability.

Next, I need to keep track of where the player lands. Remember, in the dice roll, the player rolls two 6-sided dice. This is a different distribution than one 12-sided dice (remember from Chapter 29), so I didn't put =RANDBETWEEN(1,12). Instead, I used two separate =RANDBETWEEN(1,6) columns. Since I need to check for doubles (when the numbers rolled on the dice match), having two separate columns for dice is helpful, as opposed to one column with =RANDBETWEEN(1,6)+RANDBETWEEN(1,6).

It is highly unlikely that the player will roll enough doubles of a low number that the game will not end by the eleventh turn, so I simulate ten rolls. I also need to track the player's start position on each turn so that I know where on the board he lands. I also need to know how many rolls the player has left (**FIGURE 31.20**).

	A	B
1	#	Location Name
2	0	Go
3	1	Mediterreanean
4	2	Community Chest
5	3	Baltic
6	4	Income Tax
7	5	Reading RR
8	6	Oriental
9	7	Chance
10	8	Vermont
11	9	Connecticut
12	10	Just Visiting
13	11	St. Charles
14	12	Electric Company
15	13	Go to Jail
16	14	Virginia
17	15	Penn RR
18	16	St. James
19	17	Community Chest
20	18	Tennessee
21	19	New York
22	20	Free Parking
23	21	Kentucky
24	22	Chance
25	23	Go to Jail
26	24	Illinois
27	25	B&O RR
28	26	Atlantic
29	27	Ventnor
30	28	Water Works
31	29	Marvin Gardens
32	30	Go to Jail
33	31	Go To Jail
34	32	North Carolina
35	33	Community Chest
36	34	Pennsylvania
37	35	Short Line RR
38	36	Chance
39	37	Park Place
40	38	Luxury Tax
41	39	Go to Jail

FIGURE 31.19
Mapping locations to numbers.

D	E	F	G	H	I	J
Turn #	Die #1	Die #2	Start Loc	End Loc	Doubles?	Turns Left
1	3	2	0	5	Different	4
2	2	4	5	11	Different	3
3	5	4	11	20	Different	2
4	3	5	20	28	Different	1
5	6	1	28	35	Different	0
6	4	4	35	41	Doubles	0
7	3	2	41	41	Different	-1
8	3	3	41	41	Doubles	-1
9	6	5	41	41	Different	-2
10	5	3	41	41	Different	-3

FIGURE 31.20
Simulating turns.

I determine the end location by adding the two dice the player rolled to the start location. I also set up a check where if the location ends up being greater than 40. For anything after passing Go (>40), I just have the spreadsheet return the value 41. Remember, for this game, we do not care about positions beyond the player reaching Go.

Doubles are calculated with an IF statement that says that if column E is equal to column F, then the player rolled doubles. "Turns Left" represents how many turns the player has remaining after that roll. On the first row, I check if the player rolled doubles that turn. If so, it stays at 5; if not it goes to 4. On each subsequent row, I check for doubles and either repeat or decrement the row above.

In the "Hit a Go to Jail?" column, I want to know if the player has hit a "Go to Jail" spot on this roll, so I just check if the end location number matches one of the locations that say "Go to Jail" listed in column B.

Now it gets a little tricky. I want to know if the game ends on a particular throw (**FIGURE 31.21**). That way, I can calculate the result for the game. If I do not do this, then I have no idea of which throw on which to calculate the result of that game. For instance, if a player landed on Go to Jail on one throw and then on Go on the next (since I always calculate ten throws win or lose), how would the game know whether the result was $0 or $50,000?

FIGURE 31.21
Determining
game end.

D	E	F	G	H	I	J	K	L	M
Turn #	Die #1	Die #2	Start Loc	End Loc	Doubles?	Turns Left	Hit a Go to Jail?	Game Ends Here?	Game Result
1	2	5	0	7	Different	4	Safe	No	
2	3	2	7	12	Different	3	Safe	No	
3	4	3	12	19	Different	2	Safe	No	
4	3	6	19	28	Different	1	Safe	No	
5	6	6	28	40	Doubles	1	Safe	Yes	50000
6	3	2	40	41	Different	0	Safe	Done	
7	5	6	41	41	Different	-1	Safe	Done	
8	2	2	41	41	Doubles	-1	Safe	Done	
9	5	2	41	41	Different	-2	Safe	Done	
10	2	3	41	41	Different	-3	Safe	Done	

It helps to write out these conditions as a flow chart (**FIGURE 31.22**). There are three possible outcomes: either the game ends on this turn, the game has already ended, or none of the conditions have been met, and the game is still going. If I only have two conditions (the game ends this turn, the game does not end this turn), then the sheet thinks that the game can restart.

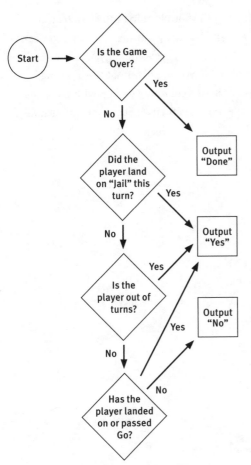

FIGURE 31.22 Flowchart for determining whether or not the game is over on this turn.

I make a flowchart because the spreadsheets allow for only one crowded line of nested IF statements. This allows me to make sure I have not missed any cases. It is easier to read than the following formula in **FIGURE 31.23**.

```
=IF(OR(L2="Yes",L2="Done"),"Done",IF(K3="Jail","Yes",IF(J3=0,"Yes",
IF(H3>39,"Yes","No"))))
```

D	E	F	G	H	I	J	K	L	M
Turn #	Die #1	Die #2	Start Loc	End Loc	Doubles?	Turns Left	Hit a Go to Jail?	Game Ends Here?	Game Result
1	2	5	0	7	Different	4	Safe	No	
2	3	2	7	12	Different	3	Safe	"Yes","No"))))	
3	4	3	12	19	Different	2	Safe	No	

FIGURE 31.23 A complicated formula can be difficult to trace.

The final column is easier and is represented by the flowchart in **FIGURE 31.24**. If the result in the previous column is "Yes," then calculate the winnings. Only one row can be "Yes." Every other row must be "Done" or "No," so this should only give one result for the whole table. When the game is not over, I have the cell output ""— nothing is outputting. This way, when I sum all the cells in this column, I end up with the game result. This also works if you have it output 0, but the null (two quotation marks indicating no character) looks cleaner.

FIGURE 31.24
Flowchart for determining the final value.

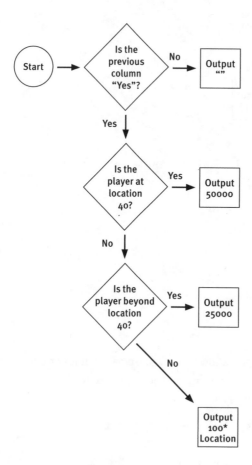

This process results in only one number popping up in the column for each game. From this, I can generate a data table of game results and then calculate the summary statistics or create a graph (**FIGURE 31.25**).

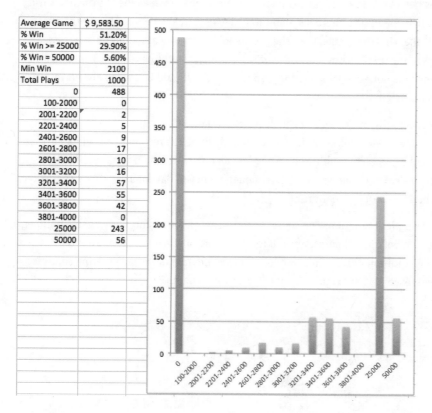

Average Game	$ 9,583.50
% Win	51.20%
% Win >= 25000	29.90%
% Win = 50000	5.60%
Min Win	2100
Total Plays	1000
0	488
100-2000	0
2001-2200	2
2201-2400	5
2401-2600	9
2601-2800	17
2801-3000	10
3001-3200	16
3201-3400	57
3401-3600	55
3601-3800	42
3801-4000	0
25000	243
50000	56

FIGURE 31.25 Simulated "Once Around the Board" games.

The original question was to find out whether the game would cost the producers more than $12,000 per episode. Over 1,000 games, this is not likely. Considering that there were only 13 episodes of the actual Monopoly game show, it was possible that all the wins would cluster in the first 13 shows. You can use this spreadsheet to determine the number of times that would happen. This analysis is great to show the producers because it answers many other questions. For instance, the producers probably do not want a final round to never end in a win, because that would make for bad television. However, they also do not want a final round that gives away too much money. This analysis shows the producers exactly how often the players win and how much they win.

Martingale Betting

Gamblers like to believe they can develop systems to beat the odds. One such system that has been around since at least the 18th Century is known as the *martingale betting system*. In it, a gambler bets a set amount. If she loses it, she bets double on the next game. If she wins that game, then she is back to the starting amount and she resets the bet back to the original amount. Otherwise, she keeps doubling the bet. Theoretically, the gambler is bound to win eventually, and thus she should be able to always return back to her original pot size.

Does this actually work? Let's bias in favor of the gambler and provide a game with a 50-percent win rate. This is obviously better odds than you receive in a casino. Further, let's give the gambler humble aims. The gambler enters the casino with $100 in her pocket. She leaves either when she has enough money to pay for a satisfying sandwich on the house (+$10) or is bankrupt.

This is a simple simulation. The columns of the sheet should start with a game number, a balance, a bet for that game, a result for that game, and a balance for after the game is complete. Additionally, a column should indicate if either of the terminating conditions has been reached (Bankrupt or Sandwich) (**FIGURE 31.26**).

FIGURE 31.26
Martingale simulation setup.

	A	B	C	D	E	F
1	Game #	Balance	Bet	Result	New Balance	Terminate
2	1	100	1	Lose	99	
3	2	99	2	Lose	97	
4	3	97	4	Lose	93	
5	4	93	8	Lose	85	
6	5	85	16	Lose	69	
7	6	69	32	Lose	37	
8	7	37	64	Lose	-27	BANKRUPT
9	8	-27	0	Lose	-27	BANKRUPT
10	9	-27	0	Win	-27	BANKRUPT
11	10	-27	0	Lose	-27	BANKRUPT
12	11	-27	0	Lose	-27	BANKRUPT
13	12	-27	0	Win	-27	BANKRUPT

Each row checks the balance of the previous row. The first row is different since there are no previous games to check. The bet is set to 0 if one of the terminating conditions has been met, ending the game. If the player gets to $0 or $100, then the game sets the terminating condition. Running this once is interesting. But running this for a year's worth of "days" of games is better. Of those 365 days, how many days does the gambler get a sandwich and how many days does she lose all $100 (**FIGURE 31.27**)?

SANDWICH Days	330
BANKRUPT Days	35

FIGURE 31.27
The results are 35 bankruptcies if you walk in with $100.

SANDWICH Days	360
BANKRUPT Days	5

FIGURE 31.28
The results are five bankruptcies if you walk in with $500.

SANDWICH Days	363
BANKRUPT Days	2

FIGURE 31.29
The results are two expensive bankruptcies if the player walks in with $5,000.

This looks pretty good! The gambler has roughly a 90-percent chance of getting a "free" $10 sandwich and a 10-percent chance of losing $100. The expected value here is roughly 0. But what happens if I change the amount the gambler walks in with to $500 (**FIGURE 31.28**)?

Since the gambler's pockets are deeper, she goes bankrupt less often. But now for five days in the year, she is paying $500 for her otherwise "free" sandwich! The expected value of playing the game goes from $0 to negative $3.83 per day. This is, of course, examining the situation from a rational, risk-neutral perspective. What happens if the gambler racks up two bankrupt days on her first two tries? She has now paid $1,000 for no lunch at all.

Let us increase the amount the gambler starts with one more time. Now she comes in with $5,000 (**FIGURE 31.29**).

Most days, she has no problem getting a sandwich. Those very deep pockets mean that she rarely has to double to the point where she may lose her purse. However, on two days that year, she did lose out and paid $5,000 for no sandwich. The average losses that year were negative $17.45 per day!

Besides having a limited pool of money from which to draw, another reason that martingale betting systems are not feasible is that casinos often limit the amount you can bet. Thus, if our $500 gambler needs to bet $64 to get back to break-even, she might be limited to betting $50, thus capping her ability to climb back out of the hole.

The martingale betting system follows the form of what is sometimes called a "Taleb distribution," named after the author of *The Black Swan,* Nicholas Nassim Taleb.[4] In a Taleb distribution, most of the results offer a nice, steady return. But every once in a while, the bet can go extremely poorly and wipe the better out. Choosing sample

· · · · · · · · · · · · · · · · · · · ·

4   Taleb, N. N. (2010). *The Black Swan: The impact of the highly improbable fragility* (Vol. 2). New York, NY: Random House.

returns to evaluate something in a Taleb distribution is misleading. If you took ten sample days from the $5,000 martingale example, you would likely end up with ten "SANDWICH" days, leading you to believe that the betting system was foolproof. This is sometimes cited as the framework that is partially responsible for the great financial crisis in 2008: firms took bets on items with extreme tail risk but evaluated them on terms of the risk of the non-tail results.[5] This is like evaluating the martingale betting system described earlier by just looking at the proportion of the SANDWICH days and not looking at the probability and impact of the BANKRUPT days.

In games, this is important because it is the edge cases that break a system. If a multi-player game's economy works for 99 of 100 players, what impact does that 100th player have? Discounting him because of his low probability is not wise, just as discounting the low probability of BANKRUPT days on the $5,000 martingale example is not wise.

Summary

- Using examples, I have shown the wide applicability of Monte Carlo simulations for answering design questions.
- Be careful about how your chosen number of trials affects the variability of your results. If your summary statistics jump around a good deal from one simulation of trials to the next, you may not be using enough trials in your simulation.
- Drawing out flowcharts for complicated steps can help ensure that you are accurately defining all the steps you need for difficult calculations.
- Often elements of your simulation vary by different amounts with respect to your inputs. By choosing a wide range of inputs to examine, you can be sure not to miss interesting behaviors that happen outside of your simulated results.
- You must examine distributions with large events in the tail carefully. Sampling too few events without understanding the tail risk can lead to misinterpreted results.

. . . .

5   Taleb, N. N. (2010). "Why did the Crisis of 2008 Happen?" DRAFT, 3RD Version. Retrieved March 4, 2015 from www.fooledbyrandomness.com/crisis.pdf.

32

Presenting Ideas

> [W]e shouldn't abbreviate the truth,
> but rather get a new method of presentation.
>
> —EDWARD TUFTE

Poor presentation is killing creativity in corporate America as millions are forced to sit through boring, poorly thought-out, waste-of-time presentations. Earlier in my career, I was pitching a new game to a board of decision makers at Electronic Arts when one executive producer who was on his BlackBerry the whole meeting interrupted me: "Why aren't there any words on your slides? Where's the content?" I was taken a bit aback. I was talking about a visual feature, explaining it in sequence with a number of diagrams. I muttered something like "That's... that's... exactly what I'm explaining right now." He looked back down at his BlackBerry. "I don't listen to presentations. I just read the slides." If he just wanted text to read, I could have emailed it to him. That would have saved everyone time, since everyone in the group could have read it at their leisure. But a meeting was called to discuss the new idea in a group.

The problem is that most presentations are just people reading slides aloud in a group environment—an activity that wastes everyone's time and is less effective for idea retention. A kind of Stockholm Syndrome sets in and people assume that this is what presentations must be, so they build up defenses like that executive producer; he'd spend the first few seconds of each slide reading the text and the rest of the presentation on his BlackBerry waiting for the presenter to catch up. It doesn't have to be that way.

PowerPoint and other *slideware* (a term coined by Edward Tufte to describe programs such as PowerPoint and Keynote) usage is only symptomatic of a larger problem: People do not know how to organize and present ideas. In this chapter, I'll use slideware as the primary vector for delivering ideas to an audience. However, oral presentations do not always need slides. In fact, slides often hurt the audience's retention of the presented ideas. Luckily, many of the techniques I talk about here are applicable to other forms of persuasive communication as well.

The Thesis

There has to be a reason for each presentation. No one just wanders into a presentation for fun or just randomly types out words to make a slide deck. The presenter is there to get some idea across and the audience is there to understand it. The "it" is the *thesis*.

One helpful heuristic for developing a thesis is to think about Twitter. On Twitter, users are confined to completing a message in 140 characters or less. If you only have 140 characters, how will you explain your idea? This constraint forces you to boil your idea down to the essence of your tweet. Some places like to use the concept of the "elevator pitch." In it, you imagine you have a decision-maker's time only from the moment she gets on an elevator on the first floor to the time the elevator reaches the top floor and she gets off. You have a minute or less to give her the salient points. Presentations should operate similarly. You should be able to sum up the presentation itself quickly, but you should also be able to sum up each individual point quickly.

Imagine that you need to present a complex board game to a potential investor. You have done all your homework in advance—designing and refining, doing market research, estimating costs, and so forth. You have a ton of information to present. But if you have only 140 characters, what do you say? A recent study of venture capital pitches showed that slide presentations for successful pitches lasted only 3 minutes and

44 seconds on average.[1] Luckily, if you follow the procedures in this book (specifically, those in Chapter 2), you will have a problem statement from which to draw. The problem statement makes a good thesis for covering the whole "what" of a game.

Slideware suggests that users break down content into individual slides and it defaults to bulleted lists. Not surprisingly, few presenters diverge from using walls of text and bullets. When one graph of text fills up the screen, they move on to the next slide. For the typical presenter, bulleted lists serve to chop up narratives into pieces that fit visually on a slide based on arbitrary font and layout decisions instead of being based on the organization of information.

Instead, a better organizational pattern is to break up a thesis into subtopics, each with its own thesis. This ensures that each slide has a purpose and is focused on achieving that purpose instead of merely serving as a repository for text.

Text on Slides

Despite the vast repository of free and evocative images and the ease with which presenters can create graphs and charts to support their arguments, the dominant use of the slide presentation is to create bulleted lists of text items that the presenter reads. Research has shown that it is more difficult to process information when it is simultaneously spoken to an audience and presented as text.[2] So while a presenter reads a slide aloud to the audience, the audience struggles to reconcile the words it hears with the text it is currently reading. The average audience can read much faster than you can easily talk: The comparison is 100 to 160 words per minute for aural presentation to 300 to 1,000 words for visual. Avoid reading the text on your slide aloud at all costs.

The average PowerPoint slide has 40 words.[3] This is far too many. Marketer and author Seth Godin limits his slides to six words at the most.[4] Steve Jobs, who crafted some of the most effective presentations in the world, was known for slides with just a few words or a statement and a subtle gradient background (**FIGURE 32.1**).

. . . .

1   Cutler, K. (2015, June 8). "Lessons From a Study of Perfect Pitch Decks: VCs Spend an Average of 3 Minutes, 44 Seconds on Them." Retrieved June 10, 2015 from techcrunch.com/2015/06/08/ lessons-from-a-study-of-perfect-pitch-decks-vcs-spend-an-average-of-3-minutes-44-seconds-on-them/.

2   Tufte, E. R. (2003). *The Cognitive Style of PowerPoint* (Vol. 2006). Cheshire, CT: Graphics Press.

3   Medina, J. (2008). *Brain Rules: 12 Principles for Surviving and Thriving at Work, Home, and School.* Seattle, WA: Pear Press.

4   Godin, S. (2007, January 27). "Really Bad PowerPoint." Retrieved May 11, 2015, from http://sethgodin. typepad.com/seths_blog/2007/01/really_bad_powe.html.

FIGURE 32.1
Simple, effective slides augment a presentation; they are not the presentation.

In a typical presentation, the slide would perfectly augment the thesis Jobs wanted to talk about. The audience briefly scanned the information and then returned their attention to Jobs to hear continued information. Compare the slide in Figure 32.1 to one from 2010 that purported to help explain the acquisition process in the US Department of Defense (**FIGURE 32.2**).

FIGURE 32.2
This is a slide that is easy to take in at a glance, isn't it?

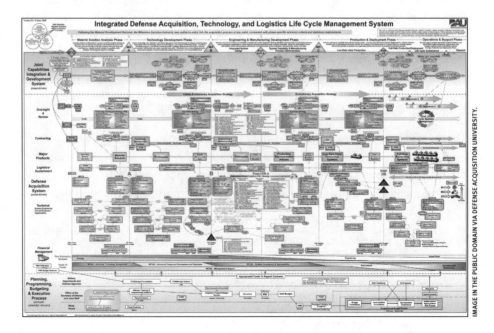

Some use slides as cue cards to remind them of what they need to talk about. There is a place for being reminded about key points to present; however, the place is not on the slide itself. It is perfectly acceptable to use cue cards to remind yourself of the order and specificity of facts. If you feel you must have a bulleted list, a private cue card is the place to print it. A visible cue card that you show to the audience, however, reveals all your information at once.

And what if you do not have anything to show at this point? Perhaps a particular point does not need any imagery or text. In that case, show nothing. Pressing B on PowerPoint or Keynote presentations brings up a black screen. Use this technique when the audience seems so into slides that they cannot focus on you. Remember that *the presenter should be the focus of the presentation*. The slides are there to augment the presenter. Not the other way around! You are not presenting to explain your slides; your slides just help you explain your thesis.

Data-Ink

In his book, *The Visual Display of Quantitative Information*, Edward Tufte relates the concept of data-ink.[5] In a presentation, *data-ink* is ink that you cannot remove from a slide without also losing information. A line that connects data points on a chart is data-ink because it shows the relationship between two points. However, a 3-D representation (**FIGURE 32.3**) of a linear relationship is non-data-ink because you can compress it to a 2-D version (**FIGURE 32.4**) without removing any information. Something with low data-ink has more of the visual representation taken up by decorative elements rather than data elements. In many cases, this makes the data harder to read. If the point of the slide is to convey data, then you want to convey that data as directly as possible.

Tufte recommends that you remove non data-ink whenever possible. However, research has shown that a minimal amount of non-data-ink can be helpful.[6]

. . . .

5   Tufte, E. R., & Graves-Morris, P. R. (1983). *The Visual Display of Quantitative Information* (Vol. 2). Cheshire, CT: Graphics Press.

6   Inbar, O., Tractinsky, N., & Meyer, J. (2007, August). "Minimalism in Information Visualization: Attitudes Towards Maximizing the Data-Ink Ratio." In *Proceedings of the 14th European Conference on Cognitive Ergonomics: Invent! Explore!* (pp. 185–188). New York, NY: ACM Press.

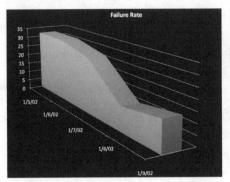

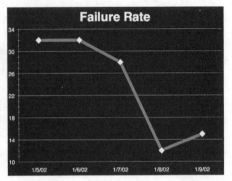

FIGURE 32.3 A low data-ink slide. You do not need the slide to have perspective and a depth dimension. It makes it harder to read where the graph intercepts the date and rate elements. For instance, what is the failure rate on January 7th?

FIGURE 32.4 A high data-ink version of the graph. This is much easier to evaluate. The failure rate on January 7th was around 28 percent.

Anyone who has sat through many presentations, especially those from novices, has been subject to the presenter who is in love with splashy transitions, sound effects, and other flash. Even if the content of the presentation is good, audiences have to wait for noisy transitions to build, wasting audience time and adding often undue pauses to the flow of information. A good rule of thumb here is to remember that no one ever closed a deal by having clever transitions; they closed deals by being persuasive. Leave the animations at home unless they help illustrate a point.

Data-ink is a more precise way of measuring the signal-to-noise ratio of a presentation. What elements of the presentation are "signal," that is, communicating persuasive information? What elements are "noise," that is, existing as excess elements that distract from the persuasive elements? A presentation designer's job should be to eliminate noise whenever possible.

A list of common "noise" elements in presentations include:

- Irrelevant images
- Bullet points when items do not work as a list, or a bulleted hierarchy when items are not hierarchical
- Text that is too small or too low-contrast for an audience member in the back row to easily read
- A company logo or template cruft on every slide (nobody cares about your company's logo except your company)

- Long animations that do not deliver information
- Unnecessary font or color changes
- Sound effects or video that do not deliver information
- Gradients that make text or images ugly or difficult to read

Do Not Waste Time

I listen to many student presentations every year. Nearly every single one contains extraneous time wasters. One of the biggest time wasters I come across is students explaining the obvious. If I have scheduled time to watch your project presentation, you do not need to say, "Hi, my name is Adam Fakename, and this is my presentation for GDN-1234 for Mr. Hiwiller's class." I know all that. That is why I'm here. And it's already on your title slide.

Team presentations are even worse at controlling overhead. I have lost count of the number of team-based presentations I have seen in my life where the team of four splits 20 slides into four equal parts. At the end of every fifth slide, the presenter goes, "And now I will hand it off to Steve, who will talk about the demographics." She hands the clicker to Steve and he begins: "Hi, I'm Steve, and I'm the market research analyst for the team and I will be talking about the demographics." He then clicks to a slide that says "Demographics."

What a waste of time!

If the audience sees you handing off the slide advancer, they will not go, "Whoa, what's happening? Did she quit?" All audience members understand that different people can present. You don't have to have an introduction and conclusion for every few slides. In this example, how many times did "Demographics" need to be said aloud? The answer is zero. Once on the slide was enough. The first speaker should conclude her section, hand off, and Steve should start into his spiel. It should be like a NASCAR pit crew: change the tires and speed off. Do not give the audience time to let their attention wander.

If you think this is just me as a listener being impatient, you are only partially right. It turns out that redundancy in information presented simultaneously verbally and visually makes the material harder to remember, especially if there are other distractions.[7]

▶ **NOTE** Prezi, while a wonderful presentation tool in many ways, makes it easy to add nausea-inducing camera movements that are completely unnecessary. Prezi is great if you need to show part of a larger figure and need to reiterate the relationship of parts to a whole, but it is noisy when you use it just to fly around a largely text-based presentation.

. . . .

7   Moreno, R., & Mayer, R. E. (2002). "Verbal Redundancy in Multimedia Learning: When Reading Helps Listening." *Journal of Educational Psychology*, 94(1), 156.

Documentation

So far, I've focused on what not to do. Here I relate a process for creating effective presentations.

First, you must understand the point of your presentation and the thesis you are trying to deliver. Only after that should you determine how you want to relate that information. For instance, do you have supporting data or anecdotes that could help you prove your point?

Start by either writing all of these elements down on paper or in a word processor. Use a free-form style. Don't open a slideware program yet. You need to know what you want to say before you can determine how to say it.

Garr Reynolds' excellent book *Presentation Zen* suggests you should make three arti-facts.[8] Most presenters only have one: the slide deck. Having only the slide deck makes the slide deck attempt to perform triple duty, and as such, it does none of its duties well. Here are the three jobs for which you may need artifacts:

- To remind yourself of the essential points and order of the presentation
- To support your presentation by showing the audience data or images
- To give the audience something to take home remember your presentation

All presentations don't need all three artifacts. Yet most slide decks attempt to be all three. The presenter should not use the slide deck to remind them of what to say because having such elements on the slides renders the presenter useless. The audience will read ahead. Because of this, the slides should be fairly incomprehensible without the presenter's narration to go along with them, so the third job also cannot be served by the slide deck alone. Instead, spend your time making three things:

- Private notes
- Slide deck
- Take home documents

The *private notes* are just for you. Depending on the complexity of the presentation equipment, you may be able to keep your notes within the slide deck on a hidden notes field that only you can see during the presentation. This is slick, but some notecards with just a few words written on them are just as useful.

. . . .

8   Reynolds, G. (2008). *Presentation Zen: Simple Ideas on Presentation Design and Delivery*. Berkeley, CA: New Riders.

The *slide deck* is for supporting data and images that go with your narration. You won't know what to put in your deck until you have your notes arranged.

The *take-home documents* are for you to distribute after the talk—they should be your presentation in a written form. Do not distribute this before the presentation or your audience will read ahead and there will be dissonance between where they are and what you are trying to present. An additional benefit of take-home documents is that they can contain more data and information than is easily readable on slides.

A disturbing trend in academic and professional conferences is that presenters are often required to send slides early for review and distribution. Your slides should be fairly incomprehensible on their own, so if you are planning to present at a conference that requires this, I recommend that you email the organizers to see if you can send your take-home documents instead.

Acquiring Images

Many presenters who decide to use images in their presentation simply go to Google Image Search, punch in a keyword, and grab the first image they find. This has numerous problems. First and most importantly, the image you find may not add anything but decoration to the presentation. Images should not just be thematic; they should support the presentation's thesis or subtheses in some way, and if they don't, they can just be distracting. For example, if you are pitching a new fighting game, a picture of *Street Fighter V* may be relevant, but unless you are showing how a particular competing feature is presented, the audience will be thinking about *Street Fighter V* instead of what you are trying to present.

Secondly, presenters often try to stretch low-resolution images to fit the size of the screen, which makes them pixelated and blurry. Or the presenter tries to cram many small, low-resolution images onto one slide. Both techniques make for poor legibility. The rule of thumb is that text and images should be easily legible by the audience member in the farthest back row of the presentation room.

Finally, in most cases, a copyright holder owns the images you find online, so you do not necessarily have the license to use them in your presentations.

You can acquire high-resolution, freely usable images through stock image sites, such as freeimages.com (formerly sxc.hu), and free vector-based art at thenounproject.com, but be careful that the images you choose do not distract from your points.

▶ **NOTE** You can scale up vector art without loss of fidelity.

FIGURE 32.5 This image has action centered.   **FIGURE 32.6** This image has action offset.

Using a company or conference logo on each slide can also be distracting. Having this on the first slide is fine, but having it on every slide simply wastes space that you could use for helpful images, text, or even just pleasing negative space. Avoid using templates that waste space on unnecessary boilerplate.

A final point to consider when placing images is what photographers call the *rule of thirds*. This is a heuristic that recommends that you place the focal point of a slide along the grid that divides the slide into threes rather than center an image. This provides a more visually pleasing aesthetic and it also gives you room for a caption word or phrase if necessary. Let's compare some images.

When I place a 3×3 grid over **FIGURE 32.5**, you can see that the action is largely contained in the center and top of the figure.

FIGURE 32.6, however, has been cropped so that the action follows the left-most vertical divider while the right side of the image serves largely as negative space.

Although the image centered in Figure 32.5 is acceptable, it does not provide enough room for notation (**FIGURE 32.7**), whereas the image with the negative space in Figure 32.6 has a more natural place for labels (**FIGURE 32.8**).

FIGURE 32.7 Labeling the centered image is okay...

FIGURE 32.8 ...but the negative space in the offset image provides a more balanced and attractive presentation.

Example: State of Mobile Games 2014

Here is a walkthrough of a simple presentation I gave to an audience of simulation experts who wanted to know about the mobile games industry in 2014. First, I had to come up with a thesis. That was easy. I opened a word processor and wrote the following:

> Thesis: While mobile games as a whole sector are making money, most individual app developers do not make money.

Next, I needed to decide the beats or subtheses that my argument would take. Eventually I settled on the following. Note that each is tweet-length and so already summarized:

- There are a huge number of submissions to app stores.
- Most apps do not make money, according to surveys.
- Some apps make a ton of money.
- If apps follow the Pareto distribution, then this is predictable.
- Using Swrve's published monetization data, we can create simulated app releases to gauge likelihood of profitability.
- These simulations show that 85.3 percent of apps will not break even given past results.

Each of these is short and not easily compressible to make an even shorter list. As I developed the presentation, I had to expand on some to help support the overall thesis.

After I settled on the list, I had to figure out how to best relate these points. In the interest of space, I'll only walk you through how I did this for the first point.[9]

App stores have a large number of games. How should I best represent this? My target audience grew up playing games on the Nintendo Entertainment System (NES). Thus, if I can relate the situation to that, it could help strengthen my point. Some quick Internet searches revealed that there were 822 published games for the NES. Additional research showed me that there are over 400,000 games on the Google Play store alone. An NES library's worth of games are submitted to the Google Play store every week. The discrepancy in these numbers was enough to make my point.

I decided that this point could be enhanced with a visual, so I started my slide software (Keynote) and made the graphic in **FIGURE 32.9**.

FIGURE 32.9
Representing the discrepancies visually provides a powerful perspective.

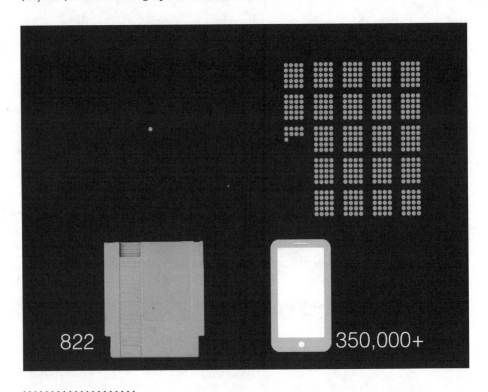

9   I will also not cite the facts from this presentation here as the relevant citations are all in Hiwiller, Z. (2014, April 24). "ECGC 2014: Design Lessons from Pareto." Retrieved December 8, 2014, from www.hiwiller.com/2014/04/24/ecgc-2014-design-lessons-from-pareto.

I had the slide reveal itself in build steps. First, the audience only sees the left side. After a click, they see the right side. The slide serves as a visual hook to the points that I made verbally about the differences in the number of games. Although there is some redundancy in data-ink, it serves to emphasize the point being made.

This image does not contain all the information I wished to talk about. Some information was relegated to my notes:

- 822 NES games were released between 1985 and 1994.
- The tiny blue dot represents every game you cherished from that time: *Mario 3*, *StarTropics*, *Contra*, *DuckTales*, *Duck Hunt*, and so on.
- The same number of games are released on Google Play in less than a week. There are over 350,000 games on the App Store. That means there are 448 times as many as the 822 NES games. The blue dot is lost in the sea of red dots representing mobile apps.

Had I put those bullets on the slide shown in **FIGURE 32.10**, the audience would have read ahead by the time I talked about them. If I had used the slide of text, I would have had little to say beyond what was on the slide.

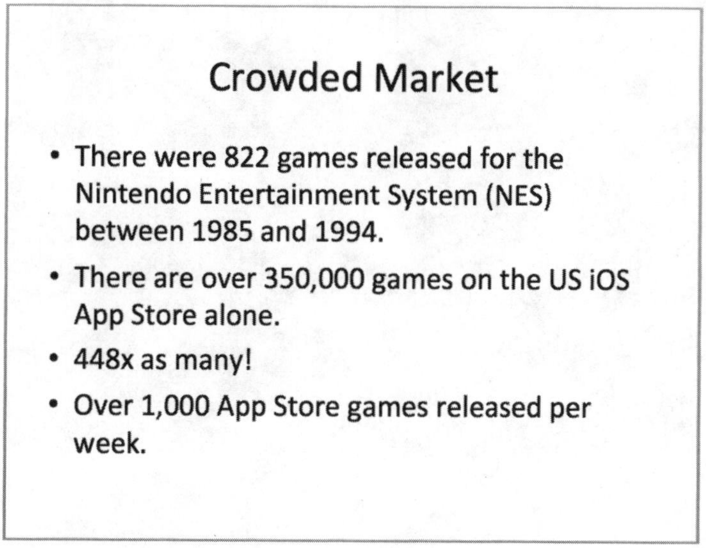

Crowded Market

- There were 822 games released for the Nintendo Entertainment System (NES) between 1985 and 1994.
- There are over 350,000 games on the US iOS App Store alone.
- 448x as many!
- Over 1,000 App Store games released per week.

FIGURE 32.10
Notes as slides don't work.

For each of my subtheses, I completed this process. Some required multiple slides because I had too much data to succinctly show it all at once. For each slide, I created notes, then the slide itself. When the presentation was complete, I wrote my notes as a handout, which I put on the web, and I shared the link at the end of the presentation.

Risk

Risk comes from not knowing what you are doing.

—WARREN BUFFETT

In 2012, award-winning author Neal Stephenson set up a Kickstarter project to fund his idea called *CLANG*, which was to be a multiplayer one-on-one sword-fighting game that focused on realism. *CLANG* would come with its own unique motion-based controller custom-built for the game. Stephenson's fans ate up the presentation, pledging over $500,000 for the title. In the Kickstarter pitch, Stephenson noted that the game had "a simple and attainable goal; we don't want to mess this up by overreaching."[10]

In 2014, *CLANG* was unceremoniously canceled by an update to the Kickstarter page. Stephenson noted that after spending the half-million, they had a prototype that "was technically innovative, but [not] very fun to play." The money was gone and backers were reasonably upset (**FIGURE 32.11**). What happened?

FIGURE 32.11
CLANG is a great case study in understanding risk at an early stage.

CLANG IS © 2013 SUBUTAI CORPORATION.

10 Stephenson, N. (2012, June 9). *CLANG* by Subutai Corporation. Retrieved May 21, 2015, from www. kickstarter.com/projects/260688528/clang/description.

Development structures differ in how they handle the riskiness of projects. For instance, a waterfall type project (Chapter 3) is not very risky if the team is making a known quantity with known resources. You do not need much iteration because the problem is well-understood up front. However, a project with less than well-understood requirements has risk in many different areas and is thus more suited for an iterative model.

Risks are elements that may diverge the final product from the planned product. Risks in games manifest mainly in three ways:

- **DEVELOPMENT RISKS** are ones that are associated with the project not finishing on time because of elements of building the project itself. These include technical limitations, personnel limitations, funding limitations, and business limitations.

- **MARKET RISKS** are ones that are associated with the project underperforming because of elements external to the team. Examples are not being able to launch a branded game with its tie-in movie, or that the market does not care about your type of game anymore. Another market risk is that you are unable to sell or explain the game to the market. This is often the case in riskier, more experimental projects.

- **DESIGN RISKS** are ones that are associated with the project underperforming because of what the project is. For instance, you may think that making an ultra-realistic sword-fighting game is an excellent idea, but you may not realize all the dependencies in animation and communication that such a design implies. These risks show themselves late in a project when you have a functional game that is not fun or a game that cannot be completed to design specifications.

Risk Analysis

To understand the risks involved in a project, it helps to play devil's advocate and enumerate all the weak points in the project or areas where things could go wrong. This is difficult to do because of ego-related blinders when this is a project you are working on, so it makes sense to practice first with other projects to which you have no personal ties. For instance, a quick look at the risks of *CLANG* reveals the following:

DEVELOPMENT RISKS

- The development team is unknown. Have they worked on games before? What kind? Does the team have an experienced producer to manage the project or will Stephenson manage the project?
- Has Stephenson or members of his team ever developed hardware peripherals before?

- Who is manufacturing the peripheral? What is their history?
- Where is the development team based? Will a $500,000 budget be enough? What are other sources of income in case the development goes longer?
- How will the team implement online play? What technical dependencies exist due to choices of technology? Is the technology chosen tested for this type of gameplay? How much online work will be required to create versus out-of-the-box solutions?

MARKET RISKS

- If the project is banking on selling a prototype to future investors, what if the prototype is no good? What other funding options exist?

DESIGN RISKS

- The pitch identifies this as being wildly innovative design work. What if the design does not work? When will prototypes be tested and completed?
- Neal Stephenson is a successful author and knows vast amounts about medieval-style sword fighting, but has he ever been the creative director in a video-game project, which is a wildly different medium?
- What if realistic sword fighting is not fun?
- What animation system dependencies are needed to provide realistic fighting?
- How will the game teach players to use the peripheral and fight effectively?
- How will the game give feedback to the player without the tactile feedback of actual sword fighting?
- How will the game limit player motion to realistic maneuvers?

For what it is worth, the *CLANG* Kickstarter pitch tackled proposed answers to many of these questions. Unfortunately, the project crumpled around the weight of these and other risks.

Yooka-Laylee is a 2015 Kickstarter project that raised over $3 million.[11] It's a game by former developers of the influential studio Rare Entertainment to make a spiritual successor to their 1998 hit *Banjo Kazooie*. The team is loaded with professionals who have made this kind of game before successfully, which somewhat mitigates development risk. They choose to use the popular Unity engine, which has been used to make other 3D platform games successfully. Market risks are largely mitigated by the

---

11 "Yooka-Laylee—A 3D Platformer Rare-vival!" (2015). Retrieved June 1, 2015, from www.kickstarter.com/ projects/playtonic/yooka-laylee-a-3d-platformer-rare-vival.

Kickstarter model and the large amount of money raised given the scope. The team provides a budgetary breakdown in their original pitch that makes a backer relatively confident that they understand where the money goes. The design risks are mitigated by a tightly controlled design that essentially promises that if you liked *Banjo-Kazooie*, that they will make more of that, with periodic design check-ins with the community during development to help steer particular features. Since the team has already made a similar game before, some of the remaining outstanding risks are the team's ability to develop in a multiplatform environment, the logistic problems in fulfillment, and the design risk of over-scoping given their Kickstarter largesse.

By explaining these risks and how they attempt to address them within the pitch in Kickstarter itself, the *Yooka-Laylee* team showed that they are much more prepared to deliver a project than the largely speculative pitch of the *CLANG* team, and because of that, they are much more likely to deliver a product.

Pitch Questions

There is one question above all others that has to be answered clearly and quickly in any game pitch presentation:

What does the player do?

Think about how you would explain some of your favorite games. *Super Mario Bros.* is about jumping on platforms and dodging enemies, not about defeating an evil turtle. *Katamari Damacy* is about rolling up objects in size order to make your ball larger and larger. *Splinter Cell* is about using the environment (breaking lights, using alternate routes) to sneak through an area where you are outgunned.

▶ **NOTE** Or at least, earlier titles in the series were about this.

All of these explanations tell you what the player does. They do not focus on the story or the aesthetics. The explanation of *Splinter Cell* could easily be "You play a secret agent who is trying to stop a terrorist threat." That is an accurate explanation of the game, but it does not explain to an audience what the player does. That explanation could just as easily have been appropriate for a movie or a book. But you are not pitching a movie or book; you are pitching a game. Focus your explanation on what the player does.

When I ask students to pitch me their game, I usually go through the following questions to judge a game pitch:

- **MOST IMPORTANT QUESTION:** What does/do the player(s) do? Is what the player does effectively communicated? Can this action be interesting to do?

- **RULES:** Are the rules needed to understand how this game would work effectively communicated? This does not mean that every rule needs to be enumerated and cross-referenced as if in a game design document, but the audience needs to understand what the boundaries of the interactions are and how they are determined.

- **GOALS AND OPPONENTS:** Is/are the player's goal(s) effectively communicated? Are the forces that stop the player from that goal effectively communicated? Do these seem reasonable?

- **THEME AND PERSPECTIVE:** How does the game look and feel? Do the theme and perspective make sense? This does not need to be exhaustive and final. However, in many games the theme is essential to understanding the game itself, so a broad understanding of the theme may be necessary. This and all aspects may change by the time the game is actually made.

- **INTERACTION:** Is it clear how this game is played/controlled? This does not mean that buttons are called out, just that the audience knows what they manipulate.

- **NOVELTY:** Are the elements that make this unique or similar to other games effectively communicated? Is the game sufficiently different from existing games in a way that would be meaningful to players? There are many platforming games. One that stars a snail would be different, but is that meaningfully different? Would players care?

- **FUN:** Does the presentation show how what is presented suggests fun or interesting interactions? Not all games need to be fun first. *This War of Mine* is a great game that is incredibly bleak. Nonetheless, it has extremely interesting interactions.

- **RISKS:** Does the pitch address obvious risks? If you plan on making an MMO in six months with a three-person team, do you understand what you are getting into?

- **HOOK:** Is there an interesting hook for the game that is effectively communicated? This should be given early! The hook does not have to be what makes the game novel, but it should be something that draws the player in.

- **RELEVANT INFORMATION:** Is all pitch information relevant? Did the presenter waste time with story elements or other elements that are not relevant to any of the other questions? Does the presenter make unsubstantiated claims ("deep strategic gameplay," "epic boss fights," "possibilities are limitless," and so on)?

If you and your team cannot answer any of the questions or cannot answer them sufficiently, this serves as a prompt that you need to go back and more effectively address them. Some questions may not be relevant. If I were using this as a guide to pitch a new feature to an existing franchise, then theme and perspective may not be relevant. However, each point is worth considering as a whole to examine areas of vagueness. Answering each ensures that the audience knows exactly what is being pitched and why.

Summary

- Do not read slides to your audience.
- Do not waste the audience's time.
- Create separate artifacts for your presentation notes, for the data and graphics shown to the audience, and for the audience to take home. Do not use the slides themselves to fulfill all three jobs.
- Although it is exciting to pitch the possibilities in a game idea, it is irresponsible to ignore the various risks that can hold the project back from developing those ideas to their full potential.
- When pitching games, it is important to communicate what the player does.

8 The Game Design Business

If it's a thing worth trying, you should be a little afraid.

—SAMUEL R. DELANEY, BABEL-17

Game design rarely happens in a vacuum. Even the hobbyist game maker who releases her work for free online must decide if work on a game is worth the time and effort she will put into it. More often than not, a game's creators hope to recoup the time and resources and turn a profit that they can then use to finance their next project. When game teams involve full-time workers who need to be paid, offices with rent and bills, and distribution channels that require certain financial objectives to be met, the business end increases in importance.

Designers can pretend to be "above" the discussion of dollars and cents. Many claim that because what they do is art, it cannot be contaminated by the base concerns of finance. This attitude is akin to burying one's head in the sand. Whether a designer admits it or not, every design decision has the possibility of affecting the bottom line. And the bottom line affects whether or not you get to continue to design games. Given the low probability that any individual game will make its money back, a small percentage of games must cover the costs for all of a studio's work. Designer Dan Cook estimates that a successful game might need to make more than 10 times the average cost of making a game to keep a studio afloat (www.lostgarden.com/2015/04/minimum-sustainable-success.html).

For a designer or team to not do everything they can to ensure their work is financially successful is akin to fiddling while Rome burns. Unless the design makes the work sustainable, there will not be much more work to be had. With the vast volume of games competing for player dollars, the days where a team could just make something and rely on someone else or "the market" to find and reward them are long gone (if that time ever existed at all). The designer and the team must be acutely aware of the market considerations of what they do.

As the business landscape of games constantly changes, there are not a lot of timeless lessons that can be related. However, there are a few topics that are relevant regardless of the current business conditions.

33 Profit, Loss, and Metrics

Growth and profit are a product of
how people work together.

—RICARDO SEMLER

Games often require a huge capital investment. Investors who put up resources to finance a game will want to know what the odds are that they will get their money back. One way to attempt to predict this is to create a *profit and loss statement* or P&L. The P&L lists all the costs and various projections of the revenues for the project to give investors an idea of the potential profit. This statement usually takes the form of a spreadsheet.

Profit and Loss

TABLE 33.1 is a spreadsheet for a hypothetical mobile racing game that would have a retail cost of $2. Revenue estimates are based on three scenarios: a worst-case scenario, an average scenario, and a best-case scenario. These numbers are not pulled from thin air. The sales numbers in Table 33.1 were pulled from similar games with similar business models in the genre.

TABLE 33.1 Basic Profit and Loss

	Worst-Case Scenario	Average Scenario	Best-Case Scenario
Units	5,000	20,000	500,000
Sales	$10,000	$40,000	$1,000,000
(Less Platform Cut)	($3,000)	($13,333)	($300,000)
Total Revenue	$7,000	$27,667	$700,000
Staff Costs	$900,000	$960,000	$960,000
Production Costs	$10,000	$10,000	$10,000
Marketing Costs	$90,000	$90,000	$90,000
Total Costs	$1,060,000	$1,060,000	$1,060,000
Total Profit (Loss) Before Taxes	($1,053,000)	($1,032,333)	($360,000)

▶ **NOTE** A number of different services used to estimate game sales pop up and close down with regularity. VGChartz estimates retail console sales. SteamSpy helps estimate Steam users and sales. AppData counts daily active users of Facebook games. App Annie is a source for information about mobile games. However, do your own due diligence, because most of these services make only estimates.

Of course, the developer does not see all of the $2 when a user buys the game. In this case, the platform holder will take 30 percent of revenues. At the time of this writing, Apple and Google Play both take 30 percent of revenues for hosting a game on their store. If you plan on publishing on Apple's App Store or the Google Play store, then you have to agree to pay them to use the platform. Similar costs exist with other platform holders, such as Sony, Microsoft, or Nintendo. Multiplying sales by price and then subtracting the amount paid directly to the platform holder leaves you with the total revenue for the game. In the example, total revenue can range from $7,000 to $700,000.

Next, you look at costs. It may be tempting to give a range of possible values for this because these too are future estimates. However, in order to have an easier analysis, you want to have only one independent variable, so keep the costs static across estimates unless the number of units sold greatly affects costs. Additionally, you should run analyses with differing cost estimates.

▶ **NOTE** A man-month is a measurement of one staff member working for one month.

Staff costs are generally the highest cost for video-game production. A common estimate for the value of a man-month is $10,000. This, of course, varies wildly by role and location. An artist in Romania will likely have a different cost than a tools programmer in Silicon Valley. Nonetheless, the $10,000/man-month is a widely used heuristic. Remember that staff costs include not just salary, but any health benefits, insurance, payroll taxes, seat licenses, and other perks that require the developer to pay on a per-person basis.

The example in Table 33.1 estimates a project of 96 man-months. This is a very small project.

Production costs include all the fixed costs of running the studio during the project. The provided example assumes that the studio has no physical office and instead just needs to pay for normal business filing and legal expenses.

Many novice game makers believe that all you have to do to assure financial success is make a "good" game (whatever that is), tell reviewers, and set up some social accounts. Unfortunately, the odds of stumbling into a financial success seem larger than they actually are because of availability bias. We are able to rattle off the names of games that were done by a small team with little to no resources only to become huge hits, but we are unable to name many from the much larger proportion of games that had the same level of polish and preparation that died on the shelf.

It is naive to think that you can release a game with no marketing budget because hundreds of iOS games are released every day.[1] Numerous services claim to be able to boost an app into the high visibility realm of the top charts, allowing organic growth to drive further purchases. One such service costs $90,000, so I have used that estimate, despite doubts of its current efficacy.[2]

Various services can help you estimate the *cost of user acquisition*. Fiksu estimated the cost of acquiring users who open an app three or more times to be $2.80 per user in February 2015.[3] When factoring out the loyalty of users, Fiksu estimated the cost of acquiring a user was $1.28 on iOS and $1.51 on Android. Research firm SuperData

. . . .

1   "App Store Metrics." (n.d.). Retrieved March 23, 2015, from www.pocketgamer.biz/metrics/appstore/submissions.

2   Koetsier, J. (2013, June 4). "How $90,000 Can Buy You a Top 10 Ranking in the U.S. App Store." Retrieved April 2, 2015, from http://venturebeat.com/2013/06/04/how-96000-can-buy-you-a-top-10-ranking-in-the-u-s-app-store.

3   Fiksu Resources. (n.d.). Retrieved April 2, 2015, from www.fiksu.com/resources/fiksu-indexes.

estimated the cost of an iOS user to be $2.30.[4] If the number of games released per player willing to pay for them continues to rise at such a high rate, expect the cost of user acquisition to continue to rise.

In the example, costs sum to $1,060,000. Even in the best-case scenario, the game generates a loss.

Metrics

Games that exist as a service rather than as a boxed copy have the ability to change on the fly through live updating via the Internet. This connectivity allows designers to better understand how real players are using their game in the wild to better educate themselves on what design decision to make. Metrics are measurements of real player behavior generated by the game and analyzed by the designers. Metrics can measure any behavior of interest. However, there are some metrics that are commonly used across projects.

Free-to-Play Metrics

The advent of the *free-to-play* (F2P) business model has ushered in some new terminology useful for making estimates on these kinds of games. First, a user for a free-to-play game may spend no money or may spend a lot of money, so you cannot use users as a way to estimate revenue as you could with a fixed-price game.

The *conversion rate* is the percentage of players who spend money in a game. If a game has 100,000 users and 97,000 users never spend any money at all, then the game's conversion rate is 3.0 percent. Various sources indicate that a 1 percent to 5 percent conversion rate is reasonable.[5] A free-to-play game can still be successful even if there are 99 freeloaders for every paying customer.

The conversion rate tells you how many players have paid, but it does not break down how much. *ARPPU* is an acronym for "average revenue per paying user." It's the average amount that each converted player has paid. You can calculate this by taking total revenue and dividing it by the number of paying players. ARPU is another commonly

. . . .

4   "Brace Yourself for the Mobile User Acquisition Bloodbath This Holiday Season." (2013, November 25). Retrieved April 2, 2015, from www.superdataresearch.com/blog/user-acquisition-bloodbath.

5   Purchese, R. (2014, April 22). "Don't Be Surprised That Just 2.2% of F2P Players Spend Money." Retrieved April 2, 2015, from www.eurogamer.net/ articles/2014-04-22-dont-be-surprised-that-just-2-2-per-cent-of-f2p-players-spend-money.

used (and confused) metric that divides total revenue by total players to get an "average revenue per user" (**TABLE 33.2**).

TABLE 33.2 Calculating Revenue

In a retail or "premium" game	Revenue = Users * Average Price
In a free-to-play game	Revenue = Users * Conversion Rate * ARPPU
	or
	Revenue = Users * ARPU

Naturally, you will not know your total revenue because that is what you are trying to estimate. However, you can estimate the ARPPU by giving an honest guess as to what the average player will spend his money on within the game.

Note that all paying users do not spend equal amounts. The derogatory terminology that the industry uses for high-paying players is "whales." I'll use that term here for familiarity despite its obvious distastefulness.

Spending in F2P games is Pareto-distributed, which means that a small percentage of the players spends a large amount of the total revenue in the game. One report from analytics firm Swrve found that only 1.5 percent of users converted into paying customers and that the average spend per month was \$15.27 (ARPPU).[6] However, only the top 0.45 percent of players ever paid more than the average. The top decile of paying users (1 in approximately 700 users) paid an average of \$77.70 and resulted in over 50 percent of the average game's total revenue. These are the "whales."

I recommend the following shot-in-the-dark as a reasonable model for estimating F2P sales. The following models the general shape of F2P spending, however it will necessarily be different as project and market changes shift behaviors. Let X be some small amount of user spending for the platform, like \$2 or \$3:

- Top-Spenders: 0.2% of users, \$20X/user
- Medium-Spenders: 0.5% of users, \$5X/user
- Low-Spenders: 0.7% of users, \$$X$/user
- Non-Spenders: 98.6% of users, \$0/user

. . . .

6   Hiwiller, Z. (2014, April 24). "ECGC 2014: Design Lessons from Pareto." Retrieved December 8, 2014, from www.hiwiller.com/2014/04/24/ecgc-2014-design-lessons-from-pareto.

Virality

If a game cannot make more money from a user (on average) than it costs to acquire that user, then the project will lose money as it gains users. Some social and online games try to escape the costs of user acquisition by increasing the virality of their game. *Virality* is accurately named because it's both a measure of how well a game spreads to new users and because this term brings with it the connotation of sickness and disease. Early measures of virality were based on how *FarmVille* used its players' Facebook feeds to spam messages about lonely cows. New players who had not heard of *FarmVille*, clicked into the game to see what this new thing was that was clogging up their news feeds. Due to the copycat nature of social game development, others quickly followed and Facebook had to change its rules for how messages were automatically generated and shared on players' news feeds.

Virality is simply a factor of how many new users each user brings in. One formula for virality (k) is written as follows:

```
k = i * c
```

The virality factor is k. The number of invitations each user sends is i. The conversion rate of those invitations into new players is c. If k $>$ 1, then the game is growing depending completely on users spreading the game on their own. For example, if the average user sends 100 *FarmVille* invites to his feed and 3 percent of those invites turn into actual players, then k is 3. The first player (Patient Zero) sends out 100 invites and three of them turn into new players. Those three players send out 100 invites each and they recruit, in total, nine new players. Those nine players send 900 invites and recruit 27 new players. And so on.

Obviously, this cannot continue forever. More accurate measurements of virality are much more complicated and take into account the time it takes to complete a cycle of invitations, the effect of multiple cycles of invitations, and the rate at which players disappear.

It used to be a common technique for a studio to buy its way into the top sales charts by spending large amounts on early customer acquisition. The idea was to spend a lot of money early, and then rely on a k $>$ 1 to acquire users over time.

This technique is no longer popular because it's not as foolproof as it once was considered to be. k is determined in retrospect and is constantly evolving. In theory, a game or app with k > 1 should do nothing but try to ensure continued virality and rake in additional users. Unfortunately for modern designers, they cannot use epidemiological models and call it a day. Game designers still need to consider design, community, marketing, and economics in order to succeed. Virality is a side effect of effective game design, not a component.

Retention

Another important metric is *retention*. Retention measures how many players "stick around." For a given time period, a game's retention is the percent of users that started that time period and remain players at the end of the time period. Take a long tutorial for example. It has ten steps: Users select a name for their character, then a race, then a class/job, such as warrior or wizard. They learn how to fight, how to cast spells, and the differences between realms. Then they are asked to send invites to their friends. After that, they learn about crafting, read and sign the EULA, sign up for the email newsletter and then finally they begin the game. Let's say 10,000 users start the process and, through metric collection, the number of users is counted at every step as reflected in **FIGURE 33.1**.

FIGURE 33.1
Retention over a tutorial's steps.

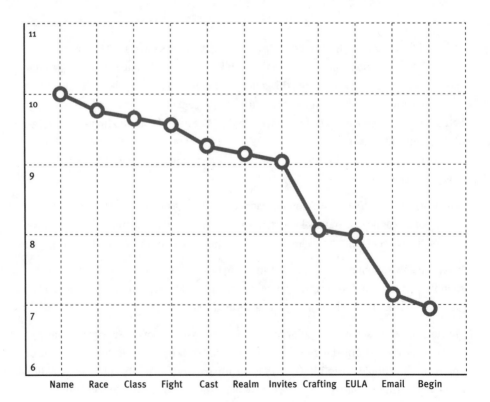

Approximately 7,000 users make it to the end of the process of the original 10,000. Overall, the tutorial process has a retention rate of 70 percent. But by looking at each step in isolation, the retention for each step can be determined. You divide the number of users in step $n+1$ by the number of users in step n to get the retention from step n to step $n+1$.

In **FIGURE 33.2**, the view of retention by step shows a huge dip in retention during the invitation step and the EULA step, with smaller dips in the naming and fighting steps. Using this information, the team can come up with ideas to make these steps more palatable. Something is causing users to abandon the game at these points where the retention rate dips.

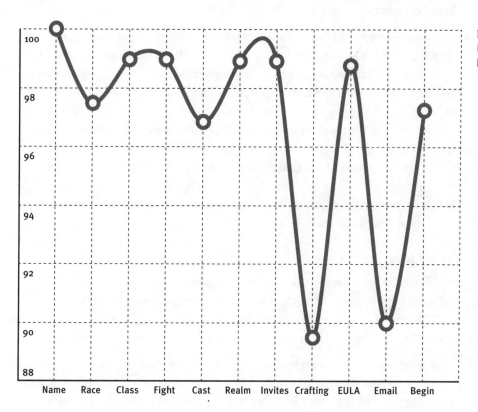

FIGURE 33.2
Retention rate
by step.

Retention generally dips fairly regularly over time as users get satiated with a game and drop off. However, any sudden dips are usually the result of a bad experience for the player. Sometimes those bad experiences are necessary, such as losing a first battle against a difficult boss. Sometimes these bad experiences are the result of confusing text or unnecessary mechanics. By collecting this information, the design team can better understand what works and does not work with players. Players who do not stick around are not likely to give you any money.

Another popularly used term is *churn*. Churn is simply the opposite of retention. Where retention measures how many users stay over a given period of time, churn measures how many users give up over a given period of time. If retention is 70 percent, then churn is 30 percent.

Users are often measured over two spans of time: monthly and daily. *Monthly active users* or MAU are those who sign in to the game at any time during a given month. *Daily active users* (DAU) are those who sign in on any given day. Looking at the ratio between these values tells a story about player retention. If tons of players show up on Day 1 and get bored and leave before Day 30, then dividing the DAU/MAU on Day 30 will result in a low number. For instance, say I had 100,000 users over the month, but only 1,000 remained by Day 30; my DAU/MAU would be 1 percent. A perfect game where players never leave would have a MAU/DAU of 100 percent because every player in the MAU would be represented in the DAU. DAU/MAU is an imprecise measurement because there is no way to retroactively count a new user in the MAU and there is no way to flag a MAU as having quit the game for good.

Other Metrics

Many analytics packages are available for digital games that allow teams to better understand the behavior of players. Often, the software provides what are called "hooks" to the analytics package that can be inserted into code to send data to the analytics software. Teams can then use that data to answer questions about their game.

When developing *Sudoku Together*, the team at Sky Parlor Studios was interested in knowing whether the coins that players collect in the games are spent or hoarded. If the coins were hoarded, then it might mean that players did not see anything in the store worth buying. Or it might mean that they were saving up for something expensive. If the coins were spent, then it might mean that the cheap items were too inexpensive or that players did not believe they could ever afford the expensive items. Nonetheless, they had nowhere to start without collecting data.

FIGURE 33.3 is a chart generated by the analytics package Swrve. It showed on a day-to-day basis how many coins were given to players and how many were spent. The area between the curves shows how much was hoarded that day. If players did not spend the coins, the spend line would be fairly flat. If this continued to increase over time, the team would know there was some kind of problem. However, the data showed fairly normal usage. When the amount of coins given spiked, so too did the amount of coins spent, indicating that users would likely spend coins as they were received right away rather than saving them. These conclusions warranted the collection of other data, but decisions were based on this data rather than gut feelings or sampled interviews.

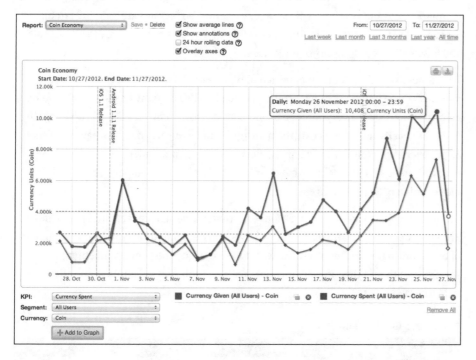

FIGURE 33.3
This Swrve output showed metrics of an in-game economy.

Cash Flow

As games become active services, the game business has to deal more and more with the problem of *cash flow*. Cash flow is the liquidity of a business, or more specifically in this setting, the ability of a business to pay its employees. Cash flow issues have caused many game studios to close their doors.

Cash flow is a simple concept. Take the cash on hand. Add to it any cash coming in and subtract any cash going out.

Here is an example. Say a team has released a game through a publisher. That publisher promises to pay out revenues within 60 days (January revenues are paid in March, February revenues are paid in April). This 60-day gap is common in royalty payments and is sometimes as long as 90 or 120 days.

The game takes off better than expected and the team has to continually buy more and more servers to handle the increased player loads. The company has to spend $100,000/ month on their staff. Every 100,000 users requires them to buy increased server space and other overhead, which costs them an additional $1/user. The users pay, on average, $2 per user each month after the publisher's cut. The first month the game launches with 100,000 users and doubles every month thereafter. The company starts off with a nice cushion of $2 million in cash.

On the surface, this looks like a reasonably profitable game. Players pay $2/user/month. The costs per user are $1/user for server costs and then $100,000 split over the number of users. Since the first month starts with 100,000 users, the team should break even the first month and then grow from there, making $100,000 in February and $300,000 in March (**TABLE 33.3**).

TABLE 33.3 Good-looking P&L

	January	February	March
Players	100,000	200,000	400,000
ARPU (Less Publisher Cut)	$2.00	$2.00	$2.00
Total Revenue	$200,000	$400,000	$800,000
Staff Costs	$100,000	$100,000	$100,000
Server Costs	$100,000	$200,000	$400,000
Total Costs	$200,000	$300,000	$500,000
Total Profit (Loss) Before Taxes	$0	$100,000	$300,000

Now consider the game from a cash flow perspective. The team starts out with $2 million in January. The team has to pay out the costs for their staff and the ever-increasing server costs as they scale up, yet the team does not get the payoff for that increase for two months. You might think that it should be OK since the game is profitable and the team has $2 million in the bank. However, take a look at **TABLE 33.4**.

TABLE 33.4 Cash Flow Crisis

	Jan	Feb	Mar	Apr	May
Users (millions)	0.1	0.2	0.4	0.8	1.6
Starting Balance	$2,000,000	$1,800,000	$1,500,000	$1,200,000	$700,000
Publisher Payment	—	—	$200,000	$400,000	$800,000
Staff Costs	($100,000)	($100,000)	($100,000)	($100,000)	($100,000)
Server Costs	($100,000)	($200,000)	($400,000)	($800,000)	($1,600,000)
Ending Balance	$1,800,000	$1,500,000	$1,200,000	$700,000	($200,000)

In just five months, the team's cash cushion is exhausted. They will have to find a way to finance more money or simply not make payroll. Even though the game is growing and the business model is profitable, the company faces insolvency. This is the danger of ignoring cash flow.

Summary

- Develop profit and loss statements based on a range of different estimates for uncertain values.
- Games now use a variety of metrics to inform designers how to change a game while it is live.
- In free-to-play games, generally the majority of the money spent is spent by a small proportion of the total players.
- By measuring the number of players who reach a specific step in a game's progression, a game team can identify what steps or features are hampering retention.
- Do not ignore cash flow. When you get paid can be as important as how much you get paid.

34 Sustainable Lifestyles

> One hundred idiots make idiotic plans and carry them out. All but one justly fail. The hundredth idiot, whose plan succeeded through pure luck, is immediately convinced he is a genius.
>
> **—IAIN M. BANKS, "MATTER"**

Many books and articles have been dedicated to the topic of informing people on how to pursue a career in games. Often these takes are idealized, relying on wishful thinking and anecdotes of the successful to supply enthusiasm rather than paint an accurate picture of the realities and the trade-offs involved. Making a career in games simply is not for everyone.

Life in AAA Digital Game Development

A modern middle-class life is possible when you are working for a video-game studio in many roles: art, animation, programming, design, testing, and project management. Generally, game studios provide a competitive salary (although lower than comparable fields), health insurance, and often, good fringe benefits.

However, video-game development is often quite unlike a "normal" job. One of the grim words that come up quickly when you start talking about the game development lifestyle is *crunch*. The "crunch" is a period of extended work hours that may include 12- or 16-hour days up to seven days a week. Crunch is excruciatingly tiring and often leads to high developer burnout. Crunch happens for a number of reasons: inefficiencies caused by turnover, lack of direction from management, disrespect between management and workers, and/or lack of a clear and accurate schedule.

One of the few defenses for crunch claims is that creating extraordinary entertainment titles requires an extraordinary amount of effort. If Company X spends 40 hours a week to make Game X, and Company Y spends 50 hours to make Game Y, then all else being equal, Game Y should be better than Game X.

The research team behind the Game Outcomes Project used a wide database of project information and metrics to try to distill principles of game development that would lead to exceptional outcomes. They put this theory to the test.[1] The data was clear. Crunch leads to poorer outcomes with a high degree of certainty. Projects made without crunch had higher scores on both subjective outcomes (the team was satisfied with the game) and objective outcomes (such as critical reception measured by a Metacritic score, or financial returns based on initial investment). The Game Outcomes Project's analysis of the topic is fascinating, but it is beyond the scope of this discussion.

Many studies confirm that crunch gives a small boost early, but that early gain is eaten up by lower productivity later. A greater-than-40-hour week does not increase overall productivity.[2] Henry Ford understood this 100 years ago, but we seem to have forgotten it in the meantime.[3] Nonetheless, the game industry tends to expect it. There is a reason

. . . .

1   Tozour, P. (2015, January 20). Gamasutra: Paul Tozour's Blog—"The Game Outcomes Project, Part 4: Crunch Makes Games Worse." Retrieved April 7, 2015, from http://gamasutra.com/blogs/ PaulTozour/20150120/234443/The_Game_Outcomes_Project_Part_4_Crunch_Makes_Games_Worse.php.

2   Thomas, H. R. (1992). "Effects of Scheduled Overtime on Labor Productivity." *Journal of Construction Engineering and Management*, 118(1), 60–76.

3   A great reminder from a games' industry perspective can be found in Cook, D. (2008, September 28). "Rules of Productivity Presentation." Retrieved April 24, 2015, from www.lostgarden.com/2008/09/rules-of-productivity-presentation.html?m=1.

that the common profile of game industry professionals is largely childless 20-somethings. In fact, 70 percent of game developers are under the age of 34.[4] Older professionals find that the long hours and lack of creative freedom are not beneficial to having a family and a fulfilling career.

If you are looking for a job in this industry, the Game Outcomes Project has some guidelines on what successful game industry teams do.[5] By finding teams that do these things well, a potential employee can hopefully avoid spending their energy on a dysfunctional team. Some of the highlights of their analysis are as follows:

- Great teams have a clear, shared vision of the game design and a plan on how to get there. The Game Outcomes Project found this to be the most important factor in the success of the team. This singular vision and buy-in kindles enthusiasm. Every team member feels important. A lack of enthusiasm is almost always a warning sign.

- Great teams understand and manage their risks. Ignoring risks and putting them off in order to "cross that bridge when we get there" is dangerous. Design elements in a game change. This is necessary for iteration. How that change is carefully managed and how negative effects to the team are mitigated is a measure of the future success of the team.

- Great teams avoid crunch and do not make it a part of their corporate culture. This is not to say that a great team never crunches, but a great team takes great care to avoid it. The Game Outcomes Project makes explicitly clear that crunch, even small amounts of it, leads to myriad negative outcomes and that it harms employee health, productivity, and decision-making.

- Great teams allow team members to feel safe in risk-taking. This encompasses the psychological safety related to expressing problems to bosses, along with the freedom to try novel and creative ideas without the possibility of punishment for failing, assuming that those ideas can fit within the team's development plans. Failing is not taboo. It is something that is discussed and learned from rather than stigmatized.

- Great teams give the team members autonomy to determine how their tasks are completed under the team's production methodology.

. . . .

4   Remo, C. (2010, May 21). Study: "Game Developers Increasingly Newcomers to Business." Retrieved April 7, 2015, from www.gamasutra.com/view/news/118984/Study_Game_Developers_Increasingly_Newcomers_ To_Business.php.

5   Tozour, P. (2015, January 26). Gamasutra: Paul Tozour's Blog— "The Game Outcomes Project, Part 5: What Great Teams Do." Retrieved April 7, 2015, from http://gamasutra.com/blogs/PaulTozour/20150120/234443/ The_Game_Outcomes_Project_Part_5_What_Great_Teams_Do.php.

- Great teams work together. They resolve conflicts between members instead of letting them stew and simmer. Team members support each other, praise successes, and make sure that each member feels mutually respected.

- Great teams minimize turnover. This is something an interviewee can ask directly in an interview.

- Great teams give individuals timely and relevant feedback on their work. This includes code reviews, which help minimize software defects.

- Great teams are conscious about being great. Each individual holds herself and other members to high standards and is self-reflective to a degree where she can under-stand, in real time, when she is not living up to her own standards.

Life as an Independent Developer of Digital Games

Life as an indie developer anecdotally meets the stereotypical features of the idealized artist. The indie developer has a great degree of creative freedom, but often struggles to make ends meet. Even extraordinarily successful independent developers often need to supplement their income. *Canabalt* designer Adam Saltsman relies on contract work and his wife's income to support his independent games work.[6] There are more routes than ever before to fund independent development, but there are also more independent developers competing for those crowdfunding, grant, or patronage resources.

Anecdotes abound of small game successes. Early app store developer Steve Demeter made $250,000 in two months.[7] *Flappy Bird* made $50,000 a day on ads alone.[8] Vlambeer's *Ridiculous Fishing* made over a million dollars.[9] I would be remiss to leave out Markus "notch" Persson's solo-project-turned-cultural-juggernaut *Minecraft*. Persson sold his company to Microsoft in 2014 and netted $1.4 billion.[10]

. . . .

6   Francis, B. (2015, March 25). "Let's Get Real about the Financial Expectations of 'Going Indie.'" Retrieved March 25, 2015, from www.gamasutra.com/view/news/237046/Lets_get_real_about_the_financial_expectations_of_going_indie.php.

7   Chen, B. (2008, September 19). "iPhone Developers Go From Rags to Riches" *WIRED*. Retrieved March 25, 2015, from www.wired.com/2008/09/indie-developer.

8   Hamburger, E. (2014, February 5). "Indie Smash Hit 'Flappy Bird' Racks Up $50K per Day in Ad Revenue." Retrieved March 25, 2015, from www.theverge.com/2014/2/5/5383708/flappy-bird-revenue-50-k-per-day-dong-nguyen-interview.

9   Parkin, S. (2014, April 3). "The Guilt of the Video Game Millionaires." Retrieved March 25, 2015, from www.newyorker.com/tech/elements/the-guilt-of-the-video-game-millionaires.

10 Associated Press. (2015, September 15) "Microsoft Buys 'Minecraft' Maker for $2.5B." Retrieved March 25, 2015, from http://nypost.com/2014/09/15/microsoft-buys-minecraft-maker-for-2-5b.

▶ **NOTE** Power law and Pareto are mathematically different, but similar enough for the purposes of this discussion.

However, these are examples of the top results in what is called a *power law* or *Pareto distribution*. Power law distributions are found in many natural and interpersonal examples from wealth distribution to the population of the world's cities, to the distribution of letters in words, to the number of connections in a social network, to the severity of earthquakes. Pareto distributions are characterized by most of the effects of a distribution falling under a small number of the causes.

For instance, in a sales force of 100 salespeople, a Pareto distribution is one in which the top 20 salespeople make 80 percent of the sales (**FIGURE 34.1**). If they sell 1,000,000 widgets as a group, these top 20 salespeople sell 800,000 of them, while the remaining 80 salespeople sell only 200,000. The Pareto distribution goes further, however. If you look at only these top 20, the top 20 percent of those (or the top 4 salespeople) make 80 percent of the sales of that group. So the top 4 salespeople made 640,000 sales. This means the top 4 contribute more than the remaining 96! Keep in mind that if you use the average to look at these salespeople, the average salesperson has 10,000 sales. However, only the top 24 of the 100 salespeople is above "average" because of the skew. The median salesperson has only 3,000 sales.

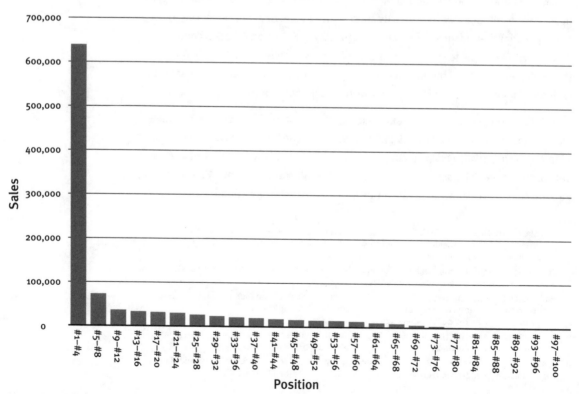

FIGURE 34.1 Power law skew.

Pareto distributions are very common in situations with positive feedback (Chapter 17). The popular aphorism is that it takes money to make money. This is partially due to the fact that money allows for greater reach, and that reach reveals more opportunities to make money. An app's popularity, for instance, influences both how the app spreads by word of mouth (virality, see Chapter 33) and by its likelihood of coming up in searches or featured apps. An app with a million downloads has a million potential advertisers, giving it a wide reach. An app that only 100 people know about has fewer avenues to spread.

In 2015, estimates were that the top 870 of the 1.2 million iOS App Store apps (or 0.07 percent of the apps in the store) made 40 percent of all the revenue.[11] Less than 3,200 apps (0.26 percent) made enough revenue to make a developer the median 2014 US household income. It's unclear whether this analysis includes the taxes and fees that the creator has to pay to be in business. In this survey, the bottom 47 percent of apps earn less than $100 a month. In another survey, the figure was 35 percent of iOS apps and 49 percent of Android apps made less than $100 per app per month.[12]

Life in Tabletop Game Development

The vast majority of people producing games in the analog (tabletop) space are hobbyists and part-time workers. Some game designers have been able to make enough from royalties to make it a career.[13] This model is similar to how book authors receive payment. However, the market for books is large, whereas the market for tabletop games remains quite niche. Probably only a few dozen tabletop game designers in the world make enough from their game design work to support themselves. Tom Vasel, designer and host of the popular tabletop video review and podcast series The Dice Tower, estimates that only 20 people worldwide make a living as full-time tabletop game designers.[14] Nearly all of them started making games for nothing as a hobby. It's not prudent at the time of this publishing to pursue a career in tabletop game development on its own without supplemental income from another source.

. . . .

11 Perry, C. (2015, January 19). "The Shape of the App Store." Retrieved March 25, 2015, from http://metakite.com/blog/2015/01/the-shape-of-the-app-store.

12 DeveloperEconomics.com. (2015, February 17). "Developer Economics Q1 2015: State of the Developer Nation" *Developer Economics*. Retrieved March 25, 2015, from www.developereconomics.com/reports/developer-economics-q1-2015.

13 Tinsman, B. (2003). *The Game Inventor's Guidebook*. Krause Publications. Kraus Publications, Iola, Wisconsin.

14 Vasel, T. (Host). (2015, April 22). "The Dice Tower #402" [Audio podcast]. Retrieved from http://itunes.apple.com.

Market Luck

Luck is quite often ignored as a possible determination of success. It may be that game designers work so hard at creating systems that respond to player input to determine success that they are unwilling to accept that their own success is not determined solely by their own input. Every Game Developers Conference (GDC) is glutted with talks about how an indie studio was successful that year with the hidden subtext (although often not hidden, nor subtext) that if you just complete the same steps as they did, you'll be successful too. If designers believe that luck is a huge factor, then all our hard work on design and analytics seems like a waste of time. Naysayers to luck fall into confirmation bias. They choose not to remember the games they have played that were good, but not commercially successful, or games that were commercially successful, but not good. Instead, they only remember games that were good *and* commercially successful and conflate that they were commercially successful because they were good. Maybe we do not choose to ignore them. Events like GDC reinforce a selection bias. Besides the niche "Failure Workshop," no one gets invited to talk about games that did not go gangbusters. And in the odd cases in which those talks are accepted, they do not fill up like the talks for the latest successes.

Over 11,000 games were submitted to the iOS App Store in February 2015 alone.[15] Hundreds of thousands of games are available at any given time, just on that platform. If there was a special sauce to success, then the average game would make a sustainable income—not, at the most generous estimate, $4,000.[16] Minimum wage is, in most cases, a better bang for your buck.

That does not mean that making games is a fool's errand. I teach students every day whose dream is to make games. If I believed that there was no reason to do so, I could not morally do what I do every day. What should be resisted, however, is the notion that those who are successful became so in a deterministically reproducible way. This is why some clones succeed and some fail. *Temple Run* got lucky in a world of exploding endless runners. Then they built off that fame. *Flappy Bird* had singular organic growth where thousands of similar quick-twitch games failed. The clones that followed and mirrored it in every way, and even those that improved on it, did not have that the seed of luck. Hard work on design and implementation matters, but at some point, you must submit to the random permutations of the market.

. . . .

15   App Store Metrics. (n.d.). Retrieved March 23, 2015, from www.pocketgamer.biz/metrics/appstore/submissions.

16   Louis, T. (2013, August 10). "How Much Do Average Apps Make?" Retrieved March 23, 2015, from www.forbes.com/sites/tristanlouis/2013/08/10/how-much-do-average-apps-make.

Summary

- *Crunch* is the practice of working extended hours in an attempt to accelerate development.

- Crunch allows for increased productivity in the very short term. However, that boost is offset by reduced productivity later.

- Find a good team to work with that communicates well, understands and prepares to take reasonable risks, and is open and transparent regarding what does and does not work.

- Revenues in the game industry are Pareto-distributed. There are a small number of big winners and a large number of releases that have no reach at all.

- Hard work and careful practice are controllable determinants of success. However, they are not the sole determinants.

Conclusion

To err and err and err again, but less and less.

—PIET HIEN

A work is never completed except by some accident...

—PAUL VALÉRY

Writing a conclusion for a game design book, especially a conclusion for a book such as this, seems inappropriate. A conclusion is supposed to wrap up the topic. However, if I was successful here, you should not feel like you are ready to wrap up anything. Instead, you should be inspired to learn more about all the possible areas of knowledge that a designer can leverage. For practical reasons, this book could not cover all the areas of interest to a designer. As a result, its mission was destined to be incomplete. Hopefully, I have been able to help cultivate the curiosity you need to become a successful game designer.

The thesis of this book has been to open your mind to all the disciplines of knowledge in the world. For that, our education is never complete. As we end here, I wanted to point out a few avoidable dangers that can keep you from success in this area:

- **CONFUSING "WHAT I LIKE" WITH "WHAT IS GOOD"**—This is so universal that I see it in myself, in students, in new professionals, and in established game design veterans. Your taste is a useful barometer for directing your focus. It's easier to make something good if you can use yourself as an infinite playtest loop, judging every design decision upon your own personal subjective metrics. But what you like is not necessarily what is best for the game. For most people "This game is good!" is an equivalent statement to "I like this game!" Many design arguments end up boiling down to "I Like X!" versus "I Don't Like X!" That cannot be resolved. As an example, I find *Minecraft* incredibly tedious. But it is undeniable that the game is good in myriad ways. The *Dark Souls* games I find to be painfully unenjoyable. Yet I can admit games like these exhibit masterful cultivation of "fiero." *Dead Rising* is one of my favorite video games of all time, but I can admit that it makes dozens of design mistakes along the way.

  Instead, use a framework that lets you focus on the design goals of the game that you are designing and let that line of thinking guide you. I may really enjoy collection mechanics, but is that necessarily appropriate in my arcade shooter? Possibly. Do I want to include it because I like it or because it will be best for the game?

  I see a lot of the games designed around the "retro" visual and gameplay aesthetics of the late 1980s and early 1990s as an expression of this. The designers likely grew up with games of that aesthetic and since they were foundational for them, they end up expressing that through their design, whether or not it's needed to solve the problem statement of the game.

  This problem also exists when discussing game design itself. Much of what has been written on the topic can be distilled down to "I Like X, so X is good game design." Be wary of that. I tried my best to avoid that in writing this book. The risk is that you limit your craft to an echo chamber of possible design ideas. There is nothing wrong with considering the things you like. After all, you picked up this book, so you have marvelous taste. But do not consider *only* the things you like.

- **DRAGGING DOWN INSTEAD OF BUILDING UP**—Crabs reportedly exhibit a bizarre behavior. If you put one crab in a bucket, it will easily climb out and escape. Put a bunch of crabs in a bucket, however, and they will pull each other down in their own efforts to escape and none will be able to climb out.

In my early years as a designer, all I could see was poor design everywhere I looked. My newfound skills helped me determine rough edges to which I had previously been oblivious. And so I was noisy about them. This can be for spiteful reasons ("I don't know why people like this, it is so broken! I'm so much smarter than they are!") or for helpful reasons ("Your game would be better if you did this."). Regardless, in both cases, it serves as criticism. Jean Sibelius is credited with the quote that "a statue has never been set up in honor of a critic."[17] Although not empirically true and likely too extreme of a position, Sibelius' point was to discount critics as unworthy of giving meaningful feedback. If you act consistently as a critic, you will likely also be seen as a naysayer or as unhelpful.

The fear of this criticism keeps novice designers from releasing something until it is perfect. They toil to buff out all the rough edges in an endless stream of perfectionist busy work and end up never releasing anything. Designers who do not fear the crabs pulling them back down release, even though it may not be perfect, and they constantly get better because of it.

Remind yourself of the beauty that is found everywhere. What is markedly harder to do is to celebrate the things that are great instead of pointing out the things that are not. This is especially true because of my final point.

- **THE "INDUSTRY" IS RATHER SMALL**—LinkedIn recently released a report that showed that the industry in which it matters most to have a network of people you can trust in order to find a job is "computer games."[18] When LinkedIn users started a new job, it was more likely in computer games than in any other industry (almost twice as likely as in the average industry) to already have been connected long-term to someone at the hiring company.

When I was a sophomore in college, I got a job in a dorm as a resident assistant. I really did not like the head RA, who was an upperclassman. He represented everything I disliked about college, and so I was an insufferable jerk around him and actively worked to undermine him with the residents every chance I got. At one point, our feud got to be too much, and one of the professional staff pulled me aside and told me that although it was obvious we had a dislike for each other, I needed to step back and consider what this acrimony was doing to my ability to be trusted as a leader and to get things done in the community. That, of course, is a sanitized version of it. In reality, he told me what a jerk I was being and told me to shape up.

. . . .

17 De Törne, B. (1937). *Sibelius: a Close-Up*. Boston, MA. Houghton Mifflin Harcourt.

18 Rigano, P. (2015, March 9). "Industries Where Your Network Matters More Than You Think." Retrieved July 21, 2015, from http://blog.linkedin.com/2015/03/09/ industries-where-your-network-matters-more-than-youthink.

Something about that intervention really clicked with me. When I acted more like an adult, I became much more successful at getting events organized and buy-in from other people because I stopped radiating jerk particles.

I see students going through this transition (both successfully and unsuccessfully) all the time. Convinced they are "right," they do everything they can to prove it, regardless of the collateral damage. In proving they are smart or right or clever, they ruin their relationships with their peers and signal to others than they are not a positive force to work with.

The professional community talks with each other at conferences and online. Designers get reputations. But do not focus just on the "torpedoed career" end of the spectrum. The designers who get reputations for being awesome, positive people are in high demand. Would you not rather be that designer? Those who believe that they will work solo forever and never need another human being are living in a fantasy that ignores the fact that even solo developers need others to get the word out to create a community and for financial or critical success.

When you consider all the terrible, back-breaking labor that the world employs to prosper, making games for a living has to be seen as a good way to spend that time of your life that you designate as "career."

I cannot image myself doing anything else. Even when my career shifted away from making games to teaching others about making games, I kept making them. There must be something deep inside me now that requires me to do so. I cannot put that genie back in the bottle. Why would I want to?

Ludography

Digital Games

Alan Wake. [Computer software]. (2010). Espoo, Finland: Remedy Entertainment.

Assassin's Creed II. [Computer software]. (2008). Montreal, Quebec: Ubisoft.

Azurik: Rise of Perathia. [Computer software]. (2001). Redmond, California: Microsoft.

Banjo-Kazooie. [Computer software]. (1998). Twycross, England: Rare.

BioShock. [Computer software]. (2007). Boston, Massachusetts: Irrational Games.

Braid. [Computer software]. (2008). San Francisco, California: Number None Inc.

Buzz!: The Music Quiz. [Computer software]. (2005). Brighton, United Kingdom: Relentless Software.

Canabalt. [Computer software]. (2009). Austin, Texas: SemiSecret Software.

Chrono Trigger. [Computer software]. (1995). Tokyo, Japan: Square.

Civilization IV. [Computer software]. (2005). Hunt Valley, Maryland: Firaxis Games.

Civilization Revolution. [Computer software]. (2008). Hunt Valley, Maryland: Firaxis Games.

Clash of Clans. [Computer software]. (2012). Helsinki, Finland: Supercell.

Corrypt. [Computer software]. (2013). Auckland, New Zealand: Smestorp.

Dark Souls. [Computer software]. (2011). Tokyo, Japan: FromSoftware.

Dead Rising. [Computer software]. (2006). Osaka, Japan: Capcom.

Dead Rising 2. [Computer software]. (2010). Vancouver, British Columbia, Canada: Capcom.

Destiny. [Computer software]. (2014). Bellevue, Washington: Bungie.

Dino Crisis 3. [Computer software]. (2003). Osaka, Japan: Capcom.

Divekick. [Computer software]. (2013). Chicago, Illinois: Iron Galaxy Studios.

Donkey Kong. [Computer software]. (1981). Kyoto, Japan: Nintendo.

Dragon's Lair. [Computer software]. (1983). El Cajon, California: Cinematronics.

Dwarf Fortress. [Computer software]. (2006). College Station, Texas: Bay 12 Games.

The Elder Scrolls III: Morrowind. [Computer software]. (2002). Rockville, Maryland: Bethesda Softworks.

The Elder Scrolls V: Skyrim. [Computer software]. (2011). Rockville, Maryland: Bethesda Softworks.

Family Feud. [Computer software]. (2011). Montreal, Quebec, Canada: Ludia.

FarmVille. [Computer software]. (2009). San Francisco, California: Zynga.

FarmVille 2. [Computer software]. (2012). San Francisco, California: Zynga.

Final Fantasy VII. [Computer software]. (1997). Tokyo, Japan: Square Enix.

Fire and Dice. [Computer software]. (2012). Orlando, Florida: Sky Parlor Studios.

Flappy Bird. [Computer software.] (2013). Hanoi, Vietnam: Nguyên Hà Đông.

flow. [Computer software]. (2006). Tokyo, Japan: Sony Computer Entertainment.

Flower. [Computer software]. (2009). Los Angeles, California: Thatgamecompany.

FTL. [Computer software]. (2012). Seattle, Washington: Subset Games.

Gone Home. [Computer software]. (2013). Portland, Oregon: Fullbright.

GoPets. [Computer software]. (2005). Seoul, South Korea: GoPets.

Gunvalkyrie. [Computer software]. (2002). Tokyo, Japan: Sega.

Guitar Hero. [Computer software]. (2005). Boston, Massachusetts: Harmonix Music Systems.

Grand Theft Auto V. [Computer software]. (2013). Edinburgh, Scotland: Rockstar Games.

Habbo Hotel. [Computer software]. (2000). Helsinki, Finland: Sulake.

Habitat. [Computer software]. (1985) San Francisco, California: LucasArts.

Half-Life 2: Episode One. [Computer software]. (2006). Bellevue, Washington: Valve.

Halo. [Computer software]. (2001). Bellevue, Washington: Bungie.

Heavy Rain. [Computer software]. (2010). Paris, France: Quantic Dream.

I Love Bees. [Alternate reality game]. (2004). Burbank, California: 42 Entertainment.

Jelly no Puzzle. (2013). Tatsunami Qrostar.

Just Dance. [Computer software]. (2009). Paris, France: Ubisoft.

Katamari Damacy. [Computer software.] (2004). Tokyo, Japan: Namco.

L.A. Noire. [Computer software]. (2011). Sydney, Australia: Team Bondi.

League of Legends. [Computer software]. (2009). Santa Monica, California: Riot Games.

Legend of Grimrock II. [Computer software]. (2014). Espoo, Finland: Almost Human.

The Legend of Zelda: Ocarina of Time. [Computer software]. (1998). Kyoto, Japan: Nintendo.

Lego Star Wars: The Video Game. [Computer software]. (2005). Knutsford, England:
    Traveller's Tales.

Lemonade Stand. [Computer software]. (1973). Brooklyn Center, Minnesota: Minnesota
    Educational Computing Consortium.

LittleBigPlanet. [Computer software]. (2008). Guildford, England: Media Molecule.

Madden NFL 2005. [Computer software]. (2004). Maitland, Florida: Electronic Arts.

Mafia Wars. [Computer software]. (2009). San Francisco, California: Zynga.

Mario is Missing. [Computer software]. (1992). Sherman Oaks, California: The Software Toolworks.

Mario Kart 64. [Computer software]. (1997). Kyoto, Japan: Nintendo.

Mass Effect. [Computer software]. (2007). Edmonton, Alberta, Canada: BioWare.

Mega Man 3. [Computer software]. (1990). Osaka, Japan: Capcom.

Metroid Prime. [Computer software]. (2002). Austin, Texas: Retro Studios.

Minecraft. [Computer software]. (2011). Stockholm, Sweden: Mojang.

Minesweeper. [Computer software]. (1990). Redmond, California: Microsoft.

NBA Live. [Computer software]. (1994). Burnaby, British Columbia: Electronic Arts.

NBA Street. [Computer software]. (2001). Burnaby, British Columbia: Electronic Arts.

NCAA Football 08. [Computer software]. (2007). Maitland, Florida: Electronic Arts.

One Pawn Army. [Computer software]. (2013). Mark Diehr.

Oregon Trail. [Computer software]. (1974). Brooklyn Center, Minnesota: Minnesota Educational Computing Consortium.

Out There. [Computer software.] (2014). Lyon, France: Mi-Clos Studio.

Peggle. [Computer software]. (2007). Seattle, Washington: PopCap Games.

Penn & Teller's Smoke & Mirrors. [Computer software]. 1995. Upper Saddle River, New Jersey: Absolute Entertainment.

Pokemon. [Computer software]. (1996). Kyoto, Japan: Nintendo.

Portal. [Computer software]. (2007). Bellevue, Washington: Valve.

Professor Layton and the Curious Village. [Computer software]. (2008). Fukuoka, Japan: Level-5.

Professor Layton and the Unwound Future. [Computer software]. (2010). Fukuoka, Japan: Level-5.

Project Gotham Racing. [Computer software]. (2001). Liverpool, United Kingdom: Bizarre Creations.

Quake II. [Computer software]. (2007). Mesquite, Texas: Id Software.

Rampage. [Computer software]. (1986). Chicago, Illinois: Bally/Midway.

Realm of the Mad God. [Computer software]. (2011). Los Altos, California: Wild Shadow Studios.

Resident Evil. [Computer software]. (1996). Osaka, Japan: Capcom.

Ridiculous Fishing. [Computer software]. (2013). Vlambeer.

Rock Band. [Computer software]. (2007). Cambridge, Massachusetts: Harmonix Music Systems.

The Room. [Computer software]. (2012). Guildford, United Kingdom: Fireproof Studios.

Rule of Rose. [Computer software]. (2006). Tokyo, Japan: Punchline.

Shadow of the Colossus. [Computer software]. (2005). Tokyo, Japan: Sony Computer Entertainment.

SimCity. [Computer software]. (1989). Emeryville, California: Maxis.

SpaceChem. [Computer software]. (2011). Chesterbrook, Pennsylavnia: Zachtronics.

Space Invaders. [Computer software]. (1978). Tokyo, Japan: Taito.

Spelltower. [Computer software]. (2011). New York, New York: Zach Gage.

Spent. [Computer software]. (2011). Durham, North Carolina: McKinney.

The Stanley Parable. [Computer software]. (2013). Austin, Texas: Galactic Cafe.

Streak for the Cash. [Computer software]. (2013). New York, New York: ESPN Internet Ventures.

Street Fighter IV. [Computer software]. (2008). Osaka, Japan: Capcom.

Sudoku Together. [Computer software]. (2012). Orlando, Florida: Sky Parlor Studios.

Super Columbine Massacre RPG!. [Computer software]. (2005). Danny Ledonne.

Superman Returns. [Computer software]. (2008). Maitland, Florida: Electronic Arts.

Super Mario Bros. [Computer software.] (1985). Kyoto, Japan: Nintendo.

Super Metroid. [Computer software]. (1994). Kyoto, Japan: Nintendo.

The Talos Principle. [Computer software]. (2014). Zagreb, Croatia: Croteam.

Team Fortress 2. [Computer software]. (2004). Bellevue, Washington: Valve.

Temple Run. [Computer software]. (2011). Raleigh, North Carolina: Imangi Studios.

Tetris. [Computer software]. (1984). Moscow, Russia: A. Pajitnov.

This War of Mine. [Computer software.] (2014). Warsaw, Poland: 11 bit studios.

Tomb Raider. [Computer software]. (1997). Derby, England: Core Design.

Tom Clancy's Splinter Cell. [Computer software.] (2002). Montreal, Quebec, Canada: Ubisoft Montreal.

The Walking Dead: Season One. [Computer software]. (2012). San Rafael, California: Telltale Games.

World of Warcraft. [Computer software]. (2004). Irvine, California: Blizzard Entertainment.

WWE SuperCard. [Computer software]. (2014). Novato, California: 2K Games.

Zork. [Computer software]. (1980). Cambridge, Massachusetts: Infocom.

Board, Card, Tabletop, and Physical Games

Abbott, E. (1949). *Candy Land*. Pawtucket, Rhode Island: Hasbro.

Aoki, M. & Wiseley, C. (1992). *Loopin' Louie*. Springfield, Massachusetts: Milton Bradley.

Baer, R. (1976). *Simon*. Springfield, Massachusetts: Milton Bradley.

Beaujannot, G., & Monpertuis, J. (2015). *Flick 'em Up!* Rigaud, Quebec, Canada: Pretzel Games.

Bauza, A. (2010). *7 Wonders*. Brussels, Belgium: Repos Production.

Bauza, A. (2010). *Hanabi & Ikebana*. Lyon, France: Les XII Singes.

Bauza, A., Maublanc, L. (2013). *Terror in Meeple City*. Brussels, Belgium: Repos Production.

Bulmahn, J., et al. (2009). *Pathfinder Roleplaying Game*. Redmond, Washington: Paizo Publishing.

Darrow, C. & Magie, E. (1936). *Monopoly*. Salem, Massachusetts: Parker Brothers.

Freise, F. (2004). *Power Grid*. Bremen, Germany: 2F-Spiele.

Funk, J. (1966). *Cross Sums* (aka *Kakuro*). Norwalk, Connecticut: Dell Magazines.

Garfield, R. (1993). *Magic: The Gathering*. Renton, Washington: Wizards of the Coast.

Gilbert, B. (2013). *The Other Hat Trick*. Good Little Games

Gilmour, J. Vega, I. (2014). *Dead of Winter: A Crossroads Game*. Addison, Texas: Plaid Hat Games.

Gygax, G. & Arneson, D. (1974). *Dungeons & Dragons*. Lake Geneva, Wisconsin: TSR, Inc.

Knizia, R. (2004). *Ingenious*. Stuttgart, Germany: Kosmos.

Lamorisse, A. (1959). *Risk*. Salem, Massachusetts: Parker Brothers.

Launius, R. & Wilson, K. (2005). *Arkham Horror*. Roseville, Minnesota: Fantasy Flight Games.

LCR. (1992). Bonita Springs, Florida: George & Company.

Leacock, M. (2007). *Pandemic*. Mahopac, New York: Z-Man Games.

Leacock, M. (2008). *Roll Through the Ages: The Bronze Age*. Leitchfield, Kentucky: Eagle-Gryphon Games.

Lehman, T. (2004). *Race for the Galaxy*. Rio Rancho, New Mexico: Rio Grande Games.

Looney, A. (1996). *Fluxx*. College Park, Maryland: Looney Labs.

Mcdaldno, A. (2013). *The Quiet Year*. Vancouver, British Columbia: Buried Without Ceremony.

Moon, A. (2004). *Ticket to Ride*. Los Altos, California: Days of Wonder.

Morningstar, J. (2009). *Fiasco*. Chapel Hill, North Carolina: Bully Pulpit Games.

Tevis, P. (2009) *A Penny for My Thoughts*. Silver Spring, Maryland: Evil Hat Productions.

Peterson, P. (1998). *Guillotine*. Renton, Washington: Wizards of the Coast.

Renin. (1991). *Nurikabe*. Tokyo, Japan: Nikoli.

Robbins, B. (2011). *Microscope*. Seattle, Washington: Lame Mage Productions.

Rosenberg, U. (2008). *Agricola*. Berne, Germany: Lookout Games.

Rosenberg, U. (2013). *Caverna*: The Cave Farmers. Berne, Germany: Lookout Games.

Roubira, J. (2008). *Dixit*. Guyancourt, France: Asmodee Editions.

Sackson, S. (1980). *Can't Stop*. Salem, Massachusetts: Parker Brothers.

Seyfarth, A. (2002). *Puerto Rico*. Ravensburg, Germany: Alea.

Seyfarth, A. (2004). *San Juan*. Ravensburg, Germany: Alea.

Sun, R. (1988). *Twenty Four*. Suntex. Easton, Pennsylvania: Suntex.

Teuber, K. (1995). *The Settlers of Catan*. Stuttgart, Germany: Kosmos.

Trzewiczek, I. (2014). *Imperial Settlers*. Gliwice, Poland: Portal Games.

Vaccarino, D. (2008). *Dominion*. Rio Rancho, New Mexico: Rio Grande Games.

Wernhard, H. (1960). *Hi-Ho! Cherry-O*. Park Ridge, Illinois: Whitman Publishers.

Index